THE MODERN
YUGOSLAV CONFLICT
1991–1995

In this book the author bridges the gap between the common perception of the modern Yugoslav conflict as portrayed in the media and the actual grim reality with which he was dealing as a European Monitor on the ground. Drawing on original source material from both the United Nations (UN) and the European Community Monitor Mission (ECMM), he critically re-examines the programme of violence which erupted in 1991 and eventually culminated in 1995 in the vicious dismemberment of a sovereign federal republic with a seat at the United Nations General Assembly. In doing so, he highlights the duplicitous behaviour of all parties to the conflict; the double standards employed throughout by the United States in its foreign policy; the lengths to which the Sarajevo government manipulated the international media to promote a 'victim' status; the contempt in which UN peacekeepers were ultimately held by all sides; and the manner in which Radovan Karadzic was sacrificed at the altar of political expediency when the real culprits were Slobodan Milosevic and his acolyte, General Ratko Mladic. This book, the first comprehensive evaluation of the conflict by an EU Monitor, tells the story of the modern Yugoslav conflict, 1991–1995, from the unique perspective of one who was there, drawing on all of the authors' published work to date.

Brendan O'Shea is an officer of commandant rank (major) in the Irish Defence Forces, with 29 years' military service. He served in the Former Yugoslavia with the ECMM and later with the Organisation for Security and Co-operation in Europe (OSCE) as an international election observer. He has also served on a number of occasions with the United Nations in the Middle East and holds a Ph.D. in History from University College Cork where he teaches Humanitarian Law and Humanitarian Intervention.

CASS CONTEMPORARY SECURITY STUDIES SERIES

MILITARY STABILITY IN EUROPE
The CFE treaty
Jane M. O. Sharp

MACMILLAN, KHRUSHCHEV AND THE BERLIN CRISIS, 1958–1960
Kathleen Newman

US NUCLEAR NON-PROLIFERATION POLICY 1989–1997
Tess Oxenstierna

NATO'S SECRET ARMY
Operation Gladio and terrorism in Western Europe
Daniel Ganser

THE US, NATO AND MILITARY BURDEN-SHARING
Stephen Cimbala and Peter Forster

RUSSIAN GOVERNANCE IN THE TWENTY-FIRST CENTURY
Geo-strategy, geopolitics and governance
Irina Isakova

THE FOREIGN OFFICE AND FINLAND 1938–1940
Diplomatic sideshow
Craig Gerrard

RETHINKING THE NATURE OF WAR
Edited by *Isabelle Duyvesteyn and Jan Angstrom*

THE MODERN YUGOSLAV CONFLICT 1991–1995
Perception, deception and dishonesty
Brendan O'Shea

THE MODERN YUGOSLAV CONFLICT 1991–1995

Perception, deception and dishonesty

Brendan O'Shea

First published 2005 by Frank Cass
This edition published 2012 by Routledge
2 Park Square, Milton Park, Abingdon, Oxon OX14 4RN
711 Third Avenue, New York, NY 10017, USA
Routledge is an imprint of the Taylor & Francis Group, an informa business

First issued in paperback 2012

© 2005 Brendan O'Shea

Typeset in Times by Wearset Ltd, Boldon, Tyne and Wear

All rights reserved. No part of this book may be reprinted or reproduced or utilised in any form or by any electronic, mechanical, or other means, now known or hereafter invented, including photocopying and recording, or in any information storage or retrieval system, without permission in writing from the publishers.

British Library Cataloguing in Publication Data
A catalogue record for this book is available from the British Library

Library of Congress Cataloging in Publication Data
O'Shea, Brendan
The Modern Yugoslav Conflict, 1991–1995 : perception, deception and dishonesty / Brendan O'Shea.—1st ed.
p. cm.
Includes bibliographical references and index.
1. Yugoslav War, 1991–1995. 2. Just war doctrine. I. Title.
DR1313.O83 2005
949.703—dc22
2004013320

ISBN 978 0 4156 5024 3

Having established that Yugoslavia was a big lie, the Great Manipulators and their well equipped teams (composed of writers, journalists, sociologists, psychiatrists, philosophers, political scientists, and ... generals!) began the process of dismantling the big lie. And then they stopped to rest from their work and suddenly noticed that the country was still whole. So then they set about dismantling the country. But in order to awaken the dormant national consciousness it was necessary quickly to establish differences: in what way were we different, that is better than them. Colleagues, university teachers, linguists, journalists, writers, historians, psychiatrists, worked fervently in the teams to secure the dormant, lost, repressed national identity

New words began to enter the language of the media; ethnically clean (territory, team, side, workforce) as opposed to ethnically unclean ones. 'Clean' and 'Unclean' quickly spread to the 'dirty war' with accompanying formulations (cleansing terrain, ethnic cleansing). Every day new maps of Yugoslavia surfaced in the media with differently coloured patches: everyone experienced some colour and patch as threatening. And of their own accord people began to proffer their own behinds, asking the Great Manipulators (the fathers of their nation, their defenders, their leaders) to brand them.

Dubravka Ugresic, *The Culture of Lies*

CONTENTS

The main protagonists   ix
Abbreviations   xii

Introduction   1

1 1991   9

The Karadjordjevo meeting 9
Violence erupts 10
Declarations of independence 12
The quest for recognition 14
The Brioni Agreement 15
War in Croatia 16
Worthless agreements 17
Demonising the Serbs 18
Enter Ratko Mladic 18
A divided European response 19
Trouble looms in Bosnia 20
Lord Carrington takes control 21
Vukovar falls 22
Dubrovnik 24
Recognition 25

2 1992   30

The Vance plan 30
More designs on partition 31
Violence erupts in Sarajevo 33
The Cutilherio plan 34
Marching for peace 35
The bread queue massacre 37
Ethnic cleansing 40

CONTENTS

The prison camps 43
Kovacevic and Kozarac 47
Karadzic's culpability 48
International reaction to the prison camps 49
Annex A 59
Annex B 60
Annex C 62

3 1993   63

The Vance–Owen Peace Plan 63
Reaction by the UN Security Council 68
Airdrops and lies 70
Abusing humanitarian aid 72
The first siege of Srebrenica 73
The peace process rolls on 75
Srebrenica becomes a 'safe area' 78
Ahmici 80
Division amongst the Serbs 82
Something must be done 85
Advent of a war crimes tribunal 86
A culture of deceit 88
Fikret Abdic 94
Talking in Geneva 99
Americares 102

4 1994   107

The market square bomb 107
The Federation begins 109
Gorazde 111
The Contact Group 116
NATO strikes back 120
Serb against Serb 121
Bihac 124
Deception and reality 128
Strange solutions 130
Turanj and Batnoga 133
Misery for the refugees 135
Karadzic makes an offer 138
Dudakovic attacks southwards 139
UNPROFOR in chaos 141
Boutros-Ghali in Sarajevo 143
The Economic Agreement and the Z4 plan 146
Bangladesh pays a heavy price 147

Jimmy Carter goes to Sarajevo 148
Fighting in Bihac 154

5 1995   157

Croatia's attitude to UNPROFOR 157
The international response 158
Preparations for war 160
Flights over Tuzla 161
Reality in Bihac 166
New arrangements 167
End of the COHA 170
Unification of the Serbs 173
Tensions rise between Knin and Zagreb 177
Trouble on the roads 180
Croatia launches a special police action 181
Leaderless in Knin 188
The fall of Srebrenica 193
A storm blows through Krajina 195

6 The End State   201

Notes	212
Select bibliography	233
Index	235

THE MAIN PROTAGONISTS

Serbia

Slobodan Milosevic	President
Mirjana Markovic	Wife of Milosevic
Borisav Jovic	Former President of Yugoslavia
General Veljko Kadijevic	Defence Minister of Yugoslavia

Croatia

Franjo Tudjman	President
Gojko Susak	Minister for Defence
Mate Granic	Foreign Minister from 1993
General Janko Bobetko	Chief of the General Staff

The Republic of Srpska Krajina

Milan Martic	President
Borislav Mikelic	Prime Minister
Milan Babic	Foreign Minister
General Milan Celeketic	Chief of Staff

Bosnia-Hercegovina

Alija Izetbegovic	President
Ejup Ganic	Deputy President
Haris Silajdzic	Prime Minister
Muhamed Sacirbey	Ambassador to the UN
General Sefer Halilovic	Commander of the Army
General Rasim Delic	Successor to Halilovic

THE MAIN PROTAGONISTS

Bihac Pocket

Fikret Abdic	Founder Autonomous Province
General Atif Dudakovic	Commander, 5th Corps, 1993–1996

Republic Srpska

Radovan Karadzic	President
General Ratko Mladic	Commander of the Army
General Manojlo Milovanovic	Chief of Staff

Croatian Community of Herceg-Bosna

Mate Boban	President
Kesimir Zubak	President of the Muslim/Croat Federation in 1994
General Tihomir Blaskic	Commander of the Army (HVO)
General Zarko Tole	Chief of Staff

Montenegro

Momir Bulatovic	President

Slovenia

Milan Kucan	President

Macedonia

Kiro Gligorov	President

The United Nations

Civilian

Boutros Boutros-Ghali	Secretary-General
Yasushi Akashi	Special Representative

Military

General Lewis MacKenzie	UN Commander in Sarajevo in 1992
General Phillipe Morillon	UN Commander in Bosnia in 1993
General Sir Michael Rose	UN Commander in Bosnia in 1994
General Rupert Smith	UN Commander in Bosnia in 1995

THE MAIN PROTAGONISTS

General Bernard Janvier — UNPROFOR Commander, 1994/95
Lieutenant Colonel Bob Stewart — Commander 1 Battalion, Cheshire Regiment

The European Community Monitor Mission (ECMM)

Ambassador Jean Paul von Stulpnagle — Head of Mission from 1 July to 31 December 1994
Ambassador Albert Turrot — Head of Mission from 1 January to 30 June 1995
Klaus Krammer — Head of Operations Division in 1994
Jean Michel Happe — Head of Operations Division in 1995

The Mediators

Lord Peter Carrington
Colm Doyle
Lord David Owen
Cyrus Vance
Thorvald Stoltenberg
Vitali Churkin
Carl Bildt
Charles Redman
Peter Galbraith
Richard Holbrooke
Jimmy Carter

ABBREVIATIONS

Military

Armija	Bosnian Muslim Army
BSA	Bosnian Serb Army
HV	Croatian Army
HVO	Bosnian Croat Army
JNA	The Old Yugoslav National Army
SARSK	Serbian Army of the Republic of Srpska Krajina

Political

APWB	Autonomous Province of Western Bosnia (Fikret Abdic)
HDZ	Croatian Democratic Union (Franjo Tudjman)
SDA	Party of Democratic Action (Alija Izetbegovic)
SDS	Serbian Democratic Party (Radovan Karadzic)

International

EC	European Community
ECMM	European Community Monitor Mission
ECTF	European Community Task Force (Humanitarian)
ICRC	International Committee of the Red Cross
NATO	North Atlantic Treaty Organisation
NGO	Non-governmental Agency (Humanitarian)
UN	United Nations
UNHCR	United Nations High Commission for Refugees
UNMO	United Nations Military Observer
UNPROFOR	United Nations Protection Force
UNSC	United Nations Security Council

INTRODUCTION

In the October 1997 issue of the *American Historical Review*, Sarah A. Kent wrote that readers should not seek the 'truth' in relation to the Former Yugoslavia's wars of dissolution because she believed it was an exercise best left to politicians, who purported to know it, and the Almighty, whom she hoped actually did. She went on to state that Bosnia had confounded the international community and raised crucial questions about existing instruments for conflict resolution because specialists had failed to achieve agreement on even a simple interpretation of the facts. She further identified that few authors had presented either the Bosnian Croat or Bosnian Serb side of the story and that simply attempting to categorise the conflict legally had become a hotly disputed issue – the Bosnian Muslims believed they had fought in a war of aggression, while the Bosnian Serbs, on the other hand, were adamant they had fought a civil war.[1]

Sarah Kent's assessment was correct on all counts. Throughout the wars of dissolution, and in the conflict-resolution phase thereafter, attempting to establish the 'truth' of what happened became an almost impossible task. Each party had their own concept of the truth, their own version of events, and their own interpretation of Balkan history. Equally, those *internationals* who came to help brought with them a variety of preconceptions and agendas, and, depending on what they actually experienced on the ground, then went away to write their memoirs doggedly determined to support one side or the other. Very few found themselves in positions whereby they could monitor the big picture and thereby offer balanced objective assessment and evaluation.

In September 1994 I was selected to join the European Community Monitor Mission (ECMM) in the Former Yugoslavia and after a time as a monitor and team leader in eastern Slavonia, and then as a monitor in the Krajina near Bihac, I was appointed to the Headquarters' Staff in Zagreb as the officer responsible for evaluating and reporting on the war in Bosnia together with the general situation in Serbia, Montenegro, Macedonia and Kosovo. In this capacity I was afforded the opportunity to work with the 'big picture', where my job was to make some sense of the conflict in order to better inform the policy-makers of the European Union. Our reports eventually found their way to EU HQ in Brussels, the foreign ministries of all EU governments and to the United Nations in New York.

However, it also became apparent at an early stage that irrespective of what my colleagues and I actually wrote, in the world of *realpolitik* individual agendas were still pursued relentlessly with the best and worst example unquestionably being Germany's single-minded determination to recognise Croatia when the Badinter Commission, Lord Carrington and EC monitors on the ground all advised against it.

Equally, when former US president Jimmy Carter and Radovan Karadzic had managed to secure the Cessation of Hostilities Agreement (COHA) in December 1994 I believed this success could and should have been built upon in a serious and meaningful way. Unfortunately the leaders of the international community thought otherwise and followed their own agendas, determining that there would be no place for an indicted war criminal at the peace-conference table – and a unique possibility for progress was squandered.

Nevertheless, ECMM continued to gather information and make evaluations. With teams spread right throughout the region, daily, weekly, monthly, and special reports on the military, political, economic and humanitarian situations came flooding into the headquarters in Zagreb and were processed through a complex evaluation system. Thereafter assessments and predictions were distributed internationally and either accepted or rejected by those who read them. ECMM's mission statement was simple. We were in theatre to observe and report at first hand on the Former Yugoslavia's wars of dissolution – and for the most part I am satisfied that we did it well.

However, it was also during this time that I first became aware of the chasm which existed between the common perception of the conflict as portrayed in most of the popular media and the actual grim reality which I was dealing with on the ground. There was a difference, and in many instances it was huge.

In order to address these issues, therefore, and drawing on all resources available, including original unclassified material from both UN and ECMM sources, this book seeks to identify the origin of the Former Yugoslavia's wars of dissolution and thereafter critically examine the programme of violence which erupted between 1991 and 1995 culminating eventually in the vicious dismemberment of a sovereign federal republic with a seat at the United Nations.

It also seeks to identify the duplicitous behaviour of all parties to the conflict; the double standards employed throughout by the United States in its foreign policy; the lengths to which the Sarajevo government manipulated the international media to promote a 'victim' status; the contempt in which UN peacekeepers were ultimately held by all parties to the conflict; and the manner in which Karadzic was sacrificed at the altar of political expediency when the real culprits were Slobodan Milosevic[2] and his acolyte General Ratko Mladic, whose barbarous behaviour in the eastern Bosnian towns of Srebrenica and Zepa in July 1995 is now well documented by the international community.[3] The case against Karadzic has always been a separate matter, and debate continues as to whether or not he deserves to be vilified in the same manner.[4]

Karadzic's indictments relate primarily to the fact that as per the Constitution of the Republic Srpska he was *de jure* the 'Superior Authority' within that so called 'State' and as such the 'buck is deemed to stop at his desk'.[5] As far as the international community was concerned it had a scapegoat. Karadzic was typecast as a psychopath, a butcher and the architect of genocide,[6] and the campaign to bring him to justice served as a convenient distraction from criticism of the international community itself and its abysmal failure to either convince or coerce any of the parties to the conflict to respect even the basic tenets of international humanitarian law. Perception was everything. Guilt had been assigned.[7] That Karadzic might well have had a significantly lesser case to answer was never even considered.

For the duration of the 1991 Gulf War journalists, would-be authors, academics and the media all found their movement on the battlefield strictly controlled by specially appointed Coalition media liaison officers. Most were adamant that when the next conflict erupted they would never again accept the same restrictions – and right on cue Yugoslavia imploded enabling hundreds of journalists and media personnel to descend first on Slovenia, then on Zagreb, and thereafter on Sarajevo. This time around most were prepared to take incredible risks in order to ferret out the 'truth' and many died because they paid insufficient attention to their own basic safety. Others lost objectivity in their reporting as they came face to face with scenes of savagery and brutality. *Slaughterhouse* by David Rieff,[8] *A Witness to Genocide* by Roy Gutman[9] and *Seasons in Hell* by Ed Vulliamy,[10] all recount what the authors believed they discovered in north-central Bosnia during 1992 when they visited prison camps run by the Bosnian Serbs. Generating public outrage became their objective in the hope that Western governments might be compelled to intervene. As far as they were concerned there was only one truth – these were concentration camps of the Second World War era. Ed Vulliamy was clear: 'There is no attempt [in this book] to be objective towards the perpetrators of Bosnia's ethnic carnage and those who appease them.'[11]

Equally, Rieff was unapologetic for his failure to be dispassionate in the face of what he perceived to be mass murder, and he later went so far as to accuse agents of the international community of distorting reports from the ground in order to maintain the line that all parties to the conflict were equally to blame. What Rieff and his colleagues failed to appreciate was that by standing one pace removed from the conflict the key international figures, and their agents scattered throughout the region, were far better placed to make balanced evaluations and assessments.

In this regard Lewis MacKenzie, Michael Rose, Bob Stewart, Milos Stankovic, Yasushi Akashi, David Owen, Cyrus Vance, Thorvald Stoltenberg and Lord Carrington all formed the view that none of the parties were innocent when it came to the violent dismemberment of Yugoslavia. All were deemed to have copious amounts of blood on their hands, an assessment which was amply supported by thousands of reports compiled by both ECMM and UNPROFOR operatives deployed in towns and villages right across the former republics. My own experience copper-fastened this view and I absolutely concur with David Owen's assessment that 'never before have I had to operate in such a climate of dishonour, propaganda, and dissembling. Many of the people with whom I had to deal in former Yugoslavia were literally strangers to the truth.'[12]

By failing to attribute all blame to the Serbs (be they in Croatia, Bosnia or Kosovo) accusations were then levelled that those expressing an alternative view were 'anti-Muslim' – something which was patently untrue. However, when some members of the international community took matters further and tried to expose the devious double games being played throughout by the Sarajevo government they in fact risked death or personal retribution. One such example was the former UN civil affairs officer in Sarajevo, Philip Corwin, who admitted that on 13 July 1995 the Sarajevo government minister, Hasan Muratovic, actually threatened to kill him if he continued working with the Bosnian Serbs, a job for which he was specifically employed by the UN.[13] And indeed I experienced these tactics myself in February 1995 when the then mayor of Bugojno, Dvezd Mlaco, threatened both myself and the others members of an ECMM team when we asked him a series of questions in relation to the distribution of humanitarian aid.

In the course of this research I have focused on the work of those who had no axe to grind in Yugoslavia save a compelling desire to find a peaceful resolution of the conflict. I believe that it is in the written work of soldiers, monitors, force commanders, peace-builders, humanitarian workers and human rights observers that the truth can be found – if it can be found at all. These were the people who came to know and understand all of the parties to the conflict and they compiled a thorough picture of exactly who was operating to what agenda. In short, these were the people who lived and worked at the coal-face for almost four and a half years and a consistency runs right through their writing which in my opinion is not found elsewhere.

For example, when General Rose states that throughout 1994 Ratko Mladic travelled to Belgrade each Tuesday and took his orders directly from the JNA HQ there (translate: Milosevic) I believe him because I know how that piece of information was obtained and processed.[14] Equally, when Philip Corwin writes that by the end of June 1995 Mladic (and not Karadzic) was in charge in the Republic Srpska, and that he briefed General Rupert Smith to this effect on 25 June stating that Karadzic had by then become merely a figurehead, this corroborates Rose's earlier assessment.[15]

Corwin also wrote to Yasushi Akashi on 28 June 1995 stating that the Sarajevo government was increasingly using the cover of UN facilities, as well as hospitals and schools, to provoke Bosnian Serb counter-attacks.[16] This assessment is again consistent with several of Rose's own evaluations, as it is with reports from the Dutch battalion immediately prior to the fall of Srebrenica that July.

In the same vein, one of the more critical incidents of the entire war was the bread queue massacre in Sarajevo on 25 May 1992 after which General Lewis MacKenzie's assessment became the focus of intensive critique by those who had other agendas to follow. Writing in his diary two days beforehand he had noted:

> Watching TV news (BBC and CNN) one gets the impression the Serbs are 100 per cent to blame. Some of the reports are unbalanced, based on what we know. Serbs bear a majority of responsibility but Izetbegovic has done an excellent job mobilizing world opinion on his side, which covers up his hidden agenda. I'm convinced he wants massive international military intervention.[17]

Then, when the bomb went off, he wrote:

> Disaster in Sarajevo. People lined up for bread were attacked and at least seventeen killed. The Presidency claims it was a Serb mortar attack. Serbs claim it was a set-up using explosives. Our people tell us there were a number of things that didn't fit. The street had been blocked off just before the incident. Once the crowd was let in and had lined up the media appeared but kept their distance. The attack took place and the media were immediately on the scene. The majority of the people killed were 'tame' Serbs. Who knows? The only thing for sure is that innocent people were killed.[18]

In fact, the only thing for certain was that this assessment would turn out to be perfectly consistent with several other reports compiled subsequently as the war went on, which indicated clearly that not everything was black, white or straightforward. Attempts to discredit MacKenzie have continued to this very day, but taken in the context of the conflict as a whole, and the duplicitous behaviour of the Sarajevo government throughout, I am satisfied that his version of 25 May was then, and still is, most probably correct.

In fact, following another mortar attack on the marketplace in Sarajevo almost two years later on 5 February 1994, in which 68 civilians were killed, Akashi wrote to the UN secretary-general, Boutros Boutros-Ghali, stating that the mortar could have been fired by the Bosnian Muslims in order to induce NATO intervention. Boutros-Ghali informed the US secretary of state, Warren Christopher, accordingly, who replied that he had seen many intelligence reports which went both ways. There are several other similar examples.

Understanding the barbarity of the fighting was also something no journalist managed to capture fully either. However, Milos Stankovic provides an insight like no other when, writing on the 1992 Croat–Muslim war in central Bosnia, he recorded the words of a local interpreter, Edi Letic, who was fighting in the trenches:

> I'm in this trench with a radio and with a whole load of other Muslims. The Croats are charging us, firing, and we're firing back, and then suddenly something snaps. Everyone around me leaps up screaming and shouting, mad, with red rage. They drop their rifles and charge forward with axes, knives, meat cleavers and bayonets and they hack away at each other. That's what it's like here. It's not enough to shoot. Better to make a real job of it with axes and knives.[19]

Similar accounts from Anthony Loyd reveal the inhumanity of the conflict and make it clear beyond doubt that the Serbs did not have a monopoly on savagery. Working in central Bosnia during the winter of 1993, Loyd, a retired British army officer, witnessed three Muslim soldiers returning to their own lines having been released by the Bosnian Croats:

> Now forced back across no-man's land they lurched unnaturally up the hillside. Their hands were strapped to their waists. Improvised claymore mines were attached to their chests and linked to the Croat houses by coils of wire that unravelled slowly with each step of their robotic progress. The human bombs were returning home. As the distance narrowed a [Muslim] officer shouted at his men to shoot them. They refused. Some of the soldiers ran back from the trench to their bunkers. There were three individual explosions so close together as to roll into one protracted thunderous roar that bounced echoes between the cold black hills. Blood, shrapnel, and tissue sprayed the trees. For a few seconds there was silence. A couple of soldiers peered cautiously over the edge

of the trench. In the shredded, ankle high scrub before them they could make out three pairs of legs. It was all that was left of their friends.[20]

When the war eventually spread to Bihac Pocket the first available information came from ECMM teams operating on the ground, and reports filed by Hugh O'Donovan represent the best evidence of impartial war reporting that I have ever seen. His work was followed in turn by that of Mark Etherington, Klaus Kramer and Bill Foxton, as the conflict evolved over three years. Between them they contributed to the compilation of a huge database of information which is richer than anything the print media had to offer and far less biased than the glowing reports of 5th Corps' successes produced by others throughout the period.

Of greater value in the context of this study, however, are the original letters and dispatches which I managed to collect during my period in theatre. The correspondence between Karadzic and Akashi subsequent to Boutros-Ghali's refusal to meet with Karadzic on 30 November 1994 is particularly illuminating,[21] as is the letter in which Akashi is eventually forced to include a map delineating where the UN declared 'safe area' of Bihac was actually supposed to be.[22]

Later, at the beginning of August 1995, the supposedly imminent collapse of Bihac was used by the Croats and their American advisers as the excuse to launch the full weight of the Croatian army against the Krajina Serbs when in fact no such collapse was about to take place. This is clear from ECMM reports of that time which indicated that the Pocket was not about to fall. Nevertheless the attacks commenced, leading to the conclusion that some other agenda was at work – and it was.

In an interview with Tim Ripley on 21 December 1997 US ambassador to Croatia, Peter Galbraith, admitted that the Croatians had told him they were about to go to war and that given the attacks on Bihac (which were not in fact about to cause a collapse of the 5th Corps of the Bosnian army) the US decided not to dispute their right to intervene. Splitting hairs on the issue Galbraith went on to say:

> It was not an agreement, just a 'no objection' ... On 1st August we issued a definitive demarche to Tudjman. We said 'whatever you do is your decision but if you do not give a warning you will face sanctions'.
>
> We stressed that this did not constitute a 'green light', and that the Croats on their own must protect Serb civilians and UN personnel. It was 'no light' at all.[23]

In reality President Tudjman interpreted all of this as a definite green light and promptly set about conducting the largest ethnic-cleansing operation of them all. By the time his soldiers were finished over 300,000 Croatian (Krajina) Serbs had been brutally driven from their homes. If there was ever any doubt what actually constituted the special position of Serbs in Croatian society, as enunciated in the Croatian Constitution, there was absolutely none now – and nobody intervened to stop this outrage, which was captured live on international TV. In fact, but for the presence of EC monitors on the ground in Bihac history might well have recorded that Tudjman's attack was justified in order to save the safe area. Having filed their reports throughout the period, and stored them safely in ECMM's database in Zagreb, that interpretation is not now possible.

Sadly for the entire Krajina Serb population, who were condemned to life as refugees in Serbia and beyond, this provides little consolation. As far as they are concerned Tudjman got his way, Croatia is now ethnically clean, and the main players in the international community raised not one finger to help them. This is how they perceive their reality now. Unfortunately, it is also the truth – and few if any want to know of their plight.

Accordingly, the purpose of this book is to record the story of Yugoslavia's dissolution from the perspective of those who worked at the coal-face – attending meetings, arranging body and prisoner exchanges, organising humanitarian aid convoys, observing and reporting as each shot was fired, and often ending up being shot at themselves. There was no monopoly on truth in Yugoslavia and this book makes no exclusive claims. Rather it seeks to unravel what transpired in order to search for truth while accepting completely that in order to find it one must first do battle with what Dubravka Ugresic correctly identified as *'The Culture of Lies'*.[24]

1
1991

The Karadjordjevo meeting

Responding to repeated attempts by Slobodan Milosevic to circumvent, and then manipulate the federal presidency in pursuit of his own agendas, Croatia and Slovenia signed a Mutual Defence Accord in February 1991 in what effectively was the first step on the road to secession.[1] Identifying the commencement of disintegration, Alija Izetbegovic, the president of Bosnia-Hercegovina, continued to argue the case for a federal state but the architects of anarchy had already moved on. Meeting at Tito's old hunting lodge in Karadjordjevo, Vojvodina, on 25 March Tudjman and Milosevic had already made plans to carve up the region, leaving 'a little bit of Bosnia for the Muslims', as Tudjman later put it.[2]

Of course this was not a new idea – a similar proposal had been negotiated back in August 1939 in order to facilitate the participation of the then Croat leader Vladko Macek in a coalition government with his conservative Serb counterpart, Dragisa Cvetkovic.[3] The difference in 1991 was that this new deal had been negotiated in secret.[4] The only matter remaining unresolved, apparently, was how to implement it. This task was left to the then Croatian prime minister, Hrvoje Sarinic, and Milosevic's counsellor, Smilja Avramov, who met on at least 30 further occasions to discuss the population transfers which would be necessary to effect it.[5]

In a meeting at the time with Ambassador Zimmerman, Izetbegovic remarked that 'If Croatia goes independent Bosnia will be destroyed.'[6] This was a profound forecast, and together with Kiro Gligorov, the president of Macedonia, he went to a meeting of the federal presidency in Belgrade on 5 April and proposed a new mechanism whereby the Federation could be held together. Notwithstanding the presence at the meeting of an EC delegation, the proposals fell on deaf ears. Milosevic and Jovic had already decided that all Serbs (including the Bosnian Serbs) should now live in one state, and Tudjman was preaching a ludicrous philosophy that Bosnia had always been a part of Croatia and that in fact the Bosnian Muslims really considered themselves to be Croats.

Violence erupts

As summer approached the seeds of conflict began to germinate. Milan Kucan had set mid-June now as his deadline for Slovene secession and he began the organisation of paramilitary units which would be employed to defend the new republic. In Croatia the situation was also tense – but for different reasons. A number of Serb villages had mobilised self-defence militias and on 1 April the village of Glina, 50 km south-west from Zagreb, declared its secession from Croatia.

This was followed by the similar secession of 28 other Serb communities in the municipality of Sisak, and the following day barricades went up around Serb villages in eastern Slavonia in the vicinity of Vukovar, Osijek, Vinkovci and Dalj. Then, to make matters worse, Vojislav Seselj,[7] a radical politician and paramilitary leader from Serbia, arrived in Borovo Selo on the outskirts of Vukovar allegedly responding to a request for help from the local Serb militia leader Vukasin Soskocanin. He brought with him a group of paramilitary fighters who had been armed by the Serbian police;[8] the relationship here between Seselj and the Belgrade authorities is of critical importance. Reflecting on the matter in 1994 Seselj was unambiguous: 'Our first contact with the police was in the summer of 1991. Then we began to receive arms directly. The first man who we had such contacts with was [Mihalj] Kertes. Later when the army entered the war the army gave weapons to us. We were given busses [*sic*], and a barracks and seated on these busses we went to the front.'[9]

This connection establishes a direct link to Milosevic because Kertes was one of Milosevic's closest aides. It was Kertes who masterminded the mass demonstrations in Vojvodina which led to the collapse of the government there on 5 October 1988; it was Kertes who rose high in the ranks of the new government which subsequently emerged; it was Kertes whom Milosevic appointed as Serbia's chief customs officer in 1994; and it was Kertes who bank-rolled the latter stages of the Milosevic regime until it finally collapsed on 5 October 2001.[10] Kertes was there at the beginning and there at the end. He was one of the very few to achieve that dubious distinction.

Of course, Kertes was not operating alone – back in 1991 he was ably assisted in recruiting these so-called 'volunteers' by the then Serbian interior minister, Radmilo Bogdanovic, the secret police chief, Jovica Stanisic, and his two deputies, Franko Simatovic ('Frenki') and Radovan Stojicic ('Badza').[11] For the likes of Seselj it was comforting to know that the full weight of Serbia's political apparatus was squarely behind him, and in December 1991 all volunteer units, including the Chetniks, were fully integrated into the JNA order of battle.[12]

The overall situation in Croatia was now deteriorating by the hour and came to a head on 8 April when it was announced in Zagreb that the courts martial of Martin Spegelj and the 'Virovitica Four' had been discontinued in response to mass demonstrations and riots on the streets. This sent the wrong message entirely to the simple Serb peasants of eastern Slavonia who genuinely believed that the Croats, aided and abetted by Germany, were now about to attack them. These fears were increased by the rhetoric of Seselj, and gained further credence when they witnessed the hurried arrival of other groups of 'volunteers'. Both Serbs and Croats in Croatia were now genuinely and legitimately afraid for their lives, and escapades like that undertaken by Tudjman's defence minister served only to confirm their worst nightmares.

On 1 May Defence Minister Susak had gone to Osijek and, enlisting the aid of the police chief, Josip Rechil-Kir, went on a night-time excursion to Borovo Selo in order to fire three missiles into an apartment complex in the predominantly Serb suburb of Vukovar. For many Serbs this legitimised the presence of Seselj's thugs, and the following day two bus-loads of Croatian police were ambushed in the centre of Borovo Selo – 12 died and a further 22 were wounded.

Croatia was now steadily sliding towards full scale civil war as the extremists on both sides took control, a fact evidenced by the death of Rechil-Kir himself, who, having subsequently voiced his objections to what Susak and his colleagues had done, was then murdered by a local HDZ activist, Antun Gudelj, who then made a 'miraculous' escape from the region notwithstanding that several police road blocks were actually sited in close proximity to him at the time.

Five years later Susak would deny that he had anything to do with the firing of rockets into Borovo Selo. He did, however, admit that he had been in the area at the time, and confirmed that he had 'visited the Croatian soldiers, and crawled for three hours in the mud towards the barricades'.[13] This 'explanation' serves only to raise further questions, and it most certainly does not rebut the testimony of Jadranka Rechil-Kir in relation to who bears responsibility for the cold-blooded murder of her husband.

From this point onwards the flames of ethnic hatred would be vigorously fanned by political leaders on all sides and at all levels, and literally within days both communities became engulfed in a crisis, the origins of which they barely understood. Harassment, intimidation, tit-for-tat killings and indiscriminate attacks on towns, villages and private houses, quickly became the norm. Law and order effectively died in Croatia on the night that Josip Rechil-Kir was murdered.

In tandem with the growing violence the result of a referendum in Croatia published on 20 May established that 92 per cent of those who voted did not want to remain within federal Yugoslavia, and the unveiling of the new Croatian National Guard on 28 May indicated clearly that Tudjman too had passed the point of no return, notwithstanding that Serb autonomous regions were springing up all over the place – Knin, Plitvice, Pakrac and Vukovar to name but four.[14]

Declarations of independence

Against this volatile political backdrop James Baker, US secretary of state, arrived in Belgrade on 21 June fresh from the Conference on Security and Co-operation in Europe (CSCE later OSCE) meeting in Berlin where a resolution had been adopted calling for the 'democratic development, unity, and territorial integrity of Yugoslavia and continued dialogue between all parties'.[15] The message he delivered to Milosevic was straightforward – the US and OSCE did *not* support dissolution and all parties should work to find a resolution.

Ambassador Zimmerman is clear that there was no ambiguity. 'The message was simple', he says. 'Baker told him dissolution was not an option.'[16] This was consistent with what President Bush had already told Federal Prime Minister Markovic on 28 March when he said that the US would not encourage or reward those who broke up the country. Baker then went to Tudjman and Kucan and told them the same story, emphasising that the US would not support unilateral secession – but his message fell on deaf ears.[17]

Four days later, on 25 June, Slovenia and Croatia declared themselves sovereign and independent states and at 8 p.m. that evening, on the tenth anniversary of the alleged apparition of the Virgin Mary in the Bosnian-Croat town of Medjugorge, and speaking to a packed Croatian Sabor in Zagreb, President Tudjman declared that he was 'calling on all parliamentary democracies to recognise the will of the Croatian people to join the society of free and independent nations'.[18] Later that evening the Slovenes did the same, and fighting began almost immediately when at Milosevic's bidding the remnants of the Federal State Council, presided over by Jovic, approved Federal Prime Minister Ante Markovic's directive that the JNA intervene in order to protect Yugoslavia's international borders. And thus the dissolution of Yugoslavia commenced when all the old border crossings and customs posts with the West fell into direct Slovene control and goods in transit and customs revenue became forfeited to the Slovene exchequer.

The ten-day war which followed was a half-hearted affair with neither the JNA nor Milosevic having the stomach for all-out conflict. Armoured units did move into Slovenia on 27 June following a main axis from Karlovac and Zagreb to Ljubljana, with a second axis further north from Varazdin, but the fighting which ensued could only be described as 'patchy', given that all main roads into Slovenia were mined and the secondary routes were covered by fire at critical points.[19]

Eventually, after an ill-fated ten-day adventure in which little military progress was made, and 37 Yugoslav army and 12 Slovene deaths were recorded, the JNA gave up. That the campaign concluded as quickly as it did was an interesting story. Five months previously, on 24 January to be exact,[20] Kucan and Milosevic had discussed a potential Slovene breakaway and the Serbian president agreed to allow the Slovenes to depart on condition that Kucan supported Serbia's claim to incorporate all Serb-populated areas elsewhere in Yugoslavia into Serbia proper. 'We both know what is going to happen', Milosevic said. 'You Slovenes want to leave, so let's make a deal. Let's rewrite the constitution and extend the right to secede, not just to the republics, but to all ethnic groups as well.'[21]

But Kucan knew that a promise from Milosevic was all but worthless and was aware that armoured columns were on the way from Croatia. At 5 a.m. on the morning of 27 June he went on Slovene Television to confirm his decision to fight. 'The Republic of Slovenia will take all necessary measures to defend our independence against the Yugoslav army', he said.[22] In the first few hours the JNA had tried to deploy just under 2,000 troops (mostly untrained conscripts) to the border crossings, but this had been resisted. The bulk of JNA troops garrisoned in Slovenia remained confined to their barracks, which from the army's perspective proved to be a huge tactical mistake because very quickly the *ad hoc* Slovene militia (perhaps 35,000 lightly armed volunteers) encircled these barracks and effectively trapped the occupants inside. Colonel Aksantijevic, a JNA commander in Ljubljana, admitted as much later on, and when it became clear that any resupply by air would almost certainly be shot down, the only options open to the federal troops were to fight their way into the country, and out of their barracks, if in fact they had the stomach for it – and in the majority of cases they did not.

The Slovenes also scored a major victory in the propaganda war and quickly had the international media reporting Serb atrocities when nothing of the sort was taking place. This was achieved by skilful media manipulation, and the hundreds of journalists who descended on Ljubljana were made most welcome. Thereafter they were corralled into a bunker beneath the Ministry of Information (allegedly for their own safety) and fed a steady diet of events taking place above ground – from the Slovene perspective.

The Serbs were portrayed as violent communists who dropped cluster bombs on innocent civilians, the struggle being thus portrayed as one between Good (in the guise of Slovenes and Croats) and Evil (personified by the Serbs). In this way a fictional blow-by-blow account of the ten-day war was fed to the media by a team of young multilingual patriotic volunteers (mostly university students aged between 20 and 30), and, unable (and/or unwilling) to venture over-ground to confirm these stories, when editorial deadlines arrived the official Slovene version of events was broadcast as fact.[23] Equally, when selected journalists (i.e. those disposed to the Slovene struggle) were allowed to venture up into the streets much of what they witnessed was stage-managed and choreographed.[24] Not for the first time in the Balkans truth had become the first casualty of war – and it would not be the last occasion either.

As an EC delegation of foreign ministers was dispatched to Zagreb, General Kadijevic was proposing massive military intervention in Slovenia at the Yugoslav State Council in Belgrade. On the verge of ratifying this course of action, Serbia's representative, Borisav Jovic, then voted 'no' and vetoed the plan. He later admitted that 'Serbia had no territorial claims there. It was an ethnically pure republic – no Serbs. We couldn't care less if they left Yugoslavia. With Slovenia out of the way we could dictate terms to the Croats.'[25]

However, this admission contains a number of truths. First, it would have been impossible to justify a military clamp-down in Slovenia on the basis of relieving an oppressed minority because there was none. Second, the Slovenes had far more in common – culturally, economically and geographically – with their Italian and Austrian neighbours than they ever had with Belgrade. Third, Milosevic probably believed he still had a deal with Kucan *vis-à-vis* his plans for Croatia, and there was no need to jeopardise it. And fourth, the Slovenes had already won the media war by opening up their country to journalists from all over the world and then successfully feeding them their own side of the story.

In fact, Slovene propaganda was so successful that Hans Dietrich Genscher, the German foreign minister, was invited to Ljubljana at the start of the war and fed a steady diet of Slovene perspective. When he then went before a press conference he accused the JNA of 'running amok' in Slovenia. This accusation was totally untrue, but it served its purpose, as indeed did calls from Senator Bob Dole in Washington demanding that Milosevic halt his supposedly violent crackdown on democracy and human rights.

Clearly Dole had little understanding of reality on the ground either – but the damage was done. International public opinion had been formed and the Slovenes were home free. Milosevic's decision to let Kucan go was utilitarian – he had no strategic interests in Slovenia. However, Croatia would be a different matter altogether.

The quest for recognition

Initially the United States continued to support the concept of an integrated federal Yugoslavia as Lawrence Eagleburger, at the State Department, and Marlin Fitzwater, at the White House, threw their collective weight firmly behind Federal Prime Minister Markovic as he set about preserving the unity of his country. The European Community, on the other hand, called upon the Conference on Security and Co-operation in Europe (CSCE) to dispatch an investigation team to the region as an internal row broke out over how to deal with the situation.[26] Germany, in the persons of Chancellor Kohl and Hans Dietrich Genscher, began to advocate recognition of a right to self-determination for Croatia and Slovenia which they incorrectly claimed to be contained in the UN Charter. Britain, France, Spain and Italy, on the other hand, continued to support the concept of an integrated federal Yugoslav state.

As a compromise, a troika of EC foreign ministers, Gianni de Michelis (Italy), Jaques Poos (Luxembourg) and Hans Van den Broek (the Netherlands) were dispatched to Belgrade in an attempt to find a solution. Prior to departure in Luxembourg, Foreign Minister Poos declared to the assembled press corps that 'this is the hour of Europe; it is not the hour of the Americans'. Europeans had decided to take the ball and run with it – and they would live to regret it.

'Croatia can't just walk out', Milosevic told the trio, '600,000 Serbs live there and they want to stay in Yugoslavia'[27] – and as far as he was concerned that was the end of the matter. For the troika, optimism about their mission was soon replaced by pragmatism, then by pessimism, and eventually by sheer frustration. Yugoslavia was certainly Europe's problem, but there was no obvious solution and the omens were not good.

In a parallel move Genscher attempted to broker a number of cease-fires in Slovenia but failed miserably, while Volker Ruhe, the chairman of the ruling Christian Democrats in Germany, continued to call for international recognition of Croatia and Slovenia in clear disregard for official EC policy on the matter. Tension between France and Germany then began to rise on this issue and only subsided slightly when the troika appeared to make some progress.

On 29 June, four days after declaring independence, Croatia and Slovenia agreed to suspend their departure from the Federation for three months to see if some progress could be made – but fighting continued nonetheless. The following day Stipe Mesic, a Croat, became president of the Yugoslav Federation, Serbia having previously blocked his appointment since 17 May, and in Slovenia the JNA recalled all operational troops to barracks. One could have been forgiven for thinking that some progress was in fact being made.

The Brioni Agreement

Watching events unfold on TV back in Belgrade Milosevic quickly understood that Serb ambitions were not best served by images of JNA fighter aircraft dropping bombs on Ljubljana or Brink airport, and therefore quickly agreed to talks between representatives from the European Community, Croatia, Slovenia, Serbia and the federal government. These took place on the island of Brijuni, just off the Istrian coast from the port of Pula, on 7 July. The document which all parties signed was to become known as the Brijuni (or Brioni) Agreement and allowed, for the first time, a deployment of European Community monitors (ECMM) to supervise the withdrawal of the JNA from Slovene territory.

Little else was agreed, but Europe's interest in the region was now clearly established and henceforward new EC monitors would fly the blue flag with 12 gold stars right across Yugoslavia in support of an agreement which from day one meant totally different things to the various parties involved. It certainly meant little or nothing to the JNA tank units operating in eastern Slavonia who shelled the centre of Osijek that very same evening. The war in Croatia had begun in spite of Brioni, but the EC in particular, and the international community in general, would be slow to admit that a real tragedy was beginning to unfold.

Nevertheless, as July wore on it initially appeared that some political progress was being made. The first ever EC Ministerial Conference on Yugoslavia convened in The Hague on the 10th, the European Community Monitor Mission (ECMM) established its permanent headquarters in the relative luxury of Hotel 'I' in the south-eastern suburbs of Zagreb on the 13th, and the Presidium of the Federal Republic of Yugoslavia announced on the 18th that the JNA would withdraw to Serbia and Bosnia-Hercegovina within three months.

On the ground, however, the reality was different as inter-ethnic violence continued to erupt throughout Croatia with the JNA actively supporting local Serb communities on the pretext of interposing between both sides. For example, the police stations in Glina and Kozibrod were attacked on 2 July. The following day a huge column of armoured vehicles poured into eastern Slavonia from Serbia and two soldiers and ten civilians quickly lost their lives. Then on the night of 6 July General Kadijevic and Milosevic appeared together on Belgrade TV calling all citizens to come to the defence of Yugoslavia.[28]

War in Croatia

Against this backdrop President Tudjman walked out of the Federal Presidium session being held in Ohrid, Macedonia, on 22 July, forcing the EC Council of Foreign Ministers to reconvene in Brussels on the 29th in the presence of the federal Yugoslav prime minister, Ante Markovic, his foreign secretary, Budmir Loncar, and representatives from Bosnia-Hercegovina and Macedonia. A six-point peace plan was unveiled, but fighting continued in all the disputed regions of Croatia as ethnic polarisation continued.

Red Cross figures indicated that by the end of July 1991 48,000 Croats and 31,000 Serbs had fled their homes in Croatia, the majority of which were then systematically destroyed.[29] The sacking of the Croat village of Kijevo typified what was happening countrywide.[30] A further example was the village of Skela where Serb irregulars massacred several people and every house was systematically destroyed. For both sides attack was fast becoming the best form of defence, and calls by the ICRC for restraint were having no effect whatever.[31] Certainly the overall political and military situation was confused, but this neither absolved nor mitigated the criminal behaviour being perpetrated by key players in the emerging conflict.

There was also a body of customary international law in existence in 1991 which governed the conduct of armed conflict. The Socialist Federal Republic of Yugoslavia had ratified all four Geneva Conventions on 21 April 1950 and Additional Protocols I and II on 17 April 1990. All senior military and political leaders throughout the six republics and two autonomous provinces should have understood their legal obligations when they decided to plunge their peoples into what became a savage and bloody war. Unfortunately most of them simply did not care

If a defence is open to any of them it would probably revolve around the proposition that at this point in time international law itself was defective because depending on how you defined the actual situation on the ground you could end up with completely different legal consequences.[32] In so far as this argument goes it would most likely hinge on whether the fighting in 1991 constituted an international or internal armed conflict.

Either way, Article 3, common to all four Geneva Conventions, governs the treatment of persons not involved in the fighting,[33] and Additional Protocol II of 1977 elaborates on these prohibitions – particularly in relation to attacks on civilians.[34] Customary international law then supplements these Conventions and in this way becomes 'absolute law' with all parties to the conflict, irrespective of how they might choose to define their involvement, bound by international humanitarian law (IHL) and thereafter accountable for their actions. By targeting civilians and persons *hors de combat* the essential provisions of common Article 3 and Protocol 2 were clearly violated, and no justification can be offered by any of the perpetrators, either for what they did or the indiscriminate manner in which they did it

Worthless agreements

With the conflict intensifying in Croatia, and the remainder of Yugoslavia in the throes of dismemberment, the International Conference on Yugoslavia managed to convince all six republics to send representatives to the Netherlands where, on 5 November at The Hague, all delegations signed up to a 'Statement on Respect for Humanitarian Principles' which contained a summary of the basic rules of international humanitarian law (the law applicable in armed conflict).

The following day Croatia and the federal Yugoslav authorities concluded a further agreement under the auspices of the European Community which dealt specifically with creating a mechanism for exchanging persons who had been detained up to that point by both sides.[35] Three weeks later a further 'Memorandum of Understanding' was signed in Geneva under ICRC auspices by representatives of the Federal Authorities in Belgrade, the JNA, and the governments of both Croatia and Serbia[36] in which virtually all IHL general principles were acknowledged, and the ICRC was even given responsibility for setting up a commission to investigate allegations of IHL violation.

At face value, then, one could certainly have been forgiven for thinking that the parties to the conflict actually wished to invoke the 'rule of law' in order to regulate their dispute, and to alleviate an evolving human tragedy which the ICRC was now estimating to involve a displacement of over 48,000 Croats and 31,000 Serbs in Croatia alone.[37] In fact, six months later both sides signed an addendum to the Memorandum[38] which purported to take account of Croatia's recognition by the European Union and the consequent requirement by both sides to apply the full rigours of IHL; that is, customary international law, the four Geneva Conventions, and Protocol I.[39]

Demonising the Serbs

It was also at this point that a campaign began in Germany to demonise the Serbs. Led by the conservative daily newspaper, *Frankfurter Allgemeine Zeitung* (FAZ), its editor Johann Georg Reismuller launched daily attacks in which he described the Serbs as 'oriental militarist Bolsheviks who had no place in the European Community'.[40] In the Bundestag the leader of the Green Party, Joschka Fischer, doubled on this sentiment and screamed for a disavowal of pacifism in order to 'combat Auschwitz', in effect equating all Serbs with the Nazis.

Thereafter politicians across the spectrum voiced the opinion that now was the time to shoulder the military responsibility for dealing with this problem, and soon thereafter, in the name of human rights, Germany abolished its ban on conducting military operations outside the NATO defensive arena.[41] Within weeks the effect of this propaganda had spread far and wide and taken firm hold in the minds of those who only wished to see the conflict in terms of 'black and white'. Unfortunately for the Serbs the evolving common perception was not assisted in any way by the antics of several eccentric and brutal military commanders.

Enter Ratko Mladic

In 1991 the commander of the Knin Corps of the Yugoslav army (JNA) in the Krajina region of Croatia was busy fighting what he believed to be a war of liberation for the ethnic Serbs whose ancestors had lived there for hundreds of years and who now had no wish to become second-class citizens in what they perceived to be an emerging fascist Croatian state. With the social and political fabric of Yugoslavia crumbling all around him this officer strode to centre stage and began to play a leading role in the developing conflict. Just turned 48, the colonel's name was Ratko Mladic.[42]

Mladic was born on 12 March 1943 in the village of Bozinovici, near Kalinovik, in eastern Hercegovina. Two years later his father had been killed while leading a partisan attack on an Ustashe village, and this appears to have left an indelible mark on his personality. Motivated by the memory of this 'heroic sacrifice' the young Mladic left home at 15 and enlisted as an apprentice in the military-industrial school at Zemun. Later he moved on to the military academy in Belgrade and was commissioned as a second lieutenant in 1965 at the age of 22.

A varied career followed – platoon commander in Skopje, battalion commander in Kumanovo, brigade commander in Stip, chief of staff of the JNA's 9th Corps in Knin, and in 1991 he became its commander. Unshakably loyal to Tito and the communist ideology while it served his purposes, Mladic progressed swiftly through the ranks and was ready and waiting for an opportunity to avenge the death of his father when war eventually broke out.[43]

He quickly ditched the old communist doctrine and re-emerged as a Serb officer working to defend Serb people against fascists and fundamentalists. This was very much the ideology being preached by the regime in Belgrade and Mladic soon became identified as someone who could be relied upon when the going got tough. Accordingly his methods were frequently overlooked by his political masters, and as the conflict spread Ratko Mladic was well on his way to becoming a modern Balkan legend – for all the wrong reasons.

By this stage he had already opened several detention centres and the unfortunate people, both male and female, whom he incarcerated in places like Bileca and Stara Gradiska, were systematically raped, starved, beaten and shot.[44] There were no excuses for the savagery which took place and no explanation will ever be adequate.

A divided European response

By now Europe was so hopelessly divided on what to actually do in Yugoslavia that the possibility of an agreed political position effectively became unattainable. France advocated the deployment of EC troops under a Western European Union (WEU) flag to support the monitors already deployed on the ground. However, when the Germans expressed an interest in this proposal the British immediately became suspicious and opposed it.

Accordingly, by the time the EC foreign ministers reassembled in The Hague on 7 September 15 per cent of Croatia had fallen to Serb control. Of course there was no shortage of new proposals – a new meeting of the CSCE; the involvement of the UN; military intervention; and last but not least, recognition of Croatia and Slovenia – but there was still no consensus and no identifiable common EC policy.

The one decision which the foreign ministers did actually make was not to recognise any territorial change achieved in Yugoslavia by force. However, this was immediately 'misinterpreted' in Belgrade to justify ongoing military action in Croatia, which in turn served only to escalate the situation further. In response the Croatian and Slovene foreign ministers travelled to Bonn in August for a meeting with Foreign Minister Genscher. While nothing of substance emerged, Genscher did threaten the Yugoslav ambassador in Bonn with immediate German recognition of Croatia if the fighting failed to stop.

On 28 August the EC finally issued what effectively amounted to an ultimatum to the six republics, demanding that they either agree to an immediate ceasefire or accept punitive international economic and military action. Surprisingly this warning was heeded, at least officially, and when Hans Van den Broek managed to secure Serbian compliance a ceasefire was signed in Belgrade on 2 September. In the longer term, however, the only tangible result of this agreement was a visible increase in the number of EC monitors on the ground and the extension of their mandate to Croatia. On the battlefields nobody paid the slightest attention – and the fighting went on.

Trouble looms in Bosnia

Meanwhile, the situation in the hitherto peaceful republic of Bosnia-Hercegovina had also begun to change. In mid-August President Alija Izetbegovic announced that it was also his intention to hold a referendum on the matter of his country's independence, because as matters currently stood he felt he had no other option. Radovan Karadzic, leader of the Bosnian Serbs, was already having discussions in Belgrade about the creation of a 'Greater Serbia' which would include Serbia proper, the Krajina regions of Croatia, Kosovo, Vojvodina and huge chunks of Bosnia.

In this scheme Croatia was to be compensated by getting those tracts in Bosnia populated by Bosnian Croats, and the Muslims could more or less fend for themselves. Izetbegovic also knew that if the situation in Croatia deteriorated much further Bosnia could not remain unaffected, especially if the bulk of the JNA currently deployed in Croatia were eventually withdrawn into Bosnian towns like Banja Luka, Zenica, Tuzla and Sarajevo. So having initially supported the continuation of the Yugoslav Federation and the policies of Markovic and Loncar, he too decided the time had come to plot a new future.

In theory Bosnia should have stood a better chance of survival as an integrated entity because no one ethnic grouping had a majority. The election results of November 1990 yielded 86 seats for the Muslims (SDA), 70 seats for the Serbs (SDS) and 45 seats for the Croats (HDZ), and theoretically future Bosnian politics should have revolved around shifting coalitions and democratic values. But that was not to be. On 4 September a gang of Bosnian Serbs killed two Muslims in clashes near the town of Bratunac, and this was followed a few days later by the declaration of a Serb autonomous region on the Bosnian–Montenegrin border.

The fragmentation of Bosnia had begun and Milosevic was once again in the thick of it. In a taped conversation with Karadzic, a transcript of which was produced to Federal Prime Minister Markovic on 19 September, evidence of Milosevic's involvement in Bosnia was clear for all to see.[45]

Lord Carrington takes control

On 3 September in The Hague, Lord Carrington, the former UK foreign secretary and former secretary-general of NATO, was appointed chairman of the Peace Conference on Yugoslavia. Signs were ominous from the beginning when his first attempt to organise some dialogue was rewarded by Slovenia's and Croatia's formal secession from federal Yugoslavia on 7 September. Then, while Europe concentrated on the establishment of a Commission to determine criteria for granting international recognition,[46] Macedonia voted for independence, the JNA brutally dispersed a civil protest of 15,000 ethnic Albanians in Kosovo, the Krajina Serbs succeeded in cutting Croatia in two when they captured the Maslenica bridge on the Dalmatian coast north of the city of Zadar, and Federal President Mesic publicly accused the JNA of having effectively carried out a coup as they now refused to take any orders from him.

It was against this back-drop of violence, compounded by a statement from US Secretary of State Baker attributing responsibility for the current bloodshed directly to the JNA,[47] and with one-third of Croatia under Serb control, that on 17 September Carrington produced his first ceasefire plan in the town of Igalo, in Montenegro, and, remarkably, managed to convince Tudjman, Milosevic and Kadijevic to sign it. However, the ink was barely dry on the paper before the Yugoslav navy began a blockade of all Croatia's Dalmatian ports and Federal Prime Minister Markovic took the unprecedented step of calling on General Kadijevic, the JNA's commander-in-chief and Yugoslavia's defence minister, to resign.

Significantly, on 22 September Kadijevic rejected this call on the basis that as he understood the situation Yugoslavia no longer existed, and the army was now taking certain decisions into its own hands. This included the continued shelling of Vukovar and Osijek, assisting local militias in eastern and western Slavonia, mounting air attacks against Zagreb, and launching naval bombardments against the cities of Zadar and Split. Carrington's first ceasefire lay in tatters!

In the wake of this failure the United Nations Security Council (UNSC) adopted Resolution 713 embargoing the sale and delivery of weapons and military equipment to all parties in Yugoslavia. Accompanied by a statement from the US secretary of state, in which he accused the JNA of complicity with Serb militias and irregular forces in Croatia, this was not just another ritual condemnation. In fact, when taken in tandem with the arms embargo it actually represented a turning point in US policy because it also recognised that hope for the continuation of a federal state was fast disappearing.

Throughout the autumn of 1991 numerous further attempts to stop the fighting proved unsuccessful, and a major row developed between Federal Prime Minister Markovic and Milosevic over the use of the JNA in what Markovic now regarded as essentially Serbian expansionism in Croatia. His assessment was correct, especially since Kadijevic was firmly installed in the Milosevic camp. In fact the JNA and Serbia had come to represent one and the same thing – different sides of the same coin – and with a predominance of Serbs in the officer corps perception and reality quickly became one.

Nevertheless, Lord Carrington continued his attempts to bring the sides together, and again on 4 October he managed to acquire the signatures of both Milosevic and Tudjman to a ceasefire – but it altered little on the ground. Interestingly, Serb indifference to this latest agreement was exemplified by an incident which occurred a few days later when, without warning, the JNA launched an air raid on Zagreb and bombed the presidential palace which contained at the time President Tudjman, Federal President Stipe Mesic and Federal Prime Minister Ante Markovic. Nobody was injured, but it clearly would have mattered little to the JNA leadership if three of the most senior political figures in Yugoslavia had been killed.

Vukovar falls

As the year drew to a close more attempts were made in The Hague on 10 October to negotiate a JNA withdrawal from Croatia; these came to nothing. Five days later Tudjman and Milosevic were summoned to Moscow for consultations with Mikhail Gorbachev and Boris Yeltsin, but this achieved little. The EC then threatened economic sanctions if the republics failed to agree on a loose type of confederation, but this warning also fell on deaf ears. Meanwhile, the first assembly of ethnic Albanian leaders took place in Kosovo, the Bosnian Serbs walked out of the Republican assembly in Sarajevo and established their own parliament in the ski resort of Pale, and extreme paranoia took hold of General Kadijevic when the German government announced that they were almost ready to recognise Croatia and Slovenia.[48] Incredibly he proclaimed that Germany was about to attack Yugoslavia for the third time that century!

And then, to make a bad situation worse, on the 18 November the town of Vukovar in eastern Slavonia finally fell to the combined Serb forces after an 86-day siege. This once beautiful town on the banks of the Danube river was 'liberated' by turning it into a pile of rubble. What was predominantly a Croat town before the conflict now became almost totally Serb by virtue of the facts that (a) it was located within the evolving Republic of Srpska Krajina; (b) the JNA had flattened all resistance in conjunction with flattening the town itself; and (c) virtually the entire Croat population packed their bags and left, having decided they would fare better as displaced persons in camps and hostels in Croatia rather than remain as second-class citizens in the physical, social and political debris which once was their home town.

Those who remained were condemned to a life of existential boredom devoid of money and food with nothing save sheets of white plastic emblazoned with 'UNHCR' logos to block up their empty broken window frames which had been shot to pieces by the JNA gunners on the far side of the river. After three months of battle Croatian losses were 2,000 dead, 800 missing, 3,000 captured, 42,852 people displaced and 25,580 out of 28,184 houses damaged or destroyed.[49]

Losses on the JNA side were still unconfirmed as late as 2001, but were probably less than 2,000. The Croats fought long and hard to retain control of Vukovar. They dug in and fought savagely[50] until eventually overwhelmed by superior firepower. Michael Ignatieff is correct in his criticism of the JNA when he identified that they could have bypassed Vukovar and sent their tanks down the Highway of Brotherhood and Unity all the way to Zagreb had they wanted to. Instead they chose to sit on the far side of the Danube and pound Vukovar into rubble.

Ignatieff also correctly identified that the entire event was a product of the 'politics of hate',[51] and this probably goes a long way towards explaining why the post-'liberation' treatment of those Croats still remaining in Vukovar's hospital became the subject of a war crimes investigation. Over a period of three days the surviving Croats were rounded up by the conquering forces of the JNA and the paramilitary thugs authorised by Milosevic to join them. Lined up, and made to walk to detention centres, the paramilitaries pulled people out of the line at random claiming they were 'war criminals', and the new security chief in the city, Major Veselin Sljivancanin,[52] stood by and permitted it all to happen.

On 20 November the killing started when those already selected were taken to the Ovcara farm near Petrova Gora outside Vukovar and systematically executed. Of the 15,000 people known to have remained in the town when the siege ended, 3,000 were soon reported missing presumed dead. Two hundred and sixty-one of them, mostly patients from the hospital, ended up beneath the congealed mud of the Ovcara farm as Milosevic's acolytes and henchmen murdered, raped and pillaged their way through Vukovar and its hinterland drunk on the rhetoric of ethnic hatred.[53] Back in Belgrade most ordinary people could barely believe what was happening as Radio Television Serbia (RTS) spat out nightly broadcasts portraying the Serbian nation rising up to defend itself from its enemies.[54]

And it worked! For the ordinary people watching RTS each night this convoluted and contrived 'reality' was pumped into their living rooms in much the same way as a programme called *Insurrection* celebrating the 1916 rising was drip-fed to an unsuspecting Irish population in 1966. And they, like us, began to believe it. In fact the RTS campaign became so one-sided that the independent radio station B92 commissioned a film called *Vukovar 1991* in an attempt to show the other side of the story and thereby deconstruct the government's concept of 'liberation' – but alas too late. 'Without the role played by TV the war would not even have happened, or at least it would not have been so bloody', contended novelist Filip David correctly to B92.[55] The key problem was that Milosevic had now come to control virtually the entire electronic media in Serbia and thereby ensured that whatever message he chose to deliver received no widespread criticism. In Croatia the media was also being manipulated in similar fashion, with the plight of Vukovar receiving equally distorted coverage on Hrvatska Television (HTV). Again a feature film on Vukovar was made and ran for months in cinemas throughout the country delivering the Croatian perspective and accusing the Serbs of heinous acts of barbarity. Subsequent films depicted the existential boredom of those displaced from Vukovar and now living in railway carriages in the town of Vinkovci.

One particular scene shows a father taking his young son to the front line to look at their burned-out home close to the water tower in Vukovar. While they are looking a Serb sniper spots them and mercilessly takes the life of the father with one bullet to the head. That the front lines were not configured in such a way as to allow this type of activity bothered no one, nor did the fact that the water tower in Vukovar could not be observed with such clarity from anywhere in Vinkovci. Reality had become distorted for the Croats too, but very few were prepared to question the propaganda diet they were fed.

Dubrovnik

Meanwhile, on the Adriatic coast, another saga was unfolding in Dubrovnik where JNA artillery continued firing primarily against Croatian military units. The city had first been attacked on 26 September just as the fourth round of Lord Carrington's peace talks commenced in The Hague. Four days later the Yugoslav navy set up a maritime blockade and thereafter the city was on the receiving end of daily shelling.

Meanwhile, representatives from the Croatian army and the JNA were busily trying to hammer out details of a ceasefire back at ECMM HQ in Zagreb,[56] and General Kadijevic and President Tudjman immersed themselves in a process to achieve agreement on the withdrawal of all JNA troops from Croatia within 30 days.[57] However, heavy shelling was reported again on 18 and 20 October and culminated in the arrival of a UNESCO delegation to the city on 25 October at the very moment JNA general Strugar was allegedly demanding its surrender. And so it went on, with images of Dubrovnik broadcast nightly on CNN.

Like all other aspects of this war reality was not quite as presented in the media. In fact, evidence has now emerged that the so-called 'devastation' of Dubrovnik was for the most part a staged event. Certainly shells were fired at the city and its environs on a regular basis, but Florence Hamlish Levinsohn is adamant that the Croats piled tyres behind the walls of the old city and then set them on fire to create the impression that the city was ablaze as a result of shelling.

These pictures were then captured from out at sea by CNN and other networks, who in turn broadcast them as fact without confirming their veracity.[58] Levinsohn's version of events is corroborated by Professor J. P. Maher of Northeastern University, Chicago, who states that he actually walked through the old city on 25 March 1992 and found only evidence of 'slight damage'. The city had certainly not been destroyed.[59] Perhaps this explains the failure of the Croatian authorities to lodge any serious claim that the JNA shelling was not justified by military necessity and therefore constituted a grave breach of the Geneva Conventions![60]

Recognition

Meanwhile, at the end of November another ceasefire agreement was signed in Geneva and Resolution 721 was passed by the UN Security Council authorising the deployment of up to 10,000 UN peacekeepers in Croatia – but the resolve of some of the main players was now faltering. On 5 December Stipe Mesic, the federal president, resigned. For him it was simple – 'Yugoslavia no longer exists', he said. There was no point going on. Fifteen days later Prime Minister Markovic followed suit having failed to curtail the federal budget allocation to the JNA for 1992. For Markovic, federal Yugoslavia was now a lost cause. In tandem with these resignations pressure to recognise Croatia and Slovenia internationally continued to mount and resulted in a decision by the EC foreign ministers on 16 December to grant recognition *after* 15 January 1992, provided both republics had;

a accepted the UN Charter and CSCE Helsinki Accords,
b guaranteed the rights of ethnic minorities,
c respected internationally recognised borders,
d upheld arms control and disarmament treaties, and
e supported political resolution of disputes.

Nevertheless, three days later, and apparently without any consultation with her EC partners, Germany went ahead of her own volition and formally recognised Croatia and Slovenia. This no doubt came as a very timely Christmas present for President Tudjman, and was certainly designed to appease the 700,000 strong Croatian community domiciled within Germany itself. It also underlined the tension and divergence within the European Community itself.

This unconditional and unilateral recognition appeared to fly in the face of the Badinter Commission, which had only just published its findings the day before the German announcement. Badinter clearly stated that only Slovenia and Macedonia fulfilled the Commission's criteria for recognition and he rejected Croatia's claim on the indisputable grounds that the administration in Zagreb was not in full control of all its territory, and that the rights of Croatia's minorities, particularly the Krajina Serbs, were not adequately safeguarded.

Croatians will argue to this day that the Krajina Serbs were accorded *special* guarantees to civil liberty under the Croatian Constitution, and this is true. But Serbs, on the other hand, argue cogently that it was precisely this 'special' status which ensured they would always be treated as second-class citizens. And if one takes that in tandem with the programme of demotion and expulsion of Serbs from jobs in both the public and private sectors at the time, then it's not particularly difficult to see their point of view.

The Croatian (Krajina) Serbs did have valid concerns in 1991, and these should have been addressed properly by the new ruling administration. They were not addressed because Croatian society had become completely polarised and concerning oneself with the welfare of Serbs was not a route to political or social success. The Croatian legislature's failure to develop its constitutional law at this time in a manner consistent with proper guarantees of civil, political and human rights for all her citizens was lamentable. Making special cases, whatever the motivation, served only to further alienate the already apprehensive Serb community scattered throughout the country. Had sincere and determined efforts been made to accommodate the Krajina Serbs, and thereby allay their genuine fears, the outcome might have been totally different. Instead old fears and old scores re-emerged in a climate of evolving hatred and anger, and for this situation the leadership of the HDZ, and Franjo Tudjman in particular, bear a huge responsibility. When it was most needed they displayed no political or moral judgement whatsoever.

Equally, while the German decision to recognise was probably permissible within the terms of international law, it certainly appeared to make a public mockery of the Badinter Report and completely undermined the ability of the EC Council of Ministers to formulate a common policy on Yugoslavia. All the rules were discarded with German recognition of Croatia and Slovenia, and the legitimate claim of Macedonia was completely ignored. Four years later, when Lord Carrington was asked to review the continuing conflict, he was adamant that the single biggest mistake in the whole sorry sequence of events was Germany's decision to accelerate international recognition of Croatia, and the corresponding failure of the European Community to resist it.[61]

In his 1997 *Report on State Practice and International Law in relation to Unilateral Secession*, James Crawford, Whewell Professor of International Law at the University of Cambridge, clearly states that in international practice there is *no* recognition of a unilateral right to secede[62] based on a majority vote of the population of a sub-division or territory, whether or not that population constitutes one or more 'peoples' in the ordinary sense of the word.[63]

However, the European Community foreign ministers were nowhere as clear in their thinking, and in a 'special report' written by the political section of ECMM during the German presidency in December 1994 evaluating the process it is stated that 'the denial of recognition had an increasingly counter-productive effect on the peace efforts. Only two reactions were possible: to block the Serb policy of force by military means, or at least internationalize the conflict by formally recognizing the imperiled republic. Serbia was using the negotiations as a diplomatic shield to continue the war and the arms embargo enabled her to go unpunished.'[64]

The report goes on to state that 'it became clear to EC member states that the recognition of the republics seeking independence could no longer be delayed ... it was only a matter of choosing the time and modalities'[65] – and it also claims that the initial decision to recognise them was taken at a meeting of EC foreign ministers in the Dutch town of Haarzuilens on 6 October 1991. Four days later the Dutch foreign minister met with Tudjman and Milosevic in The Hague and told them that there was now a 'time limit of one month or at the most two', and at the next meeting of foreign ministers in Brussels on 28 October a decision was taken that if Milosevic continued in his attempts to block the recognition process then they would continue without him.[66]

Thereafter it appears that Lord Carrington was operating in parallel, but not in tandem, with the foreign ministers. While they were all in agreement on the 'principles for a political solution' they were certainly not at one in relation to the modalities. In fact, the evidence suggests that this may well have been a deliberate tactic, because when Carrington temporarily suspended negotiations with Belgrade the report states that the

Council of Foreign Ministers took this as 'proof' that 'it was futile to wait any longer'.[67] When Badinter then produced his report on 7 December the Council took from it what it wanted to hear and the German interpretation was that it was the Serbian leadership itself that, by systematically unchaining Serb nationalism since 1987, had made the decisive contribution in undermining the multinational state created by Tito.

Equally, the report states that Germany was satisfied that Croatia had fulfilled the main condition for recognition when it included special provisions for the Krajina Serbs in its Constitution, but it omits to mention that these very provisions fell well short of full integrated citizenship, and also short of the Badinter criteria which demanded that any republic to be recognised should be in full control of all of its territory.[68]

In summary, then, it appears that irrespective of Carrington's work on the ground the EC Council of Foreign Ministers, presided over by Hans van den Broek but driven by Germany, was pushing along towards recognition of Croatia regardless. The choice, it claimed, was simple – either support the Croats militarily in their fight against the Serbs or recognise them. In this context Carrington's work was rendered all but irrelevant.

However, the fact that three years later German civil servants were still issuing position papers in order to explain their decisions and persisting in attempts to rubbish Carrington and his work speaks volumes. It also raises the question of what might have been achieved had the EC Council of Foreign Ministers actually been operating in tandem with Carrington, and not, as it now transpires, blatantly working against him?

Given this level of instability within the European Community, and Carrington's known opposition to the decision of 16 December, perhaps it was not surprising that Milan Babic, the mayor of Knin, responded on 19 December by declaring the establishment of a *Republic* of Srpska Krajina which he claimed would now amalgamate with the previously announced 'autonomous region' of eastern Slavonia, Baranja and western Srijem. Babic, representing over 300,000 people, had just taken control of one-third of Croatia![69] The following day, and not wanting to be left out of developments, the Bosnian Serbs announced that they too were opting for independence, and on 22 December Alija Izetbegovic, fully understanding what was about to unfold, requested the immediate deployment of UN troops in Bosnia.

The Sarajevo government was now trapped in a catch-22 situation: a push for recognition would inevitably alienate the Bosnian Serbs, but acceptance of the new order would find them a minority within a Greater Serbia. Ejup Ganic, Izetbegovic's deputy, summed up the dilemma when he explained: 'of course we are going to move ahead with recognition. With Croatia and Slovenia now gone we can't consign Bosnia to a truncated Yugoslavia controlled by Serbia.'[70]

Izetbegovic, for his part, was also given to understand that if a referendum produced a simple majority in favour of independence then Germany would recognise Bosnia also. This left him with Hobson's choice: either stay in what remained of Yugoslavia dominated by Milosevic and Serbia, or hold the referendum, secure the required majority, and alienate Bosnia's 1.3 million Serbs in the process.[71]

2
1992

The Vance plan

On 2 January 1992 Croatia formally accepted the Vance plan, the authorities in Belgrade having agreed to it on New Year's Eve. What was envisaged involved the implementation of a ceasefire, deployment of up to 14,000 UN peacekeepers (military, civilian and police), and the withdrawal of the JNA and Serb irregulars from Croatia. The areas to come under UN control would be called UN Protected Areas (UNPAs), and once the international troops were deployed on the ground a process of local demilitarisation would commence permitting in turn the safe return of thousands of displaced people.

At this point, however, the Krajina Serbs controlled almost one-third of Croatia and had no intention of giving any of it back. The Croats for their part were equally intransigent. They wanted all of it and were completely unconcerned where their Serb brothers might end up in the process.

It was Alija Izetbegovic who came out most strongly in favour of Vance, although its terms had only peripheral applicability to Bosnia. However, it did propose to locate the new UN force headquarters in Sarajevo, together with a small number of military observers, and this, he believed, would prove crucial to preventing war in Bosnia in the longer term. Other Bosnian officials were less confident and appealed directly to the UN to deploy troops immediately in Bosnia as a pre-emptive measure, but this appeal was ignored. Instead a truce was signed on 2 January in Sarajevo between Defence Minister Gojko Susak, on behalf of Croatia, and General Raseta representing the JNA. This became effective at 6 p.m. the following evening, but the plight of Bosnia was ignored.[1]

In the climate of relative calm which followed, politicians from all sides began to consider 'Vance' with a view to interpreting it to their own advantage. Milan Babic at first rejected it out of hand, but on 9 February a high-level delegation led by Milosevic's messengers Branko Kostic and General Blagoje Adzic, the JNA chief of staff, arrived in Knin. Immediately they addressed the Krajina parliament and convinced it to support the plan.

Babic then tried to organise a referendum on the matter but the parliament voted to impeach him. Seventeen days later Babic was gone and Goran Hadzic became the new president of the Republic of Srpska Krajina. Not surprisingly his first decision involved pledging support for the Vance plan, a policy that prevailed amongst the Krajina Serbs virtually until the very end.[2]

When the ceasefire appeared to be holding President Tudjman claimed he was giving the plan his unconditional support, but this outburst may well have had more to do with the euphoria which prevailed in Zagreb following Croatia's recognition by the EC on 15 January, and the overt support they were now obtaining from Germany, than on anything else.

For his part Milosevic publicly advised all Serbs to co-operate with the UN, and in what appeared to be a public act of good faith he ensured the departure of General Kadijevic as federal defence minister. This new situation was not, of course, without incident. Ceasefire violations continued, although the scale and frequency were considerably reduced, and a major tragedy befell ECMM on 7 January when one of their white helicopters, with five monitors on board, was mistakenly shot down by a JNA jet fighter over the village of Podrute, in the north of Croatia near the town of Varazdin. Ironically they were on their way to a meeting in Belgrade at the time.

Meanwhile, in Bosnia, Izetbegovic was faced with new developments. Taking the lead from their Krajina brothers, the Bosnian Serbs had declared their own autonomy on the basis that the Bosnian government supposedly no longer represented the interests of Bosnia-Hercegovina's Serbian people in international forums. Then there were accurate reports of a meeting on 11 January between President Tudjman and a prominent member of the Bosnian Serb leadership, Nikola Koljevic, at which the partition of Bosnia between Serbs and Croats was allegedly discussed. Paranoia broke out in Sarajevo.

More designs on partition

Warren Zimmerman, the US ambassador, is quite adamant that both Tudjman and Milosevic made no effort whatever to conceal their designs on Bosnia from him, and at a meeting in the autumn of 1991 Tudjman launched into a policy statement on the matter: 'They're dangerous fundamentalists and they're using Bosnia as a beachhead to spread their ideology throughout Europe and even the US', he said. 'The civilized nations should join together to repel this [Muslim] threat. Bosnia has never had any real existence. It should be divided between Serbia and Croatia.'[3]

This allegation was totally without foundation of course,[4] but that didn't worry President Tudjman who was in fact merely spouting the same kind of rhetoric first argued by Croats like Ante Starcevic in the 1860s when he claimed that Greater Croatia actually stretched all the way to the Bulgarian border.[5] Clearly there was no point letting the truth get in the way of his expansionist aspirations, and at a second meeting with Zimmerman early in January 1992 Tudjman continued the argument by spending over an hour trying to convince the ambassador that Bosnia should be divided. This time he claimed that the Sarajevo government actually intended to flood the country with 500,000 Turks and that Izetbegovic had a secret policy to reward large families in order that within a few years Muslims would form the majority group.[6]

He went on to claim that Izetbegovic's plans included the creation of something called 'The Zetra', a swathe of territory dominated by Muslims stretching from Bosnia through Kosovo to the Sandzak of Novi Pazar on the Montenegrin border, and then on into Turkey. He further claimed that Izetbegovic was in fact nothing more than a 'fundamentalist front man for the Turks' and that it was all a conspiracy to create a 'Greater Bosnia'.[7]

In response Zimmerman warned that the United States would not support any division of Bosnia but Tudjman ignored the message and continued that Bosnia, 'doesn't really exist – it was created by colonial powers and reaffirmed by the communists'.[8] When asked how he could possibly do business with Serbia[9] on this venture while their proxies, the Krajina Serbs, controlled one-third of Croatia, Tudjman came up with an even greater gem of wisdom when he said: 'Because I trust Milosevic.'[10]

Faced with this scenario Izetbegovic was forced to take some initiative, although the best he could offer was yet another proposal to turn Yugoslavia into an association of six independent republics. However, on this occasion he also called for a referendum to decide the question of Bosnia's own independence, something which would ultimately signal the beginning of the end for Bosnia because it played right into the hands of Radovan Karadzic and his sponsor in Belgrade. Here for the first time it could be reasonably argued that the Serbs did indeed have some kind of a quasi legal right to remain in federal Yugoslavia if they clearly wished to do so. And the reason was simple – there were 1.3 million of them.

However, it was also abundantly clear that an accommodation of this nature would prove impossible to achieve because the demographic spread was such that all ethnic groupings – Muslim, Croat, Serb and others – were what could best be described as 'mixed'. Bosnia-Hercegovina was for the most part a multi-ethnic society and it would be virtually impossible to draw lines on a map and divide it all up unless a huge voluntary transmigration of people commenced and/or they were encouraged to move by the employment of military force. In the spring of 1992, while coercion tactics had not yet commenced, the antics of all sides ensured that the country remained on course for upheaval, and talks about partition continued to keep the situation volatile.[11]

Violence erupts in Sarajevo

Far more disturbing, however, was the bombing of the sixteenth-century Ferhadija mosque in Banja Luka just two weeks before the referendum. This signalled the start of indiscriminate attacks on Muslim property right across Bosnia and should have been read in tandem with what Karadzic was now spouting to anyone who would listen to him. 'If the Bosnian government continues its efforts to gain independence', he threatened, 'one nation will disappear.'[12] Instead, Izetbegovic claimed that the bombings and intimidation were the work of extremists and urged his supporters not to blame the Serb people. If this was his genuine perception, and the evidence suggests that it was, then he was totally and utterly incorrect. The tragic consequence, however, was that no alarm bells began to ring within the international community and no EC government took any action because no one really understood the mentality of the main leaders, or the potential they possessed to generate catastrophe.

It was in this context that the constitutional referendum on Bosnia's independence, in compliance with the EC criteria for recognition, took place over two days at the end of February 1992,[13] and of the 63 per cent who voted, 99.4 per cent of them opted to secede from Yugoslavia. Most Serbs (32 per cent of the total population) followed Karadzic's advice and boycotted the proceedings, leaving the Serb leadership to announce that if Bosnia was recognised internationally they would militarily defend the territory they now held. On 1 March the first shots were fired in Sarajevo when gunmen opened fire on a Serb wedding party which was marching through the predominantly Muslim neighbourhood of Bascarsija. The bridegroom's father was killed and an Orthodox priest wounded.[14]

Izetbegovic immediately condemned the murder, and Selim Hadzibajric, the mayor of old Sarajevo, apologised, but to no avail. Having threatened before the referendum that Northern Ireland would look like a holiday camp compared with what Bosnia was going to turn into, Karadzic now believed his prophecy to be vindicated and claimed that the murder was evidence of what would happen on a large scale to the Bosnian Serb population. Within hours Bosnian Serb thugs had set up barricades all over the city and in some cases were conducting their own patrols armed with hunting rifles, machine guns and anti-tank rockets.

This was not a spontaneous reaction – the speed with which armed thugs appeared on the streets confirmed that. In an *Osobodjenje* commentary the following day Gordana Knezevic and Rasim Cerimagic suggested that the whole incident had probably been a set-up orchestrated from the beginning by the Bosnian Serb leadership. The paper was vilified for such a suggestion, but right from the outset it was clear that the story was probably right.[15] Nevertheless, Izetbegovic persisted with the argument that he had an electoral mandate from his people, and, disregarding the growing civil unrest, he proclaimed the independence of Bosnia-Hercegovina on 3 March.

The Cutilherio plan

Realising that disaster was now incubating, a variety of Western diplomats launched themselves into a series of initiatives designed to contain the situation, if not resolve it. Cyrus Vance was first off the mark and managed to get all sides together in Sarajevo on 6 March pledging to resolve their differences by peaceful means. Three days later Lord Carrington assembled Croat and Muslim delegates in Brussels and for the first time succeeded in getting them to talk about the concept of a 'federation structure' for Bosnia. However, the main effort was launched on 18 March when the Portuguese foreign minister, Jose Pires Cutilherio, introduced what was to become known as the 'Cutilherio plan'.

The plan envisaged that Bosnia would be composed of three constituent units, based on national principles, using the Swiss cantons as a model, and taking account of economic, geographic and other considerations. It would remain an integrated unitary state and none of the constituent parts would encourage or support territorial claims that might be made by neighbouring states; that is, Croatia and Serbia. Free elections would take place, human rights would be respected, and freedom of political and religious expression would be guaranteed.

To ensure that these principles had equal application within each region a tribunal composed of representatives from all ethnic groupings, together with independent international observers, would ensure compliance. Then, for the first time, a map was produced proposing the division of Bosnia-Hercegovina into three cantons, and a debate began which was to see map after map produced in the coming years – each being more problematic than the one before.

But for now Cutilherio's proposals represented the first serious attempt to resolve the problem rather than just contain it, and the sincerity of his proposals was reflected in the fact that all three leaders signed up to them in Sarajevo without reservation – Izetbegovic for the Muslims, Karadzic for the Serbs and Stepan Klujic for the Croats.

Alas, this collective goodwill lasted just one week and by 25 March Izetbegovic was backtracking furiously, insisting that the division of Bosnia along ethnic lines should be rejected at all costs. He further stated that he had only signed the plan because the EC had made acceptance of it a precondition for international recognition, something which he could never subsequently substantiate.

Two days later the Bosnian Serbs also decided to go their own way, and a meeting of their so-called 'parliament' in Pale approved a constitution for their new 'Serbian Republic of Bosnia-Hercegovina' (Republic Srpska) which they ultimately hoped to incorporate into an all-Serb state of Yugoslavia. Within nine days both sides had moved from a common position to ones which were diametrically opposed, thereby leaving Cutilherio's plan destined for the garbage bin and war about to engulf them all.

Marching for peace

The signs were ominous early on the morning of Sunday, 5 April, when several Serb members of the Sarajevo police department failed to report for duty. They had disappeared the previous evening and taken weapons and equipment with them. In other places across the city Serb workers also stayed at home. At midday a demonstration for peace got underway from the suburb of Dobrinja and by the time they reached the parliament building several thousand people had joined in. However, armed Serbs manning barricades across the Miljacka river in Grbavica were not impressed and fired some shots in the air. Incensed by this action a number of demonstrators approached the bridge, but the Serbs responded by firing into the crowd. Suada Dilberovic was hit and died shortly afterwards. Many others were wounded.

At this point the crowd moved away from the bridge and stormed the parliament building, with 2,000 of them staying there overnight. The following morning further crowds arrived and by midday the plaza outside was thronged with people. Then, just after 1 p.m. gunshots rang out from the upper floors and the roof of the Holiday Inn across the street. Panic broke out as people lay bleeding and wounded all over the place. 'There was no question as to who was responsible. The Holiday Inn was under control of the Serbian Democratic Party; its leader Radovan Karadzic; and his pack of bodyguards.'[16] For once there was no confusion between perception and reality.[17]

Left with no other option, Izetbegovic now appealed to his followers to mobilise and ironically his instructions were issued at the very time both the EC and US decided to recognise the independence of Bosnia-Hercegovina. Immediately the two Serb members of the collective Bosnian presidency, Nikola Koljevic and Biljana Plavsic, resigned and walked out to take up prominent positions in the new Republic Srpska. There would be no going back.

Throughout the country heavy fighting erupted as people of common ethnic origin banded together and armed themselves with whatever they could muster in an attempt to defend their towns, villages and homes from those on the other sides whom they believed were attempting to redraw the map of Bosnia and put demarcation lines in places where none had ever existed before.

Shootings were reported from several places as each side made pre-emptive strikes against the others. The Croats took the town of Kupres from the Serbs and then turned their attention to expanding the size of their enclaves in Muslim-held central Bosnia. The Serbs attacked the Croats in Bosanski Brod while also intensifying their shelling of Mostar. Sarajevo was hit repeatedly, and Cutilherio and Vance continued trying to negotiate a new ceasefire which was no sooner agreed by the politicians on 12 April than the military decided to ignore it and fighting continued on the ground. The manner in which the town of Bosanska Krupa in the Bihac Pocket region of north-west Bosnia stumbled into war was typical of the country as a whole with local Serb militias now at liberty to use tanks, artillery, mortars, anti-aircraft guns and helicopters, more or less at will, thus leaving the beleaguered Muslims in the unenviable position of trying to hold the line with just the handful of rusty muskets, an assortment of shooting rifles, and whatever bits and pieces they could manage to pilfer from the JNA in the days before they left.

The CSCE and the US State Department issued stern warnings to the Serbs on 20 April, but nobody listened. Then Lord Carrington and Cutilherio thought that they had successfully brokered a deal on 23 April, but the military ignored them too. At UN headquarters in New York several delegations demanded that the secretary-general, Boutros Boutros-Ghali, should immediately send UN troops to Bosnia. He refused on the basis that there was no peace to keep, leaving the Bosnian presidency to call on the JNA to leave the country. The Serb generals refused, claiming that they were entitled to defend Serb-controlled areas.

In the midst of this confusion Serbia and Montenegro proclaimed the formation of a new Yugoslavia, the Federal Republic of Yugoslavia, and Milosevic actually renounced Yugoslavia's claims on any other territories – but nobody believed him. Likewise Karadzic's claim that he no longer had any aspiration to unify the Republic Srpska with Serbia proper, but was now intent on developing a separate state, was greeted with equal disbelief. It was perfectly clear that the old Balkan maxim, 'the only truth is the lie', still had direct application in modern Yugoslav politics.

As the situation in Sarajevo continued to deteriorate Izetbegovic had a narrow escape on 2 May and was fortunate to avoid imprisonment when he was arrested by Serb militiamen at an impromptu checkpoint. However, after UNPROFOR officers intervened his release was secured, thereby allowing him to sign a truce with the JNA three days later. Alas, this limited success was overshadowed by news filtering through from Austria which indicated that Karadzic and the new Bosnian Croat leader Mate Boban had met in Graz on 6 May and agreed to stop fighting one another and then partition Bosnia on ethnic lines.

By this point the general security situation had become so bad that the EC felt it necessary to order the evacuation of its monitors from Sarajevo, and EC ambassadors were withdrawn from Belgrade. Warren Zimmerman was recalled to Washington, and the CSCE, while still allowing representatives from Belgrade to attend its meetings, banned them from participating in debates on the war.[18]

And then to compound the situation further the UN secretary-general refused to commit any peacekeeping troops to Bosnia, other than the UNPROFOR headquarters personnel who were already deployed in Sarajevo under the Vance plan, because of what he claimed to be the 'brutal pitch of the fighting' – and then on 13 May he further proposed that this group leave as well.[19] This was quite understandable, given the graphic reports which were originating from all over Bosnia detailing a phenomenon which would become known as 'ethnic cleansing' – the forced migration of whole communities as a result of threats, direct violence and oppression. For example, 83 Muslims were reported as rounded up and shot in Zaklopace,[20] and a further 50 were killed near Zvornik. Additionally, an ICRC relief convoy was ambushed en route to Sarajevo and its leader, Frederic Maurice, killed on 18 May.

These represented just some of the statistics for a 48-hour period in May, by which time UNHCR reports estimated that 1.2 million people in Bosnia had become refugees or displaced persons, and the casualty figures since March had risen to a staggering 2,225 killed, 7,660 wounded and 2,555 missing.[21] Sadako Ogata, the senior UNHCR official in the region, further estimated that in addition to Bosnia there were now 598,000 refugees in Croatia, 70,000 in Slovenia, 382,000 in Serbia, 48,000 in Montenegro and 69,000 in the UNPAs in Croatia. Her warning that 'we may find ourselves stranded with an open ended relief programme and a massive permanent refugee problem in the heart of Europe' proved to be prophetic.[22]

It was in this context that the UN General Assembly took its decision to admit Bosnia, Croatia and Slovenia as full members of the United Nations Organisation in the hope that official recognition would make it clear to all manner of Serbs that further agitation and violence was pointless. James Baker, US secretary of state, followed this lead on 22 May by ordering the closure of Yugoslavia's consulates in the US and the expulsion of her military attachés from Washington.

It was hardly surprising, therefore, that the tone of the Lisbon Peace Conference which began on 24 May should be decidedly anti-Serb, and with James Baker castigating Europe for its inactivity and lack of progress, pressure started to mount for the imposition of a range of political and economic sanctions.

The bread queue massacre

Then, on following day, 25 May, with the Conference in full session, reports began to filter through of an incident which had just happened in Sarajevo. Civilians queuing for bread in Vase Miskina Street, in the heart of the city, had been shelled, and the graphic pictures which were flashed around the world provided the anti-Serb brigade with ample evidence to condemn Karadzic and his supporters. Seventeen people died that day and over 160 others were wounded when a salvo of mortars smashed into the tightly packed street and the Bosnian Muslim delegation, led by Haris Silajdzic, walked out of the building in protest.

However, when the matter was investigated by the UN it became very unclear whether the incident had in fact been perpetrated by the Serbs at all. The poor people of Sarajevo could just as easily have been shelled by their own troops, on the instructions of their own government, in order to provoke international reaction in Lisbon – and have the Serbs condemned for it. This was unequivocally the view of General Lewis MacKenzie who by now had set up UNPROFOR operations on the ground in the city,[23] and as far as he was concerned the events on 25 May merely confirmed this.[24]

Colm Doyle, Lord Carrington's special envoy, who was a participant at the conference in Lisbon when the news from Sarajevo came in also believed that as far as the Sarajevo leadership were concerned international military intervention was what they wanted and they saw it as the key to their survival.

They were convinced that having achieved recognition the international community would now intervene militarily to protect their sovereignty against Serb aggression and that '[i]n the pursuit of this goal the Muslim interest in a negotiated settlement was less than enthusiastic. The mere possibility of some sort of intervention, especially a US military one, encouraged them to continue military action rather than concentrate on the peace negotiations.'[25] The attack on the bread queue caused an immediate cessation of the peace talks, and the prospect of a negotiated settlement with the Serbs was [successfully?] removed from the agenda.

Whatever the truth of the matter in Sarajevo that afternoon, the Serbs got all the bad press that was going, because for right-thinking people it was simply inconceivable that the Bosnian Muslims would shell their own people, or alternatively fire at the Serbs from the centre of the city in order to provoke them into firing back once they had located the original gun position. On 27 May there had been no outgoing fire from the area of the bread queue in the market. This leaves only two possibilities. Either the Serbs did fire and were incredibly accurate with what are notoriously inaccurate weapons. Or alternatively somebody else detonated an explosive device in pursuit of a political agenda.

UNPROFOR officers in Sarajevo did not believe the Serbs were to blame; MacKenzie is on record as stating that his people told him 'a number of things did not fit'; Doyle in Lisbon was far from convinced either; and both Lord David Owen and Yossef Bodansky have seen fit to record their reservations in book form.[26] In any evaluation of this incident it is therefore incumbent to ask why all these people were unable to accept the common media perception of an incident which was flashed around the world and became instant reality.

What was not revealed to anyone at the time was that lurking in the background were the hands of Ruder Finn Inc., the US public relations firm which the Sarajevo government had retained since they first saw what they had achieved for the Slovenes in 1991.[27] A single message was broadcast from Sarajevo that day – the Serbs were to blame, and anyone who offered a different version (including MacKenzie) was vilified as being anti-Muslim.

There was to be no debate on this issue and within days the UN's own report on the bombing/explosion disappeared and remains of such sensitivity that it cannot be accessed from UN resources. The author has also spoken to one UN official who was involved in the investigation, but he remains unwilling to confirm or deny anything lest he be denied future employment in the UN.

When these very questions were put directly to Haris Silajdzic, the Bosnian prime minister, by the BBC's John Simpson in the course of a *Panorama* investigation in January 1995, Silajdzic either refused to answer or claimed it was all anti-Muslim propaganda. His denials, such as they were, served only to make the case against him stronger and to perpetuate confusion.[28] But therein lies the whole problem of understanding Balkan politics at the end of the twentieth century because in the majority of cases the only truth is still the lie. The events on Vase Miskina Street would be repeated again and again as the conflict went on. Confusion would continue to reign, and attributing actual responsibility would remain an impossible task. And thanks to media-generated perception, and good public relations by the Sarajevo government, rightly or wrongly the Serbs would continue to take the blame.

There was, however, one interesting development in Lisbon which has until now gone unreported. By the time Sky News flashed pictures of the carnage in Sarajevo around the world the Peace Conference had been in session for eight days and was making very little progress. The four negotiators, Cutilherio, Soarez, Darwin and Doyle, had become more than a little tired of the alternating hourly sessions during which the Serbs, Muslims and Croats were equally unprepared to make the slightest compromise.

It was more than a little surprising, then, when Radovan Karadzic stormed into the room shouting, 'We did not do it, we did not do it.' Jose Cutilherio (who would later be appointed secretary-general of the Western European Union) turned to him and said: 'It really doesn't matter whether you did or not. You will be blamed for it anyway.' With Karadzic in a vulnerable position and an agitated state, Colm Doyle seized the opportunity and suggested that he would have to concede something tangible if his credibility was to be restored. Doyle suggested that Sarajevo airport should be reopened immediately and put under UN control.

Karadzic was outraged at this suggestion and launched into a tirade of abuse against the UN, accusing them of smuggling arms to the Bosnian Muslims, but Doyle, an Irish army officer, was equally appalled at this allegation and proceeded to make it very clear to the Serb leader that his position was becoming more untenable by the minute. Eventually Karadzic calmed down and before he left the room had signed an agreement to re-open Sarajevo airport the following week, the details of which would be sorted out by General MacKenzie and his staff.

Nevertheless the Bosnian Serbs lost badly as a result of the bread queue massacre, and Western leaders took from this incident only what they needed to justify and bolster their own policies, prejudices and political positions. Unfortunately for the Serbs this incident in Sarajevo also coincided with renewed shelling in and around Dubrovnik and the resumption of hostilities between the JNA and the Croatian army along the Dalmatian coast on 29 May.

Yet again few reporters displayed any interest in the facts of the matter, which indicated that in fact it had been Croatian troops who had renewed this particular campaign in an attempt to push JNA units away from the coast and thereby re-open the only road into the area which they had deemed critical for their own re-supply operations. So the JNA had in fact only been responding to Croatian attempts to relocate the front line and this version of events might have helped explain why shells were dropping in the vicinity of Dubrovnik[29] – but nobody was interested in that type of interpretation because once again it did not fit the perception TV networks wished to peddle to their unsuspecting international audience.

That their case should have been treated more equitably is not an issue – it is a fact. There were after all 1.3 million of them and by any standard one cares to employ they were entitled to their point of view, and to have it aired. The problem was, however, that they never managed to put this case before the international community, and whatever marginal support they might have had was lost when one report after another was published citing horrific evidence of something which came to be known as 'ethnic cleansing'.

Ethnic cleansing

The term itself concealed the actuality and reality of the situation because there was nothing remotely 'clean' about this barbaric process. Although it all sounded clinical, sanitised and even painless, in reality the programme was both savage and brutal. Pain and torture, both physical and mental, and of an intensity and scale unimaginable in modern civilised Western society, became the sadistic tools used to evict hundreds of thousands of

Muslims, Croats and Serbs from towns and villages where their ancestors had lived for generations.

It started first in the towns nearest to the border with Serbia proper where yet again groups of so-called 'volunteers' arrived from Belgrade to promote what they considered to be the pan-Serb cause. Behaving in like manner to the original 'volunteers' who had descended on eastern Slavonia in 1990, these latest recruits quickly became a law unto themselves with the local political authorities either ignoring what was happening or tacitly supporting it, while the Serb-dominated local police and military were probably glad of some assistance, at least initially. Thereafter, as events began to spiral out of control, most of Bosnian Serb officialdom became implicated by association with the 'volunteers', and the easier option for most of them was simply to go along with what was happening. Few if any had the courage to speak out in opposition, and even if someone had it would probably have made no difference.

The most notable of the 'volunteer' groups operating in eastern Bosnia at this time was a gang of thugs from Belgrade called Arkan's Tigers. These were a mob of pathological criminals led by a self-styled anarchist called Zeljko Raznjatovic, who later became a member of the Serbian parliament representing Kosovo – which of course was 85 per cent ethnic Albanian! These thugs, who had previously involved themselves in the siege of Vukovar in 1991, decided to once again pursue the goal of Serb supremacy by violently subjugating all minority opposition they encountered. In the climate of fear, uncertainty and ignorance which prevailed at the time their possibilities were endless as they exploited the confused situation to the maximum.

Initially they aligned themselves with the local police or militia on the pretext of protecting the Serb community from potential attack, but then commenced a campaign of systematic terror against Muslims and Croats in their immediate vicinity.[30] Where the Muslims decided to resist what was happening they then had to contend with General Mladic and his JNA-supported military who were every bit as methodical as Arkan in subjugating anyone who dared confront them.[31]

For those Muslims who remained in Bosnian Serb-controlled areas the regime they endured had become intolerable.[32] There are no excuses whatsoever for what was allowed to happen, nor can there be any absolution for those who permitted it to continue, but by Balkan standards this was nothing new and most of the adult population had seen it all before during the Second World War. For many of the perpetrators it was simply a case of the boot now being on the other foot.

The question arises as to whether Karadzic and the Bosnian Serb political leadership knew what was going on? The answer is that it would have been virtually impossible for them not to, which in turn begs the question of what, if anything, they could reasonably have been expected to do about it? Would a public condemnation have made any difference? Probably not.

Equally, the concept of 'right and wrong', as understood in the Judaeo-Christian tradition, had never much to do with reality in Yugoslav politics where history was, and still is, often justified on the basis of the last atrocity. So the Bosnian Serb leadership said and did nothing.

However, the critical issue here is whom the international community decided to hold responsible for the atrocities taking place across the country. It was not Radovan Karadzic who was singled out for criticism, nor was it the Republic Srpska against which economic sanctions were imposed. Instead, when the UN Security Council met in New York on 31 May it acted with a clear conscience based on the relevant information available to it and passed UNSC Resolution 757 which imposed economic sanctions against Serbia and Montenegro – the regime of Slobodan Milosevic. The vote was 13–0. Even Russia could not defend what at face value appeared to be indefensible behaviour.[33]

The government in Sarajevo had also succeeded in having its position legitimised at the highest levels. The politics of lies, hate and double-think had become the standard all round. And a mass exodus of terrified, simple, ordinary people had begun. Their only crime, by and large, had been to worship a different God and to be perceived as a threat. Unfortunately it was all about to get worse.[34]

With sanctions now in place Milosevic suggested that if this was the price to be paid for keeping all Serbs together then so be it,[35] but Izetbegovic decided that enough was enough and proclaimed a state of war to exist in Bosnia, ordering a general mobilisation on 20 June. Karadzic, for his part, continued to offer one ceasefire plan after another, but none of them ever came to anything largely because his target audience never kept an open channel on which to receive him.

Eventually, on 29 June, and following on directly from the visit of President Mitterrand to Sarajevo, the UN secretary-general agreed to the deployment of peacekeeping troops in Bosnia. By now, though, there was no prospect whatsoever of immediate peace. The three ethnic groups were all busy setting up their own republics, the latest of which was the Croatian Republic of Herceg-Bosna (CRHB),[36] and the best that new peacekeepers could hope to achieve would be to interpose between the factions and try to keep them apart.

As July wore on every political action which took place was interpreted by the Serbs as justification for reaction. Tudjman and Izetbegovic succeeded in signing a variety of agreements[37] which brought the two governments closer together, but in response the Serbs continued with the military campaign, and in Bosnia particularly continued the systematic removal of thousands of non-Serb people from their homes and communities.[38]

Those who survived this appalling treatment were lucky. By mid-August almost 2 million Bosnians had been driven from their homes; thousands were killed or missing; and those still alive were either on the move, incarcerated in prison camps or sleeping in temporary accommodation. Europe was witnessing the largest forced movement of people since the days of the Third Reich.[39]

In Sarajevo, Izetbegovic now pleaded for Western military intervention and the positioning of troops along the Drina river (Bosnia's border with Serbia), but the main focus of the UN's operations involved keeping Sarajevo's airport operational in order to receive and distribute humanitarian aid. On 17 July Lord Carrington managed to get the three warring leaderships to round-table talks in London and agreement was reached to begin a 14-day ceasefire prior to substantive talks thereafter. Within three days the ceasefire was in shreds, and no heavy weapons had been surrendered. However, it was at this point that General MacKenzie began looking at the possibility of setting up a regular UN peacekeeping mission and suggested that 40,000 troops would be needed to do that job in Sarajevo alone. As a stop-gap measure the UN secretary-general tasked UNPROFOR on 2 July to set up heavy weapons collection points

The prison camps

When the parties did come back to the table in London on 28 July new EC proposals to turn Bosnia-Hercegovina into a series of cantons, similar to Switzerland, were again rejected out of hand by Haris Silajdzic, the Bosnian prime minister. Instead the conference became consumed with a totally different issue which arose from media reports that the Bosnian Serbs were operating 'concentration camps' in which Muslim prisoners were being detained and maltreated.[40]

When this was put to Karadzic at the London Peace Conference he refuted all allegations and invited anyone who wanted to visit the camps to do so.[41] If he personally knew of prisoner abuse it is inconceivable that he would have made this public gesture, but the revelation of the existence of these camps, and apparent confirmation by US agencies, did irreparable damage to the Serb cause and consolidated the emerging perception that the Serbs were basically evil people. From that day forward Karadzic's credibility as an international statesman evaporated and for as long as he made any attempt to justify the existence of the camps he remained contaminated by them. In this context much was also made of the fact that the bulk of these so-called 'detention centres' were located in the north-west corner of Bosnia, in close proximity to the infamous Second World War camp at Jasenovac, and it was alleged by many commentators that this in some way represented a manifestation of evil reincarnate. The fact that it was Croatian Ustashe who had run Jasenovac was ignored completely in the rush to demonise the Serbs.

When the first journalists were eventually admitted to the Omarska iron-ore processing plant in August they reported scenes allegedly not seen anywhere in Europe since 1945. They reported on men caged like animals, with heads shaved and ribs protruding from famished bodies, barely able to move and unable to adjust their eyes to direct sunlight. They claimed they had found thousands of Muslim men crammed into the equivalent of a huge chicken coop, immobile for 24 hours of the day, lying in their own excrement, overpowered and overcome by claustrophobia and the stench, with some dying slowly of asphyxiation. On top of all that there were allegations of all kinds of atrocity, with some allegedly perpetrated by the inmates upon one another, and while this was bad enough it was further alleged to be far worse for those prisoners who were removed from the group because these unfortunates were then set upon by elements within the sadistic regime which ran these places. Killing, torture, humiliation and savage cruelty were allegedly the order of the day – everyday – and hundreds of years of pent-up historical hatred were apparently let loose in a daily torrent of sadistic abuse and maltreatment, not just in Omarska but in several other similar places as well.

The names Keraterm, Luka, Susica, Manjaca and Trnoploje all held terrible significance for those unfortunate enough to be detained within them. And it was not confined to the men. In schools, halls and large private houses all over the country Muslim women and children were rounded up and imprisoned in appalling conditions and subsequently set upon by their guards and other Serb soldiers. It was as if these Serbs believed that by defiling them they were trampling a people into extinction and thereby ensuring that they would never rise again. It had, of course, exactly the opposite effect and this explains the continuing hatred which predominates Bosnian Muslim thinking right to the present day.

There is no debate about the existence of these camps, and volumes have been written recording in graphic detail what journalists found when they visited them. People were killed, women were raped, others were abused in one way or another. However, it is also a fact that in all wars prisoners are taken, they are detained, and in spite of the existence of legal conventions governing how prisoners and detainees should be treated, rarely if ever is this subject a priority for commanders in the context of the main war effort.

In civil wars it is even less so and invariably the task of managing these prisons becomes the responsibility of people who were already on the fringe of their own society prior to the war, have no legal training whatever, never previously wore a uniform of any description and have quickly become divorced from whatever they previously perceived to be reality. This was the case in Bosnia where the ICRC identified and recorded that by 1 September 1992 prison camps being run by all three sides in the conflict had the following numbers of registered detainees:[42]

Croatian-controlled camps (913)
Bosanski Brod	139
Mostar prison	192
Ljubuski	92
Bosanski Brod Krindija	382
Capljlna	50
Livno prison	58

Serb-controlled camps (8,320)
Bileca	456
Manjaca	2,884
Trnopolje	3,500
Omarska	200
Batovic	1,280

Muslim-controlled camps (916)
Zenica prison	289
Visoko	210
Celebici	287
Konjic	130

It is also a fact that journalists and others were shocked at what they found in these camps, and the inmates they interviewed recounted stories which could not have been contrived. Countless people died in detention and countless others were abused – but it happened on all three sides. The Serbs had more detainees and correspondingly the numbers killed and abused were greater. For this they were apportioned the lion's share of guilt, and based on numbers alone this point is not arguable. However, the manner in which the Serbs as a nation were demonised certainly is.

In *Seasons in Hell* Ed Vulliamy recounts what he discovered in north-central Bosnia during the summer of 1992 (there are several other similar accounts), and it is a shocking tale of man's inhumanity to man and woman. At Trnopolje he met Fikret Alic,[43] a young man with a famished torso and xylophone rib cage, whom Vulliamy claimed had been starved into this dismal malnourished condition after 52 days of imprisonment in Keraterm. This was correct. He also claimed that this image of Alic had now become the symbol of the war. This was correct also because pictures of Alic subsequently appeared in publications worldwide. What Vulliamy did not mention (and of which he was perhaps unaware at the time) was that Alic was suffering from tuberculosis and had been for some time. His famished condition was not due solely to his incarceration, and when one looked more closely at the photography it became quite clear that those standing in the background behind him were not similarly malnourished.

Equally, the fence behind which they were standing was of the single strand barbed wire variety with the nails on the inside!

Therefore neither the structure of the fence, the nature of the prison, the number of the detainees, nor the general condition of the majority of prisoners in any of these camps could in any way be equated or compared to the real concentration camps of the Second World War. This was not Belsen, this was not Auschwitz, this was not Stuthoff, and a hitherto unpublished ECMM Report complied by EC monitors Barney Mayhew and Charles McLeod provides a less emotive, better-balanced and more relevant account of what was actually taking place.[44]

Writing in the *Financial Times* throughout this period, Judy Dempsey corroborated virtually all of ECMM's findings. However, she also discovered an issue of *Epocha*, the weekly magazine of Serbia's (Milosevic's) Socialist Party, which contained the following passage:

> This region (north west Bosnia) is now cleared of Croats and Muslims. Our Army surrounds Muslim villages. If the Muslims do not raise the white flag we raze the villages to the ground. Serb villages will be built there ... Those people not from mixed marriages can go to Izetbegovic, or to Croatia. Those from mixed marriages who have not fired at Serbs can choose to remain. In Kotor Varos (once a town of 36,000 east of Banja Luka) there are no longer ethnic minorities.[45]

Dempsey went on to identify that all sides were involved in this 'cleansing' and also reported that the Muslim-run camp in Konjic, previously identified by the ICRC as containing 130 detainees, now contained over 3,000 Bosnian Serbs who were imprisoned in a damp, dank, dark, disused railway tunnel. What she did not elaborate upon, perhaps because she did not make the connection, was the fact that by publishing 'progress reports' on ethnic cleansing in *Epocha* Milosevic and his cohorts effectively endorsed what by now had become a clear and unambiguous policy. The army referred to as 'our army' was the newly formed Bosnian Serb army (BSA), staffed and equipped from Belgrade and led by General Ratko Mladic.

Mladic had become the leader of this group because Milosevic promoted him into the job. The chain of command for 'our army' was very simple: it ran from the thugs on the streets to the commanders who supervised them, to the general staff of the BSA, to Ratko Mladic, and, finally, to Slobodan Milosevic himself. Radovan Karadzic may have been nominally the president of the RS and *de jure* the commander-in-chief of the BSA, but he did not have any *de facto* position within its chain of command, a point which arose again and again for those who wished to see it. In this context, then, the question arises as to who bears ultimate responsibility for what happened in Kozarac?

Kovacevic and Kozarac

Born on 10 February 1941 in the village of Bozici, near Prijedor, in northwest Bosnia-Hercegovina, Milan Kovacevic spent his first years interned with his mother in the Second World War Croatian concentration camp at Jasenovac where tens of thousands of Serbs, Jews and gypsies were being systematically exterminated. By 1992 he had risen to become an anaesthetist by profession and also vice-president of the local Serbian Democratic Party's 'Krizni Stab' (Crisis Committee) in Prijedor.[46]

Of course his 'official title' was prone to change depending on whom he was talking to. One day he was the 'executive mayor', the next he was the 'city manager', and the day after he could be the 'president of the municipal council'. But by whatever title one chose to address him Kovacevic was in charge and not much happened in Prijedor that he had not authorised. It was from this 'exalted' position, that he empowered himself to oversee a wholesale alteration to the demographic balance in the town, which prior to that had been the second largest city in northern Bosnia with a population of 112,000 – over half of whom were Muslims.

With Bosnia spiralling out of control, nationalist Serbs led by Kovacevic organised a night-time coup against the elected Muslim authorities and the following morning had taken control of the town and surrounding municipality. There was little if any fighting. The Serbs controlled the local territorial defence units, which were well armed, and consequently the Muslims offered little or no resistance. They were not prepared for a fight; they were not prepared for war; and they were certainly not prepared for the criminal savagery which followed.

Once Kovacevic and his cohorts had control of Prijedor and its hinterland the majority of the region's Muslim men were marched off into several *ad hoc* prison camps – Keraterm, Omarska and others. Many Muslim women were incarcerated in a camp at Trnopolje where rape and torture were carried out. Then they turned their attention to the nearby town of Kozarac, just six miles away, which had a population of 25,000, the majority of whom were Muslim. The town was quickly surrounded by Serb tanks and on 24 May 15 shells impacted in the town every minute, having whistled through the air from 12 different directions. The cleansing of Kozarac turned out to be one of the most vicious episodes of civilian slaughter in the entire war.[47]

Of course Kovacevic did not accomplish all of this on his own. He was ably assisted by a variety of underlings, not least amongst whom were the likes of the now-convicted war criminal Dusan Tadic, and the self-styled 'police chief' of Prijedor, Simo Drljaca. However, it is crucial to point out at this juncture that when in August 1992 Radovan Karadzic authorised the international media to travel to Prijedor to visit the prison camps scattered nearby it was Milan Kovacevic and his colleagues the journalists discovered to be clearly in charge of the region – including the camps themselves.[48]

Life in north-central Bosnia in the summer of 1992 was savage, brutal, primitive and tribal. Kovacevic told Ed Vulliamy that it was, in his opinion, 'a great time for the Serb nation'.[49] It was not. It was evil personified, and in this regard the journalists and reporting agencies were as one. For once there was no divergence between perception and reality.[50]

In late August Lara Marlowe managed to travel as far as Kozarac and found Serb militiamen now sitting in houses amongst the personal effects of the former Muslim residents. She spoke to one of them, Dragan Zamaklaar, and discovered the complexities of the whole cleansing phenomenon:

> I feel nothing for the Muslims who lived in the house we have taken. Muslims moved into our home in Kladusa [the town of Velika Kladusa in the Bihac region]. They killed my uncle last spring. How would you feel if you saw Muslims slit your uncle's throat or if you saw them throw Serb women and old people out of windows? The house we built in Kladusa had ten rooms and a basement but now six of us live in a house with just four rooms.[51]

Marlowe went on to meet Zamaklaar's mother, father, grandmother, sister and brother, all of whom had no income and spent most of their time sitting in the house trying to figure out what had actually happened to them. She also discovered that notwithstanding the tit-for-tat nature of the conflict, and however those involved might rationalise their predicament, in actual fact all of them were only succeeding in impoverishing one another.

Karadzic's culpability

The matter of Radovan Karadzic's culpability in all of this now needs to be examined. In the first instance it is a matter of fact that he had no direct or personal control over the actual camps themselves, and there is direct evidence that he issued instructions to his army commanders in June 1992 ordering them to obey the rules of international humanitarian law.[52]

There is also the undisputed fact that when journalists first accused him of running 'concentration camps' he immediately invited the international media to come and visit them, which is how Gutman, Vulliamy, Burns and all the others, actually got permission to go to Omarska and Trnopolje in the first place. Accordingly, it is not at all clear whether back in 1992 Karadzic

> individually, or in concert with others, planned, instigated, ordered, or otherwise aided and abetted in the planning, preparation, and

execution of, the persecutions on political and religious grounds, of Bosnian Muslim and Bosnian Croat civilians, or knew, or had reason to know that subordinates were about to do the same or had done so, and failed to take the necessary and reasonable measures to prevent such acts or to punish the perpetrators thereof.[53]

In fact it is perfectly arguable that he made a reasonable effort to stop what was taking place in the camps, but this reality was certainly not perceived by those who filed their copy, and Western editors had already decided anyway who the good and the bad guys actually were.

Granted, if one accepts that 'the commander-in-chief is always responsible for all his men do and fail to do' then the case against Karadzic is closed. If, however, one is prepared to concede that he never had full control over Kovacevic and others like him, and failed to take action against them because he genuinely failed to comprehend the gravity of what was taking place, or actually thought people were obeying his order of 13 June, then perhaps he should be allowed to plead to lesser charges. But that also depends of course on how you interpret other things he did in the course of the following three years.[54]

International reaction to the prison camps

August 1992 was marked by continuing international outrage over the discovery of the camps in the Serb-controlled areas of Bosnia, and the US State Department was first off the mark to condemn Karadzic and immediately began to call for the establishment of a war crimes tribunal. Images of Serb atrocities were flashed around the globe, ensuring that from now on it would become virtually impossible for the international community to retain any objectivity in their dealings with Karadzic, notwithstanding that he had issued further orders to his subordinates.[55] Yet again there is evidence to suggest that Karadzic did indeed issue these and other orders to his subordinates, but in the media this was ignored. The Serbs would never again get the benefit of the doubt in all that was to follow, even on occasions when they were perfectly entitled to it.

That said, there were some writers who chose to challenge the Ruder Finn Inc. version of events, and in 1999 Norma von Ragenfeld Feldman set about a comprehensive deconstruction of what Pulitzer prize winners John Burns and Roy Gutman had been writing. Firstly, attacking Burns and the reports he filed for the *New York Times*, Feldman was critical of the fact that from her perspective he had been far too close to the presidency in Sarajevo and not objective in his continual condemnation of the Serbs for all kinds of atrocity. She also claims that in Gutman's case much of his reporting was based on the testimonies of just two witnesses and as such it amounted to little more than hearsay.[56]

Certainly Burns relied heavily on the story of a Serb soldier, Borislav Herak, to identify the criminal behaviour of the Serbs, and Gutman was deeply concerned at what he perceived to be the lot of Fikret Alic. Whether their reporting was sufficiently researched (irrespective of their prize winning) is now a moot point, and one can legitimately ask whether even taken in the context of the time some deeper probing should have been undertaken. But the main issue concerns the manner in which their work was exploited by the PR people in Sarajevo who in the early days of August, following the visit of an ITN news crew to Omarska and Trnopolje, immediately generated an international debate comparing the camps to those of the Nazis, and the overall situation to the Holocaust.[57]

The Serb regime was not comparable to that of the Nazis, nor was it correct to compare the general situation on the ground to the Holocaust. Certainly criminal acts were perpetrated in the conflict up to that point, but they were perpetrated by all sides. The critical difference was that Serb abuses were more widespread and the Sarajevo government was adept at managing the international media. Feldman's assessment was that the steady stream of information issuing from Muslim (government) officials was extremely biased. She called it 'a stream of misinformation, twisted facts, and deceiving photographs', and her assessment is supported in large measure by both ECMM and MacKenzie. It is also supported by the French journalist Jaques Merlino (deputy editor-in-chief of France 2 TV) who examined the connection between the media and public opinion in the Former Yugoslavia at this time and concluded that a number of news reports were deliberately aimed at misinforming the (international) public. In fact he went on to claim that a large number of accusations made against the Serbs were unfounded, or at least greatly exaggerated, and following an interview with James Harff of Ruder Finn Inc. he stated that he was frightened and profoundly saddened to find that so many intellectuals had allowed themselves to be duped by an indistinct American who was simply a professional PR man doing his job, and doing it without any remorse, and thinking only about the profits to come his way.[58]

Equally, the US journalist Peter Brock's accusations of pack reporting and journalistic negligence in the media caused immediate controversy – but there was more than a ring of truth to it. He claimed that the media campaign vilifying the Serbs, and designed to force Western governments to intervene militarily, was an unprecedented and unrelenting onslaught combining modern media techniques with advocacy journalism. In other words, a combination of bold headlines, multi-page spreads of gory photographs and gruesome video footage designed to shock Western leaders into reaction on the Muslim side.[59]

The reality was that all sides in the conflict ran detention camps. Some were worse than others. The Serb camps were of the kind that could be found in any war zone worldwide. They were not nice places. Prisoners were starved, beaten and sometimes killed. And rapes did take place. But this was not the Holocaust and the Serbs were not Nazis. Unfortunately, however, this typecasting stuck and the damage to the Serb cause was done long before they even realised it. The media had struck the first decisive blow in the battle for the hearts and minds of the Western public and their political masters.

In an attempt to introduce some balance into the equation an Expert Commission was established pursuant to UNSC Resolution 780 of 6/10/92 to examine in detail the question of detention camps in Bosnia and it visited ten prison/detention camps throughout Bosnia, reporting blatant human rights violations by all sides.[60] This finding was always predictable because no one side ever had a monopoly on savagery in any previous Balkan conflict either, but the international political establishment was not impressed. Instead there were continued screams for retribution against the Serbs, typified perhaps by the reaction of Lawrence Eagleburger, the US deputy secretary of state, who began calling for war crimes investigations.[61]

Another distortion of reality was also exposed at this time when General MacKenzie identified Izetbegovic's strategy and tactics. In spite of MacKenzie's best efforts he (Izetbegovic) would not meet with Karadzic to discuss anything. He was willing to talk to Belgrade, or the JNA, or the UN – but never Karadzic. In this way he sought to delegitimise the Bosnian Serb leader and again he was successful. He also sought by every available means to have the arms embargo lifted, or failing that to have his own troops equipped covertly. When asked if there was anything which would immediately improve the situation, MacKenzie was unequivocal: 'Yes – and the Presidency [of Bosnia] will hate to hear me say this: negotiations with the Serbian side within Bosnia.'

When asked about whether the different leaders actually had control of what was happening on the ground he had this to say: 'There are large numbers of individuals and units that are out of control. But they are out of control within a defined chain of command. There's ample evidence of units operating to their own agenda.'

And when asked why he refused to blame the Serbs for all of Bosnia's ills he maintained that the situation was more complex than that: 'What we now see from the Bosnian Presidency's side is that it is in their interests to keep the thing going and get the Serbs to retaliate in order to convince the international community that intervention is a good idea. So I blame both sides.'[62]

MacKenzie had correctly identified that the intolerance emanating from Sarajevo was every bit as bad as anything coming from Pale, but this assessment flew in the face of the preferred international perception which portrayed Izetbegovic as legitimate, sincere, honest, peace-loving and an elderly statesman. Sarajevo's public relations operation pushed this perception unrelentingly, and it was crucial to their strategy. When Karadzic actually made an offer to return to negotiations on 11 July his call was effectively ignored. He had called for the three parties to sit down together, claiming that he controlled 70 per cent of Bosnia now but only wanted 64 per cent.

However, Izetbegovic completely ignored this offer of talks and called instead for international military force to be used against the Serbs. There is the possibility (perhaps probability), of course, that Izetbegovic was correct in his evaluation and that Karadzic may not have been serious anyway, but no international pressure was brought to bear on Izetbegovic to explore the proposals, and all one can do now is speculate on what might have been.

For those who would claim that Karadzic might well have been sincere in his proposals (and the author is one of them), then this episode potentially represents another opportunity which was lost, and the blame for that loss did not, on this occasion, lie with the Serbs. But there were few, if any, who wanted to take this approach. Instead the West continued a frantic search for its own solution, with senior politicians and diplomats stumbling from one peace conference to another. Each new agreement was heralded as the final solution but inevitably yielded nothing, and on 25 August Lord Carrington resigned, having spent almost a year trying unsuccessfully to find a peaceful resolution to the conflict.

He summed up his frustrations with the whole process as follows:

> All those leaders – almost without exception will agree to anything. They'll put their name to any bit of paper with not the smallest intention of doing anything whatever about it. There's no good faith in practically any of the people I dealt with there. It's much more difficult to negotiate with people who don't mean what they say, because how do you negotiate?[63]

Carrington also identified very clearly that as far as he was concerned the international community was also culpable for recognising Croatia and Slovenia before all other matters were settled:

> From the outset the prospect of recognition had been the one real instrument to keep the parties engaged in the negotiating process. As a result of that December decision (by Germany) the original concept of the Peace Conference unraveled and we had no real leverage which we could bring to bear.[64]

Certainly Carrington had a point of view in this regard and his own perceived failure bore heavily upon him. With the benefit of hindsight it is possible to say that his assessment of the situation was probably correct.

What was not obvious to him at the time was why the parties, and particularly the Muslims, operated as they did. That would become obvious to the man who replaced him – Lord David Owen, the former UK foreign secretary and latterly leader of the SDP.

So the talking continued and the next attempt to solve Bosnia's problems by discussion took place between 26 and 28 August, and became known as the London Conference. All the main players and representatives of over thirty other interested states attended and decided that any attempt to find a solution to the conflict should now be co-ordinated by both the EC and the UN.

To this end Lord Owen for the EC and Cyrus Vance for the UN were appointed as co-chairmen of a Permanent Peace Conference. The Bosnian Serbs agreed to lift the siege of Sarajevo and other towns, to close detention camps, to co-operate with humanitarian relief operations, and to turn over their heavy weapons to the UN.

The international community, for its part, reaffirmed its commitment not to recognise any territorial gains achieved by force and put in place a no-fly zone over Bosnia.[65] As the Conference closed Milosevic expressed his hopes for a successful implementation of the accord but stated that he really had little control over the activities of the Bosnian Serbs. This was not true. Dr Karadzic was equally adamant that his people had nothing to do with attacks on Sarajevo, and this was not true either. Whatever the motivation for these denials – it was not clear then and it is less so now – the meeting was barely over before Lawrence Eagleburger was again planting doubt and articulating his worst-case scenario by stating that he 'did not have any particular confidence that Milosevic would live up to his end of the bargain'.[66] Once again he might have made a greater contribution had he let Milosevic and Karadzic carry on with their gamesmanship and said nothing to distract them.

In any event it was not the Serbs who chose to escalate the situation on the ground that evening as the conference broke up. Instead it was Croatian paramilitary elements who slaughtered 53 women and children in an attack on a convoy of buses near Mostar, and Izetbegovic's own Armija who cut down 20 Serbs as they were attempting to flee the eastern enclave of Gorazde, and no doubt that news gave the Serb leaders something to think about as they made their way home from London.

They were also probably interested in the news that the Western European Union (WEU) had decided to make over 5,000 soldiers available to the UN for the protection of humanitarian convoys in Bosnia, although no decision to do this had yet been made by the UN, and perhaps this influenced them on 30 August to call off their four-month siege of Gorazde.

As the Peace Conference moved on to Geneva[67] the handing over of heavy weapons proved to be a little more complicated than was originally envisaged because neither side was willing to part company with all of their equipment. On top of that the leadership of the HVO announced that they also intended to remove themselves from the jurisdiction of the Bosnian government and called for the division of the country into three distinct entities. This particularly unhelpful announcement was prompted by their belief that the Bosnian Croats could now adequately defend themselves, thanks to recent deliveries of weapons and troops from their sponsors in Zagreb. Such was Croatia's 'good faith' response to the London proposals. Into this simmering cauldron the UN now decided to deploy 6,000 more troops to protect humanitarian activities in Bosnia,[68] bringing the total troop levels to 12,000 in Croatia and 7,500 in Bosnia.

We had now arrived at a point where the international solution to each new escalation of the conflict seemed to be to throw more troops at it without necessarily giving them any clear directive as to what they might be expected to do. Equally, in Croatia all was not well either as violations of the Vance plan ceasefire were being reported daily by ECMM and the UN, and ongoing activities by Serb paramilitaries in eastern Slavonia continued to change the ethnic balance of the region.

In Baranja, for example, the Serb proportion of the population had jumped from 25 per cent before the war to over 70 per cent now, as Croats continued to be expelled in order to make way for Serb refugees from elsewhere in the country, and from parts of Bosnia as well.[69] While the Croatian authorities in Zagreb were outraged at what was happening, and made huge political capital out of it in the international media, it must be pointed out that Croats were performing exactly the same type of ethnic cleansing in western Slavonia in places like Pakrac, Daruvar and along the infamous Dragovic Road.[70] The evidence in all of these areas was incontrovertible, and remained so well into 1995, with the broken shells of thousands of houses lying derelict and empty, deliberately destroyed to ensure that the previous, legitimate and legal occupants could never return.

In any event, on 18 September all sides managed to commence the first round of talks as agreed in London, but any possibility of progress was dealt a severe blow when Karadzic began outlining his plans to resolve matters peacefully by dividing up Bosnia between Croatia and Serbia. Needless to say this was unacceptable to the Muslims, and Izetbegovic immediately departed for the UN in New York where he denounced any plan that would reward ethnic cleansing.

He remained there long enough to witness the expulsion of Yugoslavia from the General Assembly on 22 September – the first such instance in the history of the UN – and the establishment of the UN's own investigation into the camps.[71]

With fighting continuing in several places more foreign troops arrived in theatre, 2,400 of them from Britain, but the only real contribution the international community could still make was to pump in additional humanitarian aid. EC president Jacques Delors sanctioned an increase in the flow of food and medical aid to a total of US$600 million for 1992, but for the Sarajevo government this could never be enough and Haris Silajdzic, the Bosnian prime minister, continued to appeal for the arms embargo to be lifted. And at one level he had a case.

The Armija could not be compared to either the HVO or the BSA, both of which had sponsors across the borders. The Muslims were stuck in the middle with no sponsor, little or no equipment, and they were quite unable to resist any serious operations that were mounted against them because in many places they were still nothing more than mafia gangs in disguise. And they were also faced with the dilemma that even if perchance the Armija were upgraded, the Croats (HVO), and more particularly the Serbs (BSA) would then almost certainly use this as justification to escalate their own operations even further. This catch-22 situation led some in Sarajevo to suggest that it was perhaps better to tolerate this imbalance in the relative strengths of forces, and thereby contain the conflict, rather than achieve parity and risk a huge escalation – but they were a minority.[72]

Then as October drew to a close tensions between the Armija and the HVO continued to surface. In the wake of bitter clashes between the sides at Novi Travnik and at Gornji Vakuf, a climate of mutual distrust developed which culminated in a point-blank refusal by the Armija to accept HVO assistance in defence of the central Bosnian town of Jajce against a concentrated Serb attack. While both sides skirmished with one another, the Serbs advanced on Jajce, took the town, and up to 30,000 Muslims were forced to pack what few belongings they could find and then flee the town and its hinterland. Thereafter they began to pour into Travnik, Vitez and the Lasva valley, places which were in no way able to accommodate them.

Most international observers were unable to comprehend why the Muslims and Croats had failed to combine in the face of this new Serb onslaught, but in fact they had little if any knowledge of what was really taking place on the ground. Lieutenant Colonel Bob Stewart and his battalion of Cheshires now found themselves caught right in the middle of this human disaster as they attempted to deploy in the area and set a headquarters at a school complex in Vitez. While the first British troops were settling into an environment of confusion, disorder and fear, which was deteriorating further by the day, the latest set of proposals from Owen and Vance were being offered to the three warring parties in Geneva on 27 October. These were of little interest to the poor misfortunate people now squatting in Travnik and elsewhere who had run from their homes with nothing save the clothes on their backs and the few miserable possessions they could carry. The entire social structure of the area quickly disintegrated and the inability of Muslims and Croats to pull together in the face of such appalling adversity said it all.

This intransigence would dominate relations between the two from this point onwards and it served to justify all attempts to exterminate one another, as well as validating rejection of all attempts to implement some kind of federal political system. As far as the Muslims were concerned the Serbs might have been annexing huge tracts of land in central Bosnia, but the HVO were doing exactly the same in the south culminating in their eventually taking control of Mostar City on 25 October and then proclaiming it to be the capital of the Croatian community of Herceg-Bosna.

And then, as if to complete the polarisation, news began to filter through that the leaders of the Bosnian and Krajina Serbs had got together in the railway town of Prijedor, in north-west Bosnia, and signed an agreement designed to unite both entities politically, create a joint military and legal system, and thereafter fulfil their aspiration for the 'unification of the whole Serbian nation'.[73] Jajce fell on 3 November, and Bosnian government officials walked out of discussions with Vance and Owen in Geneva. It was clear there would not be any sign of peace before Christmas – but nobody felt inclined to predict what the new year would bring. In Bihac, for example, over 200 people were now dead and 1,600 wounded. This typified the overall situation – with the Muslims taking most of the casualties.

But the advent of winter, and with the first falls of snow imminent, saw the overall situation across the country begin to stabilise to some extent as all sides concentrated on surviving the next few months. The UN immersed itself in discussions on lifting the arms embargo, enforcing no-fly zones and implementing naval blockades. This was due in no small measure to sustained pressure from Islamic countries to have current policy revised. However, no change was made, mainly because neither Lord Owen nor Cyrus Vance would agree to it. Owen suggested on 6 November that any lifting of the arms embargo would be equivalent to 'pouring oil on an already burning fire'. Vance, for his part, also rejected the pressure on 13 November on the basis that 'it taxed credulity to suggest that lifting the arms embargo for only one of the parties would be either feasible or desirable'.

Nevertheless, at the political level Izetbegovic, Tudjman and Boban did hold a variety of meetings and exchanged several documents with the expressed intention of strengthening political, economic and military ties between the three groupings in the face of a common enemy. This unfortunately did little to pacify any of their military personnel on the ground, resulting in clashes at Prozor between the Armija and the HVO which claimed the lives of 30 people; in addition, large parts of the town were destroyed.

Boutros Boutros-Ghali's report to the Security Council on 24 November on the situation pertaining in Croatia did not seem to worry any of them unduly either, but it was quite damning in its findings. Among other things he reported that 'murders, burning and demolition of houses, destruction of churches, killing of cattle and domestic animals, and armed robberies and assaults were aimed at members of national minorities' – that is, the Serbs.

However, in spite of all this an interesting meeting took place in Sarajevo, though it went largely unnoticed as a consequence. On the 26th, the new Croatian chief of the General Staff, General Janko Bobetko, had lengthy discussions with the new supreme commander of the BSA, General Ratko Mladic. The detail of the talks remains unknown, but it was highly significant that Bobetko felt able to represent all Croat forces (HV and HVO) and that Mladic was able to represent all Serbs (BSA and SARSK). This clarifies the relationship between the HV and HVO at this time and for all that happened subsequently. It also clarifies the chain of command and puts the head of that chain firmly in Zagreb. The relationship between Mladic and the RSK was never a matter for speculation. His personal involvement in establishing the SARSK in the first place, and his continued close contacts with the Knin leadership, gave substance to the popular belief that Mladic would never abandon Krajina. As events unfolded this would prove to be yet another lie.

And so as 1992 drew to a close the prospect of a settlement seemed as far away as ever. The Organisation of Islamic States began to call for military intervention in Bosnia and the arming of the Muslims as UNHCR figures indicated that there were now 3 million refugees displaced within the Former Yugoslavia, with 1.7 million of them in Bosnia. President Tudjman continued to push for Western military intervention to halt what he regarded as Serb aggression, both in parts of Croatia and in Bosnia, and he also called for the international supervision of Serbia's borders to ensure that supplies were prevented from coming across.[74]

These calls represented classic double-think as far as Tudjman was concerned because he conveniently omitted to mention that his own troops were involved in their own expansionist endeavours in eastern Hercegovina against the Bosnian Serbs. These activities resulted in the proclamation of a very strong warning from Belgrade that if the HV/HVO failed to desist, the JNA would be employed directly against them in order to preserve the integrity of the Montenegrin border.

On the political front the year ended with Milosevic under severe pressure in Belgrade as the new federal president, Cosic, threw his weight behind Federal Prime Minister Panic on 14 December in the latter's attempt to oust Milosevic at the forthcoming presidential election in Serbia. And as another round of peace talks got under way in Geneva on 16 December, Lawrence Eagleburger was again on the anti-Serb bandwagon, this time seeking the indictment of a list of people whom he wanted tried before a 'Nuremberg'-type tribunal; needless to say the names of Milosevic and Karadzic were right there at the top of it. Having also demanded the enforcement of a 'no-fly zone' and a lifting of the arms embargo, he then took it upon himself to speak on behalf of the 'West', declaring 'we [?] have concluded that the deliberate flaunting of Security Council resolutions and the London Agreements, by the Serb authorities, is not only producing an intolerable and deteriorating situation inside the Former Yugoslavia, it is also beginning to threaten the framework of stability in the new Europe'. He concluded by insisting that the West 'would stand for nothing short of the restoration of the independent state of Bosnia-Hercegovina, with its territory undivided and intact; the return of all refugees to their homes and villages; and indeed a day of reckoning for those found guilty of crimes against humanity'.[75]

Eagleburger had in fact hit upon a key issue without, I suspect, actually realising it. He correctly identified the criminal behaviour of the Serbs but omitted to criticise the equally criminal activities of the other two parties. In so doing he effectively gave both the Croats and Muslims his blessing to continue with their policies of exacting retribution and *de facto* endorsed what they were doing on the ground. By failing to state that *all* of the parties to the conflict were guilty to some degree or other, Eagleburger gave the philosophy of hatred and vengeance as practised in the Balkans both his personal and official stamps of approval, which in turn served only to further inflame an already volatile situation. If nothing else this spoke volumes about the vacuum that had become US foreign policy in the region at the time.

As the year drew to a close Tudjman, Izetbegovic, Vance, Owen and Mate Boban met in Zagreb on 17 December to hammer out an agreed position that could be brought to the Peace Conference; the UN Security Council was directed by the General Assembly on 18 December to review the arms embargo and consider the possibility of military intervention against Serbia and Montenegro; Radovan Karadzic, a Montenegrin psychiatrist, was elected the first president of the Republic of Srpska on 19 December; Slobodan Milosevic was re-elected as president of Serbia on 20 December;[76] on 28 December President Bush began threatening the Serbs that the US was ready to use force against them; and all interested parties assembled in Geneva in order to be presented with a new map of Bosnia which sought to divide the country into ten largely autonomous provinces under a loosely organised central government. This was to be the new territorial and constitutional solution for Bosnia and Hercegovina and quickly became known as the 'Vance–Owen plan'.

Initial hopes for success were high, but soon evaporated when news began to filter through that over 10,000 Muslim troops were gathered to the south of Sarajevo, on Mount Igman, in preparation for an assault on the city in order to lift the siege which had been running now for nine months. The fact that this military activity was permitted to take place at this particular time certainly calls into question the sincerity of Izetbegovic and his immediate entourage *vis-à-vis* the entire peace process in which the international community was heavily investing both time and money.

In this regard, on New Year's Eve Boutros Boutros-Ghali and Cyrus Vance flew to Sarajevo to plead with Izetbegovic in the hope that he would call off his planned New Year offensive against the Serbs, but instead of thanking them for their efforts as they made their way through the city streets bystanders hurled abuse at them and called them fascists and criminals, among other things. Arguably the situation was not improved when later that evening Boutros-Ghali spoke to the international press corps and addressed the people of Sarajevo by saying: 'I understand your frustration, but you have a situation [here] that is better than ten other places in the world. I can give you a list if you want it.'

These words of wisdom were not any comfort or consolation to the hundreds of helpless people whom he was addressing. Exposed to the bitter cold of Bosnia's winter, devoid of gas to heat their homes, and fighting to defend their place in the queues for bread and water, the people of Sarajevo were not impressed with the secretary-general. Izetbegovic was well aware that this was the case, and from his perspective what harm if he exploited the discomfort. The problem was that both Boutros-Ghali and Vance had come to help, and in spite of a worsening predicament the Sarajevo government were completely reluctant to take it. This was no accident. It was a policy decision. Other agendas were being followed.

Annex A

REPUBLIKA SRPSKA
PRESIDENCY

Number: 01–53/92
Date: June 13, 1992
Duplicate issued: 21–32/92

In accordance with Article 174, Section 1, Paragraph 14 of the Law on the Army of the Serb Republic of Bosnia and Herzegovina ('Official Herald of the Serb People in BiH', number: 7/92), the President of the Presidency of the Serb Republic of Bosnia and Herzegovina hereby enacts the following

Order

regarding the implementation of international war law conventions in the Army of the Serb Republic of Bosnia and Herzegovina

1   The Army of the Serb Republic of Bosnia and Herzegovina ('the Army') and the Serbian Ministry of Internal Affairs in armed conflict

apply and respect the international war law conventions. International war law conventions referred to in Article 1 above are understood to include the following: international agreements signed or ratified or otherwise endorsed by the former Socialist Federal Republic of Yugoslavia; customs and conventions of international war law; generally recognized principles of international war law.

2   *Responsible for the implementation of international war law conventions are commanders and commanding officers of the Army as well as every member of the Army or other armed formation participating in armed operations. The commanding officer is responsible for initiating procedures for the issuance of a sentence in accordance with the law against individuals in violation of international war law conventions.*

3   *The Minister of Defense of the Serb Republic of Bosnia and Herzegovina is hereby authorized to issue instructions for treatment of war prisoners.*

4   *Training is to be scheduled regularly in order to familiarize members of the Army with international war law conventions.*

5   *This order becomes effective on the day it is published in the 'Official Herald of the Serb People in BiH' and an integral part of this order are instructions for treatment of war prisoners.*

PRESIDENT
SERB REPUBLIC OF BOSNIA AND HERZEGOVINA
Dr Radovan Karadzic

Annex B

REPUBLIKA SRPSKA
PRESIDENCY

Number: 01–530/92
Date: August 19, 1992

TO THE GENERAL STAFF OF THE REPUBLIKA SRPSKA ARMY, THE MINISTRY OF INTERNAL AFFAIRS AND ALL SECURITY SERVICE HEADQUARTERS

In accordance with our act of June 13, 1992 regarding respect of international war conventions, I again

Order

1. That all subjects realize their responsibility to adhere to international humanitarian law, especially Articles 3 and 4 of the Geneva Convention;
2. That orders be issued to all fighters and all employees of the Ministry of Internal Affairs to respect prisoners, civilians, medical facilities, private and public facilities, the emblem of the Red Cross and personnel and property of the United Nations;
3. That forcible relocation and carrying out other illegal measures against the civilian population be prevented and eventual certificates of sale of property or statements that refugees will not return have no legal validity and are hereby declared invalid;
4. That immediate steps be taken to improve conditions in all prisons in Republika Srpska in accordance with recommendations given during the visit of the International Red Cross to those locations. In accordance with a previous Decision, all war prisoners who are not in good health, that is, who will be unable to serve in the enemy army in the near future, are to be unilaterally released;
5. That the International Red Cross be informed immediately regarding all prisons in Republika Srpska and that lists of people in those prisons be submitted to this institution;
6. All members of the Army and Police of Republika Srpska are responsible for lending every form of assistance to organizations of the International Red Cross, the United Nations High Commissioner for Refugees and other humanitarian organizations. Full security for these personnel and their access to all prisons for war prisoners must be provided.

General position:

Every organ of the Army and Police in their area of jurisdiction is responsible to carry out energetic investigation with respect to any suspicion or sign of violation of international humanitarian law.

PRESIDENT
REPUBLIKA SRPSKA
Dr Radovan Karadzic

Annex C

REPUBLIKA SRPSKA
PRESIDENCY

Number: 01–532/92
Date: August 19, 1992

TO THE MINISTRY OF INTERNAL AFFAIRS OF REPUBLIKA SRPSKA
There are indications that five civilians of Muslim nationality were murdered in the village of Bastasi near Celinac. I

Order

that a most thorough investigation be conducted, the perpetrators be identified and brought to Justice.

Employees of the Ministry in the Security Service Headquarters in Banja Luka and the Public Security Office in Celinac must undertake all measures to protect the civilian Muslim population of Celinac municipality which, according to our information, has no military organization and is not preparing for military intervention against the Serb people.

PRESIDENT
REPUBLIKA SRPSKA
Dr Radovan Karadzic

3
1993

The Vance–Owen Peace Plan

In what had now become almost 'tradition', the New Year in the Former Yugoslavia was welcomed with another spate of ethnic violence. While the politicians in Geneva debated the colours and contours on the proposed new peace plan map, in Gornji Vakuf units of Armija from Zenica, Travnik and Bugonjo launched a combined attack on HVO elements from Gornji Vakuf and nearby Prozor. The ensuing battle achieved nothing as equal casualties were taken on both sides, but several outlying villages were destroyed and further damage was done to the town itself.

Of far more significance, however, was the fact that the Bosnian Croat pockets in central Bosnia were now completely cut off from the rest of the Croatian Republic of Herceg-Bosna (CRHB), and as such were under permanent threat from the Armija. It was therefore more than a little ironic that just as the political leaders were supposedly struggling to find agreement in Switzerland on the delineation of new provinces etc., their agents on the ground were actively involved in extensive preparations to physically redraw the boundaries on the ground by force. In classic Balkan style the politicians were discussing the possibility of a formal, legal, binding document, while their own military commanders were pursuing a totally different agenda, and indeed it is well nigh impossible to accept that this was just coincidence.

An insight into these events is to be found in the explanation given to Colonel Bob Stewart by Enver Hadzihasanovic, the commander of the Armija's 3rd Corps, in the immediate aftermath of the killing of Lance Corporal Wayne Edwards in Gornji Vakuf on 13 January. Edwards had been shot in the head while driving his UN Warrior armoured vehicle through the town as an escort for an ambulance full of wounded civilians.[1]

Stewart and his soldiers were screaming for answers and Hadzi-hasanovic began by explaining that prior to the fall of Jajce the Croats had been deliberately creating trouble for the Muslims in Prozor in order to distract them and thereby ensure that Jajce fell more easily. He further claimed that the problems in Gornji Vakuf were but an extension of a policy which was designed to divert Muslim attention and resources away from other problems at Turbe.

He further claimed that this was all part of a secret formal pact between the Croats and Serbs which was evidenced by a marked decrease in Serb activity whenever the other two were at one another's throats.[2] While Colonel Stewart found this interpretation very difficult to accept he was nevertheless forced by circumstances on the ground to concede that it was also perfectly possible.

But for the most part international attention remained firmly focused on Geneva where the Vance–Owen plan was unveiled. Basically the proposals revolved around (1) reorganisation of Bosnia into ten provinces, (2) the creation of a new constitution which would provide for provincial autonomy within a decentralised state, and (3) the establishment of a permanent ceasefire throughout the country. Within the ten provinces the Muslims and Serbs would have an absolute majority in three each, with the Bosnian Croats equally dominant in two. One province would deliver a simple majority to a Muslim/Croat combination, while the last province, Sarajevo, was to become an open city. Thereafter five secure corridors, protected by the UN, would guarantee 'full freedom of movement' to all citizens between the various parts of the country and there were to be no ethnically clean areas.

On the face of it, this was a reasonable attempt to solve the problem and might have provided a framework within which more progress could have been made. But for that to happen all sides would have had to display some flexibility and awareness of just how critical the overall situation had become. Not surprisingly these criteria were not in evidence. First to disagree with the proposals was Karadzic, who cynically offered to stay at the conference table for ever but was completely unwilling to relinquish any Serb-held territory, insisting instead on the continuation of a separate Bosnian Serb state. To add insult to injury he also stated that he was unwilling to relinquish claims to tracts of land which at that time were still under Muslim and Croat control.

The Bosnian Croats for their part were very satisfied with the plan and signed it on 4 January, while Vance and Owen pleaded with Milosevic to exert some pressure on Karadzic. It didn't work, and the conference broke up with Izetbegovic departing for the United States in an attempt to muster support for his position. Meanwhile the situation on the ground continued to deteriorate when a Bosnian deputy prime minister, Hajika Turajlic, while being transported to Sarajevo airport in a French APC, was stopped by Serb irregulars at a checkpoint. A stand-off developed which culminated in the Serbs gaining access to the vehicle through the rear door and then spraying the interior with machine-gun fire. Turajlic was killed.

This situation was further complicated when it emerged that EC investigators had allegedly discovered that up to 20,000 Muslim women had been raped in the course of a systematic programme of ethnic cleansing by the Bosnian Serbs. And as if that was not bad enough, Karadzic was then quoted in *Globus*[3] as stating that in his opinion 'it is not difficult to procure nuclear weapons on the open market'.

There seemed to be little common ground anywhere now, but undeterred, and refusing to accept that no progress could be made, the mediators continued to pressurise Milosevic. This paid off and on 11 January, following a public apology by the Bosnian Serbs for the death of Turajlic, all sides returned to the table in Geneva. The following day, 12 January, Karadzic announced that he would recommend Vance–Owen to his assembly in Pale, although most observers believed that this was nothing more than a tactical move.

Nevertheless, albeit under threat of EU economic and diplomatic sanctions, Karadzic did place the Vance–Owen plan before his Assembly, advocating that perhaps Muslims and Serbs could live 'beside one another' if they couldn't live together. Eventually the plan was approved, by 55 votes to 15, on 20 January. Then, just when it looked as if the political situation might be improving, the military situation in both Bosnia and Croatia flared up again.

In Gornji Vakuf the fact that Vance and Owen thought they had successfully negotiated a ceasefire between the Muslims and Croats was totally ignored on 20 January, while near Zadar the Croatian army launched a completely new offensive against the Krajina Serbs on 22 January in an attempt to retake the Maslenica bridge, the recovery of which was critical to their main supply route to the southern coast.

The areas under attack were all within the designated UN protected area, but this technicality was of little interest to the advancing Croats and when the Security Council unanimously condemned the 'operation'[4] that resolution was also ignored. After three days of vicious fighting, and with the land connection to Zadar re-opened, President Tudjman announced that the offensive was over; but that was not how matters materialised on the ground. Instead, both sides continued the struggle and Zadar was shelled daily in response to continued skirmishing by the Croats all along the front line.

Then, in response to the deaths of two French peacekeepers on 25 January, Boutros Boutros-Ghali threatened to withdraw the 16,000 UN troops now deployed in the UNPAs. Nobody paid much attention to him either, as fighting worsened with the commencement of a Serb counter-offensive. Further east along the confrontation line Croatian troops evicted the Krajina Serbs from the Peruca dam but had no sooner done so than mines and explosives were set off which were designed to destroy it. Frantic repair work prevented a major catastrophe.

Meanwhile back in Geneva some progress was being made as the

Muslim and Bosnian Croat positions appeared to converge following a series of concessions by Izetbegovic on 25 January. However, this atmosphere was short lived when on the following day the *Washington Post* carried reports of yet another secret meeting, this time between Milosevic, Tudjman and Cosic, the Yugoslav president, as a result of which they had all apparently agreed to co-operate in dismantling Bosnia.

In an attempt to salvage something from what was now turning into a debacle another proposal was put on the table on the 29th which was designed to establish an interim National Council, comprised of three members from each side, which would govern the country pending the result of free elections. This was to come into effect immediately upon acceptance of Vance–Owen by all three sides and looked at face value like a reasonable compromise. However, the Muslims rejected it out of hand claiming for the first time that they would not participate in any power-sharing arrangement with people they considered to be 'war criminals'.

A basic interpretation here might suggest that they were simply unwilling to give up power and its trappings, and up to a point that was true. However, a better evaluation would once again identify the silent presence of Ruder Finn Inc. because the Sarajevo government had launched a deliberate campaign to delegitimise the Bosnian Serbs by branding them as war criminals – and this was a significant and deliberate move. From this point onwards every government minister, official and spokesperson pumped out the same message whenever a TV camera appeared before them. The administration in Sarajevo was a 'government' and the Bosnian Serbs were 'war criminals'. This was a public relations ploy – and it worked.

Then on 30 January the talks in Geneva broke down completely and all sides went home, each intent on pursuing their own military offensives. And to make a bad situation worse Tudjman announced on the following day that his government now intended to liberate every inch of Croatia by force.

At this point Vance and Owen moved to secure American acceptance of the plan, and to this end Karadzic was granted a limited visa to attend peace talks in New York while Lord Owen attempted to persuade the Clinton Administration to endorse the plan and deploy US troops on the ground to enforce it. He was disappointed on both counts. *Time*, *Newsweek* and the *Washington Post* were all lined up against the plan because Ruder Finn Inc. had done their work and convinced them it would reward Serb aggression, while in the White House it was still party time following Clinton's inauguration on 20 January and the lightweight politicians who would form his inner cabinet neither understood the problems in Bosnia nor really cared much about them.[5]

As far as Madeleine Albright was concerned it was a European problem, and Al Gore wanted to weigh in on the Muslim side. Their cumulative failure to support Vance–Owen was seen in Sarajevo as proof positive that sooner or later Clinton would throw his lot in with them, when nothing of the sort was the case. The reality was that Bosnia was of little interest to the Clinton Administration. The very last thing any of them wanted was to become involved in a Yugoslav war, but nobody was prepared to come out and say so. This left Vance and Owen in an untenable situation where effectively all they could do was make public appeals for support on the grounds that their plan was the only plan on the table.

However, this appeal fell on deaf ears and once again Izetbegovic came out rejecting it, using soundbites. 'We will not accept the plan because it implies that genocide can be carried out and rewarded', he declared. Karadzic, on the other hand, was delighted to have an international audience in the US and advocated acceptance of the plan by all sides, announcing that the Serbs were not born fighters and 'would much rather drive Toyotas than Tanks'. And so it went on, with little progress, much debate, and no acceptance of the plan.

Then on 10 February, in a surprise move, US Secretary of State Warren Christopher unveiled his own six-point plan, stating that as far as the Clinton Administration was concerned 'the continuing destruction of a new United Nations member challenges the principle that internationally recognised borders should not be altered by force'. He was adamant that all parties 'must' negotiate a settlement, and to help them concentrate their minds he began advocating the implementation of further economic sanctions, the establishment of a war crimes tribunal, and stricter enforcement of the no-fly zone over Bosnia. Izetbegovic gave the initiative his qualified support while Karadzic also accepted the move, notwithstanding that most of the rhetoric which accompanied it was decidedly anti-Serb and directed specifically against him.

It was no coincidence either that at that very moment, on 11 February, a US human rights group had begun legal action against Karadzic in a New York Federal Court on charges that he had ordered the mass rape of Muslim women by the Bosnian Serb army, something which he had always dogmatically denied. The pressure on Karadzic was now intense as virtually all media soundbites attempted to delegitimise him publicly. He had walked into a trap in the US; he never saw it coming, and was effectively ambushed.[6]

Meanwhile, back in Sarajevo, the City Council, on orders from Izetbegovic, ordered the boycotting of all UN relief aid on the basis that the UN was not doing enough to deliver supplies to the starving inhabitants of the eastern enclaves. At face value this was a classic case of 'cutting off one's nose to spite one's face', but there was more to it than that. The stopping of relief was specifically designed to frustrate the international community in the one area where it could actually achieve something in Bosnia. It was also designed to generate more hysteria in the media, which would in turn force Western politicians to intervene on the Muslim side. This resulted in the stoppage of all relief flights into Sarajevo because with the distribution of aid stopped the warehouses remained crammed to capacity. Then, to make capital out of the situation, on 16 February Bosnia's ambassador to the UN, Muhamed Sacirbey, announced to the world that because there was no distribution of food Muslims in the eastern enclaves of Srebrenica, Zepa and Gorazde had resorted to cannibalism in order to survive!

This was not true. It amounted to nothing more than a blatant attempt to inflame an already volatile situation. This particular claim also defied basic common sense, but he got away with it because the media were steadily becoming conditioned to a perception of beleaguered Muslims under attack by the Serbs and abandoned by the West. Most of the media chose to re-broadcast his outlandish claims without ever bothering to establish the truth and, satisfied that this new approach was working well, it was quickly adopted by several other Muslim politicians with Haris Silajdzic and Ejup Ganic being the worst offenders.

Reaction by the UN Security Council

With no apparent let up in the violence, and even less prospect of an agreed political solution now emerging, the UN Security Council decided on 22 February that an International Criminal Tribunal would be established 'for the prosecution of persons responsible for serious violations of international humanitarian law committed in the territory of the Former Yugoslavia since 1991'. For all right-thinking people this was a welcome development and while it by no means guaranteed that any of the perpetrators were about to be brought to justice it did represent a significant policy shift on the part of the Security Council, whose record on the Former Yugoslavia up to that point had been abysmal.

Resolution 764, in July 1992, had simply declared that all parties to the conflict had obligations under international humanitarian law (IHL), and in particular the Geneva Conventions of 1949, and that persons who had committed, or ordered the commission of grave breaches of the Conventions, were individually responsible in respect of such breaches.[7]

One month later the Security Council expressed 'grave alarm' at continuing reports of widespread violations of IHL in the Former Yugoslavia, and specifically in Bosnia. These reports contained detailed information on all of the following: forcible expulsion and deportation of civilians; imprisonment and abuse of civilians in detention centres; deliberate attacks on non-combatants, hospitals and ambulances; impeding the delivery of food and medical supplies to the civilian population; and wanton devastation and destruction of property. Again the Security Council strongly condemned all these violations, demanded that all parties to the conflict immediately cease what they were doing, and that they desist from further breaches of the law.

Next came Resolution 771 in August 1992 calling upon the states themselves, and also international humanitarian organisations working on the ground, to start gathering evidence relating to violations of IHL and to make this available to the appropriate authorities (who ever they were?). The Security Council also decided that pursuant to Chapter VII of the UN Charter it had the authority to instruct/order all parties to the conflict, others actively involved and all military forces operating in Bosnia, to comply with the provisions of Resolution 771 – or else it would take further unspecified measures.[8]

Needless to say, none of the parties paid much attention to this having little or no respect for the rule of law in the first place, and so, left with no option, the Security Council instigated these 'further measures'. An impartial five-member Commission of Experts, chaired by Professor Frits Kalshoven from Holland,[9] was established to furnish the secretary-general with an evaluation of the evidence currently available of grave breaches of the Geneva Conventions and other violations of IHL.[10]

In any event, by 9 February 1993 the secretary-general was ready to submit Kalshoven's 'Interim Report' to the Security Council, concluding that grave breaches and other violations of international humanitarian law had indeed been committed in the territory of the Former Yugoslavia, including wilful killing, ethnic cleansing, mass killings, torture, rape, pillage, destruction of civilian property, destruction of cultural and religious property, and arbitrary arrests. The report concluded by noting that should the Security Council, or another competent organ of the United Nations, decide to establish an *ad hoc* international criminal tribunal, such a decision would be consistent with the direction of his work.[11]

Accordingly, and perhaps having little other option, the Security Council adopted Resolution 808 on 22 February 1993, stating that it was determined to end these crimes and to bring to justice those who had been responsible for committing them. For the second time this century Europeans were about to be charged with war crimes, genocide and crimes against humanity.

The establishment of a tribunal should have taken effect after the conclusion of treaty negotiations between the parties to the conflict and then adopted by the UN General Assembly or a specially convened conference, following which it would be available for signature and ratification. (The theory here is that if the parties to the conflict can actually bring themselves to sign the treaty in the first instance then there exists a reasonable prospect that they will subsequently co-operate with its officials as persons are located and brought to trial.) Unfortunately, in this case the secretary-general was forced by circumstances to operate in an interventionist capacity because he could not rely on the co-operation of any of the parties involved.

Therefore in strict legal terms the Security Council would be taking an enforcement measure under Chapter VII of the UN Charter in order to establish a subsidiary organ of a judicial nature within the terms of Article 29. This organ would then perform its functions independently of any political considerations and would not be subject thereafter to the authority or control of the Security Council in relation to the performance of its judicial functions. And finally, the lifespan of the tribunal was to be directly related to the restoration and maintenance of international peace and security, taking account of all previous and subsequent Security Council resolutions. This was not an attempt to establish a general international criminal jurisdiction, nor was it intended to pave the way for the creation of an international criminal court, although the success or failure of the tribunal would of course give rise to increased debate on these very issues.

Airdrops and lies

Meanwhile, on 17 February UNHCR decided enough was enough and shut down all relief operations in Bosnia on the basis that political leaders across the board were making a mockery of UNHCR's work – and they were. Humanitarian aid had become a hostage to politics, and aid distribution was being abused by all sides. After five days the boycott was lifted, but the prospect of US airdrops to resupply the enclaves was still on the cards. Four days later this was the subject of a NATO foreign ministers' meeting in Brussels, and on the 28th three unescorted US transport planes dropped 21 tonnes of relief aid near the village of Cerska in eastern Bosnia. The operation went well, but was barely concluded before the Bosnian vice-president, Ejup Ganic, began criticising the policy demanding that it now be repeated over and over again. Ganic's objective was to ensnare the US and then keep it involved, and he was prepared to use any means whatsoever to achieve that. But he would be disappointed. In what was passing for US policy on Bosnia at this time, long-term intervention was not an option.[12]

Furthermore, Ganic was far from honest in his assessment of the problem at the time and he failed utterly to explain why the eastern Muslim enclaves were under such intense pressure from the Serbs in the first place. But telling that particular story was not in his interest. In actual fact Muslim troops led by Naser Oric had mounted a series of fighting patrols from Srebrenica on 7 January and attacked and trashed several Serb villages along the Drina valley. The object of these attacks was primarily the civilian population, and innocent Serb women and children were forced to flee from their homes terrorised by Oric and his soldiers.

Not surprisingly the Serbs went crazy and launched their own attacks on Muslims near Zvornik, at Cerska, and down the length of a valley called Konjevic Polje.[13] Of course, by that time Oric and his entourage had returned to Srebrenica and were holed up in defensive positions, while Muhamed Sacirbey set about regaling the international media with further tales of Serb aggression and cannibalism.

Yes, the poor people of Srebrenica were hungry. Yes, they were cold. And yes, their lives had been turned upside down. But they had not resorted to eating one another. And by and large the reason they found themselves in this predicament in the first place was because their leaders had embarked on a ridiculous hit-and-run campaign which by any yardstick one cared to use had no prospect whatsoever of being successful. This version of events was not reported because no international reporters were working in Republic Srpska and the Sarajevo government were only divulging those aspects of the situation which served their own purposes. Perception was not reality in eastern Bosnia during the early days of 1993 where a dirty war was being played out – instigated for the most part by the Muslims.

As the Serbs continued harassment shelling of Sarajevo, EC monitors began submitting more reports of ethnic cleansing in Croatia in order to facilitate the accommodation of other Croats who had been displaced in Bosnia and the Krajina. Nobody paid much attention to the passing of UN Resolution 808 which empowered the UN secretary-general to establish a war crimes tribunal within 60 days, nor did anyone become particularly excited by the commencement of another round of the peace conference in New York on 1 March.

At this point Izetbegovic had effectively won the 'perception war'. The international community was now also calling the Bosnian Serb leaders war criminals, and his position not to talk to them under any circumstances was justified. Judging that Karadzic was about to be marginalised further, a Russian proposal emerged in the shape of an 'eight-point-plan'. This was primarily focused on tightening the arms embargo against Croatia, but no one displayed much interest in it. Instead all parties became more entrenched in their own positions, and the activities of Karadzic at this time provide a useful insight into his convoluted thought process.

The small town of Cerska remained surrounded by the Bosnian Serb army, and the plight of the Muslim inhabitants had only marginally improved in the aftermath of food drops. On 2 March the indications were that the town was about to fall, but UN officials were prevented by the local Serb military from evacuating the wounded. Allegations of plunder and murder were then made against the Serbs by the government in Sarajevo. Instead of countering this by co-operating with the international agencies in the distribution of aid and evacuation of the wounded, Karadzic firstly threatened that further US airdrops to the enclaves would cause an escalation of the war. Then realising his mistake he called another press conference and attempted to pass the blame for what was happening to renegade elements whom he claimed were out of control because they had supposedly witnessed atrocities committed by the Muslims. Nobody believed any of this, and seemingly oblivious to the fact that fighting was continuing around Cerska, Karadzic then tried to portray himself as an international statesman willing to participate in the democratic process and ready to redraw of the political map of Bosnia at the conference table in New York.

This Balkan logic was completely unintelligible to all save his fellow Slavs, and not surprisingly the conference ended without agreement on 6 March. Two days later the Muslims decided to launch a huge attack on Serb positions in eastern Bosnia. The fact that a major humanitarian relief operation was being mounted, from which both sides could benefit, was of no concern to either of them as they unleashed their vengeance and hatred each upon the other. They had assessed that aid would still be available when they had tired of fighting – and of course they were right.

Abusing humanitarian aid

This pattern would repeat itself over and over again as the year wore on. The Christian charity of innumerable Western agencies would be used and abused by all three arrogant and corrupt regimes as they exploited the innocence, humanity and bravery of thousands of genuine ordinary decent people. When Western humanitarian agencies had given the last penny from their limited resources nobody said thanks – they just demanded more.

It is therefore perfectly reasonable to ask whether it might have been better had all aid programmes been suspended indefinitely at this time, pending a permanent and lasting solution. Perhaps this kind of action might have brought all of them to their senses. Innocent people would still have suffered in the short term – there is no question about that – but it might just have forced their leaders to try harder to find a solution. Instead billions of ECU were poured into the region and ended up in one guise or another as payment in lieu of wages for the fighting soldiers on all sides – with the residue more often than not being sold for high profit on the thriving black market.

Of course, humanitarian and relief agencies will argue that there are equally valid arguments for persisting with humanitarian operations even where only a fraction of the aid ends up where it is supposed to, and the airdrop programme to the eastern enclaves during March of 1993 was consistent with this thinking. In that case particularly, most of the food went directly to the military because they were the ones who controlled the drop zones and retrieved it. This ensured that they at least could continue their activities with comparatively full bellies.

The first siege of Srebrenica

With the plight of the civilian population deteriorating dramatically in the eastern enclaves humanitarian convoys remained unable to acquire permission to cross through Bosnian Serb lines, notwithstanding daily guarantees from Karadzic that they could do so. Frustrated with the stalemate the UN commander in Bosnia, General Phillipe Morillon, took it upon himself to go to Srebrenica in the hope that his personal intervention might break the deadlock. What he found when he got there on 11 March was an enclave which had been under siege for 11 months and where World Health Organisation officials were recording the deaths of between 20 and 30 people every day as a result of shelling, starvation and the non-existence of basic medicines.

He also discovered an appalling overcrowding situation where countless numbers spent the night-time walking the streets in temperatures of −20°C because there was simply nowhere else to go. By day these poor souls crept into beds vacated by those who had managed a night's sleep only to repeat their nocturnal meanderings the following night. The general was about to have plenty of time to observe life in the enclave because, unknown to him, decisions were being taken behind the scenes which would directly affect him.

Naser Oric,[14] the Armija commander in Srebrenica, had in fact received a coded message from Murat Efendic, a government official in Sarajevo, which clearly instructed him to hold onto Morillon until he guaranteed the safety of the enclave. Quickly a demonstration was organised and erupted in frenzy just as the UN party attempted to leave. At this point Morillon was *de facto* a prisoner. He did not have any freedom of movement, he was not free to leave, and the pleadings of the population were anything but spontaneous. This was a trap, and the Sarajevo government were holding a UN general as their hostage. Morillon had been kidnapped, but this was not obvious to him at the time because communications with Srebrenica were poor to begin with and the official story being fed to the media in Sarajevo was that it had been the plight of people which convinced Morillon to remain amongst them.

Overwhelmed by these 'pleas for assistance', and unable to leave now anyway, Morillon made his way into the post office building and, using a loud-hailer to address the crowd which had gathered outside, he told them: 'I deliberately came here and I have now decided to stay here in Srebrenica. You are now under the protection of the United Nations.' In a symbolic gesture he unfurled a UN flag and hoisted it over the building. The crowd applauded, perhaps believing that the presence of UN troops amongst them would improve their lot, but it was anything but clear what all of this was supposed to mean.

For the Serbs the presence of the UN 'hostages' in Srebrenica certainly complicated matters, and after prolonged discussion with Mladic, and his deputy Manojlo Milovanovic, a ceasefire was eventually arranged on condition that Morillon went back to Sarajevo. Fearing another Balkan double-cross Morillon decided to stay a little longer, and eventually, four days later on 19 March, 68 tonnes of food and other supplies arrived in Srebrenica – the first ground delivery of food since 10 December. However, the food had barely arrived before another row broke out over what to do with the sick and wounded, and this was only resolved when Morillon announced that he had brokered a reciprocal exchange – 240 Serbs detained in Tuzla would be released as a quid pro quo for the evacuation by helicopter of those Muslims most in need of medical attention.

But again the Sarajevo government had other ideas, and employing the ruse of blaming the authorities in Tuzla for disobedience they decided that in fact only 46 Serbs would be permitted to leave. Izetbegovic and his advisers were now playing with the lives of their own sick people in Srebrenica in order to gain some political leverage. None of this was happening by accident and neither was it simple opportunism. It was, in fact, part of their grand strategy.

Of course the UN also complicated matters by trying to insert a platoon of French troops into the enclave, complete with a satellite communications system, and when they were discovered on board the incoming helicopters the Serbs became hostile and immediately set about ripping the aircraft apart on the pretext of carrying out an inspection. Furthermore, Maggie O'Kane from the *Guardian* newspaper and Brian Hulls from the BBC were also discovered on board, and when Hulls' videotape was played it transpired that he had been filming all the Serb military positions on the Vis feature on the inward flight. Both were arrested because neither was supposed to have been there in the first place.

However, three French UN helicopters did eventually make it into Srebrenica to evacuate a number of the seriously wounded, but because the whole deal was falling apart the Serbs reacted violently on 24 March by shelling the landing site with artillery on the pretext that they believed the helicopters were bringing in weapons to the Muslims. With two Canadian peacekeepers injured, and one of them dying if he could not be evacuated, Lieutenant Commander George Wallace (UK) flew back into Srebrenica and winched the casualties to safety. Later the exchange of the 46 Serbs went ahead in full glare of Bosnian Serb TV – but the day itself had been a disaster.

Justin Webb of the BBC, reporting from Tuzla that night, was correct when he said that the problem had been the politicians' failure to control their military personnel on the ground. What he failed to point out was that Mladic was the one who had disregarded Kradazic's orders to comply with the transfer arrangement and it was Mladic's troops who had deliberately shelled the helicopter landing zone as the wounded and sick were being evacuated. Naser Oric, on the other hand, had done exactly what he had been told to do by his political overlords in Sarajevo, as had the authorities in Tuzla who reneged on the agreement to release all 240 Serbs. Neither side had much concern for those who were the subject of the agreement and even less regard for the UN who were only trying to facilitate a humanitarian exchange.

Frustrated now beyond toleration Morillon knew that the key player on the Serb side was not Karadzic. He knew where the real power actually lay in the Republic Srpska – Slobodan Milosevic in Belgrade – and there was no mystery about that on 25 March 1993 or any time thereafter. Having been refused permission to cross the border at Kalesija by the Bosnian Serbs Morillon returned to Tuzla,[15] contacted Milosevic in Belgrade, and went to see him. Soon thereafter negotiations restarted in Bosnia which resulted in another ceasefire being agreed in Sarajevo on 28 March, thereby enabling a further busload of Serbs to be released from Tuzla with 19 UN relief trucks permitted to travel to Srebrenica to commence the evacuation of 2,300 women, children and old men on the following day. Satisfied that something of substance had been achieved at last Morillon then returned to Sarajevo.

De facto he had been held hostage in Srebrenica for 17 days on the instructions of the Sarajevo government, but incredibly the UN decided not to interpret the matter in this way and set about forgetting the entire episode as quickly as possible. In hindsight this was a mistake because the UN's inaction was interpreted in Sarajevo as a sign of weakness and effectively opened the door to further abuse of the UN in the months ahead. Nevertheless it must be said that had Morillon not been prepared to accept the risk to his personal safety in the first place it is certain that nothing whatever would have been achieved at this time. People on both sides owe him a debt of gratitude for persisting in his attempts to make the exchange process work. He deserved great credit, but in typical UN fashion received almost none.

The peace process rolls on

While all of this was going on in Srebrenica political pressure mounted on all sides to accept Vance–Owen, with NATO offering a multinational force of over 50,000 troops to implement the plan if and when it was ever signed. The two mediators had begun to make some progress with Karadzic when on 17 March the Sarajevo government arrived with a new proposal redrawing the map once again, and this time advocating 13 provinces instead of ten. Karadzic's response to this was to accept the proposal on condition that the areas held by the Serbs in provinces to be controlled by Croats and Muslims could be swapped for Muslim and Croat areas in the provinces which were to be controlled by the Serbs. This would have involved a huge transfer of people, culminating in a situation whereby each province would be ethnically clean.

Needless to say this was greeted with contempt by everyone save the Serbs, but had it been accepted Bosnia might just have been spared the horror and bloodshed which was to follow. The land-swap idea was rejected largely because Karadzic had suggested it, but it could have been the solution to all their problems – especially in light of the fact that large-scale fighting between Muslims and Croats had again broken out in central Bosnia on 10 March.

Nevertheless, Izetbegovic signed the third and final section of the plan on 25 March. Two out of three had now signed all sections of the agreement. It only remained for Karadzic to come on board as well, and there is little doubt that he was under severe pressure from Russia to sign. However, just when he might have put his name on the paper the UN Security Council passed Resolution 816[16] on 31 March authorising NATO to commence enforcement of a 'no-fly zone' over Bosnia on 7 April. This was a disastrous development and begged the question whether there was any co-ordination whatever between UN HQ in New York and its officials and representatives working on the ground.

Not surprisingly Karadzic immediately threatened to pull out of the peace talks altogether if the resolution was enforced, and the situation was further complicated by an announcement from the Sarajevo government to the effect that two Bosnian Serbs, Borislav Herak and Sretko Damjanovic, had been tried for the war crimes of murder and multiple rape, found guilty, and were both sentenced to death. Once again timing was everything – and this was not coincidence.

General Morillon was sufficiently outraged by this announcement that he launched into a stinging attack on the Sarajevo government for their insensitivity in pursuing this issue at the very time the peace process was so fragile. He knew, as did ECMM, that Sarajevo was not committed to the plan and had signed up to it only because they expected Karadzic would not. Now when it looked as if by some quirk of fate he might just come on board some other distraction had to be arranged to dissuade him. How convenient, then, that they just happened to have a couple of convicted Bosnian Serb war criminals available to parade in public before they decided to execute them.

If nothing else Radovan Karadzic was always predictable, and true to form he swallowed this ruse hook, line and sinker. In a matter of minutes the peace process (such as it was) had been successfully derailed – not by Karadzic, but by Izetbegovic and his inner circle in Sarajevo.

Unable to tolerate any more of this Balkan double-think, Cyrus Vance stated that attempting to mediate in the Former Yugoslavia had been 'the most difficult task that he had ever witnessed', and promptly announced his resignation as mediator with effect from 1 May. Norwegian foreign minister, Thorvald Stoltenberg, was nominated to replace him and against a backdrop of renewed shelling in Srebrenica the Bosnian Serb Assembly duly obliged on 3 April and rejected the peace plan by 68 votes to 0, calling instead for the creation of ethnically pure provinces. Announcing to the media that 'the peace plan is dead, long live the peace process', Karadzic did nothing but add to everyone's frustrations, and his suggestion that the plan could still constitute the basis for a new agreement fell on deaf ears.

Grasping now at straws, Warren Christopher said he still believed that the door was open for further peace talks, but this interpretation was very difficult to reconcile with ongoing fighting all over Bosnia and a chronic humanitarian situation in Srebrenica, where in spite of Morillon's best efforts the evacuation of refugees was still proving impossible. Even when the Serbs granted permission for a controlled exodus from the enclave the local Armija military commander, Nasir Oric, ordered the people back to their homes on the spurious grounds that the more of them that left the more vulnerable the rest of them would become.

This was not a reasonable military assessment in any shape or form, and neither was it something Oric thought up on his own. There were 60,000 dirty, starving, miserable people now crammed into Srebrenica and it suited the Sarajevo government to keep them where they were and have the Serbs continually blamed for their condition. In fact it is perfectly arguable that Sarajevo had a vested interest in actually making the plight of their own people worse – the more inhumane their circumstances the more vilification that could be heaped on the Serbs.

Understanding the situation for what it really was the Serbs had no compunction about renewing their onslaught on the enclave, justifying their action on the basis that the Muslims had been given an opportunity to leave and had for one reason or another decided to stay put. Seething with frustration Morillon called a press conference on 7 April and announced he was going back in and intended to stay there until the matter was resolved. The next day, en route to Srebrenica, his party was surrounded by 300 Serb 'civilians' who demanded that he turn around and go back to Tuzla. He persisted in his demands for freedom of movement, but eventually had to face reality.

Then to add insult to injury, just as he was about to leave, a helicopter landed nearby and a Bosnian Serb officer dismounted, offering to 'rescue' Morillon from the mob and air-lift him to safety. This was a gratuitous insult but begged the question what was happening in relation to the alleged imposition of a 'no-fly zone'. This was precisely the point the Serb leadership wished to make – and the relentless shelling of Srebrenica went on.

On the international front reaction to the perception that 'the Serbs were to blame for everything' was predictable, with leading figures all threatening forms of punishment if Karadzic failed to come on board.

Lord Owen indicated to the BBC that military force would very likely be necessary to win the Bosnian Serbs' acceptance of the Vance–Owen plan. This was followed by a recommendation from Senator Joseph Biden, chairman of the US senate's European Affairs Subcommittee, that the arms embargo should be lifted and selective bombing of Serb artillery positions commence immediately. A US State Department report, commissioned by President Clinton, was also published and advocated US military involvement, while Margaret Thatcher, the former UK prime minister, launched a scathing attack on all Western nations for their handling of the situation. She too called for an immediate lifting of the arms embargo and the bombing of Serb artillery positions. The EC, she said, was acting like 'accomplices to a massacre'. Sarajevo's gospel message now had many disciples.

Meanwhile at the UN HQ in New York pressure was mounting to tighten sanctions against Serbia for her continued support of the Bosnian Serbs, but Russia managed yet again to postpone any vote on the matter until after 25 April. On the ground the situation escalated further on 12 April when 60 Dutch and French aircraft began enforcing the 'no-fly zone' and the Serbs replied by shelling Bihac, Kladanj, Olovo, Sarajevo and Srebrenica, where one shell landed in a school yard killing 14 children and wounding several others. In total 55 people died in Srebrenica that day and the entire affair was witnessed by 16 international staff, both military and civilian, whom Morillon had left behind on his previous visit.

Srebrenica becomes a 'safe area'

When word of this got out Larry Hollingworth of UNHCR went before the media screaming that he hoped the Serb commander who ordered the shelling would burn in hell.[17] Then, two days later, Naser Oric announced that he was going to surrender. Of course he had no intention whatever of doing this, and the enclave was not about to fall, but once again the plight of Srebrenica's poor people was being manipulated in Sarajevo to induce the international media to cry in unison that 'something must be done'.

The following day Oric pretended to surrender formally and pressure increased proportionately on the international community. Working frantically at both military and diplomatic levels the UN Mixed Military Working Group in Sarajevo rushed to obtain agreement on any interim measure and eventually came up with a scheme which would allegedly demilitarise the enclave, insert 140 Canadian peacekeepers and permit 500 wounded to be evacuated by helicopter. Those who wanted to would be free to flee to central Bosnia and the enclave would remain in Muslim hands. On the following day the Security Council of the United Nations passed Resolution 819 declaring Srebrenica to be a 'safe area'. Sarajevo had scored a huge diplomatic victory. Their 'government' had been supported by the highest political body, and better still – having declared Srebrenica to be safe, the responsibility for keeping it safe would now belong to the international community as well.[18]

The next day the Security Council, prompted by the non-aligned members and France, approved UNSC Resolution 820,[19] which would further tighten sanctions against Serbia, in the form of a maritime exclusion zone and the freezing of Yugoslav assets abroad – unless the Bosnian Serbs signed up to Vance–Owen within eight days. No sooner was this announced than news of another peace agreement brokered by Morillon began to filter through, which indicated that significant progress had been made.

The 'Srebrenica Agreement'[20] (or the Airport Agreement, as some commentators would later call it) was to include the following: an immediate ceasefire; the evacuation of sick and wounded from the enclave; the creation of corridors to allow for unrestricted relief convoys; the disarming of defending Armija troops within 72 hours; the installation of Canadian UN peacekeeping troops; recognition by all sides of the principle that Srebrenica was now a 'UN safe haven'; and the creation of a 'liaison board' to oversee the implementation of the agreement.

Morillon had pleaded with New York not to vote on Resolution 820 until his agreement was given some time to work, but nobody in New York was prepared to wait and they went ahead anyway. Consequently two very contradictory messages were sent to the Bosnian Serbs, leaving even non-committed observers wondering if the UN's right arm knew what its left was doing.

The following day 130 Canadian troops arrived in Srebrenica, beginning the immediate evacuation of the more severely wounded, and Eduard Balladeur, the French prime minister, announced that General Morillon's appointment as UN military commander in Bosnia had been extended. This put paid to a variety of rumours that he was about to be dismissed, which had mushroomed since his outspoken attack on the Bosnian government, and were apparently originating from the ranks of his own colleagues in the French General Staff in Paris. Jealousy may well have had something to do with it. In any case the extension of his appointment would allow him time to figure out what actually constituted a 'safe haven' because at that time nobody in Sarajevo, New York, Zagreb or anywhere else had the remotest idea what they were talking about. Nobody had thought this concept through and it was now left to Morillon's officials on the ground to make it up as they went along.

This 'ad hockery' in 1993, while admittedly resolving an immediate and chronic problem, would ultimately lead to the fall of Srebrenica two years later. Had any attempt been made at this time to establish specific criteria for the creation of a 'safe area', and if some form of agreement had been obtained from the warring parties, it is just possible that the concept could have worked and a great many lives saved in the process. Unfortunately all sides went on to develop their own understanding of what constituted a 'safe area' and in time this would lead to even greater conflict than that which Morillon's plan was supposed to stop.[21]

Back in Srebrenica the airlift into the enclave began early on the morning of Sunday, 17 April. Milos Stankovic flew in on the second wave[22] with a copy of Morillon's Agreement in his pocket. He had been tasked to deliver it to Oric. When he eventually found him he handed it over, noting that someone from the Armija's 2nd Corps in Tuzla had scribbled four sentences in red ink at the bottom.

When Oric finished reading he looked at Stankovic, smiled, and said: '[W]e will do everything to comply with this agreement and co-operate fully with the United Nations, but as for freedom of movement – there is none. No-one will leave this enclave, not even the United Nations.'[23] Clearly Oric had just received new instructions which were completely at variance with what had been agreed in Sarajevo.

The following day, at Oric's first official meeting with the UN, he issued a list of demands for reconstruction of the enclave and was seemingly oblivious to the suffering of the town's inhabitants. In relation to demilitarisation Oric would only agree to demilitarise the town itself (and not the environs), so once again the goal posts had moved. Everyone present knew the Serbs would not accept this, but they also knew that the UN had insufficient troops to enforce compliance. Therefore in reality the UN had been lured into this situation by the Sarajevo government because it suited their purposes completely to have foreign troops now effectively embroiled in a problem which their agents (read 'Oric') had created in the first place. The Canadians did try to demilitarise the town, but Oric only permitted the submission of equipment which was bordering on obsolete or broken.

The Serbs were anything but pleased because they knew exactly what armaments were in the enclave, and Karadzic declared that he was about to withdraw from the peace talks and never sign up to Vance–Owen. Nevertheless, in Srebrenica the cease fire did begin to take hold largely because both sides were exhausted and for once calls for the massive military intervention by Lord Owen provoked no reaction. And then the eastern enclaves became overshadowed yet again by reports of further bouts of savagery between Muslims and Croats in central Bosnia.

Ahmici

The excuse for this latest round of bloodletting was ostensibly the kidnapping of a Croat military commander in the predominantly Muslim town of Zenica. Apparently Colonel Totic and his bodyguards had been ambushed in broad daylight with three of them killed and Totic taken prisoner. The problem was that nobody was really sure what had happened. Colonel Bob Stewart, who had operational responsibility in the area, was unable to clarify the matter either, preferring instead to explain the incident by reference to what Colm Doyle, Lord Carrington's special envoy, had once said to him, the gist of which was that all sides were perfectly capable of killing their own people if they thought there was some benefit to be derived from it.

In any event, the situation soon got out of hand. 'All hell broke loose in Vitez in the early hours of the next morning', wrote Colonel Stewart. 'Gun and artillery battles broke out right the way through the area ... We estimated that up to possibly three hundred people on all sides had died in the latest batch of fighting.' His account of what happened in the village of Ahmici near Vitez on 16 April, when over 107 innocent Muslim civilians were slaughtered by Bosnian Croat soldiers, indicates the type and scale of savagery of the war.[24]

Another account of what happened in Ahmici is even more vivid because it comes from a 17-year-old girl, Elma Ahmic, who lived through the attack and has been haunted by it ever since:

> About 20 people surrounded our house shouting to get out of here. This is Croatia not Turkey. My father came out and asked them what they wanted. They took my father and went behind the house and killed him. They shot my brother when he was coming down the stairs. Then they shot my grandfather and my two uncles in the front yard. Many of the people who killed my family are still there. I know who killed them.[25]

Martin Bell, to his great credit, compiled his BBC report on the Ahmici killings whilst standing amongst the charred remains of a complete family, who having been unable to escape their attackers were locked into their home, had petrol poured in on top of them, and were then burned alive. This atrocity, while admittedly a product of the war culture, had nothing whatever to do with military strategy, or even military tactics at the lowest level.

It was quite simply a crime against humanity, perpetrated by pathological criminals who were either unanswerable to their political masters or, alternatively, doing their bidding.

Back in Srebrenica the Canadians were now considered by UN HQ in New York to have successfully disarmed all Armija elements in the enclave, although how this was supposed to have happened was not explained. Oric knew this was not true, the Serbs knew it wasn't true, the Canadians certainly knew it was a lie, as did UNPROFOR both in Sarajevo and in Zagreb. Nevertheless, the Canadians were now tasked with defending the 'safe area'. How exactly they were supposed to achieve this with only 130 lightly armed troops against the tanks and guns of the Bosnian Serb army was never explained. Their mandate did not include actually defending civilians, but this issue was never addressed either.

From the Serb perspective this disarmament was considered a farce right from the beginning and it in no way satisfied General Mladic's demands.[26] Not for the first time UN troops were now deployed keeping a peace, the terms of which were interpreted completely differently by all of the groups who were party to it, thus making the UN's 'safe area' policy *de facto* unworkable right from the very start.

Division amongst the Serbs

It was also decided in New York to send a team of UN observers to monitor traffic on the Danube in an attempt to enforce the sanctions against Serbia and Montenegro strictly while all international representatives on the ground simultaneously stepped up the pressure on Karadzic to sign Vance–Owen. In a very strange development both Milosevic and Cosic, the Yugoslav president, sent a letter to Bijeljina where the Bosnian Serb Assembly was in session.[27]

The letter described Vance–Owen as an honourable peace, and concluded by issuing an incredibly strong warning which stated that in the matter of opting for war or peace they were choosing peace. They also made it clear that the Bosnian Serbs did not have a right to endanger the future of ten million people living in the new Yugoslavia.[28] No message from Belgrade could possibly have been clearer, but it made little difference because the Bosnian Serbs went on to reject the plan by 77 votes to 0. On foot of this decision the threatened sanctions against Yugoslavia became effective immediately.

This was probably the point when Milosevic decided that the Bosnian Serb political elite were no longer serving his purposes. They had become an embarrassment and he was losing face internationally as a consequence of his apparent inability to control them. Worse still, the international community was no longer prepared to distinguish between Belgrade and Pale, and all were now being tarred with the same brush. The time had come to cut Karadzic and his cronies adrift, but the problem was how to do this without damaging his own position in domestic public opinion. Serbia's broken economy was now about to suffer further because of Pale's intransigence. For Milosevic this was unacceptable – the Bosnian experiment had been all very well but it paled in significance when compared with political survival at home.

That said, an open conflict with his Bosnian cousins was not an option either because far too much had already been invested in Serbia's expansionist plans. Equally, removing the political elite in Pale was not a runner because these were the people who had become the managers of the black market. They were making a large fortune from their extracurricular activities and would certainly use their military and police to preserve the status quo. Therefore trying to fight them physically was not an option. In this context they could be guaranteed to fight to the last, and images of Serbs fighting Serbs splashed across the international media could only strengthen and encourage all their enemies.

Instead he would have to distance himself gradually from Pale and use every opportunity presented to him to undermine the power and influence of Karadzic and Krajisnik. The acquisition of new allies and new quislings now became Milosevic's top priority. To save Serbia he would have to sacrifice all whom he had previously encouraged to rebel. Karadzic would either do what he was told or be sacrificed at the altar of political expediency. Pan-Serbian nationalism was all very fine but now it was time to put one's priorities in order – and the political survival of Slobodan Milosevic came first. Nothing else mattered. As with Tito before him, unity would always remain subordinate to political expediency and personal power. It would take him over two years to distance himself fully from his protégés, but as far as Milosevic was concerned the respective fates of Krajina and the Republic of Srpska were now effectively sealed.

Of course none of this was ever blatantly obvious and several reporting agencies, ECMM included, remained steadfastly convinced that when the chips were down Milosevic would never desert his brothers and cousins west of the Drina river.

Now under incredible pressure, Karadzic departed for yet another round of the UN-sponsored peace conference taking place this time at the Astir Palace Hotel in Athens. With Lord Owen advocating military intervention/confrontation, President Clinton wanting to toughen the sanctions still further, and Boris Yeltsin announcing that Serbs could no longer count on Russian support, finding a genuine reason not to sign Vance–Owen was becoming more and more difficult. All the main players turned up this time: Owen, Vance, Cosic, Milosevic, Tudjman, Izetbegovic, Boban, Bulatovic, Churkin and Bartholomew;[29] and left effectively with no friends at all Karadzic signed his name to the Vance–Owen peace plan on 2 May. There was, however, one caveat – his signature had to be ratified at the next meeting of the Bosnian Serb Assembly.

'A happy day in the Balkans, a day of sunshine', announced David Owen to the world's press corps, indicating his relief that something tangible had been achieved. But he of all people should really have known better! The American response was far more cautious. Warren Christopher declared himself to be 'hopeful but skeptical', while Milosevic made a public appeal to the Bosnian Serb Assembly on Belgrade TV pleading with them to reject the extremists in their midst and ratify the signature of their president.

He reiterated this point a few days later when he went before the members, having travelled to Pale especially for the meeting. In his address he stated his position very clearly. 'You have to understand', he said, 'I cannot help you any more.' The Greek prime minister, who had also arrived to attend the meeting in the old Olympic ski resort, pleaded for a positive response when he said: 'If you don't sign the plan it will be suicide', and further appeals were heard from Momir Bulatovic, Montenegro's president, and Dobrica Cosic, the federal president. All seemed to fall on deaf ears, but the critical point emerged when Ratko Mladic arrived with a number of maps indicating exactly how much territory the Bosnian Serbs would have to surrender if the plan was ratified.

From this point onwards the mood of the meeting became defiant and when Karadzic declined Milosevic's invitation to recommend the plan to the Assembly the Serbian president took the floor for the last time and put his position on the matter beyond any doubt:

> I believe there is no alternative. I believe we have to go for peace. The plan was signed by Dr Karadzic in Athens and I believe it is a good plan. It is in the interests of the Serbs in Bosnia and of all Serbs. One can sacrifice for one's nation everything except the nation itself. If you don't accept the Vance–Owen Plan you are going to sacrifice your people.[30]

A break in proceedings was then called after which the Bosnian Serbs went into closed session. Milosevic and Bulatovic tried to gain entry but were refused, and reading this to be an indication of what the Assembly was about to do the two presidents sent for their cars and left Pale without further delay. A little later that day, 5 May 1993, the Bosnian Serb Assembly voted not to ratify Vance–Owen and decided instead to put the matter before all their people by way of a referendum to be held ten days later. The international community shrugged its shoulders in total disbelief, but there was little anyone could do except wait as the Bosnian Serbs continued to struggle with whatever portion of their collective conscience still remained intact.

In Belgrade patience with Karadzic and his cohorts had now expired and the government, at Milosevic's prompting, 'officially' suspended the provision and transportation of all goods except humanitarian aid. Ironically, that very same day President Tudjman was opening an 'international' airport on Brac Island off the coast from Split. This facility would within a short time be transformed into an American airbase from which sophisticated unmanned aircraft would patrol the skies over both Bosnia and Krajina. It would also be quickly upgraded to take C-130 Hercules transport aircraft and become a staging post for supplies coming from Islamic countries (mostly Iran) en route for the Armija in central Bosnia. It must surely rank as more than a little ironic that at the very time the

Bosnian Serbs were supposedly agonising over a negotiated settlement the Croats were publicly unveiling a facility which in the near future would be used to considerable effect against them.[31]

By now the US and UN had begun to plan for military intervention in the expectation that Vance–Owen would eventually be rejected by the Bosnian Serb people in the referendum. President Clinton began urging the international community to unite and take decisive action, while the Security Council decided to flex its muscles and declared that, in addition to Srebrenica, five other places – Sarajevo, Zepa, Tuzla, Gorazde and Bihac – would all now become UN 'safe areas' as well, and the Bosnian Serbs were ordered to withdraw their forces and permit UN relief vehicles free access.

Resolution 819 had been introduced by the leader of the non-aligned bloc, Diego Arria of Venezuela, in response to the Morillon initiative, but by the time it was passed the concept of a 'safe haven' had been reduced to that of a 'safe area'. The problem was that nobody had the slightest idea what either concept entailed.

Something must be done

This new policy, while at face value indicating that the UN was about to get tough, was never properly thought out. In fact, it was essentially formulated in direct response to media-generated pressure typified by articles of the type which appeared in *Time* magazine on 3 May. 'Do Something ... Anything' screamed the headline quoting Nobel Laureate Elie Wiesel's address to President Clinton at the dedication of the Holocaust Museum in Washington DC. 'Mr President,' he said, 'I have been in Former Yugoslavia last fall. I cannot sleep since what I have seen. We must do something to stop the bloodshed. Something, anything must be done.'[32]

Standing a short distance away was none other than Croatian president Franjo Tudjman, nodding his head in agreement. The fact that Tudjman's own protégés were also raping, pillaging and burning their way happily through central Bosnia at the time seemed to bother nobody. The reason for this was that Tudjman was perceived to be the good guy. He had not been typecast as a criminal and therefore it mattered little to most people present what his thugs were doing in the Lasva valley. Clearly they could only be defending themselves from those vicious Serb criminals!

CNN then took up the 'something must be done' campaign and for 24 hours demanded the establishment of safe areas in Bosnia, even though they had no concept of what this might entail. They presented the notion that the UN was in some way a credible military deterrent in the region and that once these areas were declared to be UN-protected the Serbs would be sufficiently impressed to desist from further action. Nothing could have been further from the truth. We knew it, the Serbs knew it, and most probably CNN knew it too – but the seed had been planted and there was no going back. The force commander frantically attempted to establish criteria whereby this decision[33] could be implemented, but from the start the concept would mean totally different things as the conflict bubbled on in several disparate areas.[34]

Sir David Hannay, the British ambassador to the UN at the time, was quite prepared to admit subsequently that there never was the slightest chance of the UN protecting Srebrenica, or anywhere else for that matter either,[35] because on the ground Mladic remained defiant, demanding that his terms be met before any 'safety' matters could be discussed. Essentially this involved the surrender of all weapons within the enclaves – something which patently was never going to happen.

It later transpired that in order to get the Canadians into Srebrenica in the first place Morillon had actually advised Sefer Halilovic, the Armija supreme commander, to accept these terms publicly and thereby avoid giving Mladic the excuse to overrun the place – notwithstanding that he knew full well Oric would never disarm.[36] While this advice was no doubt well intended, and Morillon was genuinely concerned for the ordinary people in the enclave, it highlights once again the different layers of reality which could be found within the conflict if one was prepared to dig deep enough.[37]

But from May of 1993 onwards a fiction was perpetuated that the six specified locations were in some way 'safe' simply because the UN Organisation had said they were, notwithstanding that there was no way they could guarantee it. The truth and tragedy of the matter was that thousands of poor, hopeless, helpless people put their trust in the UN, and took their word at face value because they had no one else to turn to. Had this falsehood never been preached in the first instance it is perfectly reasonable to argue that many of these desolate, beaten souls, who struggled to stay afloat in the tide of broken humanity which ebbed and flowed across the Balkans, might well have moved away when the situation was less critical and more opportune. Instead they stayed put because the West said it would protect them. They died because it did not. This is the legacy of the 'safe haven policy'.[38]

Advent of a war crimes tribunal

While media attention focused on the practicalities of the war and peace, other matters were also quietly under consideration at UN HQ in New York where on 3 May the secretary-general reported to the Security Council pursuant to paragraph 2 of UNSC Resolution 808. He produced a paper for approval called Document S/25704 which contained the statute for the establishment of an international criminal tribunal for Former Yugoslavia, an institution which was to prove ground-breaking in international humanitarian law (IHL). Of critical importance was paragraph 29 of the Report which emphatically stated that the tribunal would not be making new law, and paragraphs 33, 34 and 35 established exactly what law would be applied.[39]

The Report went on to identify the central position of the Geneva Conventions in IHL and was crystal clear that they also provided the core rules of customary international law. It further identified that persons in the Former Yugoslavia who had committed, or ordered the commission of, 'grave breaches' of the Conventions were individually responsible for serious violations of IHL,[40] and Article 2 of the Statute of the Tribunal outlined precisely what these grave breaches or war crimes actually were.

Crucially, the secretary-general next identified what constituted 'violations of the laws and customs of war' and declared that the Fourth Hague Convention of 1907 Respecting the Laws and Customs of War on Land, and the Regulations annexed thereto, comprised a second important source of conventional IHL which had now also become part of customary international law, given that the original high contracting parties saw the conventions as complementing 'the principles of the law of nations, as they result from the usages established among civilised peoples, from the laws of humanity, and the dictates of public conscience'.[41]

He was further satisfied that breaches of this body of law should also be classified as 'war crimes' on the basis that the Nuremberg tribunal had already made this ruling in 1939. Accordingly, what constituted 'violations of the laws and customs of war' were listed in Article 3 of the statute.

In Article 4, the secretary-general set about clarifying what constituted the crime of genocide, and once again he decided that while the 1948 Convention on the Prevention and Punishment of the Crime of Genocide confirmed that genocide, whether committed in time of peace or in time of war, is a crime under international law, the terms of the Convention are now also part of customary international law and as such have universal application.

And finally the secretary-general addressed the matter of what constituted 'crimes against humanity', identifying that they had first been recognised in the Charter and Judgment of the Nuremberg Tribunal, as well as in Law No. 10 of the Control Council for Germany. These acts, which are aimed at the civilian population, are prohibited, regardless of whether they are committed in an international or internal armed conflict.

Having established that it was 'natural persons' who were subject to the jurisdiction of the tribunal,[42] the secretary-general then addressed the principle of 'individual criminal responsibility' and, having taken account of all available advice, decided that all persons who had participated in the planning, preparation or execution of serious violations of international humanitarian law in the Former Yugoslavia had contributed to the commission of these violations and were, therefore, individually responsible.[43]

A plea of head of state immunity, or that an act was committed in the official capacity of an accused, would not constitute a defence, nor mitigate punishment.[44]

On 25 May 1993 the Security Council adopted UNSC Resolution 827 and thereby approved the Statute for the International Criminal Tribunal for Former Yugoslavia as submitted two weeks previously in the secretary-general's report. The scope and application of international humanitarian law had now been redefined in a unique manner by an agency which up to that point was never considered to have had such competence. The secretary-general in his urgency to respond to the ever-deteriorating situation had managed to draw together all identifiable sources of the IHL and determine how all the pieces of the jigsaw should fit together.

By deciding that conventional law had over time become customary law he had managed in one fell swoop to blur the distinction between the law applicable to internal conflicts, on the one hand, and international war on the other. And perhaps this was inevitable, given the mixed nature of what was happening on the ground in the Former Yugoslavia where the conflict was in reality both internal and international at the same time, and subsequently developed into a hybrid conflict which commentators began to call 'internationalised' simply because they could not think of anything more appropriate.

In any event the core issues had now been resolved, and the law clarified for the 11 judges who would gather in The Hague 'to well and truly try' those who would appear before them.[45] Equally, it was now perfectly clear to the perpetrators of evil on all sides of the ethnic divide that their interpretation of the *context* within which they were operating had become all but irrelevant. From now on it would be the *nature* of their actions for which they would ultimately be accountable.[46] Professor Adam Roberts later summed it all up rather well: 'The situation whereby civil wars were hardly subject, even in theory, to a body of international rules was an anachronism, the ending of which should not be mourned.'[47]

A culture of deceit

Meanwhile, Boris Yeltsin and his deputy foreign minister, Vitali Churkin, continued their appeals to 1.3 million Bosnian Serbs to vote for Vance–Owen[48] – but if the ongoing destruction of mosques in Banja Luka was anything to go by the prospects were not good.[49] There was, however, some indication from eastern Bosnia of a lull in hostilities, but this was counterbalanced by news from Mostar City where Croats and Muslims had resumed fighting. If Vance–Owen was ever to have effect in Mostar it would involve the transfer of authority from Muslim to Croat, both of which had equally valid competing claims to the city, and neither of which were prepared to give them up.

Appeals by the force commander, General Wahlgren, to President Tudjman to intervene, yielded no improvement on the ground,[50] and very disturbing reports began to filter through of civil rights violations at Croat-run detention centres, specifically the one at Citluk a few miles south of Mostar itself. ECMM also received reports of another Croat detention centre which was housed on one of the islands off the coast in Croatia proper.

On 11 May Milosevic, whose patience with Karadzic had now all but expired, called for the referendum to be cancelled in order that the Bosnian Serb leaders make their way to Belgrade and settle the matter rather than continue squabbling in public. Karadzic immediately rejected this suggestion, which in turn led Boutros Boutros-Ghali to declare in frustration that no matter what result the referendum produced he personally would not accept it.

In Washington the possibility of sending US troops to Macedonia, as peacekeepers in a pre-emptive role, remained under serious consideration, but an underlying current of frustration with the whole situation in Bosnia was becoming more and more evident. The mood of Congress was articulated succinctly by Senator Joe Biden when he attacked European leaders on 5 May for what he called 'their discouraging mosaic of indifference, timidity, self delusion, and hypocrisy, which amounted to codification of a Serb victory'.

This was more than a little extreme, but it nonetheless reflected the general dissatisfaction with international policy which appeared simply to stumble from one crisis to the next. And then, as if on cue, another problem now presented itself in the form of a Croat detention centre south of Mostar in which 1,500 Muslim prisoners were incarcerated in circumstances which UNHCR officials in Mostar City described as similar to those in which the Jews were kept by the Nazis during the Second World War.

Armin Pohara, a Muslim journalist, managed to make his way into the camp which was located in the military airport and where Muslim prisoners were incarcerated in huge subterranean storage tanks previously used to store aviation fuel. The tanks were half buried in the sense that their roofs were exposed to the blistering sunshine. Conditions inside became unbearably hot and breathing became very difficult, given that aviation fumes were still present; not surprisingly many people died.[51]

The matter of responsibility for these gross human rights violations may never be adequately addressed, but Stipe Mesic was very clear where he thought the buck should stop. 'President Tudjman must have known about the camps', he said. 'I asked him who had organised them. He said "We Croats should not blame ourselves. There may be camps but the others have them too."'[52] It was no excuse, but essentially he got away with it because, as far as the Western media were concerned, 'Tudjman might well have been responsible for death camps in Bosnia – but he was on our side, and that was all right, because we had long ago established beyond doubt that the Serbs were the bad guys. Tudjman was sponsored by Germany and that made everything OK.' Sadly, this perception was reality in 1993.

With Muslim–Croat relations now going downhill rapidly, a row was breaking out between the Bosnian foreign minister and his ambassador to the UN, and with all the Serbs apparently fighting between themselves as well it was indeed difficult to see where European policy was heading at this time. A BBC report on the 14th, which indicated that that the EC was about to impose sanctions against Croatia because of their vicious offensive on Mostar, initiated an immediate response from Germany in the person of Foreign Minister Kinkel who strongly advised President Tudjman to stop the current attack. Having undertaken to intervene Tudjman did nothing, as evidenced by the fact that no change was perceptible on the ground. This proved conclusively to all monitoring agencies that it wasn't official EC initiatives alone that were ignored completely – the situation had become so ludicrous that even the Croats were not prepared to take instructions from their main sponsor and protector.

This lesson was not lost on the Serbs as they made their way to polling stations on the 15th. Neither was it lost on Karadzic, who saw no evidence to suggest that anyone had the commitment or resolve to bring the Croats to heel. All the wrong signals were now being transmitted, and in that context it is much easier to understand why the Bosnian Serbs behaved as they did. As far at they could see the Croats had been given *carte blanche* to pursue their own war. Whether this perception was correct or not essentially makes no difference. Perception was reality for all sides and in that context it is worth examining what Karadzic was actually saying about the situation at this time.

His consistent point of departure always remained that if the West wanted success they should recognise the will of the Bosnian Serb people (not unreasonable); that Bosnia, as a separate state never existed, and never would (also not unreasonable if one was prepared to accept that he had a legitimate point of view in the first place). In relation to the ongoing threat of violence against him by the Western powers he argued that 'If they want to do it they can, they have the capacity. But why would they want to come here and intervene on a single side? Why destroy a small state that now exists (Republic Srpska)? We see no reason [for them] to intervene.'

None of this was outrageous, but unfortunately Karadzic was just as likely to say something totally bizarre as produce a reasoned and balanced argument, and it is generally the latter which the media latched onto. Neither was his case helped by the public performances of his military hard man, Ratko Mladic, who continually did the Serb cause a great disservice by screaming that Western military forces 'would leave their bones in Bosnia'. Another assertion of his – that 'if the West bombs me I'll bomb London' – served only to ensure that Mladic, Karadzic and all the Bosnian Serbs were painted in black by the international media.

It also drove a wedge between the two of them personally, and for the first time Karadzic went public, calling these outbursts 'idiotic and irresponsible' and suggesting that Mladic would be reprimanded. This was wishful thinking, of course, because Mladic had long since been pursuing his own agendas, but it was nonetheless a clear indication that as far as Karadzic was concerned Mladic had now become a liability.

However, the fact that the Serbs remained painted as 'the bad guys' was also largely due to their own failure to present their case properly. Had they employed a decent public relations firm, *à la* the Bosnian government, or censored themselves strictly like the Croats, the Serb image might well have developed in a totally different way. Alas, the results of the referendum served only to compound media prejudice. Of the 1.2 million who voted, 96 per cent rejected Vance–Owen, opting instead for an independent Bosnian Serb state and Karadzic's reiteration immediately afterwards that 'the peace plan is dead, long live the peace process' was anything but helpful. In response, Russian foreign minister, Kozyrev, immediately produced a new four-point plan on 18 May in order to deflect attention away from launching a bombing campaign, and under pressure from Owen and Stoltenberg, Tudjman and Izetbegovic agreed to commence implementation of Vance–Owen in those areas of Bosnia under their control.

No sooner had this been announced than another spate of Croat/Muslim violence erupted in Vitez the following day, and it was in the course of these clashes that a hitherto unnoticed relationship between the Croats and the Serbs was exposed.

Allegations of HVO/BSA collusion had begun to surface during the HVO offensive in and around Mostar, but suspicion increased dramatically when details of Croat/Muslim battles in central Bosnia began to emerge. When EC monitors began investigating the matter they discovered that there was indeed substance to the rumours and identified that significant co-operation was taking place. Among the personal effects of a Serb officer, monitors discovered written orders to co-operate with a local HVO unit. Croat refugees and soldiers were observed returning from Serb-held territory after they had sought and been given refuge from an Armija advance.

The ICRC confirmed this when they witnessed the return of 800 HVO, with their weapons, from BSA-held territory. The UN reported incidents of open fraternisation between the BSA and HVO, while UNHCR reported that the HVO in Konjic were supplied with ammunition and food by the BSA and that they had witnessed BSA personnel and vehicles participating in HVO resupply operations. East of Kiseljak UN observers were actually satisfied that BSA elements were taking part in a combined HVO/BSA operation against the Armija in return for deliveries of fuel, and that HVO attacks in central Bosnia were designed to distract Armija attention away from the Posavina Corridor where the Serbs had a vested interest.[53] The scale of co-operation was never satisfactorily established, but all who came across it were in no doubt that it was directed by Zagreb and Belgrade as part of the master plan for the ultimate partition of Bosnia between Milosevic and Tudjman. A meeting between Radovan Karadzic and Mate Boban, which took place in Montenegro around this time, inflamed this situation even more – but officially all that either side were prepared to offer was denial.

Milos Stankovic also records direct evidence he uncovered from an Armija soldier who had been fighting near Grude in the summer of 1993. At one point the Armija gunners ran out of ammunition so they did a deal:

> You see we had money but no shells and the Serb Hercegovina Corps had shells but no money. Since we weren't fighting then down there we did a deal and bought 1,000 shells at 100 Deutschmarks apiece. But the problem we had was we had no means of transporting these shells so the Serbs fired the fire missions against the Croats for us. All we had to do was get our observers to flick to the Serb artillery net and adjust the fire ... it went so well the Serbs threw in an extra hundred shells 'za kafu' – for free.[54]

Stankovic could hardly believe this because north of Sarajevo at that very moment the Serbs and Muslims were knocking hell out of one another. This led him to the following conclusion:

> It was really a war about money, of wheeling and dealing, of local warlords making money hand over fist at the expense of the little people. Small wonder there wasn't a single offspring of any of the leaders on any of the sides who fought. The precious ones were all away in the west or in Turkey or in Belgrade studying at university or whatever. You only had to listen to stories like these to realize that policy makers in the west would never be able to sort this out.[55]

Watching this drama, with all its dark intrigue, from the security of Washington DC, President Clinton really had only one concept and he repeated it over and over again. He simply didn't want to see the United States get to a position in Bosnia which replicated Northern Ireland, Lebanon or Cyprus, and in that context as far as he was concerned the safe areas were nothing more than shooting galleries. If he got nothing else right that assessment was correct and this in turn allowed him to support a joint Russian/American/British/French/Spanish plan which was unveiled on 22 May and contained 13 proposals. Amongst these was one proposing that the UN immediately dispatch more non-American peacekeepers to secure and protect the six designated safe areas. NATO air power would be used if the Serbs launched fresh attacks and UN personnel would monitor the border between Serbia and the 'Republic Srpska' to ensure that Milosevic was not covertly sending supplies to the Bosnian Serbs. A war crimes tribunal would also be set up immediately, on top of which Croatia was to be formally put on notice that sanctions would be imposed against Zagreb if they persisted in resupplying Boban and the HVO.[56]

Taken at face value the plan had a lot of merit in that it faced up to the problems of implementing a safe haven policy and called on Tudjman to halt his clandestine expansionist endeavours in Bosnia. Karadzic welcomed the news with open arms, embracing the 'Washington Accord' and suggesting that he thought President Clinton was going to be a great president. When Izetbegovic was informed of Karadzic's reaction on 23 May he rejected the plan out of hand, saying that it was completely unacceptable because it did nothing to address Serbian aggression and genocide. Urging his people to fight on, he declared 'we are not going to waste time any longer on these futile negotiations', and this in the face of unrelenting pressure on the ground by the Serbs and daily expulsions of between 100 and 200 Muslims from Mostar – by the Croats! This logic would have been impossible to understand were it not clear that the Organisation of Islamic States also rejected the new initiative out of hand as they perceived it to support the *de facto* situation on the ground, which for Muslims everywhere was now unacceptable.

The Bosnian Serbs, having initially welcomed the plan, then appeared to backtrack and Cosic, the Yugoslav president, rejected the need for monitors on the border with Serbia – as did Slobodan Milosevic. In the midst of this shambles NATO defence ministers assembled in Brussels in an attempt to iron out the details of defending the safe areas, but nothing resulted from their deliberations. There was wholesale confusion right from the start as the US and France became locked in a conceptual debate on whether UN troops could be justified in returning fire if an attack on a safe area took place. The French position, as enunciated by Foreign Minister Juppe, would permit retaliation if the safe area itself was hit, while the US insisted that retaliation in the form of air strikes could be sanctioned to protect individual UN troops on the ground. After two days of prolonged debate no consensus could be found and a senior US official reportedly said that those in attendance were not even sure that 'safe haven' was the right phrase because it conjured up something that not even NATO itself could provide.

As the meeting broke up in disarray the NATO secretary-general, Manfred Woerner, outlined all of the questions which the ministers had been unable to resolve. These included: (1) What does 'safe' mean? (2) Who defends whom? (3) What are the rules of engagement? (4) Where is the connection to the withdrawal of Serb forces from captured territory? (5) What weapons may be used by the protectors? (6) What constituted a demilitarisation of the designated safe areas?

Nobody could definitively answer any of these questions and therefore no acceptance of the Washington Plan was possible – by the very people who proposed it![57]

Boutros Boutros-Ghali then suggested another 'London'-type conference to try and sell the plan to the warring parties, but incredibly the non-aligned bloc in the UN General Assembly spoke out on 27 May rejecting the plan on the basis that acceptance of it would turn the safe havens into what they called 'refugee camps in perpetuity encircled by Serbs'.

On 28 May he submitted a formal considered report to the Security Council which basically rejected the Washington Plan for all the aforementioned reasons, and on cue the Bosnian Serb army renewed hostilities in the eastern enclaves. The international community had sent out all the wrong signals without even thinking about what they were actually doing. In Bosnia these signs were interpreted by Ratko Mladic to suit his own purposes, and on the same day the safe area of Gorazde came under attack with Sarajevo receiving a ferocious shelling on the 29th and 30th which left 20 people dead and another 150 injured. In the midst of all of this the Yugoslav president, Cosic, was unable to win a confidence vote in Belgrade on 25 May and was replaced by Zoran Lilic. For most people this contest was irrelevant in the overall scheme of things. Nobody cared much that Cosic was gone, and clearly nobody was particularly bothered either about the fate of the six so-called 'UN safe areas'.

Fikret Abdic

It was at this time that another figure emerged from the shadows to become a major player in Bosnia's complicated conflict. His name was Fikret Abdic and his role was often misrepresented and misunderstood in the media. Born in 1939 in the small village of Donja Vidovska near Velika Kladusa in Bihac Pocket (now a UN safe area), he was the third child of a large family, and upon leaving school began working for the local agricultural co-operative which at the time employed 26 people. Twenty-five years later he had climbed to the top of this small 'Co-op' and turned it into an agricultural food processing industry called Agrokomerc with 13,500 people on the payroll. Abdic had become a man of considerable influence, with 430 farms operating in 50 villages, supporting 52 factories churning out a variety of agri-food. He joined the League of

Communists in 1959 and got himself elected as a deputy in 1963. In 1967 he had become a member of Bosnia's Communist Party Central Committee, and later that year he received Bosnia-Hercegovina's highest civil recognition when he was conferred with the King Faisal Award for his success with Agrokomerc.[58]

However, in 1987 things began to go wrong when he was charged on several counts of corruption and held in investigative detention for over two years. Apparently Agrokomerc had been effectively printing money for itself by abusing the Yugoslav 'bank bond' system on a huge scale, and the entire economy of north-west Bosnia was threatened with collapse.[59] When eventually no indictments were proffered he set about re-establishing himself in political circles and in fact became one of Bosnia's delegates to the Assembly of Yugoslav Republics. But more importantly by far he also managed to save his company by keeping open his trade corridor to Croatia by doing several deals with the Krajina Serbs.

Critically, in 1991, at Bosnia-Hercegovina's first multi-party elections, Abdic emerged as the main threat to Izetbegovic, both within the SDA and also as the potential new president of the country. When the votes were counted he emerged over 200,000 votes in front of Izetbegovic but almost immediately announced that he was not interested in the top job and was prepared only to continue as a member of the Presidential Council. In the light of subsequent events it is arguable that Abdic 'abdicated' his responsibilities, thereby allowing Izetbegovic to take control and ultimately lead the country into war.

The problem was that, notwithstanding that he had actually beaten Izetbegovic in the popular vote, he never had the backing of the SDA heavyweights in Sarajevo, nor did he have the support of the Bosnian Serb members of the presidency either. The only casualty of an attempt to force the issue at that time would have been Abdic himself, and in a 1994 interview he was quite clear on this subject.[60] While this all sounded very magnanimous Abdic conveniently omitted to mention another version of events, which took place in early May 1992, and tended to offer a better explanation of his relationship with Izetbegovic.

Returning from another failed peace conference in Lisbon Izetbegovic had flown into Sarajevo on the night of 2 May oblivious to the fact that all hell had broken loose in his absence following an attempt by the Bosnian Serbs to divide the city in two. He was also unaware that General Milutin Kukanjac, the officer commanding the JNA's Second Military District, together with his headquarters staff, were now trapped in their barracks to the east of the city, and that Sefer Halilovic was demanding their immediate surrender and a handover of all weapons.

Expecting to be met on the tarmac by UNPROFOR vehicles which would escort him back to the presidency building, he found himself instead surrounded by 30 members of the JNA with orders from Kukanjac to arrest him and take his party to the Lukavica Barracks in a Serb-controlled village on the southern edge of the city. Once there it was Kukanjac's intention to initiate a procedure whereby Izetbegovic would be released once he had successfully negotiated safe passage for his own personnel out of area held now by the government's territorial defence units.[61]

However, when Izetbegovic arrived in Lukavica he managed to gain access to a telephone and made contact with the city's TV station, via one of the very few serviceable P&T lines in Sarajevo, and confirmed that he had in fact been arrested by the JNA. He went on to nominate Ejup Ganic as acting president in his absence and then the two of them began a discussion of the situation live on air. While the conversation was taking place another twist to the story unfolded when Fikret Abdic unexpectedly walked into the TV studio allegedly enquiring as to the president's well-being.

Initial surprise at his actual presence in the studio soon gave way to total disbelief when it emerged that earlier in the evening he had successfully made his way from Bihac, travelling first to Split on the coast, and thereafter through Mostar, Zenica, Kiseljac and Visoko before eventually arriving in Sarajevo. He had managed to make his way through several Bosnian, Croat and Serb checkpoints, apparently without any difficulty whatever, a feat which was at that time justifiably considered by all parties to the conflict, and also by the UN, to have been totally and utterly impossible. When all of this emerged Ganic immediately became very suspicious and decided that an attempt was in hand, probably orchestrated by Abdic, to depose Izetbegovic.

A meeting of the government was called at once and convened in the presidency building, where the interior minister, Alija Delimustafic, opened proceedings by advocating the selection of a new president who might be better equipped and disposed to do a deal with Kukanjac and the JNA. While this suggestion certainly contained a great deal of merit Ganic rounded on the minister and the proposal was summarily quashed. However, what he singularly failed to eradicate was the lingering suspicion that Abdic had been in league with Belgrade, the JNA high command, and a number of cabinet ministers, in an attempt to remove Izetbegovic and assume control himself. There is, of course, no direct evidence that this was Abdic's intention but thereafter his political career in Sarajevo proved to be irreparably damaged, and when Izetbegovic was exchanged for Kukanjac the following day in the course of a botched operation in which six JNA officers were killed, it became crystal clear that the hardliners in the SDA were firmly back in control.[62]

Within a short period Alija Delimustafic gave up on politics in Sarajevo altogether and went to live in Austria, while Abdic knew that the longer he remained in Sarajevo the more marginalised he was destined to become. In mid-September 1992 he returned to Bihac and assumed an advisory role to the District Assembly where within a short time a political reform package appeared and had an 'Abdic philosophy' stamped all over it. His main problem was clearly going to be keeping the Bihac Pocket area out of a war which was about to engulf the rest of the country, and this was brought home very dramatically on 27 April 1993 when an attack was launched across the border by the Krajina Serbs in which they succeeded in capturing a large swathe of land in the north-east corner of the Pocket around the town of Bosanska Bojna.

When Abdic confronted the local Serb commanders they told him that this had only been a 'limited local offensive' by troops who had previously been expelled from this area by 'uncontrolled elements' and that all they were doing was reclaiming their own land. But when one delved a little deeper it emerged that the attack had been very much co-ordinated, employing infantry, armour and artillery drawn from three Serb brigades in the area. When the Armija's 5th Corps then counter-attacked they found themselves repulsed in a very controlled and orderly fashion, which in turn convinced that this was anything but an *ad hoc* incursion by a handful of frustrated displaced Serbs.

Then it emerged that the whole thing had in fact been strictly co-ordinated between the Bosnian and Krajina Serbs, and that the field commander for the attack had been a member of the Bosnian Serb army's 1st Corps in Banja Luka, and that both artillery units had opened fire at exactly the same time.[63] All of the jigsaw pieces began to fall into place. Bihac was well on its way to becoming the next Srebrenica.

The message for Abdic was clear. If he was to spare his people the savagery and brutality of all-out conflict then he would have to take the initiative himself. No confidence could be derived from any vague ill-defined announcement that the UN had declared Bihac town a 'safe area' because it had no means whatever to enforce it. And even if by some quirk of fate the Serbs decided to respect this declaration for a while there was nothing to stop them from pursuing their campaign elsewhere in the area whenever they wanted to. Furthermore, it was blatantly obvious that the 5th Corps could not be expected to initiate any significant operations of their own, and could not be depended upon to hold the line in the face of a concerted and co-ordinated Serb attack.

There was nothing for it but to negotiate with the Serbs and attempt to establish some criteria whereby everyone could live together. The first phase of this policy came into play more or less immediately when UNPROFOR suggested a demilitarisation of the disputed area around Bosanska Bojna. The plan involved the placement of French UN troops between the warring parties, policing the area with UN civil police (UNCIVPOL), and the resettlement of the original inhabitants who were now living elsewhere. The last part of this was extremely ambitious, and everyone knew it, but agreement was obtained and the situation settled down for a while.[64]

When the Washington Accord[65] failed to find acceptance in Sarajevo, Abdic became even more concerned. He believed that Izetbegovic had only rejected the initiative because the Serbs had decided to accept it, and the gulf between them began to widen and culminated in a row which erupted at a meeting of the Presidential Council on 23 June when a proposal to partition the country effectively into three ethnic provinces as a part of a negotiated settlement was being discussed.

Abdic had no difficulty supporting this proposal because he fervently believed that partition was already a reality on the ground now anyway. However, Ejup Ganic vehemently opposed him, advocating that the fight, such as it was, must go on. Izetbegovic was equally dogmatic and on 28 June proposed that government representatives should boycott the peace talks in Geneva if partition remained on the table. At this point Izetbegovic and Ganic walked out, leaving Abdic and the remaining presidency members in a quandary.

At the conference table in Geneva a few days later Abdic knew exactly where he stood. He could agree to whatever he wished, but if that did not subsequently meet with Izetbegovic's approval back in Sarajevo then all his efforts would be in vain. He was supposedly negotiating on behalf of the presidency of his country, but he could not deliver on any issue because Ganic and Izetbegovic held a veto at home. This situation was not helped either by the fact that Lord Owen had now decided Abdic was really the only one in Sarajevo he could do business with. When news of this emerged the SDA heavyweights took umbrage and set about discrediting him.

By July Abdic could tolerate the situation no longer and took the unprecedented step of writing a public letter to Izetbegovic and the other members of the presidency in which he set out his assessment of the situation and what he believed they were doing wrong.[66] What he had to say turned out to be prophetic, but like many prophets before him he would not find acceptance by all his own people. He was never going to be admitted to the inner sanctum of the SDA and consequently a great deal of bitterness is to be found in what he wrote. Nevertheless, the letter provides a unique insight into SDA politics at the time and leads one inescapably to the conclusion that perhaps there was a better way to deal with the situation had Izetbegovic been prepared to take it.[67]

Now in a minority of one Abdic was convinced that Izetbegovic had no intention whatever of entering into any form of negotiated settlement that might involve concession of some jurisdiction over their own territory to the Serbs. Whenever it looked as if a settlement might be possible Izetbegovic usually found an excuse to walk away, and as far as Abdic was concerned he had suffered enough of this folly. Quickly he came to the conclusion that there was no point whatever waiting for further guidance from Sarajevo and decided it would be better for the citizens of Bihac if they opted to fend for themselves.

Talking in Geneva

In the wider context talks were still taking place at the headquarters of the International Conference on the Former Yugoslavia in Geneva, and on 15 July the so-called 'Erdut Agreement' was signed which allowed for the placement under UNPROFOR control of the Maslenica bridge, Zemunik airport and the Peruca dam (all in Croatia), and the establishment of a UN civil police (UNCIVPOL) presence in certain villages within the Krajina.

This permitted President Tudjman and his media circus to perform 'official' opening ceremonies at Maslenica and Zemunik which reduced tensions in Croatia and Krajina sufficiently for Owen and Stoltenberg to turn their attention once again to the matter of bilateral talks on Bosnia.[68]

This resulted in an announcement on 28 July that Karadzic, Boban and Izetbegovic had all agreed to issue instructions to their respective troops to observe a ceasefire, but by the time they had all convened six days later in Geneva a section of the Maslenica bridge lay submerged in the water following several Krajina Serb bombardments. There seemed to be no way forward, and on 10 August all talking came to a halt following the reimposition of the blockade of Sarajevo by Serb forces on the ground. Then on the 16th, just when the conference appeared to be getting back on the rails, Izetbegovic sent a letter to Owen refusing to have bilateral discussions with Mate Boban until the Croats complied with the terms of the Makarska Agreement,[69] and gave full freedom of movement to all the humanitarian agencies which would in turn give access to Muslim communities in places like Mostar. Then, having overcome that problem, Izetbegovic walked out of the next meeting on the 19th accusing the co-chairmen of having decided on a plan to divide Sarajevo which would give half of it to the Serbs when nothing of the sort was the case.

At this point the process was clearly going nowhere with the best suggestion being conditional acceptance of the plan pending immediate return of all Muslim land currently held by either the Serbs or Croats. While the parliament in Sarajevo was mandating Izetbegovic to this effect by 61 votes to 11,[70] Tudjman was meeting Fikret Abdic on the island of Brijuni.[71]

To put it mildly it was very surprising that the one man who had become completely marginalised in Bosnia should now find himself advising the president of Croatia on how to proceed at the next round of international peace talks. But it was nothing short of astonishing to discover the extent of his influence, which was there for all to see in the text of Tudjman's address to the combined session in Geneva two days later.[72]

Not surprisingly nobody was prepared to accede to Izetbegovic's conditions so the Muslims did not sign, and the following day Tudjman went on the offensive again declaring to anyone who would listen that the conference had broken down because of Sarajevo's intransigence.[73]

Fortified by the support that was now clearly coming from Tudjman, and anxious to ensure that his economic links with Croatia remained intact, Abdic, in the course of an interview on Bihac TV, announced that as far as he was concerned the future of the Pocket lay in the people's own hands and not in slavishly following the dictates currently emanating from Sarajevo. Gathering together a group of like-minded associates, a meeting was held at the Agrokomerc offices in Velika Kladusa on 7 September and a committee was formed to promote what was called an 'Initiative for the establishment of the Autonomous Province of Western Bosnia within the Republic of Bosnia and the Union of Republics of Bosnia-Hercegovina'.[74]

In three days 17,238 people from all over the Pocket had put their names to the initiative proposals and the president of the Initiative Committee, Professor Asim Dizdarevic wrote to the District Assembly on 11 September inviting all the municipal councils within the Pocket to declare their position on the matter. The letter concluded with a warning: 'Until competent authorities declare themselves, and form suitable bodies, the Initiative committee will continue with its work bearing in mind that they do not have the right to ignore the plebiscitary request of the citizens in any issue.'

The following day an extraordinary session of the Bihac District Assembly was held and it was decided that if Articles 47 and 84 of the Constitution of Bosnia-Hercegovina were to be complied with the people were indeed entitled to express their opinion on the matter. The municipalities of Bihac Town, Bosanska Krupa, Cazin and Velika Kladusa were instructed to ascertain the views of the other 230,000 citizens of the Pocket immediately. However, within three days this had changed when the response from the municipalities indicated that there was no evidence of any overwhelming support for the initiative. Instead it transpired that the only people in favour were all connected to Agrokomerc in one way or another and were not representative of the population as a whole. But the seeds of conflict had been sown. Bihac was well on its way to a 'war within a war' in which Muslims would slaughter one another and everyone else would interfere.

On 27 September an assembly was established in Velika Kladusa which proclaimed the existence of the 'Autonomous Province of Western Bosnia' (APWB), an area equating roughly to the northern half of Bihac Pocket and where Agrokomerc was most influential. For the ordinary people in this part of Bosnia life had long since become simply a matter of survival, and if there was the remotest chance that their conditions and prospects were going to improve by throwing their lot in with Abdic then they were quite prepared to do so. Equally, those members of the 5th Corps and the territorial defence force (TDF), who were originally from Velika Kladusa and its environs, had no qualms about supporting the new political set-up either because they fully understood that they stood a far better chance of receiving payment for their services from the coffers of Agrokomerc than they did from the Sarajevo government.

And so within a very short period of time the Pocket had become politically and militarily polarised; in effect divided in two. Skirmishing began almost immediately near the village of Skokovi on 2 October, but undeterred Abdic announced the creation of his new political party, the Muslim Democratic Party (MDS), the following day and his disciples began settling into a new pattern of existence as towns and villages were fought over, changed hands, and then sometimes changed back again. Mediation attempts by UNPROFOR's General Briquemont on 6 October proved unsuccessful and the fighting escalated in the town of Cazin which became the first town in the Pocket to experience this new conflict. The town fell initially to Abdic forces on the 15th but returned to 5th Corps control the following day after much skirmishing.

In order to ensure that the only threat to APWB came from Sarajevo Abdic quickly moved to sign non-aggression pacts with the other Bosnian leaders, and on 21 October he travelled to Zagreb to conclude a deal with Mate Boban, representing the Bosnian Croats and specifically the HVO within the Pocket. The following day he moved on to Belgrade and entered into a similar arrangement with Radovan Karadzic. In order to complete the picture he also entered a *rapprochement* with the Krajina Serbs on 28 October which included a non-aggression pact and demilitarisation of the disputed Bosanska Bojna area in the north-east. With all external relations resolved Abdic believed he was now in a position to pursue his own objectives within the Pocket, but this would prove more difficult than even he had bargained for.[75]

In fact the Sarajevo government's problems were not confined exclusively to Bihac as several other parts of the country also began to consider organising their own affairs. Not least amongst these was the municipality of Tuzla in north-central Bosnia, where the notion of autonomy was being seriously considered. In response to the potential disintegration of Sarajevo's area of influence, and the failure of the 5th Corps to deal satisfactorily with Abdic, a decision was made which saw General Drekovic moved sideways to take command of the 4th Corps, and his deputy, Colonel Atif Dudakovic, promoted to major-general at 39 years of age, and assigned command in Bihac.

This was a shrewd move by Sarajevo in that at one level it gave the impression of radical reorganisation but at the same time retained a high degree of continuity within the 5th Corps. It also sent another message to would-be secessionists. Dudakovic was 100 per cent loyal to Izetbegovic and was now rewarded for it. He in turn set about his new appointment with relish and prepared to take the fight to Abdic in a way that Drekovic never would.

Americares

But the situation in Bihac was still only a sideshow compared to events taking place nearer home in Sarajevo. On 22 October Bosnian Croat forces (HVO) entered the village of Stupni Do at 8 a.m. and systematically burned 52 houses to the ground, killing 36 Muslims in the process. It later transpired that the villagers had been told to leave their homes a few days previously by the HVO but had decided to stay in the hope that the tension would dissipate. In any case, these poor people had nowhere else to go – but the decision to stay proved wrong.

This sent shock waves through the government in Sarajevo because now, for the first time, they believed that a combined Serb/Croat offensive might be imminent. In response the Armija high command were ordered by Izetbegovic to launch a large-scale attack on the Croat town of Vares, and operations got underway on 3 November. Faced with elements from both the Armija's 2nd and 3rd Corps the local HVO brigade quickly abandoned their checkpoints and withdrew south-eastwards across Serb-held territory to the village of Dastansko, where, with the help of some Serb mercenaries, they dug-in and managed to hold their positions.

The capture of Vares, however, gave a much-needed shot in the arm to the presidency of Izetbegovic and tactically it linked up four Armija Corps – the 2nd in Tuzla, the 3rd in Zenica, the 6th in Konjic and the 4th in Mostar. Politically it also vindicated the president's faith in the Armija General Staff, who had been so influential in having him reject the Geneva peace plan on the basis of their claims that they could, if given the opportunity, reclaim all Muslim lands which had been lost by use of force. Few observers gave this claim much credibility because their military capability consisted largely of badly armed infantry with a few light mortars, a few pieces of captured light artillery and a handful of armoured vehicles. However, things were getting better on the battlefield, evidenced by the fact that for the very first time ammunition had become available for live-fire training exercises with the full range of weapons which they possessed.[76]

A pertinent question here might have been where all this ammunition was coming from in the first place, given that there was supposed to be an arms embargo in operation. Nobody asked. Nobody was too bothered either that a number of baseball-capped, civilian-attired Americans were also wandering all over central Bosnia at this time in the company of US Senator Joe Biden. On a heli-flight into Tuzla in early April Milos Stankovic actually sat beside one of Biden's aides and was astounded to learn that these people were advocating that a huge logistics base should be established in Croatia from which arms and ammunition would then be trans-shipped into Bosnia. As far as he was concerned the UN was a shambles and it was now time for a different course of action.

A few weeks later Stankovic was again flying into Tuzla and this time encountered more baseball-capped individuals, one of these caps bearing the logo 'Americares' – a US non-governmental agency (NGO) which no one had ever heard of. Later that day Stankovic was asked to interpret for this individual at a meeting with the Armija airfield base commander. The questions were all technical in nature – depth of concrete, length of runway, alternate runway, average air temperature and density at various times of year – not the type of questions for which your average NGO would require answers.

Then it emerged that Americares was on the verge of mounting an aggressive airborne delivery of 'medical aid', which was only stopped when UNPROFOR put all the pieces of the jigsaw together.[77]

But this was just the beginning. Soon all manner of equipment would be making its way to the Armija, which in turn ensured that when Izetbegovic looked for advice from his generals the standard reply was always to continue slogging it out. Along with the leaders of both other parties, the Armija high command also had a vested interest in keeping the fight alive. They were important people while the war went on, their word was law, and they controlled both the black market and the distribution of international humanitarian aid.

If they also had a firm expectation that the US would eventually come to their assistance then there was no reason whatever to stop the fighting, and even less to sign some half-baked peace agreement. In 1993 this was the kernel of the problem on the Muslim side. Public misgivings in Geneva about land distribution etc. did not reveal the full picture. That which was perceived by Owen and Stoltenberg was not real. Reality was to be found on the ground, and as discussed with representatives from Americares and other supporters of Sarajevo.

In any event the euphoria of Vares, such as it was, turned out to be short lived because on 9 November, after very heavy shelling by the HVO, the old Turkish bridge in Mostar (the Stari Most), which had spanned the Neretva river for four centuries and survived many wars and floods, was blasted into pieces and sent crashing into the turquoise waters below. This was a poignant moment for Muslims and Croats alike, and while this senseless vandalism made it crystal clear to everyone that the values of the past were now well and truly gone it also triggered a reaction from the politicians who at least theoretically were supposed to be in control of their military.

Within three days Mate Boban had fired his top general, Slobodan Praljak, replacing him with the more moderate Ante Rosso, and in Sarajevo the Croatian foreign minister, Mate Granic, met with the Turkish foreign minister, Hikmet Cetin. Later the pair of them, together with Haris Silajdzic, signed 'A Common Declaration on an Immediate Cease-fire between the Armija and the HVO' on 11 November.

Five days later in Geneva, on 18 November, Sadako Ogata of UNHCR succeeded in extracting another signed declaration from representatives of all three sides which purported to guarantee the free passage and security of all humanitarian convoys operating in Bosnia – and when the Armija and HVO came on board on the 24th it began to look as if a major breakthrough might be achieved at last. As the year drew to a close the overall situation on the ground, while remaining totally unresolved, nevertheless appeared to be quietening down. This was, of course, as attributable to the winter weather as much as to anything else, and all the parties remained focused on their own objectives and aspirations.

Karadzic was still ready to discuss any proposals which might lead to the ultimate partition of the country, while his military commanders continued to provide local support to both the HVO and Armija in different places along the confrontation line in the hope that they would inflict further damage on one another and thereby allow the Serbs to benefit from the fallout.

The Bosnian Croats for their part became embroiled in an internal political row as their pockets in central Bosnia became even more isolated than before and could only now be resupplied by air, and that only by courtesy of helicopters on loan from the HV in Zagreb. Further HV support for the HVO was to be found in Gornji Vakuf where fighting continued unrelentingly, while in Kiseljak assistance was being provided by the nearby BSA who were more than willing to drive their tanks across the confrontation line, fire a few rounds at the Muslims, and then withdraw from whence they came.

The only consideration regulating the frequency of this kind of co-operation was the ability of the HVO to provide adequate compensation, which could range from direct cash payments in hard currency to the provision of food and fuel, and to turning a blind eye to Serb incursions into Croat territory in order to launch their own raids against Armija positions. Like everything else in the Balkans, if the price was right anything was possible.

Within the Muslim community it had now become clear, following the rejection of the Geneva peace plan, that for the moment at least the military held sway over the politicians, and Abdic's declaration of autonomy in Bihac, if it did nothing else, served to push the SDA leadership into a concentrated effort to ensure that similar problems did not spring up in other places.

They were also acutely aware that Abdic was now 'doing business' with all of their sworn enemies as a result of a meeting held on 7 November with Vladimir Lukic and Jadranko Prilic, the prime ministers of the Republic

Srpska and CRHB respectively, where apparently all three had agreed to institute a whole range of political and economic programmes.

In response, Izetbegovic began travelling extensively throughout the country attending a wide range of meetings in a gesture of solidarity with his long-suffering supporters who by now were barely eking out a subsistence existence in the hundreds of battle-damaged towns and villages scattered across a cold and barren landscape. Haris Silajdzic remained behind in Sarajevo to look after international matters, and between the two of them, while they certainly did not resolve the situation, they did manage to stabilise it for a while. In this context what they least required was more trouble in Bihac; but that was exactly what they got.

On 4 December Abdic forces launched a ground attack in the west of the Pocket using around 1,000 troops, and in a meeting with a UNMO team in Cazin General Dudakovic was scathing in his condemnation of the Krajina Serb authorities for permitting Abdic unrestricted transit through their territory in order to resupply his forward troops. While this was probably warranted, his criticism of UNPROFOR for failing to curtail these activities most certainly was not. As on previous occasions all that the UN troops on the ground could do was watch and wait as the conflict raged around them, and later on (if all went well) help to pick up the bodies and ferry the wounded to hospital.[78]

This was precisely the situation in which UNPROFOR's Polish battalion found itself during the early days of December when all they were able to do was set up dressing stations near the scene of the fighting and thereafter transport the wounded back to Vojnic hospital, and onwards to Karlovac in Croatia if so required.[79]

By 8 December, although the situation had stabilised with little gain to the APWB forces, Abdic had very definitely succeeded in forcing Dudakovic to commit troops to several new positions, which in turn made him very vulnerable to attack from the Bosnian Serbs all along the southern confrontation line. However, both sides had suffered many casualties, with over 300 dead and 1,000 wounded. EC monitors quickly suggested to all sides that their best option lay in an immediate ceasefire and shuttled between both camps, dodging incoming Bosnian Serb artillery.

In the midst of all this an amazing request was made to the ECMM team in Bihac town on Wednesday, 29 December, when Dudakovic asked them to set up a meeting between himself and the commander of the Krajina Serbs' Lika Corps, who bordered the Pocket to the south-west, and through whose area all black market goods flowed. War might well have been going on but business was still business; neither commander had any difficulty accepting this situation and working through it.[80]

Elsewhere throughout the Former Yugoslavia there was little room for optimism as the new year approached. Heavy fighting continued in central Bosnia in spite of the fact that a Christmas ceasefire had been agreed to and signed. Armija troops launched a major attack on the Croat-held Vitez Pocket on 22 December while simultaneously shelling Zepce, Visoko and Kiseljak, but after six days of fighting no significant territory had changed hands. In Tuzla, while the situation was generally quiet, tension remained very high in anticipation of the next BSA attack which recently had seen the Bosnian Serbs fire Frog/Orkan rockets and SA-2 surface-to-air missiles against ground targets in the town itself.[81]

The confrontation line in Croatia remained comparatively quiet and the seasonal truce was generally respected by both sides, with the exception of one Colonel Bosonac, a local Krajina Serb commander in the southwestern part of Sector South, who continued his own programme of daily shelling which had no tactical objective other than to intimidate the Croatians who lived on the other side of the confrontation line and anyone else who ventured into the area.

In Krajina itself the recent election results suggested that while some of the main personalities were going to change appointments little else was likely to emerge. And in Serbia and Montenegro life remained very difficult for the population as the effects of economic sanctions continued to cause hardship and deprivation.

As the last seconds of 1993 died away there was nothing whatever to indicate that 1994 would bring any great improvement to the lives of all these Slav people. It seemed to matter little what God any of them worshipped because no superior being appeared to be listening to their prayers – unless of course you consider that 'baseball-capped' agents of the United States fall into this category. Before another year would pass several more would find a premature final resting place beneath the cold and barren Balkan soil, slaughtered indiscriminately in the next round of brutal senseless savagery.

4
1994

The market square bomb

Notwithstanding that EC monitors were rewarded with the announcement of a ceasefire in Bihac on 18 January Abdic continued to blame Izetbegovic for prosecuting the war with the Bosnian Serbs. The creation of APWB, he said, was not a secession from Bosnia-Hercegovina but rather an attempt to save a part of the country from destruction and death, and to preserve some kind of economy in order that the people might not starve.[1] A bag of flour, for example, cost 7 Deutschmarks in Velika Kladusa but the same product cost over 70 Deutschmarks in Cazin, Bosanska Krupa and Bihac town – if of course one could get it at all.

However, on 16 February, having been snubbed by Sarajevo again and knowing that Colonel Legrier had been unable to extract any clear explanation of what constituted the 'safe area of Bihac' from either UNPROFOR HQ in Zagreb or from UN HQ in New York, Abdic decided to reject fresh ECMM proposals for political discussions and launched his forces on a series of offensives which successfully punched a hole almost two kilometres deep into the 5th Corps' positions.[2]

Then, to make matters worse, a journalist working for VIP News in Belgrade filed a report on 22 February which indicated that General Ratko Mladic, the BSA supreme commander, had begun co-ordinating a combined APWB/RSK/BSA attack on the Bilhac Pocket pursuant to a new agreement worked out between Abdic and Karadzic which had allegedly been signed in Belgrade in the presence of both Slobodan Milosevic and the new RSK president Milan Martic.[3] Whether any this was actually true made very little difference because the mere suggestion of such collusion was sufficient to generate wholesale paranoia amongst the besieged community in Bihac who had long since come to the conclusion that the whole world was aligned against them anyway.[4]

But no matter how bad things were in Bihac they were worse in Sarajevo where another act of unprecedented savagery took place at 12.37 p.m. on Saturday, 5 February. As the ordinary citizens went about their business in the hope of acquiring a morsel or two to eat a 120-mm mortar shell smacked into the central market square which was packed with people at the time.[5]

The reason for this unprovoked attack remains completely unclear, with some commentators suggesting that it was all an unfortunate mistake and had to do with a local ceasefire arrangement which the Serbs thought had expired and the Muslims believed had not. Others wondered if it had been part of the ongoing mafia war in the city. More suspicious observers seriously questioned where the shell had been fired from and suggested that in fact it might have been fired by the Armija themselves in order to allow government officials to yet again walk away from the ongoing international negotiations – because predictably enough this is precisely what followed.

Crater analysis by the UNPROFOR investigation team proved inconclusive. All any of those involved would admit was that the round had come from the north-east, where both sides had positions, and that the ammunition itself had been a 120-mm mortar.[6] However, somewhat disturbingly the investigation report cannot now be accessed from UN HQ in New York and the investigation team have all effectively taken a vow of silence. This is not helpful and leads one to conclude that something was discovered which did not add up.[7] At UN HQ in New York the matter was far from clear either and the secretary-general, Boutros Boutros-Ghali, later wrote:

> I told [Warren] Christopher (US Secretary of State) that Akashi reported that the mortar round that had exploded might have been fired by the Bosnian Muslims in order to induce a NATO intervention. Christopher replied that he had seen many intelligence reports and that they went both ways.[8]

In that case, and given that the US secretary of state had actually admitted his intelligence was inconclusive, the Bosnian Serbs were entitled to claim the benefit of the doubt. Only five small pieces of shrapnel were recovered from the marketplace – the rest found their mark in the bodies of almost 300 people,[9] and while rational thought finds it inconceivable that the Armija would shell their own people, the war in Bosnia produced a variety of very irrational and unsavoury individuals. These were to be found on all sides and there is no question whatever that many of them were more than capable of firing that shell and cogently justifying it to themselves thereafter.

Whatever the truth of the matter, the incident and the carnage did allow the UN to once again threaten large-scale NATO air-strikes if the Serbs refused to withdraw their heavy calibre weapons from around the city. This time the threat was serious and the Serbs knew it. Within a few days the ultimatum was complied with and resulted in what became known as the 'Sarajevo Ceasefire of the 9th of February' whereby both sides agreed to stop fighting and to withdraw their heavy weapons outside a 20 kilometre radius of the city, or put them into UN designated and controlled weapons storage sites.[10]

And then, just to prove that NATO was indeed serious in its intentions, an attack by six Bosnian Serb aircraft on the Armija's munitions factory in Novi Travnik in central Bosnia resulted in four of the Serb planes being shot out of the sky for breaching the UN no-fly zone over Bosnia. This was quite a staggering response given the inactivity and indecision which preceded it and was clearly designed to show the Serbs that a new 'get tough' policy was in place. Anywhere else this might have been interpreted as progress. Not, unfortunately, in Bosnia!

The Federation begins

However, some political/military movement was evident when on 23 February Ante Rosso, commander of the HVO, and Rasim Delic, commander of the Armija, turned up together in Zagreb and signed their names to a new ceasefire agreement. Three weeks later Tudjman, Izetbegovic, Silajdzic and Kezimir Zubak, representing CRHB, all made their way to the United States and ended up signing what became known as the Washington Agreement. This established for the first time a political federation between Croats and Muslims in central Bosnia and a confederation between this new body and Croatia proper.[11]

But the speed at which all of this took place caused huge surprise, begging the question what had happened to make the Croats and Muslims embrace each other. The answer, of course, is that this had more to do with the regional interests of the United States and Germany, and President Tudjman's long term ambitions for the creation of Greater Croatia,[12] than anything else. The Federation did not develop indigenously but was imposed from outside, and, not surprisingly, from the outset left both partners looking for totally different things from the new arrangement.

For the Bosnian Croats the main inducement was the promise of formal confederal links with Croatia proper, which in turn would provide a useful justification for the large number of Croatian troops (HV) already operating within the borders of Bosnia-Hercegovina.[13] It would also allow for much closer political and cultural links with Zagreb, and provide a stepping stone to wider Croatian objectives.

From the Muslim perspective joining the Federation at least brought the struggle with the HVO to an end, and this would in turn allow the Armija to redirect their attentions to their real enemies the Bosnian Serbs. On a more practical level both Izetbegovic and the rest of the SDA leadership were also well aware that they had arrived at a point where they risked losing considerable international support for their position unless they agreed to something soon. Entering a vague and as yet ill-defined Federation fulfilled that criterion very nicely.

The Agreement also envisaged the creation of a Federal Assembly with its own budget, army and police force, which in turn would guarantee the safety of all displaced persons as they returned to their homes. Whether the Federation would develop into anything more than a glorified ceasefire was questionable, but as far as the Croatian government were concerned their complicity was rewarded with a US$128 million loan from the World Bank.

From the American point of view bringing both sides together represented the culmination of a process which Charles Redman (Clinton's special mediator) and Peter Galbraith (US ambassador to Croatia) had been working on behind the scenes for months, but which at the end of the day they had literally to bully the Croats into signing.[14] If they failed to agree then it was made quite clear that recent US investigations into detention centres run by the Bosnian Croats might be made public, with a view to recommending prosecutions to the International War Crimes Tribunal.

Of critical importance also was the US commitment to deploy an American group called MPRI (Military Professional Resources Incorporated) in Zagreb. This US State Department-approved agency employed both the former US army chief of staff, General Carl Vuono, and the former head of the US army in Europe, General C. 'Butch' Saint. Providing training and technical support to Croatia's armed forces, and believed to have connections with the weapons brokerage firm Cypress International, MPRI's expertise would prove invaluable and also copper-fasten American support for Tudjman's long-term objectives.[15]

That this amounted to a clear violation of the UN embargo on the transfer of defence goods and services to all the republics of the Former Yugoslavia clearly bothered none of them, and so for several reasons which had precious little to do with peaceful coexistence Croats and Muslims in Bosnia were prevailed upon to stop killing one another.[16]

In tandem with all of this another series of negotiations were underway behind closed doors at the embassy of the Russian Federation in Zagreb. These resulted in another signed agreement on 29 March between the Croatian government and the Krajina Serbs. Both sides agreed to an immediate cessation of hostilities, a freezing of the military situation on the ground, the establishment of a separation zone for infantry, and 10- and 20-kilometre exclusion zones on both sides of the ceasefire line from which all mortars, tanks and artillery would have to be removed. If for one reason or another it was deemed impossible to remove these weapons the required distance then they could be retained within the exclusion zones – but only in specially designated 'weapons storage sites' which were to be controlled and monitored by UNPROFOR.

When the Separation Zone was established it would come under the exclusive control of UNPROFOR and no military, paramilitary, militia or police personnel from either side would be permitted to operate within the area. The ceasefire itself would be monitored jointly by both ECMM and UNPROFOR, using the cumbersome mechanics of the Joint Commission System to iron out any points of dispute which were guaranteed to arise between the parties.

Signed by Messrs Sarinic and Rakic on behalf of the parties, and witnessed by ambassadors Eide and Aherns on behalf of the UN and EU, in the presence of the UN force commander General De Lapresle,[17] the 'Ceasefire Agreement of the 29th of March' was a major step forward, and, taken together with the Washington Agreement, it did look briefly as if the prospects for some short-term stability right across Croatia and Bosnia appeared to be reasonably good.[18] But then, as always in the Balkans, just when it looked as if a settlement might be in the offing something else happened to divert attention away from the peace process and onto another obscure battlefield. This time the focus of attention would be a place called Gorazde.

Gorazde

The pretext for the Serb attack on Gorazde in April 1994 was provided by the Armija themselves who had continually used the enclave as a springboard from which to launch raids on Serb construction workers nearby who were attempting to build a by-pass around the area in order to provide better communications between Trebijne in the south and the Posavina corridor in the north. These raids had been ongoing for some time and continued notwithstanding (or perhaps because of) the fact that Gorazde was supposed to be a UN 'safe area'. In fact it had been clear for a long time that if this pattern continued it would only be a matter of time before the Serbs struck back, and when it eventually happened nobody was particularly shocked. The only surprise as such was the scale of the Serb response which turned out to be more vicious and sustained than anything that had gone before – but there were reasons for this too.[19]

General Mladic, who had been away from Bosnia on compassionate leave following the death of his daughter in Belgrade,[20] believed that with the prospect of an overall solution about to be imposed on all the parties there remained very little time within which to tidy up outstanding matters – and the pacification of Gorazde was for him an important outstanding matter. For a long time this enclave, with its 60,000 Muslim inhabitants, had remained a thorn in his side and amazingly managed to survive in spite of being surrounded and cut off from the rest of Bosnia for over a year and a half.[21] When Mladic's troops began tightening their grip on Gorazde in the first week of April 1994 it looked as if we were in for a repeat performance of what had happened in Srebrenica the year before. Thousands of people from outlying villages had again begun to run for their lives before a creeping artillery barrage which indiscriminately flattened everything before it – but this time the stakes were different. This time Mladic had decided to attack a designated UN 'safe area' with the intention of securing its systematic destruction. With no electricity, gas or water, and the situation getting worse by the minute, Mladic gambled that the world would not intervene.

For General Sir Michael Rose, the new UN commander in Bosnia, this development represented the first major threat to his personal authority in the region, and while he clearly wanted to respond, the use of air-strikes was very much a last option he hoped he would never need to use. He genuinely believed the use of air power to be inconsistent with the concept of peacekeeping and was acutely aware of how the Americans had got it so completely wrong in Somalia when they attempted to enforce a peace. 'You cannot fight a war from the backs of white painted vehicles', he would frequently remark, and he was determined not to step across the 'Mogadishu Line',[22] which would turn peacekeeping into war fighting and serve only to put his own troops at risk when they could barely defend themselves.[23]

The UN troops on the ground were very fortunate that Sir Michael had fully grasped what the UN could and, more importantly, could not do in Bosnia. A weaker personality might have been pushed, or tempted, to take the war to the Serbs, especially since Western public opinion, influenced significantly by the likes of Madeleine Albright at the UN in New York and Admiral Leighton Smith at NATO's base in Naples, was *de facto* demanding aggressive action.

To have intervened in this way would have sacrificed UNPROFOR's neutrality in the conflict and thereafter, from the Serb perspective, every UN soldier would have become a legitimate target. The UN Organisation as a whole was fortunate to have had Rose at the helm in Sarajevo at what ultimately turned out to be a pivotal time in the history of the whole Yugoslav conflict. His clear understanding of his mission and mandate saved his soldiers' lives. There is absolutely no doubt whatsoever about that fact.[24]

It was hardly surprising then that when news of the Serb advance on Gorazde began to filter through Rose and his staff initially attempted to downplay the situation precisely because it was unclear. Bosnian government officials led by Haris Silajdzic took a different view of the matter and, courtesy of CNN and Sky News began to peddle the line that the Muslim population of the enclave were on the verge of annihilation as UNPROFOR stood by and did nothing to help them. This was not exactly true, but when on 8 April Mladic launched a three-pronged attack and two days later bombarded the city centre with tank, artillery and mortar fire, it became clear to Rose that intervention was now crucial.[25]

At 4.25 p.m. on the 10th Rose asked Yasushi Akashi (a man who also saw no merit in crossing the Mogadishu Line either) for permission to call in close air support, and 50 minutes later it was granted. At 6.25 p.m. two American F-16Cs arrived overhead and in four minutes dropped six 250-kg bombs which obliterated a Serb command and control bunker. Mladic was not impressed. The Serb attack continued and the city centre was shelled again. The following day two US Marine Corps F/A 18A Hornets[26] operating out of Aviano in Italy were directed onto further Serb targets by British SAS personnel on the ground in Gorazde who were operating in the enclave as forward air controllers (FACs), among other things.[27]

Using six Mk82 bombs the strike successfully destroyed two armoured personnel carriers and one tank, but bad weather prevented an attack on other tanks which had been on the original 'shopping list'.[28] Mladic got the message but was not impressed and immediately ordered his troops to take UN personnel hostage against further air intervention. Quickly, over 150 UN personnel elsewhere in Bosnia were taken into Serb captivity, and Tuzla city was shelled while the attack on Gorazde continued.

On the 15th the final Serb push began and Rose decided to call once more for close air support. Again he needed Akashi's permission but was unable to contact him because he had gone to lunch with Dr Karadzic in Pale. A farcical situation then developed as Rose asked Akashi for permission to bomb Serb positions around Gorazde while Karadzic listened in to the conversation. He then picked up a second phone and spoke directly to Mladic on the battlefield who accused the UN in the enclave of being deployed in the wrong place and therefore as far as he was concerned they deserved whatever they got.

There being no way whatever to confirm any of this Karadzic then rounded on Akashi: 'They were on the front line, what were they doing on the front line, they are not supposed to be there.' In danger of being taken hostage himself if he went ahead and authorised another air-strike, Akashi declined to give permission. Mladic then continued his advance as the Muslim defences to the north of Gorazde collapsed, and two British forward air controllers were wounded when the Serbs overran their positions. One of them later died from his wounds.

Meanwhile, back in Pale Karadzic and Akashi finished their dinner without further interruption and the next day the Serbs announced to the media that they now held all the key terrain around Gorazde and were continuing to push forward. Faced now with another 'Srebrenica' Rose pleaded with Akashi once more for air support; in the afternoon he reluctantly agreed. However, by the time the planes arrived overhead the weather had closed in and their only achievement was to have a British Harrier shot down. It was hit by a surface-to-air missile. Alarmed at how the situation was escalating, Vitali Churkin, the Russian special envoy, had made his way to Pale only to discover that Karadzic, seemingly oblivious to the possibility of massive air retaliation, had gone off to Banja Luka for a series of political meetings.[29]

Undeterred Churkin contacted Akashi, who was still in Sarajevo, and informed him that he had brokered a deal with Momcilo Krajisnik, the president of the Bosnian Serb parliament, whereby in return for a cancellation of air-strikes the Serbs would stop shelling Gorazde, withdraw 3 kilometres from their current positions, and release the 150 UN hostages. The strikes were called off, but needless to say none of this happened. When Karadzic and Akashi both returned to Pale the following morning for discussions they found Churkin in a rage and so severely embarrassed that he eventually stormed out of the meeting in disgust.

The following day the Serb military push on the ground continued and the shelling resumed where it had left off momentarily the day before. While the politicians grasped at one straw after another people died on the streets of Gorazde, and in a letter to Boutros Boutros-Ghali, Izetbegovic claimed that 'the so-called safe area had become the most unsafe place in the world'.

While the international community dithered, on the 19th the Serbs raided the weapons collection point at Lukavica Barracks in Sarajevo and made off with a variety of weapons in clear breach of the Sarajevo ceasefire of 9 February; the death toll in Gorazde continued to rise.[30] The next day NATO finally managed to issue an ultimatum (notwithstanding clear policy differences between the Americans and the British) which threatened punitive air-strikes if three conditions were not met by the Serbs – an immediate ceasefire; the withdrawal of troops 3 kilometres from the centre of Gorazde by first light on 23 April; and the withdrawal of heavy weapons 20 kilometres from the centre of the town by the evening of the 26th.

Mladic chose to ignore these demands and continued to shell Gorazde, but when nothing had happened by the 23rd Admiral Leighton Smith from his base in Naples contacted Akashi, who was in Belgrade, and asked for permission to begin the air-strikes on the basis that the first condition – the establishment of an immediate ceasefire – had not been met.

Akashi refused because he said he believed the Serbs were actually withdrawing some of their heavy weapons; and in fact they were. He then ordered General Rose to deploy 247 UN troops[31] into Gorazde under cover of darkness on the night of 24/25 April, and although Manfred Woerner, NATO's general secretary, was outraged that the air-strikes had been cancelled there was little he could do. Akashi claimed he had identified gestures of goodwill from the Serbs, and for now that was good enough for him.

This time round the threat of air-strikes had been enough. Over the next few days the Serbs withdrew, burning houses and destroying the water pumping station as they left. The Armija in Gorazde handed over a small number of rusty muskets as British and Ukrainian troops were interpositioned between the opposing forces and a ceasefire was established to be monitored by a variety of agencies. But without doubt the most significant outcome by far was that the Serbs were left in control of all the high ground overlooking the town and retained the potential to shell it whenever they wanted to.

Haris Silajdzic lost no time in pointing this out and complained bitterly that some Serb artillery remained within the 20-kilometre exclusion zone. He was correct, but this issue was never dealt with properly at the time largely because a row had broken out between the Sarajevo government and Rose over what he supposedly said when he went to the enclave to visit his conglomerate force there.

In the course of a tactical appreciation of the recent conflict he had observed that the Armija appeared to have abandoned their defensive positions too quickly and expected the UN to fight their battles for them. In reality that mattered little now as once again in Bosnia a large group of Muslims had been left living in what almost amounted to one large concentration camp, isolated and surrounded, and right smack in the middle of Serb territory.

The long and the short of it was that while the enclave might not have fallen, Mladic had still won. Politically, Karadzic was left carrying the can and even more detached from Belgrade, if that were possible. Lord Owen believed that

> Relations between Karadzic and Milosevic were never the same after Gorazde. They [the Bosnian Serbs] were shown up to be bare-faced liars, all the time saying they weren't after Gorazde when they were. They lost the support of the Russians for quite a while after that. Which they deserved. It was outrageous what happened over Gorazde.[32]

But that is probably too simplistic an explanation. A better evaluation might take account of the fact that Milosevic had all but washed his hands of the Bosnian Serbs after the collapse of the Vance–Owen plan, and this latest episode was really only more of the same thing. Equally the whole Gorazde operation, the same as Srebrenica the year before, was strictly directed by Mladic, with the politicians having little or no influence.

Karadzic could and should have distanced himself totally from what had happened, but not for the first time took the wrong option. Rather than admit his impotence in this regard he ended up being photographed playing chess with Mladic near the front line while the enclave burned in the background. He was never in a position to call Mladic to heel effectively and this powerlessness may well have accounted for his absence from Pale when Vitali Churkin came to see him. Rather than admit the truth, he chose to abscond, leaving Momcilo Krajisnik behind to give undertakings which he knew would never be honoured.

Karadzic was only ever in control when Mladic decided to go along with him. In fact when Mladic initially arrived to take command of the Bosnian Serb army following his exploits in Croatia he demanded that the political leadership in Pale 'immediately and unconditionally yield all control to him and that they refrain from making any political decision without the approval of his military command'. Later on he took it upon himself to threaten the commencement of a terrorist campaign against London and Washington which forced Karadzic, on 17 March 1993, into open conflict with his general when he publicly denounced the statement as 'idiotic, irresponsible, and unauthorised'.[33]

It is one thing to blame Karadzic for everything which happened in the name of the Bosnian Serbs, but it is altogether another to determine whether he ever really had the wherewithal to actually influence the conduct of any given military operation. As time went on his relationship with Mladic would deteriorate even further, culminating at a point where he was forced to form his own 'praetorian guard' to ensure his personal safety; later again he would make several unsuccessful attempts to sack him. Instead of concentrating on the growing void between Milosevic and Karadzic, which is indisputable, it might be far more interesting to examine the relationship between Milosevic and Mladic and attempt to discover why the Serbian president never ever condemned the ex-JNA officer, even during the worst excesses of the Bosnian Serb's military campaign. If you accept that Milosevic never abandoned his dream of a Greater Serbia then what better double-cross than to vilify Karadzic publicly on the one hand while simultaneously encouraging Mladic to continue the struggle on the other. After four years of double-cross, double-think and flexible conscience – from everyone up to and including senior officials in Germany and the United States – everything was possible in the quagmire that had become Bosnia-Hercegovina at this time.

The Contact Group

While Mladic was attacking Gorazde international efforts to underpin the Washington Agreement continued in Vienna where on 8 May Kesimir Zubak and Haris Silajdzic signed what was to become known as the Vienna Agreement. In reality, of course, the new Federation still amounted to little more than a glorified ceasefire, but for the international politicians who were singing its praises it could be whatever they wanted it to be. It could be a new political departure, or a victory for Western diplomacy, or indeed a convenient way around the arms embargo.

Andre Lejoly, a Belgian EU monitor who carried out a detailed study on the implementation of both the Washington and Vienna Agreements, was absolutely correct when he observed that in real terms the Federation was nothing more than 'a reflection of the vested political interests in

Bosnia-Hercegovina'.[34] But the political circus moved on and the next performance took place on 25 May, in the town of Talloires, at the foot of the French Alps. Here for the first time Kesimir Zubak and Haris Silajdzic, representing the Federation, and Momcilo Krajisnik, representing the Serbs, were introduced to something called the Contact Group – a new body which the international community had determined would begin resolving the remainder of Bosnia's problems now that the Muslims and Croats had stopped killing one another.

The Contact Group was in many ways the logical successor to the work of Owen and Stoltenberg, but it differed from all that went before in that probably for the first time it represented a clear attempt to broaden the negotiating base by actively involving the United States and Russia in a formal structured manner. Having these two continually on the periphery had never made any sense, and Lord Owen's assessment was correct when he said: 'You had to find a way where the Americans were involved in the nitty gritty of negotiations, and in dirtying their hands in a settlement which they then had to go out and support.'[35] Within a short time Charles Redman and Vitali Churkin began to drive the process forward and a new plan for Bosnia began to emerge.

Bosnia would be preserved within its internationally recognised borders but be composed of two subordinate political entities: one Serb with 49 per cent of the territory, and the other a Muslim/Croat federation with 51 per cent. Once presented the parties would have two weeks to accept the plan or reject it. There would be no negotiation. Like Vance–Owen the year before the theory proved the easy part, but it took until the end of June before the maps outlining the detailed proposals were unveiled.

Not surprisingly, Dr Karadzic immediately began expressing reservations, and to be fair to him it would have been amazing had he reacted any differently because, with some minor alterations, the essence of the proposal was the same as that contained in Vance–Owen which had been so overwhelmingly rejected by the Bosnian Serb Assembly 12 months previously. The problem was still the same – the Serbs held 73 per cent of Bosnia and the plan would only permit them to keep 49 per cent.

The critical question was how Milosevic would react. On 6 July we got the answer. Furious with the Pale leadership since they had ignored his approval of Vance–Owen, and with Serbia's economy now crippled by UN sanctions, he had for many months been telling the Bosnian Serbs to compromise. Zoran Lilic, the president of what remained of Yugoslavia, had also issued a public warning on 7 June to the effect that ten million Yugoslavs would not be held hostage to any leader in Yugoslavia, no matter where he came from, and that included the Republic Srpska and the Republic Srpska Krajina. The message from Belgrade had been crystal clear for months, but nobody in Pale appeared to be listening.

Then on 6 July Milosevic accepted the plan and it looked as if the

Contact Group were on the verge of a major breakthrough with the British and French foreign ministers, Douglas Hurd and Alain Juppe, rushing to Pale to explain the facts of life to Karadzic. The message was very simple. If the Bosnian Serbs failed to come on board this time then Europe would reluctantly accede to US demands and lift the arms embargo against the Muslims. The problem, however, was that Karadzic simply did not believe them, and in a state of shock the ministers went home empty handed.

Accordingly the Pale leadership, together with their senior military and police personnel, were summoned to Belgrade for a lecture. Once again they were faced with the combined authority of Milosevic and Bulatovic and were left in no doubt as to what was required. Having spent long hours and many days closeted away in the Dobanovici military base trying to find a formula of words which the Contact Group would accept, Karadzic and his colleagues returned to Bosnia in defiant mood.

As had become the norm by now, an Assembly meeting was held behind closed doors in Pale, and aware that the Muslims and Croats had reluctantly accepted the Contact Group plan, and Belgrade's insistence that at the very minimum the plan should be endorsed as a basis for further negotiation, the Bosnian Serbs took their vote, wrote their decision on a sheet of paper, and then placed it in a pink envelope to be opened in Geneva at the next round of talks.

Full of drama, and with Karadzic acting out his feigned agony, it quickly became apparent that the contents of the envelope amounted to a rejection of the plan. Facing a repetition of the Vance–Owen closing scenario it was hardly surprisingly that Izetbegovic called a press conference the following evening and announced that he was withdrawing the Sarajevo government's previous unconditional approval and acceptance of the plan. As far as he was concerned, now that the Bosnian Serbs had refused to accept it he wished to add a few new conditions of his own.

With the media's attention focused firmly on Sarajevo and Geneva, President Tudjman's visit to Mostar almost went unnoticed. With a frozen smile on his face, and protected by a horde of EU officials, he went for the first time across the Neretva river and ventured onto the streets of east Mostar. With German foreign minister Klaus Kinkel outlining what the new EU Administration could do for both parts of the city, Tudjman and his defence minister Gojko Susak got a unique opportunity to witness for themselves just how effective their own artillery had been in flattening the old city, killing thousands of civilians, and forcing those who remained there to move underground and live in dank, musty cellars. That the pair of them were not taken away and lynched when the people discovered who they were must remain one of the great mysteries of the entire conflict.

Meanwhile, back on the diplomatic front a last-ditch attempt to salvage the peace talks was being made by Vitali Churkin and the Russian defence minister, Pavel Grachev, who first went to Belgrade[36] where reportedly they had an explosive meeting with Ratko Mladic. Then they moved on to Pale, but their only achievement there was to have Karadzic 'interpret' that the Russian army would come to his aid if Western forces attacked him. Grachev never intended to convey anything of this nature, nor for that matter was in any position whatever to deliver it. Nevertheless, a second Assembly meeting was called following this visit, but the response remained exactly the same. 'Acceptance of an unfinished and unknown peace plan would be the beginning of the end for the Serb people on its centuries-old territories and a prelude to national suicide', Momcilo Krajisnik said in a letter written jointly to Milosevic and Russian President Boris Yeltsin. 'Only a sovereign Serb state with compact territory and inviolable borders, with Russian, Serbian and Yugoslav guarantees, can provide for the survival of the Serbs west of the Drina.'[37]

International reaction was predictable and in Washington, Secretary of State Warren Christopher called for the world to act against the Bosnian Serbs, notwithstanding that a split within the Contact Group itself was now becoming more and more apparent. Testifying before Congress, Christopher reiterated the US position that lifting the arms embargo against Bosnian Muslims would remain an option if the Serbs persisted in rejecting the peace plan. A far better evaluation of the situation was made that day by John Steinbruner of the Brookings Institution in Washington DC, but unfortunately it received very little attention. His prediction of how events were about to unfold would prove ultimately to be far more astute than anything the secretary of state had to offer. His argument ran that Serb rejection of the peace plan would finally force the West to face up to the 'reality' of the war in Bosnia and its long-term consequences.[38]

It would take another year and a half for this 'decisive action' to be taken and many more would die in the interim, but at this point in time the foreign ministers of the Contact Group met in Geneva over the weekend of 30/31 July and adopted a number of measures following Pale's rejection of the plan. These included further tightening of the existing sanctions against Serbia and Montenegro, and a 'beefing up' of the safe areas within Bosnia. The option to remove the arms embargo was also discussed, but Russia, Britain and France remained steadfastly opposed to such a move.[39]

Unable to contain his anger and frustration any longer Milosevic launched into a public vilification of Karadzic and his colleagues and warned them that '[n]obody has the right to reject peace in the name of the Serbian people'. In a letter to the Pale Assembly he warned the members that if they rejected the plan they were on their way to committing a crime against their own people. 'You do not have the right to the lives of the citizens of Yugoslavia', he told them, but while one further Assembly meeting was held the result remained predictably the same.[40] On the night of 3 August, at yet another Assembly meeting, the plan was rejected for the third time and a referendum was called for 27/28 August to put the matter before the people for confirmation. There was little doubt in anyone's mind what the outcome of that particular exercise was going to be as both the army and those Serbs living in land designated for the Federation were guaranteed to reject it.[41]

That night Milosevic rang Bulatovic in Herceg-Novi. 'Unfortunately they rejected the Plan, we must put into force that decision to close the border. Do you agree?' Bulatovic said yes he did. 'They made their decision', said Milosevic, 'our decision takes effect tomorrow.'[42] The following day Yugoslavia's border with the Republic Srpska was closed along the Drina river. After several threats to abandon them Milosevic had finally cut the Bosnian Serbs adrift.[43]

NATO strikes back

Then, as if to prove this very point, on 5 August some Bosnian Serb troops stupidly snatched some heavy weapons, including a tank, from the UN Weapons Collection Point at Ilidiza in the Serb suburb of Sarajevo, and while making their escape fired on a UN helicopter which was following them. Totally fed up with the situation General Rose looked for an air-strike and got it. That afternoon NATO jets attacked and destroyed an armoured personnel carrier which was operating within the exclusion zone and almost immediately the Serbs offered to return the weapons they had taken that morning.[44] Momcilo Krajisnik then went into a damage limitation exercise and rang up Serge Viera de Mello, the head of UN Civil Affairs in Sarajevo, and apologised for what happened, but the question must surely be asked why the incident was allowed to happen in the first place.[45] If the Bosnian Serbs had tried to pick a worse moment to behave like a crowd of thugs they would have been hard pushed to find it. This in turn begged the question of 'what was going on'. Officially the answer was that uncontrolled elements had acted on their own – but that was a less than satisfactory explanation.[46]

Within the Bosnian Serb military very few people acted on their own. In fact nothing much happened at all if Mladic didn't know about it – but officially Mladic was nowhere to be found. In fact he had been missing from Bosnia since the Contact Group peace plan had been rejected and was staying in Belgrade at the time. This left the politicians in Pale apologising for the actions of their own military over which it was now crystal clear they had absolutely no control. A quick examination of NATO's increased involvement in the conflict at this time would also have confirmed to both Mladic and Milosevic that things were indeed beginning to change, and the fact that the air-strikes called against the 'uncontrolled elements' that Friday marked the fourth occasion the Alliance had attacked in Bosnia would not have been lost on either of them. Neither would the fact that all targets to date had been Bosnian Serb.

NATO's involvement began in July 1992 when it was decided to employ a naval force in the Adriatic to monitor compliance with UN sanctions imposed against Serbia and Montenegro, and this was soon expanded to permit enforcement. By October 1992 surveillance aircraft began monitoring the UN-declared 'no-fly zone' for military flights over Bosnia, and in April 1993 this was expanded to include combat patrolling with fighter aircraft in order to enforce what became known as 'Operation Deny Flight'. By June 1993 NATO was offering close air support (CAS) to UN troops on the ground if they came under attack, and in August air-strikes were threatened against Bosnian Serb positions if they continued to shell Sarajevo.

At a NATO summit meeting in Brussels in January 1994 all of these previous measures were confirmed and a decision was made to use air-strikes to reopen Tuzla airport for humanitarian aid flights if so required. Then in February 1994 the Serbs were given ten days to withdraw their heavy weapons from around Sarajevo and hand them over to the UN, or face air-strikes. The Serbs complied. However, US fighters found Serb light-attack aircraft violating the 'no-fly zone' and shot down four of them. This was NATO's first combat action since it was founded in 1949, and in April Alliance aircraft made their first attack on ground targets when two air-strikes were launched against Serb positions around Gorazde in order to protect UN personnel in the enclave.

Later in April NATO announced that air-strikes would be used to protect all six UN-designated 'safe areas' in Bosnia, and Mladic was given a deadline to withdraw his troops from around Gorazde. He complied. And then on 5 August NATO planes attacked the armoured personnel carrier which was violating the total exclusion zone around Sarajevo, a strike which was also in retaliation for the removal of the heavy weapons from the UN weapons collection point at Ilidiza that morning.

The following day reaction to the air-strike was unanimous – the Bosnian Serbs had got what they deserved. Moscow stopped just short of endorsing the air-strike, blaming the Serbs for bringing it upon themselves; Warren Christopher thought it was a good step forward; and in Brussels it was presented as an affirmation of EU/UN/NATO resolve to impose their will on the situation once and for all. In Belgrade all state media services launched a concerted attack on the Bosnian Serbs, and it quickly emerged that Milosevic intended to use this opportunity to topple Karadzic as well. State-controlled television interviewed a range of political figures who all in turn advocated acceptance of the Contact Group peace plan (CGPP) and denounced the Bosnian Serbs for rejecting it.

Serb against Serb

And then, almost as if it were pre-planned, the Bosnian Serb military managed to get themselves even more bad press when reports began to filter through from Peter Kessler, head of the UNHCR office in Tuzla, of their latest escapades in the north-eastern town of Bijeljina. Apparently another 64 Muslims – 47 women, eight elderly people and nine children – had been evicted from their homes in the middle of the night, and having been stripped to their underwear, relieved of their possessions and forced to sign away any legal rights to their property, they were then released into a minefield from where they were allowed to commence their lonely trek to the relative safety of Tuzla. The men apparently had been separated and taken away to begin a programme of forced labour.

The last thing Karadzic needed at that particular moment was for new 'evidence' to emerge indicating that people acting in the name of the Bosnian Serbs had not abandoned their obscene policies and that heinous atrocities were still being committed. Several agencies reporting on Yugoslavia (ECMM included) were convinced that these latest events were part of a concerted campaign and that Milosevic and Mladic were behind it.[47]

The one area in which Karadzic's remarks were not the product of paranoia was his assertion that a new Muslim/Croat offensive had begun.[48] The Armija had indeed launched a fairly large-scale offensive from the town of Vares and succeeded in retaking over 20 square kilometres from the Serbs.[49] Intent on securing the road which had previously connected Sarajevo with Tuzla, and having successfully captured the important town of Brugle, local HVO units also joined in with their Federation partners in order to exploit the situation even further.

With the eastern access routes into Republic Srpska now closed the economic blockade began to bite. Basic foodstuffs, which had never been in plentiful supply, now soared in price. Crowds began queuing outside shops in Pale and Banja Luka hoping to purchase small quantities of cooking oil, sugar, processed meat and canned food as deliveries from Serbia and Montenegro all but stopped. In fact, border guards in Serbia were so intent on complying with their new orders that UNHCR relief convoys bound for Pale were turned back at the Drina notwithstanding that Milosevic had agreed that humanitarian supplies such as food and medicine could cross.

In response to what was now approaching a crisis situation, Karadzic ordered all municipal authorities to mobilise a compulsory workforce in order to generate the best possible yield from the harvest, and as a morale booster patriotic pictures were transmitted on Bosnian Serb TV of both Karadzic and Mladic (who had now returned to the fray) working in the fields. All holidays, such as they existed, were cancelled, and a ten-hour working day was introduced.[50] Life was becoming very difficult in Pale, and Karadzic was doing his best to hold the whole thing together.

The problem was that once again Karadzic had no control over his soldiers, and the BSA artillery continued operating more or less independently. Whoever was giving the orders it was not Karadzic. The only thing he was doing was hosting strange discussions with Patriarch Pavel, head of the Serbian Orthodox Church, and several other bishops, who had come to Pale to condemn the blockade and to express their solidarity with the Bosnian Serbs in their quest for a 'just peace'.[51] Later that day Karadzic received another boost when the US State Department announced that it would be some time before any international action would be taken against the Bosnian Serbs because basically the Contact Group were unable to agree on a common course of action.[52]

Then President Clinton stated that if by 15 October the Bosnian Serbs had not accepted the CGPP he would within two weeks of that date formally introduce and support a resolution at the UN Security Council to lift the arms embargo. Translated this read that no substantive action would be taken by the international community for at least two months, and then only if the Security Council agreed.

From Karadzic's perspective this meant the Bosnian Serbs had bought themselves some time and in the normal run of events he could reasonably expect that by November another new plan with another set of maps would appear on the table – just in time for the whole process to start all over again. This was how the Serbs interpreted all of these messages and taken in that context perhaps it was hard to blame them for the manner in which they subsequently behaved. All the subliminal messages told them that the West could not find consensus, that there was no common policy, and worse still that there was no common resolve.

If this was the case, and the Serbs clearly perceived that it was, then there was no valid reason to part with one square inch of territory because it was blatantly obvious there was no one actually prepared to go and take it from them. And in the same vein it had become unmistakably clear to everyone operating in Bosnia that UNPROFOR was only involved in little more than a holding operation and could barely protect itself. And even if a decision to flex some muscle was taken by UNPROFOR commanders on the ground it was virtually guaranteed that the political masters in Zagreb or New York would overrule them. On the odd occasion when the internationals became very angry an air-strike might be called, but the Serbs could live with that. It was after all a relatively small price to pay for continually getting your own way.

Then, as if to confirm this hypothesis, Michael Williams, UNPROFOR's spokesman in Zagreb, began saying that if the US went ahead with their plan to lift the arms embargo it would be difficult to see how UNPROFOR could remain in theatre,[53] and instantly the debate shifted to the 'doomsday scenario' whereby the Muslims and Croats might refuse to let them leave. This launched the international community into another intellectual debate which would fully occupy them for the next six months, and Karadzic muddled on – another crisis had passed.

Meanwhile, back in Sarajevo, General Rose and his staff continued their efforts to make the best of a bad job and appeared to have convinced both Muslims and Serbs to agree to an 'anti-sniping agreement' which was to come into effect on Monday, 15 August. The Serbs and Muslims pledged to patrol high-risk areas with UN personnel and signed up to the proposal at Sarajevo airport on Sunday pledging to flush out and prosecute any snipers who disobeyed their new orders.

The threat of NATO air-strikes had effectively halted shelling of the city since February, but the well-hidden gunmen who maimed and killed and defied UN anti-sniping teams which were set up specifically to fire back, had continued their grisly work. However, General Rose was optimistic: 'We're looking at joint measures for the detection and final suppression of snipers who may be about in buildings', he said. 'It's a very important step towards returning the city back to normality.'

He was absolutely right, it was an important step, but it could only be implemented if both sides were willing to respect the agreement. There was no way in the world the UN could enforce it – and therein lay the source of the whole problem. With 20,000 troops in Bosnia, and a huge civil administration supporting them, all UNPROFOR could do was *ask* the warring parties to behave themselves. If that was all they could do, then surely it was time someone asked whether in fact they should actually continue to remain there at all.

Bihac

In the meantime the war in Bihac Pocket continued unabated, with Abdic hanging on to control of the northern one-third of the Pocket while Dudakovic juggled his limited resources in an attempt to keep the internal confrontation line quiet and simultaneously deal with never-ending harassment shelling[54] and regular low-intensity ground attacks by the Bosnian Serbs. Then on 16 February APWB forces launched several attacks against 5th Corps' positions and succeeded in moving the confrontation line up to 2 kilometres to the south.[55] Observers on the ground began wondering just how long this could go on, as Dudakovic appeared to be on the verge of a total collapse.[56]

The Danish UN battalion, which was stationed just north of the Pocket, also indicated that the 5th Corps would collapse within two weeks.[57] All other monitoring agencies on the ground agreed as the Bosnian Serbs launched one attack after another across the Una river and were supported by rockets, artillery and helicopters. On 11 March Bosnian Serb snipers also saw fit to take the life of a young French peacekeeper who was simply manning an observation post near the town of Otoka. He was shot twice in the back.[58]

Incredibly, and in spite of the war, business was still business, and the

5th Corps and APWB managed to organise crossing points in the front line on Mondays, Wednesdays and Fridays, where civilians could cross and re-cross in order to buy food and trade in cigarettes and other items. Equally, a formal meeting was also organised on 23 February to discuss a large-scale purchase of food from APWB by the 5th Corps itself.[59]

A Commission chaired by the chief of staff of UNPROFOR's BH Command[60] did arrive in the region on 24 February in an attempt to negotiate three separate ceasefire agreements: one between the 5th Corps and APWB; a second between the 5th Corps and the BSA; and a third between the 5th Corps and the Krajina Serbs – but it ignored three fundamental problems. First, the French battalion had no mandate whatever to go patrolling a DMZ. The UN was in Bosnia to support the distribution of humanitarian aid and nothing else. Second, the 5th Corps would never tolerate the free passage of Serbs along the railway between Banja Luka and Knin. Last, and perhaps most importantly, Izetbegovic had long since abandoned any intention of ever again negotiating with Fikret Abdic. These proposals were destined only for the garbage bin, and the virtual pointlessness of international involvement in the Pocket was well articulated by Colonel Legrier in an interview with World-wide Television News (WTN).[61]

Nevertheless, on 31 March, for no obvious reason and of their own volition, Dudakovic met with General Boric, his BSA counterpart in the 2nd Krajina Corps, and they produced a draft ceasefire agreement which apparently established an actual line on the ground across which both sides agreed not to step.[62] Dudakovic was running a new strategy now because before he could take on the Serbs again he had to deal with Abdic. If the internal situation was ever to be resolved he had no option but to temporarily close down the external confrontation line, and thereafter redeploy some of his forces to the north.[63]

It also emerged at this time that one of Abdic's chicken farms near Velika Kladusa had been turned into a prison camp where 5th Corps prisoners and others were now being held.[64] As news of this and other camps spread throughout the Pocket the ever-increasing tension got worse. The UN secretary-general's report of 16 March on the application of the 'safe area' principles to Bihac did nothing whatever to alleviate this, and in fact served only to confirm people's worst fears and suspicions.

UN policy now seemed to have lost all direction. It was unclear whether UNPROFOR had any mandate to deter attacks on the safe area from outside the borders of Bosnia-Hercegovina (i.e., the Krajina), and it was unclear whether any attempt could be made to intervene in the internal conflict if one or other of the parties decided to mount a conventional attack. And to make a bad situation worse the UN secretary-general declared that air power could only be used within Bosnia-Hercegovina – effectively declaring that UNPROFOR could not call for NATO close air support against the Krajina Serbs no matter how many shells they lobbed into Bihac town and elsewhere. None of this was helpful. And an anti-war demonstration even happened on the 20th when over 1,000 people assembled in Bihac town to protest against the UN's handling of events around Gorazde.

In Krajina a new government was appointed to preside over their non-existent economy, and the 17 new ministers elected Borislav Mikelic as prime minister.[65] This was good news for Abdic because Mikelic had been a friend of his in better times when he ran a meat processing plant in Petrinja. In fact it was generally believed that the connection was much closer and that each had shares in the other's business, which may well have been the case, but at the very minimum they could safely be considered kindred spirits. If nothing else could be guaranteed it was a safe bet that Mikelic's appointment would guarantee the continued safe passage of all kinds of goods from Croatia through Krajina to Velika Kladusa. It also virtually guaranteed continued Krajina military support for APWB.

Availing themselves of the comparative calm, EU monitors managed to visit the site of the heaviest recent fighting on the Grabez plateau and adjoining areas to the south and south-east of Bihac town. In a rare interview with Colonel Sarganovic, the brigade commander of the 5th Corps' 501st Brigade, they learned that the BSA appeared to have several brigades in reserve, but rather than commit any one unit they preferred instead to use elements from all of them simultaneously.[66] Over the next few days the 5th Corps was forced to give ground in several places as the Krajina Serbs once again supported the APWB attack with artillery.[67]

While all of this was taking place events elsewhere were about to have a profound impact on how the remainder of the APWB campaign would be conducted. Having signed the Washington/Vienna Agreements on 8 May and bowed to US pressure to behave himself in relation to Bosnia, President Tudjman was now faced with the problem of how to deal with Fikret Abdic. He had after all been an ardent supporter of APWB up to this point, and we have seen the level of influence which Abdic exerted on the president, but the time had come for another sacrificial offering to be made at the altar of expediency, and when questioned by UN Civil Affairs on 13 May, Mr Jusic, APWB's prime minister, confirmed that Croatia's support for Abdic was now finished.[68]

As if that were not bad enough the 5th Corps then regained all the ground they had lost during the previous week and elements within the APWB leadership, Jusic included, were well aware that things were about to change. The first indication that this was so occurred when UNHCR was prevented from carrying out its work in Velika Kladusa and the ordinary people, who were in dire need of assistance, were coerced into signing an oath of allegiance to Abdic before they got any humanitarian aid. Teachers who refused to sign were dismissed from their schools, which were only barely functioning anyway, and shopkeepers who refused to cooperate had their shops forcibly closed down by the APWB police. And all UN vehicles were now being stopped and searched to prevent any 'unlawful' distributions which had not been sanctioned by Jusic. The situation was slowly but surely sliding into chaos.[69]

By now the entire internal confrontation line was very hot and the mayor of Bihac instructed all international organisations operating in the Pocket to move to the Park Hotel or their security could not be guaranteed. This, of course, was just the usual excuse to lock up the foreigners while the natives got on with the business of slaughtering one another – but strangely no one ever called the bluff. When the 5th Corps liaison officer arrived later on he announced that the offensive had been ordered by Armija HQ in Sarajevo with a view to concluding the internal struggle by the end of the month.[70]

On the APWB side of the line some reinforcements were actually arriving from the north, but this was generally believed to be little more than a holding operation until the civilians living in the area could extricate themselves from the battle and the APWB wounded could be evacuated to hospital in the town of Vojnic in Krajina.[71] It then emerged that the Krajina Serb army was about to enter the conflict in support of Abdic if the 5th Corps advance transgressed a line which the SARSK generals had drawn on the map. The location of the line was known only to them, but the UN's Sector North Headquarters in Topusko were informed that they would get two hours' advance notice in order to move their troops into safety.[72]

The Serbs were indeed in a position to do this because of the huge quantities of tanks, guns, mortars and rockets which were now in position all around the Pocket.[73] This whole scenario played into Fikret Abdic's hands. If he was prepared to grease a few palms along the way then there was little difficulty encouraging some bored Krajina Serb officers to make use of these guns and tanks, which just happened to be sitting there and perfectly within range.

Whether or not Dudakovic was aware of the preparations in Krajina is not known, but either way his offensive continued to make steady progress. Radio Bihac also kept up a tirade of propaganda announcing that several villages had been liberated,[74] that 267 former APWB soldiers were now fighting for the 5th Corps, and that an APWB Brigade had that day refused to continue fighting.[75] In fact this latter information was correct and referred to the 4th APWB Brigade who had disobeyed their orders and withdrawn from Pecigrad thereby leaving the town in no man's land. The civilian population had also fled northwards and the town was now completely deserted.[76]

The casualties of the 5th Corps in the course of this particular attack were assessed by the French at 70 killed and 240 wounded, with APWB figures unknown. In a campaign such as this these figures were very high and probably had more to do with Dudakovic deciding to stall the operation than any other 'shortage of resources'.[77]

Over the next days all sides began responding to the new situation within the Pocket. The BSA reinforced their positions all along the Una valley, although the numbers varied considerably between 1,500 and 3,000.[78] UNMO's reports then began to indicate that the 5th Corps might now be in receipt of ammunition resupply, thanks to nightly helicopter flights into Coralici by the Croatian army. Initially there was no proof of this but within a few days the UNMOs could confirm that this was in fact the case, and identified the aircraft involved as two Croatian MI-8 helicopters in camouflage colour scheme with white panels upon which large red cross markings had been painted. There were also twin machine guns sticking out of the front.

These were observed unloading tank ammunition for the one tank which the 5th Corps had available to them, this providing the clearest sign yet of how the game had changed.[79] There were also reports of Iranian aircraft flying in with a variety of equipment, as well as bringing units of mujahedin fighters; but none of this could be substantiated just yet. And in Velika Kladusa Abdic started to come under pressure as it suddenly dawned on the people that from now on more and more of them were going to die if the APWB was to survive.

At 5.30 a.m. on 7 July the ECMM team in Bihac town were awoken from their slumber by 5th Corps military police and told that they were now confined to their accommodation until further notice. The entire civilian population were also put under curfew, although they did not have armed guards on sentry duty outside their homes. Zagreb radio reported that elements of the 5th Corps had mutinied, but from where the monitors and the other international agency personnel were sitting they were unable to confirm or deny it.[80]

Local radio broadcasts said that a terrorist group was operating in the area. Then, at 6 p.m., mortar fire was heard north-west of the town. The only information Team Bihac could send to Zagreb that night was that they still had no idea what was going on, but the efficient way in which the international personnel were confined suggested that whatever was happening had been well planned. This assessment turned out to be 100 per cent correct.[81]

Deception and reality

Before he could make any attempt to reverse his fortunes with the Serbs Dudakovic knew that he had first to deal with Abdic, preferably driving him out of the Pocket altogether. To this end he began planning an operation codenamed 'Tiger-Liberty', and called in his most trusted subordinate, Lieutenant Colonel Hamdo Abdic to carry it out.[82] The plan envisaged a number of 5th Corps officers convincing Fikret Abdic that they were leading a mutiny against Dudakovic and were asking for APWB support to ensure success. Then at an opportune moment they would either arrest Fikret Abdic, or kill him, and thereafter the APWB would fall apart.[83]

On 7 July Hamdo Abdic, Muhamed Babic and some other senior 5th Corps officers, made their way through the front line, eventually contacted Fikret Abdic, and convinced him of their defection, whereupon he immediately agreed to support them. Returning south the 'mutineers' then set up their headquarters near the village of Izacic, close to the border with Krajina, and received food, fuel, cigarettes, 1,200 Kalashnikov semi-automatic rifles, over 200,000 rounds of ammunition, grenade launchers and some anti-tank missiles from Abdic.[84] Then, on 8 July, several explosions were heard in Bihac town, the members of the District Assembly were arrested, road blocks were set up all over the place, and Radio Bihac broadcast a series of bulletins which indicated that a coup was indeed in progress and that Dudakovic was reported to have handed himself over to the Serbs.

This was picked up in Velika Kladusa, and Radio Velkatron, the APWB's own station; this dis-information was then spread even further afield. By nightfall the coup was declared a complete success and a victory celebration was organised in Izacic for all concerned. This was the point when Fikret Abdic was to be arrested – but for some unexplained reason he failed to turn up.

What happened next remains unclear, but when it began to emerge that the whole thing was in fact a hoax, Colonel Branko, the Krajina Serb liaison officer, apparently tried to leave the area and was shot dead in the process. Razim Bazic, Fikret Abdic's senior security officer, and his driver were also killed, while the APWB defence minister who was representing Abdic was arrested, although his driver, Addis Shabic, mysteriously vanished.

Other than these incidents the whole operation had been bloodless and later that night, when Dudakovic walked into the French UN headquarters in Bihac town dressed as a mutineer, with the tell-tale white ribbon in his epaulette, the reality of the situation began to unfold.[85] It was not until the 10th that the full story began to emerge. While some of the minor details remain disputable, the RC Zagreb Daily Report, as written up that night by Irish EU monitor Jim Bourke, gave an excellent account of what constituted the truth on the day in question.[86]

ECMM's deputy head of mission, Brigadier General Bruno Cailloux, was now dispatched into the Pocket and on the 19th met Dudakovic for lunch. Claiming to be the originator and author of the whole operation he said he was completely satisfied with the outcome.[87] Meeting Abdic in his castle fortress in Velika Kladusa a few hours later the mood was less optimistic. Operation 'Tiger-Liberty' had been demoralising and embarrassing for Abdic, but nevertheless Cailloux could not conclude that APWB was on the verge of collapse.[88] But this perception was incorrect. The APWB was about to crumble.

On Thursday, 28 July the 5th Corps launched a new offensive all along the internal confrontation line and began to make progress against what had now become a badly organised, ill-disciplined and very confused APWB force. The only group putting up any serious resistance were the 500 members of the 4th Brigade holed up in the deserted town of Pecigrad, but with the 5th Corps virtually surrounding them and bombardment of the town taking place at the rate of one projectile per minute this courageous last stand was not expected to continue much longer. However, Dudakovic was anxious to press on and rather than waste any more time on Pecigrad he decided to by-pass it and head for Velika Kladusa with all speed. When he carried out this manoeuvre he discovered that the front line had in fact moved further north and was now less than seven miles from Abdic's headquarters.

Strange solutions

Across the border in Krajina neither the Banja or Kordun Corps were sure what was going to happen next and as a contingency measure they raided the UN weapons storage sites in Sector North where they had placed their heavy equipment as part of the 29 March ceasefire agreement with Croatia. UNMOs on the ground also reported increased Serb artillery support for Abdic, but the difficulty here was that within a very short time they were going to end up shelling the outskirts of Velika Kladusa itself.[89] The following day, as Abdic sent his civil police to the front line in a last ditch attempt to keep the 5th Corps at bay, news filtered through that Pecigrad had fallen.

With the road to the north now open most of Dudakovic's military problems were solved. His dilemma was how to complete the job and push Abdic out of the Pocket completely without at the same time killing thousands of innocent civilians who had fled to the north before the 5th Corps' advance and were now crammed into Velika Kladusa and its immediate environs.

Before Dudakovic had made up his mind on how to handle this situation Abdic announced publicly on 5 August that he was ready to enter negotiations with Sarajevo. This encouraged General Rose sufficiently for him to alter his schedule and fly to Velika Kladusa to talk to Abdic. What Rose did not know was that Dudakovic was under strict instructions from Izetbegovic to finish Abdic off once and for all and to permanently resolve the military situation in the Pocket lest it redevelop again in the future and thereby distract the 5th Corps from carrying out their primary mission, which was to hold the external line against the Bosnian Serbs. Nevertheless, neither Abdic nor Dudakovic would ever be forgiven if they murdered thousands of innocent civilians. In an attempt to avert this an amnesty was offered by Sarajevo on the morning of 9 August.

While the terms were not unreasonable Abdic refused to capitulate and pledged to remain with his people, offering to open discussions with Izetbegovic through the offices of General Rose – but the Bosnian president was having none of it.[90] Abdic then asked Krezimir Zubak to become involved, but nothing materialised there either[91] and his situation became more untenable by the hour. His only consolation was that the 6th APWB Brigade had successfully disengaged from the battle west of Pecigrad. Having crossed into Krajina, where they knew the 5th Corps would not pursue them, they arrived in Velika Kladusa more or less intact.[92] With them, however, came an additional 7,000 civilians, and however happy Abdic might have been to see them an already dreadful humanitarian situation became even worse. In response to this influx, and the continuous unrelenting shelling, some 50,000 displaced people grabbed what little they could carry and moved across the border into Krajina to commence life as refugees.

And in the midst of this chaos and disorder, ECMM's head of mission, Ambassador Paul Joachim von Stulpnagel, went to Velika Kladusa on the morning of 12 August and met with Abdic who gave the impression that he was completely oblivious to the turmoil going on around him.[93]

When the meeting concluded Abdic then went through the bizarre performance of holding a press conference by phone with representatives from the world's press who had assembled in the Intercontinental Hotel in Zagreb. With his assembly speaker, Bozidar Sicel, and the prime minister of APWB, Zlatko Jusic physically present in Zagreb, Abdic announced, to the amazement of all present, that an interim solution to the problems in Bihac had been found and that he was personally prepared to fund a 'Mostar-type settlement' whereby the entire Pocket would be demilitarised and become a protectorate of the European Union with a French national appointed as the European administrator.[94]

This development came as a complete surprise to everyone present, and several others besides. It also begged the question of where this notion actually came from in the first place – or more importantly who it was that suggested it to him. In reality it could only have come from one source – ECMM's head of mission, von Stulpnagle – and this in turn raises the issue of who at European level had authorised the proposal. Had anyone consulted with the Contact Group? Had anyone discussed this with either Lord Owen or General Rose? The answer to these questions appears to be 'no', which only permits one to conclude that von Stulpnagle had gone on a solo run.

Additionally, whatever hope of success such a 'solution' might have had some months previously when both sides could have bargained from comparatively equal positions, it now stood absolutely no chance of acceptance given that the 5th Corps, and by inference the Sarajevo government, were well and truly ready for a final battle. When pressed by the media to state just how much territory his forces still retained Abdic declined to answer, and refused also to comment on the latest UNPROFOR assessment which indicated that at best he only controlled about 50 square kilometres in the immediate vicinity of Velika Kladusa. As the press conference rambled on he again said that he was willing to negotiate with Sarajevo and that he always recognised the integrity of Bosnia-Hercegovina's internationally recognised borders, but in the same breath launched into yet another verbal assault on Izetbegovic.

To those present in Zagreb it was clear that Abdic had lost all touch with reality. His troops were on the verge of annihilation and yet he still persisted with condemnation of Izetbegovic. It was also clear that if Abdic had got his Mostar ideas from von Stulpnagle then ECMM's head of mission hadn't much grasp of reality either. An EU administration of Bihac was never discussed at European Council level, or at the Contact Group, or by Vance, Owen or Stoltenberg. Throwing such a concept to Abdic as a lifebelt was disingenuous to say the least of it.[95]

A meeting between delegations from APWB and the 5th Corps did take place on the 15th, but this stalled because the APWB side were insisting on a formal ceasefire prior to political negotiations, and the Bihac authorities, including Dudakovic, wanted it the other way around. When they got together again on the 17th some progress was made until the APWB representatives began looking for a 'constitutional expert' to draw up the political settlement. Unable to proceed any further another meeting was scheduled for the 20th; it never took place.

Fighting soon erupted, and a Gazelle helicopter was seen flying some of Abdic's personal staff out of Velika Kladusa. By 5.30p.m. over 500 townspeople had decided it was time that they too departed and were now dispersed along the main road out of town leading northwards into Krajina. Another 700 miserable and confused people had gathered 7 miles further south near the village of Mala Kladusa, and as they swarmed about in the middle of the road they suddenly realised that the leading elements of the 5th Corps were almost upon them. Very quickly they organised themselves and, pointing their laden-down cars, tractors, horses, carts, donkeys, wheel-barrows and bicycles in the general direction of Krajina, they grabbed what few remaining possessions they could carry and began an odyssey into 'living hell'.

By now the APWB authorities had also started to panic and the situation spiralled out of control when the word went out that all civilians were now advised to leave Velika Kladusa by midnight. The military would theoretically remain for a further 24 hours to make sure that everyone got away.[96] Across the border in Krajina the civil and military authorities were faced with an impending humanitarian disaster as thousands of refugees began pouring into a jurisdiction which could barely sustain itself. Initially the plan was to facilitate the safe passage of all these people through Krajina and then have them disperse into Croatia proper, but it quickly emerged that this was not going to happen.

Turanj and Batnoga

When the first 59 refugees arrived at the Croatian police checkpoint at Turanj, near Karlovac, they were allowed to pass through as their documents were considered to be in order. However, when the scale of the migration became clear the Croatian government decided that it could not take responsibility for the numbers involved and the crossing point was closed. Later on when another 700 arrived they were allowed through the Serb checkpoint and into the UN-controlled 2-kilometre Separation Zone between the two forces, but when they attempted to pass into Croatia they were turned back by Croatian police. As if that were not bad enough, when they then attempted to return to Krajina the Serb police refused to let them back because another 2,000 had arrived at the checkpoint in the meantime and the place had become completely blocked.

In an attempt to bring some order to the scene an ECMM team from Karlovac sought out the local Croatian chief of police, who was now personally manning the checkpoint, and pleaded with him to give some assurance to the unfortunate people who were now trapped in no man's land. All that this futile exercise elicited was a display of arrogance by the Croat, who announced that as far as the Croatian government was concerned an agreement had been signed with UNPROFOR ten days previously in which the UN had assumed responsibility for refugees in Krajina, and as these people were still technically in Krajina the UN could look after them. As darkness fell, and unable to proceed into Croatia or return from whence they came, the only thing these victims of the conflict could do was 'bed-down' where they were and hope that things would get better in the morning. But in fact the situation got worse.[97]

At 5.30 a.m. on 21 August the final 5th Corps attack on Velika Kladusa began and quite quickly it evolved into a series of street battles which continued throughout the day. By early evening resistance had evaporated and at 8.30 p.m. Dudakovic entered Abdic's castle fortress while his troops poured onto the deserted streets, drinking and celebrating a famous victory. They also managed to plunder and loot a number of premises before a detachment of military police arrived to restore some order. Whether this was a deliberate tactic by Dudakovic remains unclear, but either way to the victors went what few spoils of war were worth taking from Velika Kladusa that autumn evening.

In the meantime, the unfortunate people who had fled the Pocket were now assembling a variety of makeshift refugee camps across Krajina. In addition to the 2,500 still trapped at Turanj more were gathered near Topusko, another group had arrived at Katinovac, but by far the largest concentration was now to be found in a miserable, godforsaken place, called Batnoga where upwards of 20,000 people were crammed into a filthy disused chicken farm. Of these, 80 per cent were women and children. As the enormity of the situation began to dawn on the international agencies UNHCR negotiated successfully with the Krajina Serbs to allow them to supply the camp with humanitarian aid. The first consignments consisted of basic requirements such as bread and water, and tentage to accommodate those who could not fit into the farm's 24 sheds.[98]

At a crisis meeting in Zagreb the following day Mate Granic, Croatia's foreign minister, and Ivan Jarnjak, the interior minister, having first discussed the matter with Bosnian prime minister Haris Silajdzic, then went to Yasushi Akashi and effectively washed their hands of the whole problem. Conveniently forgetting that in the not too distant past their president, Franjo Tudjman, had been one of Fikret Abdic's greatest supporters and had gone to great lengths to legitimise him as an international figure, the citizens of APWB were now to become the latest sacrifice at the altar of political expediency.

The rules had changed. The Americans were calling the shots now and Izetbegovic was back in favour. The two ministers spelt it out to Akashi that these refugees were in what was supposed to be a UN-protected area, so the UN could go and look after them, or preferably encourage them to go back to where they came from in the first place.[99] In typical fashion Krajina was 'occupied territory' when the Croatian government was talking politics, but someone else's responsibility altogether when there was a real problem to be dealt with. As Akashi left the meeting he was under no illusions whatever as to who would have to take up this problem and run with it. Once again it would be UNPROFOR, UNHCR, ICRC, ECTF and ECMM, with European Union taxpayers' money footing the bill for whatever relief programme was eventually put in place.

As each day passed more and more people continued to stream into the refugee camps, with Fazilla Abdic, Fikret Abdic's wife, taking on the role of a refugee leader at Turanj while her husband and his armed praetorian guard apparently enjoyed unrestricted freedom as they moved around Krajina to one meeting after another.[100] Dudakovic for his part made an appeal to the refugees to return to their homes, which he claimed were intact and untouched – but nobody was prepared to believe him.[101] ECMM's Roger Bryant noted that '[t]he town [Velika Kladusa] this morning [22 August] looked as if a disappointed English football crowd had given the centre some serious attention',[102] and Sefija Delanovic reported that 'the 5th Corps entered our village, burned our house, and took our sheep and horses away'.[103]

During the following days Dudakovic began sending most of his troops and equipment back to the south, while the streets of Velika Kladusa remained deserted. UNPROFOR figures indicated that there were at least 23,000 refugees scattered throughout Krajina and probably many more holed up in remote places that had not as yet been discovered.[104]

An ECMM team from Glina caught up with Abdic as he addressed the refugees who had gathered at Stara Selo near Topusko. His basic message was that they should continue to hold out for independence as compromise with the 5th Corps was not an option.[105] Later that evening 300 refugees on the Krajina side of the Polish UN checkpoint in the middle of Turanj surged forward and approached the Croatian police demanding to be let in. Reinforcements were summoned from Karlovac, the Croats stuck to their guns, sand bags and armoured vehicles, and the refugees remained where they were. By now a variety of celebrities, including the American ambassador Peter Galbraith, were touring the area and actively encouraging the refugees to return to Velika Kladusa where a new municipal authority led by Sefik Stulanovic was in place. Deriving no confidence from this development, largely because Stulanovic had spent the previous eight months in jail for opposing APWB rule, and with Abdic continuing his 'no surrender' routine, the numbers at Turanj continued to swell.

Misery for the refugees

By the evening of 25 August the numbers at Turanj had risen to over 12,000,[106] thanks primarily to the operation of a six-bus shuttle service which began ferrying people from Topusko. The majority of these unfortunate people were now crammed into a one-kilometre stretch between the Polish soldiers in the middle of the crossing and the Croatians on the Karlovac side. With APCs and lightly armed police at the checkpoint, more heavily armed police immediately behind them, and special police a little further to the rear, the Croats were ready to act in the unlikely event that these hungry, filthy, frightened and confused people would attempt to overthrow the Croatian state!

Even more police were on call back in Karlovac police station, and thousands of soldiers were not very far away either.[107] Just what exactly they thought the threat was remains anybody's guess![108] However, a detailed report compiled at the time by 'Feed the Children' put everything into perspective.[109]

Meanwhile, in Batnoga the situation had already taken on an air of permanence with the emergence of a refugee leader in the person of Sead Kajtazovic (one of Abdic's right-hand men) and the commencement of formal meetings between the refugees and the plethora of UN officials who had by now descended upon the place. At a meeting on the 26th Kajtazovic announced that there were now between 32,000 and 35,000 people in the camp and remained adamant that they could not return to their homes because UNPROFOR would not be able to protect them, especially at night. He then asked the EC monitors present to go back to Velika Kladusa and find out what was going on, but even as they headed off he was already looking for more transportation to accompany the 356 tractors, 112 horses and carts, and 2,500 people who were setting off across Krajina to Turanj.[110] At this point Ambassador von Stulpnagle made another foray into the countryside and again met with Abdic in Topusko. This time, however, there was no international press conference and no new international schemes were announced.

At Turanj and Batnoga EU monitors had managed to talk freely with some of the refugees, many of whom were quite willing to return to their homes and take their chances with the 5th Corps, but they maintained they really had no choice. They had to obey Abdic, and his appointed leaders in both camps.[111] The sight of Abdic walking around Batnoga in the company of US ambassador Peter Galbraith and his entourage certainly gave the impression that the Autonomous Province of Western Bosnia, 'in exile', had now attracted American support – although nothing could have been further from the truth.[112]

Galbraith then moved on to Velika Kladusa for a meeting with Dudakovic, representatives from UNPROFOR, and all the other agencies now operating there. After one and a half hours of discussion it emerged that the new authorities had agreed to establish refugee resettlement centres throughout the Pocket, and UNPROFOR, even though it had no mandate whatever for this kind of activity, and could barely protect itself, would protect the returning refugees for a period of six months. Thereafter the people could reintegrate into the community or leave and live in Krajina if they wished. None of the APWB military would be forced to serve in the 5th Corps, but if they wanted to join voluntarily then that would be acceptable.

UNCIVPOL, ECMM and the other international organisations would oversee the whole thing.[113] Sadly this solution, such as it was, was not attractive enough to encourage anyone to break ranks with Abdic.[114] The refugees stayed where they were, and the humanitarian situation got progressively worse, notwithstanding the arrival of a UNICEF mobile health clinic and the provision of two heavy duty generators from the Polish UN battalion. Grasping at every straw that was thrown to them the EU monitors attending the daily meeting in Batnoga on the 29th thought they detected a change in attitude by Kajtazovic when he indicated that he might be prepared to tell the people to go home if UNPROFOR could really guarantee their safety.

Wasting no time the monitors immediately set out for Velika Kladusa and after some discussion with the mayor he agreed to provide them with a letter for the refugees which would outline in detail the type and level of protection they could expect from the new administration.[115] Ironically, when the team attempted to get back into the Pocket the following day to collect the letter the Serb police refused to let them through on the grounds that their papers were not in order. Fortunately Team Bihac were in the area, managed to pick up the letter, and took it to Batnoga where both Kajtazovic and Abdic were having a meeting at the time. Having read the document Kajtazovic then announced to the disappointed and frustrated monitors that as far as he was concerned it was not legal as it had been issued by an 'illegal authority'.

From the perspective of the Krajina Serbs all of this was just a political side-show, but if nothing else it ensured that for as long as the crisis continued they could look forward to taking their percentage of all humanitarian aid that crossed their borders en route to the refugees. The Croats, however, had a different approach which was spelled out by the mayor of Karlovac to ECMM's chief humanitarian officer, Jan Uwe Thoms, in the course of a volatile meeting on the 30th. Unbelievably the Croats were more concerned about the 'damage' the refugees were allegedly doing to deserted Croat houses in the Separation Zone. They wanted to know who was going to pay for this. The mayor, by liberally interpreting the ceasefire agreement of 29 March, had determined that the UN should foot the bill for the alleged damage. He continued in this vein by expressing his concerns that by using water from the nearby Korona river the refugees were polluting Karlovac's water supply, which was going to pose problems for his people in the near future.

It was also clear now that the longer the situation remained unresolved the greater the risk that both refugee camps would become permanent fixtures.[116] Colonel Dequen, the new commanding officer of the French UN troops in the Pocket, also torpedoed the concept of 'resettlement centres' on the basis that he was neither mandated nor in a position to guarantee anyone's protection. As far as he was concerned the matter of resettlement was the responsibility of the Sarajevo government – and he was absolutely right. Unfortunately this development also played into Abdic's hands and he now had a statement from a senior UN officer to support what he himself had been preaching for two weeks.

In the camps themselves the law of the jungle began to set in, with weapons being fired to settle disputes at Turanj, and the camp leadership in Batnoga becoming completely confrontational with the international agencies continually berating them for supposedly doing nothing. It also emerged that the Serb militia positioned around Batnoga were also arresting people they thought were trying to escape and herding them off to prison in Vojnic and elsewhere. For those who managed to evade capture there was then the matter of mines to contend with, and the camp was alive with stories of the several unsuccessful escape attempts.[117]

Then, just when people had begun to forget the military side of life, two Orkan rockets ploughed into Velika Kladusa at 10.50 a.m. on 9 September. UNMOs confirmed that five rockets had been fired from east of Otoka in Bosnian Serb-held territory. This tied in with other attacks on Buzim and Cazin over the previous few days. The only matter at issue was which type of Serb, Krajina or Bosnian had actually fired them, and at the end of the day it hardly mattered. The message for Dudakovic was very simple – he may have won a battle but the war was far from over, and as he handed in another official protest to the ECMM team in Bihac town he was acutely aware that there was more work to be done before the Pocket could be considered secure.[118]

Throughout September the refugees became pawns in a dirty political game which revolved around keeping them where they were, for as long as possible, in ever-deteriorating circumstances. Then, when the tragedy became overwhelming, Abdic would reappear to demand international intervention, which in turn might pressurise Izetbegovic to compromise sufficiently and thereby allow the re-emergence of APWB in one guise or another. This was his strategy, but the reality of life was grim for those who followed him. In Batnoga, babies were born and adults and older children died from the usual variety of causes,[119] UNPROFOR engineers had begun to build showers and toilet facilities, and a US medical team was doing its best to provide basic services for those worst affected.[120] However, from time to time, when the leaders felt the refugees might be getting too happy with their lot, a row would conveniently break out over whether or not UNPROFOR had the requisite permission to deliver food aid to the camp in the first place!

One day the Serb militia guarding the perimeter would begin this argument,[121] while on the next the refugee leadership themselves would find a reason to turn the food away – and from time to time they even went to the bother of organising hunger strikes to protest their belief that the international community was not doing enough to help them.[122] The refugees had become an international problem,[123] and Abdic and his close associates continued to exploit the situation to further their own objectives.[124]

Some of the best reports written on this subject were compiled by Lieutenant Colonel Michael Cleary, from Athlone in Co. Westmeath, who was at that time ECTF's infrastructure and food co-ordinator in the Former Yugoslavia.[125] He visited Batnoga camp several times, and his report of 19 October in particular confirmed just how bad the overall situation had become.[126]

Karadzic makes an offer

While all of this was taking place in Krajina the political process in Bosnia was going nowhere either, especially since the Bosnian Serbs had rejected the Contact Group plan at referendum. The perception of Bosnian Serb intransigence, indifference, even apathy, was proliferated in the media on a daily basis. The message was simple. The Serbs had no interest in finding a solution, and no evidence could be found to suggest otherwise – until now.

In reality, however, Jovan Zametica, Karadzic's personal assistant, rang UN HQ in Sarajevo early in October and asked to speak to Captain Mike Stanley (Milos Stankovic).[127] He then insisted that Stanley travel to Pale immediately because the Serbs had something vital to say. When Stanley arrived Zametica immediately took him into Karadzic's office and stated that he had been authorised by Karadzic to make a proposal designed to end the war quickly. Zametica instructed that the proposals he was about to make were to find their way without delay to Rose initially and then onward to the Contact Group. The proposal was simple. In return for Croatia giving up 20 kilometres of coastline south of Dubrovnik, the Krajina Serbs would cede all of Sector West, most of Sector North and some of Sector South. In Bosnia the Muslims would give up Srebrenica, Zepa and Gorazde in return for a wide corridor linking Sarajevo with central Bosnia, and Bihac would revert to the Bosnian Serbs. In return for all of this the Bosnian Serbs would reduce their overall land share in Bosnia to 31 per cent.

Stanley believed this to be a serious proposal and immediately passed it to Rose who sent it through the Foreign and Commonwealth Office to Pauline Neville-Jones at the Contact Group. The problem was the Contact Group were not interested because as far as they were concerned their plan was the only one they were prepared to deal with, and as Karadzic was bound by the referendum result there was now no room for manoeuvre.

The international community failed in its obligations to pursue *all* avenues that might have led to a resolution of the problem when they rejected this proposal. Equally, the senior politicians and negotiators failed to do a proper estimate of the situation in relation to Karadzic and the predicament in which he now found himself. Had any of them bothered to read the detailed assessments which ECMM and UNPROFOR were churning out on a daily basis they would have easily identified just how vulnerable Karadzic's position had actually become, and why he had made this proposal in the first place. Stanley believes that that this was a lost opportunity. This author absolutely agrees with him.[128]

Dudakovic attacks southwards

On 26 and 27 October Dudakovic launched the 5th Corps on a two-pronged attack deep into Bosnian Serb positions to the south and south-east of the Pocket, which quickly took them across the Una river and into the outskirts of Bosanska Krupa from where they had been evicted over two years previously. In the days which followed they advanced south as far as Kulen Vakuf, sweeping all Serb opposition before them. However, by the 29th Dudakovic's initiative had ground to a halt, but thanks to CNN and Sky News this campaign was portrayed internationally as a legitimate military operation in pursuit of 'rebel Serb forces'. Nobody bothered to remark that it was also 'an attack out of a UN safe area'. Why? Because as far as the international media holed up in Sarajevo were concerned this was just a case of government (read 'legitimate') troops pursuing rebel (read 'illegitimate, bad, terrorist') Serbs.

But Dudakovic had moved too far too fast and his limited resources were now stretched over a distance of 80 kilometres. On 4 November the Bosnian Serb counter-attack began and by the 6th Kulen Vakuf had been retaken. During the next week the Bosnian Serbs regained over 90 per cent of the territory lost and pursued the 5th Corps back to a line just south of the Pocket. Meanwhile, in the north, 5,000 Abdic soldiers supported by Krajina Serbs launched an attack on Velika Kladusa on the 16th.[129] By 17 November the 5th Corps was once again committed on all three fronts and indications were that their position was becoming untenable.

On the 18th two Orao aircraft took off from Udbina airbase in Krajina and dropped napalm and cluster bombs on Bihac town.[130] The following day a further air attack from the same base resulted in one of the aircraft smashing into an apartment block in Cazin, causing wholesale death, injury and destruction. Significantly enough the pilot, who was born in Serbia, was flying a Bosnian Serb aircraft, from an airfield in the Republic of Srpska Krajina! This explained just how convoluted the whole conflict had become – and there were plenty of equally confusing variations on both the other sides.[131]

On 19 November the UN Security Council passed Resolution No. 958 which allowed for the possibility of air-strikes by NATO if UNPROFOR so requested. The vote was unanimous: 15–0. NATO quickly endorsed the Resolution and Madeleine Albright, US ambassador to the UN, immediately climbed on board the anti-Serb bandwagon claiming that her government was satisfied that a military response to the situation was justified, given that the 'safe area of Bihac' was now at risk. The only problem with this approach was that neither Albright, Akashi or anyone else in the UN had the remotest idea where exactly the 'safe area of Bihac' actually was.[132] Nevertheless, within the international community it was now generally accepted that NATO air-strikes were warranted, and at 1p.m. on 21 November the long-awaited air attack on the Udbina air base took place.[133] Involving 39 aircraft, this was the biggest air operation of its kind ever mounted by NATO, and was clearly designed to dissuade the Serbs from further attacks on the Pocket. As events unfolded, however, the resolve of the Serbs would prove far greater than that of the peacekeepers.[134]

By last light on the 29th it was universally accepted that if Milovanovic really wanted to take Bihac town there was no way the 5th Corps could stop him. He chose not to, and instead continued with harassment shelling in order to afford Abdic and the Krajina Serbs an opportunity to make a final assault in the north. By 9 December, however, the entire battlefield had become a complete stalemate. Having just escaped from Velika Kladusa, EU monitor Henrik Markus explained that 'soldiers from each side were crawling a few meters along hedgerows, firing a few shots, and then crawling back again, accompanied by a constant level of shelling'.[135]

UNPROFOR in chaos

In a special report to Kofi Annan on 15 November Akashi referred everything back to a Draft Report on Safe Areas which he had submitted to New York on 29 April – but upon which no decision had yet been taken.[136] In that document UNPROFOR had recommended the creation of a very limited safe area around Bihac town, purely on the basis that this was all they could reasonably be expected to defend with the resources they had available. Seven months later the manpower levels were approximately the same, although the new Bangladeshi battalion had experienced the added difficulties of deploying into the Pocket without half their kit and only one rifle between every four of them.[137]

In this context, then, it was not at all surprising to find that Akashi had correctly and succinctly assessed that '[t]he fundamental issue in dealing credibly with the Bihac situation is that UNPROFOR's responsibilities must to the extent possible be brought into line with our capabilities'.[138] Akashi did not have the capability to deal credibly with any situation which arose, in Bihac or elsewhere, and the concept of a military exclusion zone around Bihac town was never a realistic option. It wasn't his fault that UNPROFOR was left to invent limited responses on an *ad hoc* basis, and when the Security Council did choose to act on 19 November and pass UNSC Resolution 958 authorising close air support and air-strikes in Krajina, Akashi was still left to make a decision knowing that no matter what he did it still wouldn't be enough. Akashi couldn't win, but to his great credit he continued to try.

To safeguard the status of Bihac and the other five 'safe areas' in Bosnia an additional 34,000 UN troops would have been needed to do the job properly, but with the organisation barely able to balance its budget, and a complete lack of direction from the Department of Peacekeeping Operations (DPKO), it was clear there was no chance of this happening. The attack on Udbina was a punitive and disproportionate response which was not linked in any serious way to any proposals for a peaceful settlement.

Worse still, the Serbs had full knowledge the attack was coming and had diverted most of their aircraft to other places as a precaution.[139] The attack was *ad hoc*. Ultimately it served no purpose. All it achieved was to make it even more difficult for Akashi to deal with the Serbs, as he was left to jump from one crisis to another.

General Mladic responded immediately by letter to the UN force commander, General De Lapresle, in which he bluntly said: 'It is sad that you are partial ... You are, General, responsible for the escalation of the war here and your offer that you and General Rose continue to mediate in establishing a ceasefire is senseless.' Accusing UNPROFOR of being no better than 'those who from 1941 to 1945 have spread death in these areas', Mladic refused to guarantee the safety of any UN soldier in Bosnia. He concluded defiantly: 'be assured that you cannot bring peace using NATO bombers'.[140] Karadzic's letter to Akashi was even worse, threatening to treat the UN as the enemy.[141]

Not surprisingly Akashi's response was anything but resolute – but how could it have been otherwise?[142] His gesture of including a map delineating the 'safe area' as he understood it was a *de facto* acceptance that Karadzic did not in fact understand where the safe area was actually supposed to be. Equally, asking him to exercise 'maximum restraint' was a far cry from laying down the law, but of course he had no means to enforce that law anyway – and everybody knew it.

The overall situation took a turn for the worse on 23 November when at 9 a.m. two British Harriers on a reconnaissance patrol over Bihac were locked onto by an SA-2 'Fan Song' radar system, and in compliance with their orders the pilots, acting in self-defence, engaged the system with Harm missiles and destroyed it. In response NATO launched additional sorties which attacked two other SAM missile sites near Otoka and Dvor with similar effect.[143]

News of this was not well received in Pale, and all Serb checkpoints were immediately closed to both UN and civilian traffic. Flights in and out of Sarajevo were suspended following Serb threats to shoot down incoming aircraft. Numerous sniping incidents took place, including an attack on a tram just outside the Holiday Inn, while west of Sarajevo, near Ilijas, 55 Canadian UN troops were taken hostage by the Bosnian Serbs and, having been disarmed of everything except their side arms, they were then taken away to six different locations.

Further north in Brcko the UNMO team was evicted from the area and, having been sent off on the road to the Serbian border, they were then robbed of their armoured Landrover and personal belongings.[133]

In Banja Luka the UNMOs in the town were actually taken under escort to the airports at Zauani and Mahovljani and forced to sit on the runways as a deterrent to further attacks.[145] In Bihac the level of Bosnian Serb shelling increased dramatically, leading the UN to report that 'the Krajina and Bosnian Serb forces have for all intents and purposes effectively cut off Bihac town'.[146]

The next day the situation deteriorated even further when 350 UN troops – French, British, Ukrainian and Russian – were surrounded in several places by Bosnian Serb forces as they manned weapons collection/storage sites and were denied permission to leave. In response, General Rose went public with a plan to arrange a ceasefire in order that Bihac be demilitarised like Srebrenica, Zepa and Gorazde were supposed to be; Haris Silajdzic, speaking after his meeting with Rose, unbelievably went along with this.

Karadzic, on the other hand, dismissed the pair of them and continued to insist that 'Bihac will only become a protected zone when the Serbs have disarmed the 5th Corps, making it then possible for the Moslem civilian population to lead normal lives.'[147]

Then, in a surprise move, Dudakovic sought out ECMM's Francis Bonal, a French monitor who had been operating in the town on his own for over a month, and between the two of them they agreed that a ceasefire was indeed required at this time. Using the satellite phone in Bonal's Landrover they then attempted to contact Karadzic directly in Pale. Incredibly, Dudakovic knew the phone number by heart.

However, and in spite of their best efforts, they failed to raise him.[148] The unproved suspicion here of course was that Karadzic was well aware who was looking to speak with him, but availed himself of the confusion to allow Milovanovic time to press home his military advantage.

Boutros-Ghali in Sarajevo

While Rose convinced Muslim and Serb leaders to meet at Sarajevo airport[149] on the 25th, UN sources were reporting that no more than 300 members of the 5th Corps remained actively defending Bihac and that the population had swollen to over 70,000 as a result of the huge influx of displaced people. The hospital was packed with casualties, the markets and shops were completely bare, and people sheltering in their homes were reported to be weeping openly with fear. Monique Tuffelli from UNHCR believed that while the ordinary people were very angry earlier in the week at the UN's perceived failure to protect them, they were now too overpowered by events to blame anyone.

Later, as the airport talks concluded, Haris Silajdzic announced that he was willing to agree a nationwide ceasefire, but Nikola Koljevic, while accepting the need for a ceasefire, wanted further discussions before any final agreement could be reached.[150] Broadcasting on Bosnian Serb Radio News at 7 p.m. that night Koljevic insisted that Britain, France and Russia would have to guarantee the deal for the Serbs. Whether this was a serious proposal or just another delaying tactic is not exactly clear, but the international mediators were dismayed to discover that the very next item on the same news bulletin featured General Milovanovic threatening the 5th with extinction if they failed to surrender within 24 hours.[151]

Of no concern to any party was a demonstration taking place that very evening thousands of miles away in a place called Dhaka, where hundreds of Bangladeshis were marching by torchlight to highlight the plight of their troops in an obscure place called Bihac Pocket. 'We strongly protest at the UN decision to put them on high risk duty without proper logistics. Today they are just like sitting ducks', said a man whose nephew was serving with UNPROFOR.[152]

This very subject was also on the agenda when the Croatian war council met in Zagreb that night where a significant contribution was being made by an article Denis Kuljis had written in *Globus* on 25 November. Entitled '20,000 Serb Soldiers from Croatia [Krajina] and Bosnia are Entering Bihac', and conveying graphic images of helpless Muslims and Croats about to be butchered, this was a dramatic piece of propaganda. Of course it could have been easily dismissed by objective assessment, but as far as Tudjman's war council were concerned these 'revelations' could not have come at a better time.

With fighting continuing round Bihac NATO planes were ordered into action, but as the initial sortie was trying to locate a suitable target Rose had a change of heart and decided that basically the whole exercise was a waste of time. The mission was cancelled, and even though the Serbs fired two badly directed SA-2 missiles at the departing aircraft no follow-up action was initiated.[153] Clearly the spectre of the 'Mogadishu Line' had appeared once more and Rose was not prepared to send his troops across it.

This decision was greeted with derision by the government in Sarajevo, but members of other agencies in the region, and those staff officers at ECMM HQ who had previously served in other UN missions, knew that Rose was right. In real terms there was nothing he or any other foreigner could do to stop the carnage if the parties to the conflict were not themselves prepared to talk to one another. Had Rose gone ahead with the airstrike it was virtually certain that by 9 a.m. the following morning more UNPROFOR troops would have found themselves surrounded and held hostage pending the inevitable climb-down which would eventually follow, thus producing even further bad publicity.

The main problem now was that Rose got ambushed by Haris Silajdzic that night when he thought he was on his way to meet Izetbegovic at the presidency. With the entire Sarajevo press corps in attendance Rose found his way blocked on the first floor of the building as Silajdzic berated him, screaming that Rose was personally responsible for the deaths of 70,000 Muslims in Bihac. The media loved it. Rose could not escape and his discomfort was obvious. Siladjzic had all the soundbites, and the evening news bulletins pumped out the perception that UNPROFOR was to blame one more time.

It was all a lie of course, and Siladjzic's figure of 70,000 was preposterous – it had no factual basis whatsoever. But the damage was done. The Sarajevo government only wanted to exploit the situation around Bihac (which as we have seen Dudakovic essentially created himself) to draw NATO into the wider war. Bihac was important in that context. Falsifying the casualty figures was simply a means to that end.

At this point the UN Security Council empowered the secretary-general to go to Bosnia in the hope that his personal intervention might succeed where his emissaries had failed. Flying into Sarajevo on the morning of 30 November, and having written to Karadzic in advance asking for a meeting,[154] Boutros Boutros-Ghali first went to meet Izetbegovic at the presidency building. Then he gave a press conference. And then he returned to the airport for a meeting with Karadzic, who feigned outrage that the secretary-general would snub the Serbs by refusing to come to Pale.

Proposing a compromise Karadzic suggested that the meeting take place in the Serb part of Sarajevo, where all Boutros-Ghali had to do was literally walk across a bridge. Unbelievably he refused, and it was at this point that Karadzic decided he was not going to the airport. A unique opportunity was lost. At face value it certainly appeared that the UN secretary-general was intent on spending as little time as possible in Sarajevo, when in reality he should have been prepared to stay there for as long as it took to bring all of the parties to their senses. He had nothing whatever to gain from treating any of them differently, and this of course begs the question why he refused to make the relatively short journey to Pale, or an even shorter walk across the Bosna river.

Clearly he had his own perception of Karadzic and his ministers, but if he was not prepared to actually talk to them, and at least see them as equal parties to the problem, then he really had little business coming to Sarajevo in the first place.[155] His concerns revolved around the problem of attributing the perception of legitimacy to the Bosnian Serbs and their republic. This he was not prepared to do under any circumstances – thus his refusal to meet with Karadzic.

Unquestionably there was a certain logic to this argument, but it singularly failed to take account of the reality on the ground which was screaming out for resolution. Reality demanded that all parties be treated equally in order that lives be saved. Alas, for the secretary-general of the United Nations maintaining a perception was more important than dealing with the hard reality, and that was a very sad testimony indeed. This was more than a lost opportunity – it was a tragedy – and it signalled to the Serbs that they could no longer expect to be dealt with impartially by the international community, something which was quite clear to Karadzic in his letter to Akashi on 1 December.

The Economic Agreement and the Z4 plan

But it wasn't all about Bosnia. On 2 December, after several postponements, the ICFY-sponsored Zagreb/Knin Economic Agreement was signed in Zagreb. It dealt with water supply, electrical distribution, the reopening of the Zagreb/Belgrade highway through Sector West, and the opening of the oil and gas pipelines through Sector North. It was also supposed to be the basis for further negotiations between Knin and Zagreb on several other issues – the return of refugees and displaced persons, the payment of Croatian state pensions and the further opening of other roads and railways.

This was a huge step into the unknown for the Krajina Serbs, and while at one level it made perfect sense to co-operate with the Croats on these matters, on another it made none at all. One of the less enthusiastic was Milan Babic who remained firmly convinced this was but the first step in a process which would eventually erode the status of Krajina altogether. When President Tudjman then began insisting that if the agreement was not implemented in full by 20 January Croatia would refuse to extend UNPROFOR's mandate, Babic's worst fears were confirmed.

Borislav Mikelic, on the other hand, was far more upbeat and stated on Belgrade Radio that while he had not achieved all that he wanted on economic matters he had 'managed to make an agreement without preambles, Security Council resolutions, or political qualifications. Croatia has international recognition within its borders on paper', continuing, 'everything else is in our hands'. All of this no doubt went down well in Belgrade, where Mikelic was being used cleverly by Milosevic to pave the way for better relations between Belgrade and Zagreb, but it was immediately clear to all commentators that no matter what the Serbs conceded to Croatia, in the longer term it would never be enough.

With the ink barely dry on the Economic Agreement, out stepped the 'Zagreb 4', which curiously enough, and in typical Balkan fashion, consisted of five people.[156] They produced their plan for a political solution, which allegedly was aimed at the 'peaceful' reintegration of the UNPAs (i.e. Krajina) into Croatia proper.

Superficially it looked as if some progress was being made, but that was not the case. In Krajina all troops were fully mobilised and rumours abounded that the Croatian army was operating inside Bosnia's international borders in order to attack into Krajina by the 'back door'. When this was put to General Gotavina, the HV commander in Split, he responded by claiming that the Krajina Serbs were also operating in Bosnia (presumably he was referring to the area around Bihac), and that this more or less justified what his own troops were up to.[157]

Of course by any reasonable standard it did not, and UNPROFOR sources later confirmed that elements from at least three Croatian brigades (126th, 4th and 9th) were actually deployed in Bosnia in an area just north of Livno at that very time.[158] They got away with this because the international community was totally divided on several key issues, not least of which was the central matter of whether UNPROFOR stay put or go home.[159] To compound matters further the UN General Assembly conducted a vote on 9 December and for the first time labelled Krajina as 'occupied territory' within Croatia's internationally recognised borders. They also declared that any attempts to integrate these areas into a federal Yugoslavia (i.e. Serbia) would be illegal under international law.[160]

This was another serious mistake. It permitted Croatia to grab the high moral ground at the very time meaningful talks should have been taking place on an equal basis. Krajina was occupied territory all right. It was occupied by people whose ancestors had lived there for hundreds of years, and even the most basic examination of the 1991 Census, or any one of a plethora of maps illustrating ethnic distribution in the Balkans, left this matter in no doubt whatsoever. Once again the perception of legitimacy took precedence over the stark reality, and people continued to die as a consequence. The EC Summit taking place in Germany on 10 December chose not to see reality either and instead condemned the Krajina Serbs for occupation of their own homeland, and the Bosnian Serbs for their current campaign in Bihac which had in fact been initiated by the 5th Corps.

Bangladesh pays a heavy price

On Bosnia's many battlefields military commanders of all creeds now sought to exploit this political indecision. In the Livanjsko Polje the Croatian army continued their push against the Bosnian Serbs. At a press conference in New York on 10 December Foreign Minister Granic claimed that his army was only supplying 'logistic support' to the HVO, while Mario Nobilo, Croatia's UN ambassador, said that the HV were there to attract some of the Serbs away from Bihac. In their opinions this was all perfectly legal because a military agreement between Sarajevo and Zagreb had already been signed.[161]

General Rose, on the other hand, was becoming more and more frustrated. He had tried to enter Bihac but found his way blocked by a Krajina Serb checkpoint which would not move. He had undertaken the visit to rally the morale of the Bangladeshi troops and to try to re-establish a reliable supply line to them.[162] His failure to achieve even these very limited objectives provided an indication of just how difficult the whole situation had now become. Sadly it was about to get worse.

In the late afternoon of 12 December a Bangladeshi armoured personnel carrier (APC) was hit by a Sagger anti-tank missile just outside the UNPROFOR logistics base on the southern edge of Velika Kladusa. The

Reuters report that night was full of the usual soundbites: 'rebel Serbs', a 'government' enclave, etc. – and while it certainly told the story it singularly failed to explain any of it.[163]

Ismail Hassain was so badly injured that he never regained consciousness and died the following morning. It took over eight hours to evacuate the five injured Bangladeshis by road to the American field hospital at Pleso, near Zagreb, because for some inexplicable reason the Krajina Serbs refused UNPROFOR permission to conduct a medevac by helicopter.[164] In all probability this would not have saved Hassain's life anyway, but the fact that the UN were powerless to even medevac their own people was lost on no one.

In this, the most critical of situations for peacekeepers, the UN was not able to act without permission in order to save the lives of its own people. And if there had been any doubt in the past about the scale of contempt which *all* the belligerents harboured towards UN soldiers, there was none whatever now. This was a very sad day for UNPROFOR in more ways than one, and in effect signalled the beginning of the end. In the dark and cold that Monday night in a place called Velika Kladusa 'the penny finally dropped' for even the most ardent supporters of peacekeeping. There was no peace to keep, the safe areas were a joke and political direction did not exist.

Jimmy Carter goes to Sarajevo

Back in Sarajevo life went on as if unaffected by events in Bihac. The last of the detained peacekeepers were released by the Bosnian Serbs and a relief food convoy was eventually allowed through to the city, although one complete UNPROFOR fuel convoy was hijacked and the vehicles were never seen again. Then reports began to filter through that President Milosevic had managed to split the Bosnian Serbs to such a point that the Pale parliament was now allegedly operating independently of Karadzic and on the verge of accepting the Contact Group plan. It was also reported that he supported both the 'Economic Agreement' and 'the Z4 plan', and proof of this appeared to be indicated by the visits to Belgrade of prominent mediators from the Contact Group and ICFY.

In this context Karadzic made a pre-emptive strike and caught everyone by surprise when he appeared live on CNN on the night of 14 December and announced to the world that former US president Jimmy Carter was on his way to Bosnia to act as an honest broker in an attempt to hammer out a new and better settlement. He went on to confound his critics further by announcing a string of unsolicited concessions which were to become effective immediately.

It all sounded too good to be true, and no one was sure what exactly was going on, but all were agreed that if former president Carter was prepared to travel to Sarajevo, and put his considerable reputation on the line, then he at least deserved to be given a fair chance. The only unanswered questions were how this had all come about in the first place, and who had convinced Carter that he actually stood a chance of producing any kind of acceptable settlement. Like everything else in the Balkans the answers were anything but simple, and not immediately to hand.

It had all begun at a cocktail party in Santa Barbara, California, in June 1994 when Borko Djordevic, a Serb then working in America as a plastic surgeon, was introduced to Tom Hanley, a partner in the Los Angeles law firm of Whitman, Breed, Abbott, and Morgan. Neither of them spoke of the ongoing situation in Bosnia, and Djordevic made no reference to the fact that he had gone to medical school with the leader of the Bosnian Serbs. But when Karadzic contacted his former classmate in late November to enquire if some initiative could be started in the United States which might improve his precarious position at home, Djordevic thought of Tom Hanley.

In early December, with a letter from Dr Karadzic in his possession, Hanley approached the White House, the State Department and the Carter Centre in Atlanta, and invited them all to come to Bosnia in order to find a lasting settlement. Neither the White House nor the State Department replied, but after a while the Carter Centre did, and on 14 December Hanley, Djordjevic and Slavko Laserevic made their way to Plains, Georgia, where some of Carter's officials met them for a preliminary meeting in a local restaurant called The Country Corner. In the course of the meeting a waitress interrupted to say there was a telephone call for Hanley. Incredibly it was Karadzic at the other end of the line in Bosnia wanting to confirm the message which was about to be delivered to the former president. Once that was sorted out the group departed for Carter's home.

When Jimmy Carter was satisfied that the offer was genuine he phoned Karadzic in Pale and asked him to confirm once again that as a preliminary gesture all UN convoys would be permitted free movement, all UN peacekeepers released, all Muslim prisoners under 20 released also, a ceasefire honoured around Sarajevo, the airport reopened, and human rights and fundamental freedoms guaranteed throughout the Republic Srpska. Karadzic agreed immediately, and having told CNN that this new plan could bring the fighting in war-torn Sarajevo to a halt within 24 hours, Jimmy Carter was on his way to Bosnia.[165]

The development immediately drew a cool response from Western officials and diplomats. A White House spokesman said that while they were sceptical about the Bosnian Serbs' intentions, if the steps outlined by Karadzic were implemented they would help reduce tensions and ease the humanitarian situation in Bosnia. On the other hand, Lawrence Eagleburger immediately made himself available as a sort of 'unofficial spokesman', and his contempt for the initiative was obvious as he expressed doubts that Jimmy Carter actually knew where Bosnia was.

This was distinctly unhelpful, and NATO's secretary-general Willy Claes, in his attempts to reject Karadzic's offer, was not much better. 'I do not see any indication of a peace plan', he said, 'this is just an elaboration of points', while French foreign minister Alain Juppe rejected it outright. 'There is a provocative aspect to the plan which is unacceptable', he said.[166] Reaction became even colder the following morning when reports began to filter through that General Rose's helicopter had been fired upon by the Bosnian Serbs as it flew over Mount Igman south-west of Sarajevo. These reports were not true, and it later emerged that Muslim troops had done the shooting in order to have the Serbs blamed for it and thereby scuttle the Carter mission before it even got off the ground.[167]

As Jimmy Carter set out for Bosnia on 18 December White House officials continued to play down the significance of what was unfolding. Some of their remarks were nothing short of appalling. To suggest that 'he might be drawn into things he does not fully understand', or, 'it's more complicated than anything he has handled before',[168] did nothing but undermine the former president. Whether or not this amounted to a deliberate attempt to sabotage the whole process remains a very moot point. Suffice it to say that legitimising Karadzic was not on the Clinton Administration's agenda. As far as they were concerned there were predetermined 'good guys' and 'bad guys' in Bosnia, and it served their purposes best if that distinction remained intact. The fact that there were *no* 'good guys' in Bosnia, that all parties had copious amounts of blood on their hands, and that at that point in time Karadzic was the only one even vaguely attempting to improve matters, seemed to have, intentionally or otherwise, completely escaped them.

In any case, Jimmy Carter, his wife Rosalynn, and Harry Barnes and Joyce Neu from the Carter Centre, made their way to Frankfurt on a commercial flight and then on to Zagreb on board a US military plane. Hanley, Djordjevic and Laserevic were left to find their own way to Pale having been refused permission to travel on the same military aircraft! During the stop-over in Zagreb Carter met with President Tudjman, the US ambassador Peter Galbraith and the Bosnian prime minister Haris Silajdzic, who apparently voiced the opinion that Karadzic was only interested in manipulating the situation to dilute the Contact Group plan.

Later, across the city at UNPROFOR HQ, Yasushi Akashi refuted this suggestion when he voiced his opinion that he thought the former president too intelligent to be manipulated by anyone. What Akashi failed to point out, and certainly should have, was that on each leg of his journey every single person whom Carter would encounter was likely to try by fair means or foul to bring him around to their particular way of thinking. When he touched down in Sarajevo that Sunday evening Izetbegovic was the next manipulator waiting to meet him.

Arriving in Pale just after midnight[169] Hanley immediately set about briefing Karadzic for his meeting the next morning. Working through the night until just after 5 a.m. Hanley explained in detail what Carter could accept, and more importantly what he could not. In the latter category Karadzic was intent on trying to extract from Carter an assurance that the UN's economic sanctions on all Serb republics would be lifted as a *quid pro quo* for his agreement to a permanent ceasefire throughout Bosnia.

His objective here, of course, was to prove to the entire Serb nation just who their real leader was and to achieve for all of them what Milosevic had patently failed to realise. The problem was that Carter could never deliver any of this no matter what Karadzic was prepared to concede, and it took Hanley the whole night to convince his client what the real position was.

However, when Carter and Karadzic went into private session, and sat down with a laptop computer to put the final touches to the agreement, the matter of the sanctions raised its ugly head again. After two hours of argument the whole process was about to fall apart on this point – and probably would have had Djordjevic and Hanley not taken Karadzic aside and warned him that if he persisted with this approach then it would be interpreted internationally that he really didn't want peace after all. After a tense few minutes Karadzic agreed to drop the sanctions issue and signed up to a ceasefire, based on the provisions of the Contact Group plan, which would reduce Serb-held territory in Bosnia to 49 per cent.

Before returning to Sarajevo to sell the deal to Izetbegovic, Carter and Karadzic went before the media circus which had descended on Pale. It was immediately clear that something was in the offing. Praising the Bosnian Serbs for their commitment to a peace agreement, Carter said that their role in the war had been 'misunderstood', and when Karadzic denied that the Serbs had been the aggressors, the former president sent shock waves through the Sarajevo government by admitting: 'I can't dispute your statement that the American people have heard only one side of the story. The entire world is hoping and praying for peace in this country and your commitment to honour human rights'.[170]

This also sent shock waves through the White House who lost no time in pushing Dee Dee Myers before a camera to reaffirm their official position that the Serbs were indeed the aggressors in the war. Why this outburst was necessary in the middle of delicate negotiations has never been explained, but it certainly had a negative effect on Karadzic who quickly became very unsure where exactly he stood between 'official' and 'unofficial' US positions. If this was designed to unnerve him it worked, and if it was a deliberate act it was wholly despicable.

Whatever the reality, Karadzic appeared on CNN that night and gave the impression that he had not after all agreed to a four-month ceasefire but saw this as only a possibility. 'Generally speaking we have told the

Muslims we don't want any more ceasefires, we want an end to the war and not breaks for them to recover', he said. He badly needed official US support at this point, but no one in the Clinton regime was prepared to give it.

The following morning Carter went to Izetbegovic and Ganic in order to establish where exactly they stood on the matter of an immediate ceasefire, which would allow a talks process to begin. Not for the first time the Muslims were faced with accepting something which they believed Karadzic had already rejected the previous night on CNN, and although a final settlement based on the current map of Bosnia was the last thing they would ever agree to, they nevertheless agreed to come on board for Carter's 'talks process'. After a two-hour meeting Izetbegovic told reporters that his government would accept an immediate ceasefire for four months and enter negotiations on the basis of the Contact Group plan.

At this point Carter went to General Rose's headquarters and faxed a letter to Karadzic via an UNMO team who conveniently lived close to his home on the High Road in Pale.[171] Again Carter made it clear to Karadzic that without doubt he was now going to be personally blamed (again) internationally if nothing materialised from this final round of talks. This was something Karadzic simply could not risk, given Milosevic's ongoing campaign to remove him.

Accordingly, by the time Carter arrived back in Pale the decision had already been taken. After a brief meeting, Karadzic and Mladic looked on as Jimmy Carter announced his latest triumph to the world's press: 'The most significant achievement this morning was the Bosnian Serb leaders' agreement to a complete ceasefire [Cessation of Hostilities Agreement (COHA)] throughout Bosnia to be implemented on December 23rd with all confrontation lines to be monitored by UNPROFOR.'[172]

Carter succeeded where all the rest failed because he had taken Karadzic seriously. A meaningful ceasefire had been signed and all those who mattered were on board, but still international reaction was mixed, to say the least of it. In fact, sections of the British press were scathing in their remarks, with the *Independent* claiming that Carter's 'self important piety blinds him to the fact that he has played straight into the Bosnian Serbs' hands', and while the *Guardian* was not much better it did at least recognise that 'his is the only show on the road'.

Alain Juppe remained very sceptical and was adamant that 'experience in this conflict has taught everyone that the ink is never dry on agreements before they are broken', while in the US Dee Dee Myers was back before the cameras on behalf of the White House offering only a cautious welcome to the agreement. 'If those things happen certainly that's a positive accomplishment', she told reporters, while in Belgrade Slobodan Milosevic went on the record to indicate that the deal had his full support,[173] something he reiterated on CNN's *Larry King Live* later that night. Whether he actually meant any of this is debatable because the deal effectively scuttled his immediate plans to install a quisling in Pale. For the moment Karadzic was still in firm control.

Meetings got under way almost as soon as Carter had departed and all sides appeared initially to be committed to the process, notwithstanding yet another attack on Sarajevo's marketplace in which two men died.[174] This time there was no indication from where the shells had been fired, but it is not unreasonable to suggest that whoever ordered the attack did so in the hope that it would exert some influence on Akashi who was at that very moment deep in discussion with government ministers on the matter of the Armija's refusal to vacate the designated demilitarised area on Mount Igman. In spite of several difficulties Akashi remained optimistic as he shuttled between Sarajevo and Pale, and at noon in Sarajevo, or 11 a.m. GMT, on Saturday, 24 December, Jimmy Carter's ceasefire came into effect – and to practically everyone's disbelief it was respected by all sides.

Philip Watkins and Christopher Geidt, the EC's most senior monitors in Bosnia at the time, assessed the implications of the Carter mission in a report filed from the dreary surroundings of their headquarters in Zenica late on Christmas Eve.[175] They accurately identified something which practically everyone else had either missed or chosen to ignore – namely, that the Bosnian Croats had been completely forgotten in the latest peace agreement between the Muslims and the Serbs.

Equally, the fact that the Croats were not demanding to be part of the process clearly established that they were operating to a completely different agenda. For the moment they were quite happy to continue their military operations against the Bosnian Serbs near the town of Livno, especially since the Croatian army was becoming more and more involved there by the day.[176] Croatian government spokespersons had also begun indicating (leaking to the press) that President Tudjman was on the verge of telling Akashi to remove all UNPROFOR troops from his country once the current mandate had expired in January, notwithstanding that the Economic Agreement was working well and that the Serbs had withdrawn their barriers and opened up the Zagreb–Belgrade highway at 2.30 p.m. on 21 December.

The opening ceremony had been witnessed by both Milan Martic and Milan Celeketic as a procession of over 60 Croatian vehicles drove the 15-mile stretch from Kutina to Novska. This was a major concession by the Krajina Serbs, but this good will was not reciprocated with the Croats choosing to interpret it instead as a sign of weakness. Milan Babic, now Krajina's foreign minister, had never been in favour of conceding anything to Zagreb, but he was overruled by both Martic and Prime Minister Mikelic. The way events were now unfolding they might have been better served had they listened to him.[177]

Fighting in Bihac

In Bihac Pocket the 5th Corps had begun to withdraw southwards on 18 December as Abdic and the Krajina Serbs began to get the upper hand.[178] By the 21st Velika Kladusa was back in APWB hands, although Abdic controlled little more than the town itself which was extensively damaged and had no electricity, gas, water or wood available.[179]

The southern confrontation line remained active, but as the ceasefire negotiations made progress in Sarajevo there was a noticeable scaling down of operations by the Bosnian Serbs.[180] In a separate development, progress was made in relation to the passage into Cazin of a UN food convoy, which had at that point been held in Topusko for several days. It quickly emerged that a *quid pro quo* had been agreed here in relation to fuel for Abdic's people at Turanj.[181]

December 27th marked the thousandth day of Sarajevo's siege and, with only the occasional shot being fired, General Rose and minister without portfolio, Hasan Muratovic, went to Bihac in an attempt to get all sides to respect the ceasefire and thereby be included in the COHA planned now for 1 January.[182] Surprisingly, they were well received by all sides, with even Abdic agreeing to toe the line, and for the first time in years the prospect of a realistic country-wide ceasefire appeared to be on the cards. Over the next few days the level of hostilities right across Bosnia decreased dramatically and on the morning of 29 December, having obtained the necessary fuel from UNHCR,[183] between 4,000 and 5,000 refugees from Turanj began the long journey home in a convoy of 20 buses, 16 trucks, 200 cars, 200–250 tractors and 120 horses and carts. They were returning to dreadful conditions, but at least they were going home – and that would provide them with some consolation.

Dzemal Ahmetovic, who had been the refugee leader in Turanj, estimated that over 2,000 tonnes of assorted humanitarian aid would be required urgently once the refugees had returned to Velika Kladusa because another convoy from Batnoga was scheduled to arrive on the 30th. This was a conservative estimate and would take time to organise, but for the moment all UNHCR and ECTF could supply were rolls of plastic sheeting for use in lieu of window panes, and small quantities of food and water. It wasn't much, but at least it helped to fortify them against the worst of the wind, snow and hail.

By the evening of 30 December over 6,000 refugees had returned to their vandalised, looted, broken homes in the hope that their particular war was over. They were not to know it at the time, but 1995 would bring them even further tragedy, and within a short time they would find themselves back on the road again and once more dependent on charitable handouts from UNHCR and several other trusts and agencies. They could be forgiven for thinking that it was their destiny to be permanently in the wrong place at the wrong time.

The final days of 1994 were marked by frantic diplomatic efforts to ensure that when the COHA was unveiled on 31 December all sides would embrace it and make a determined effort to ensure it worked. ECMM's outgoing head of mission, Ambassador von Stulpnagle, together with Philip Watkins and Chris Geidt, visited Pale on 30 December and were granted a unique meeting with Dr Karadzic, General Mladic and Professor Nikolai Koljevic, at which, perhaps for the very first time, the Serbs explained some of their positions and why they held them.

Concerning relations between the Republic Srpska and Europe Karadzic saw the European approach to the problems in his country as one of trying to impose a solution but taking no account of the Bosnian Serbs' perspective. He felt that this approach was now softening in that he believed the Contact Group now recognised that all sides to the conflict had equal status. When pressed to allow EU monitoring teams to operate within his territory he declared himself to be hopeful that this might happen but argued that any development of this nature was likely to be linked to a full acceptance of the COHA by the Muslims and European recognition of the Bosnian Serbs' right to self-determination which he believed to be enshrined in the UN Charter.

Mladic criticised Europe for supporting the continuation of economic sanctions and for taking the side of the Sarajevo government, but he also suggested that the time was ripe for all outstanding matters to be settled by political as distinct from military means. Both of them expressed a wish for higher-level contact with the European Union, and as the meeting concluded Karadzic pointed out that a window of opportunity now existed in Bosnia, which, should it remain open, would afford ECMM the opportunity of working in his country in the future.[184]

The following afternoon Alija Izetbegovic and Rasim Delic signed the Cessation of Hostilities Agreement in Sarajevo before Akashi took it to Pale where Karadzic and Mladic signed it later that night. The entire process had been difficult and at one point, on the 31st, it looked as if the Serbs might back down. However, Milos Stankovic persisted in his role as negotiator and, thanks to satellite communications with Rose in Sarajevo, the Bosnian Serbs (all of them) eventually came on board.

Two days later Kesimir Zubak and Tihomir Blaskic signed on behalf of the Bosnian Croats, thereby bringing all sides together and thus offering a modicum of hope that within the next four months some permanent arrangement might emerge which could bring all of the suffering to an end.

And the credit for most of this, whether the Clinton Administration and the international community liked it or not, went to Radovan Karadzic. Without his approach to Jimmy Carter in the first instance none of this would have come about. It is easy to argue that Karadzic had ulterior motives for making this move, and that had he not been under serious personal threat from Milosevic he would never have even considered it in the first place. Perhaps this is so – and perhaps it is not. Either way the inescapable truth remains the same – Karadzic initiated the process, he followed through by delivering on a string of unsolicited concessions, amazingly he brought Mladic along with him, and finally he signed his name to the COHA thus providing a window of opportunity from which a lasting peace might well have emerged.

It wasn't his fault that Izetbegovic, Zubak and their international backers were not sufficiently committed to the process to actually take that opportunity and make it work, and to set aside their own longer-term agendas. This would become crystal clear in the months ahead when we discovered who was using the COHA to prepare for war.

5
1995

Croatia's attitude to UNPROFOR

In the Livanjsko Polje region of Bosnia the Croatian army (HV) was now busy building up its forces. For months large numbers of HV had been 'supporting' HVO operations with a tactical group based on the 4th Guards Brigade from Split, but also incorporating elements from a string of other professional units including the 5th Guards Brigade who had travelled all the way from eastern Slavonia to partake in 'on-the-job training'.

In Sarajevo it soon became quite clear that senior figures there were also looking for an excuse to distance themselves from the Agreement completely. In an interview at the time with ECMM's Philip Watkins, Rasim Delic, the Armija's supreme commander, made no attempt whatever to disguise his position and expressed no confidence whatever in the COHA process. Over the years, the Muslims had consistently rejected any deal that would effectively partition the country, and it was clear on 6 January that this new process would ultimately be rejected by them as well for exactly the same reasons. Not surprisingly, then, Delic was only too prepared to be distracted into other areas and immediately began demanding that the Krajina Serbs get out of Bihac Pocket as a precondition to his further participation in the whole COHA process.[1]

In this context it was not surprising either to find that the commander of the Armija's 2nd Corps in Tuzla had set about trying to wreck the Regional Joint Commission before it got off the ground. He began by complaining hysterically that a Bosnian Serb liaison officer had been installed at the UN Sector HQ without his, or Izetbegovic's permission. When he got no satisfaction from the UN sector commander he then took it upon himself to blockade Tuzla air base, where the UN were garrisoned, and effectively held all the troops therein, including the Serb officer, as hostages.

The exchange of liaison officers was specifically mentioned at para. 3 of the COHA, which both Delic and Izetbegovic had signed, yet neither of them intervened to call one of their subordinates to heel. The situation deteriorated further when Karadzic then produced a set of maps purporting to divide Sarajevo into 14 parts – seven for the Muslims and seven for the Serbs – with the equivalent of a Berlin Wall running down the middle of it.[2] As far as the Sarajevo government were concerned the COHA was just a temporary little arrangement. It gave a breathing space in which they could consolidate their forces and rearm – and that was all they wished it to be.

In Croatia at this time the situation also changed dramatically when President Tudjman went live on Croatian television (HRT) on 12 January and informed his people that he had written the following message to the UN secretary-general Boutros Boutros-Ghali: 'As the President of the Republic of Croatia, I have the honour to inform you that the UNPROFOR mandate is hereby terminated effective March 31, 1995 in accordance with Resolution 947 (1994).'[3]

He then went on to deliver an address to his people the tone of which was somewhat different: 'UNPROFOR's failure to fulfil its tasks and enable the implementation of the Vance Plan and all Security Council resolutions should be blamed on rebel Serb leaders in occupied areas and even more so on Belgrade leaders who wanted to make them part of a Greater Serbia.'[4]

From Croatia's perspective this decision was perfectly understandable, and perhaps even logical. Tudjman was absolutely correct in his assessment of what the UN was *not* achieving in Krajina, and no more than the Muslims in Bosnia he was acutely aware that the longer the situation remained as it was the greater the possibility of the Confrontation Line becoming a *de facto* and *de jure* border.

Not surprisingly, then, this move served only to further alienate those whom Tudjman wished to reintegrate into Croatia, with Milan Babic claiming that no matter what the Knin government was prepared to do by way of normalising relations with Zagreb it would never ever satisfy the Croats.

The international response

International reaction to Tudjman's announcement was mixed, with the UN Security Council reaffirming its opinion that the presence of UNPROFOR provided the best opportunity for regional peace and security, and a formal appeal was made to Croatia on the 17th to reconsider its decision.

Germany's foreign minister, Klaus Kinkel, actually admitted that he thought Tudjman was 'absolutely wrong',[5] and the US State Department expressed what it called 'disapproval', but other than that there appeared to be very little media interest in what was clearly perceived as just another move in 'Balkan political chess'.

The following day Croatian foreign minister, Mate Granic, announced that termination of the mandate was not negotiable and went on to say that Croatia had now amassed the military strength necessary to retake Krajina by force if so required.[6] This was not an idle remark because since the signing of a Memorandum of Co-operation on Defence and Military Relations between the United States and Croatia on 29 November 1994,[7] Croatia was arming itself at an alarming rate. MPRI (Military Professional Resources Incorporated) had set up their operation in Zagreb, the importation of weaponry and military equipment was proceeding through the Croatian State Agency 'ALAN,[8] and the Croatian armed forces were well on their way to becoming strong enough to contemplate a new war with as many different Serbs as cared to join them in the battle.

In 1996 *Newsweek* magazine posed the question of whether President Clinton was actually aware of Iranian arms shipments to Croatia. The answer they printed was as follows:

> *Newsweek* has learned that in early 1994 Croatian President Franjo Tudjman asked US diplomats how Washington would react to an Iranian offer to smuggle weapons to Croatia and Bosnia. That would violate the United Nations arms embargo and increase Iran's sway over the Muslim led Bosnian government. But Washington decided that levelling the military field was its top priority – even at the expense of its own policy of isolating Tehran. Tudjman was informed that Washington had no view on the matter – a diplomatic signal to let the weapons shipments proceed.[9]

In 1994 alone, Croatia spent almost US$1.4 billion on what were loosely described as 'defence affairs and services', a figure which accounted for 31 per cent of that year's total budget expenditure, or 10 per cent of GNP. Of this, US$0.7 billion was used for the illegal importation of MIG fighter aircraft, helicopters and missiles. The remainder was spent on domestic production and development which, President Tudjman confirmed on 22 December 1994, in his address to the Nation, involved ongoing contracts with 324 firms throughout the country.[10]

It was hardly surprising, then, that Granic was buoyant when recommending to the Serbs that they carefully consider something which was about be unveiled at the end of the month.[11] Entitled the 'Draft Agreement on the Krajina, Slavonia, Southern Baranja, and Western Sirmium', or better known as the 'Z4 plan',[12] this latest document purported to represent consensus between the US, Russia, the EU and the UN.

It was presented to President Tudjman on the morning of 30 January. Immediately afterwards the 'Zagreb Four', or 'Five', depending on your perspective, led by Ambassador Galbraith, set out for Knin where Milan Martic refused to even look at their proposals until the whole matter of UNPROFOR's status was resolved.

By any objective standard Martic was absolutely correct not to entertain either Galbraith or his plan. It was an insult to the Krajina Serbs as a people and confirmed each and every suspicion of what they believed life would become under Croatian rule. The Z4 plan, however, was neither fair nor reasonable, and, being drafted in various embassies in Zagreb, the only real question the Krajina Serbs were left wondering about was who had actually written it up in the first place.

Henceforward the Z4 plan would be presented regularly as the answer to all the problems in Krajina, and the Serb's failure to accept it as further evidence of their intransigence. This particular line was a lie, but thanks to persistence by the Z4 Group themselves, and the Croatian government, the perception that the Serbs were exclusively intransigent gradually began to stick. Within a short few months this perception would be used against them to devastating effect.

Preparations for war

Meanwhile, back in Bosnia the Muslim/Croat federation was beginning to stagnate until a group called the 'Friends of the Federation' emerged in an attempt to revitalise the process and a US State Department official named Robert Owen[13] was given the unenviable task of making the whole thing work.

Of course the 'Friends' turned out to be none other than the original promoters in an unconvincing economic disguise, but even promises of increased funding for much-needed infrastructural development failed to distract the parties from their overriding hatred of one another. In fact, Bosiljko Misetic, Tudjman's special adviser on Herceg-Bosna, was still talking about the 'Zetra', the conceptual Muslim kingdom stretching from Turkey in the east through Kosovo, Sandzak and Macedonia, to Bosnia. As far as Misetic was concerned Izetbegovic was the father of such a Zetra and would have to be removed.[14]

At this time the Armija High Command also began a root and branch reorganisation of their forces and for the first time brought all their elements within one single chain of command. This was not a secret, and General Drekovic, commander of the 4th Corps in Mostar, stated that the army was becoming stronger every day. 'There will be soon enough heavy weapons, and the production of weapons and ammunition is very high in our territories.'[15] If Drekovic was to be believed the existence of the UN arms embargo, and the implementation of a no-fly zone by NATO, was having no effect whatsoever. Clearly perception and reality were not at one on this issue either.

The ability of the Armija to churn out ammunition for their troops from very primitive factories was presented throughout the war as a major achievement. In Bihac, Dudakovic saw fit to give Sky News almost unrestricted access to the sheds and garages in Cazin and Coralici where everything from mortar bombs to rifle ammunition was being produced. This was good public relations, the image relayed all around the world being one of beleaguered Muslims hanging on by their fingernails thanks to their own devices and ingenuity. The reality, of course, was totally different with Croatian army helicopters flying nightly resupply missions into the Pocket and light aircraft from a variety of other airfields in Croatia engaged in similar activities.

In central Bosnia the situation was similar, with much of the civilian population employed in the production of ammunition. A case in point was the steel factory in Zenica. Although closed, it was clearly a hive of activity manufacturing industrial gases and a variety of different artillery shells.[16] This discovery by ECMM put many things in context, but one matter which could not be easily reconciled was the deployment throughout the factory grounds of several hundred Turkish UN troops complete with their battalion headquarters, and several other support establishments. Admittedly these troops were there because this was the site offered to the UN by the local municipal leadership in the first instance. But by now they had become little more than human shields behind which the Muslims, on this occasion, could manufacture whatever they wanted. And all of this apparently with the total compliance of both the Turks and UNPROFOR headquarters.

Flights over Tuzla

On the night of 10 February Captain Ovind Moldestad from UNPROFOR's helicopter section in Sarajevo was visiting Tuzla. It was a clear night and facing towards the city he saw two fighter aircraft flying overhead with the after-burners, navigation lights and strobe lights all visible. They were flying in circles at 3,000 feet but they should have been at 25,000 feet with all lights off. Moldestad then went to call his duty officer in Sarajevo only to be told that NATO had no aircraft flying that night. When he came back outside one of the guards told him that another aircraft had been flying overhead as well – a C-130 Hercules transport aircraft.

Later, when Moldestad reported the matter to Rose's replacement, General Rupert Smith, he was told not to talk about what he had seen. Later again when he went to the NATO base in Vincenza, Italy, he was taken away by a US officer, Colonel Cooper, and then interrogated by several other US officers in relation to what he had seen. Finally permitted to leave the base, a fellow Norwegian handed Moldestad a confidential document which showed that NATO had not been patrolling the 'no-fly zone' that night. The NATO AWAC had been replaced by a US Navy E2 Hawkeye and two F18 fighters from the same carrier.[17]

Then a Norwegian UN Observer in Tuzla, Lieutenant Saetersdal, reported the sighting of a Hercules C-130 transport aircraft, escorted by F16 fighters, and when UN troops attempted to visit the area into which they suspected supplies were being dropped they were confronted by heavily armed Armija troops. With the entire area cordoned off the Muslim troops refused point blank to allow the UN access to the site, and after a stand-off lasting several hours the UN personnel withdrew.[18]

While the official report into this incident recorded no more than that the investigation had been inconclusive, the force commander, General De Lapresle, nonetheless decided to cable Kofi Annan, the UN's head of peacekeeping operations in New York, with his evaluation of what was going on: 'It appears that two clandestine re-supplies have taken place. The equipment being delivered is assessed to be of a high value/high technology, such as new generation anti-tank guided missiles or perhaps surface to air missiles – the origin of the cargo or the jets is not known.'[19]

When NATO were asked to identify this air traffic it initially suggested that these were 'standard civilian flights and training missions'! Then it emerged that the AWAC's on permanent station over Bosnia to enforce the no-fly zone were not all NATO crewed, some were exclusively American, and either way it also transpired that they were actually susceptible to 'blind spots'! If it also happened that the AWACs were slightly off course for any reason then the size of these 'blind spots' became even bigger, and if any would-be arms supplier could get his hands on the AWACs' flight schedules, or knew in advance when 'friendly' planes were on station, the rest of it was simple. By 21 February, as more and more damning information began to emerge about NATO's inability to secure the skies over Bosnia, the issue began to take on the nature of a scandal, from which everyone wanted to distance themselves.

In a secret memo to Kofi Annan, Chinmaya Gharekhan, Boutros Boutros-Ghali's senior adviser, indicated that within a very short time this whole matter was going to come before the Security Council. He derided NATO's 'explanations' such as they were: 'The NATO investigators would have us believe that no unauthorised activity took place. This conclusion would severely erode the credibility of UNPROFOR reporting on any air activity. The NATO report refers to "normal civilian airline traffic patterns in Serb airspace". I wonder what is this "normal civilian Serb air traffic"?'

The following day Annan sent a cable to Akashi in Zagreb which said that Thorvald Stoltenberg had confirmed to him that notwithstanding all of NATO's explanations, the original UN reports were correct. It also emerged on the evening of 19 February that the level of Muslim air activity in central Bosnia had alarmed the UN sufficiently for Lieutenant Colonel C.A. Le Hardy, the chief operations officer at Sector North-East headquarters in Tuzla, to write to General Rose's Headquarters in Sarajevo outlining the scale of what was taking place and the procedures he was now implementing to monitor it properly. These measures included the deployment of TOW thermal sighting equipment, the use of a troop of Leopard tanks as mobile observation posts, and the establishment of several additional static observation and listening posts.[20]

So what was really going on? Well, the answer to that depends on one's willingness to accept that the United States was actively involved in a covert campaign to supply arms and equipment to the Bosnian Muslims. For those less inclined to accept this line a perusal of the *Los Angeles Times* on 5 April 1996, or the London *Independent* of the following day, might be of assistance. These new revelations indicated that large quantities of illegal arms and equipment were being flown into the Croatian airport at Pula by Iranian cargo aircraft and then transported by road into Herceg-Bosna, where after all the appropriate tariffs had been deducted what was left of the original shipment made its way to the Muslims in central Bosnia. A second supply route, subsequently more preferred, involved the delivery of equipment directly to the Armija units on the ground, and probably was activated when it emerged just how much equipment was being siphoned off by Croats of all descriptions as the convoys travelled over land.

The general consensus at ECMM and UNPROFOR was that these operations were carried out by either reserve or retired US pilots, flying specially adapted Hercules C-130s from American bases in Britain and Europe. Landing at remote airstrips in the most northern part of Cyprus they would take on board Iranian weapons and ammunition, including artillery shells, and when all was securely bolted to pallets with parachutes attached, the pilots would set a course for the Croatian coast and onwards into Bosnia.[21] In the event that they could not complete their missions in one run, Brac Island, just off the coast from Split, could be used as a staging post, and some of the local people in the island's picturesque town of Bol were adamant that American C-130s were flying in and out of their airport on a regular basis.[22] When the delivery runs were made into Bosnia they were most probably co-ordinated by US Special Forces personnel on the ground, the presence of whom, despite complete denial by the United States, was verified by Canadian UN troops in Visoko during January 1995 and accepted as a fact by the intelligence section at UNPROFOR headquarters in Zagreb.[23]

On the ground the local Armija units sealed off the drop zones in order to prevent the UN wandering in on top of them, and, flying low over the tree-tops with the back door wide open, the pallets were quickly jettisoned as the pilots endeavoured to get out of the area as quickly as possible. Mission accomplished, and with no evidence on board, the pilots were then free to land wherever they wished. ECMM discovered one such aircraft parked on the tarmac at Split airport on the evening of 23 February.[24]

The critical factor, however, was the confirmed presence in the airport building, at exactly the same time, of Colonel Kresimir Cosic, personal adviser to President Tudjman and chairman of the Croatian Defence Ministry's committee for 'international co-operation and bi-lateral projects'. Cosic, later to become a lieutenant general and Croatia's deputy defence minister, was at that time functioning as Tudjman's liaison officer with the US State Department on the activities of MPRI and the implementation of what became known as the US's Defence Training and Advisory Programme (DTAP).[25] ECMM was quite satisfied that they had uncovered yet another piece of the clandestine weapons supply jigsaw which every monitoring agency in the Former Yugoslavia was frantically trying to put together.

The story of covert resupply operations had now became 'good copy' for everyone with a story to tell, and General Mladic lost no time getting in on the act. In a letter to General De Lapresle in Zagreb and to General Rupert Smith, who had recently taken over from Sir Michael Rose in Sarajevo, he outlined what he believed was going on.

In fact, Akashi had already cabled Kofi Annan in New York on 18 July 1994 saying 'we can confirm that the BiH (Army) has been receiving new weapons'. Listing the type and calibre of what had been discovered, he concluded by adding: 'we firmly believe that such equipment is being trans-shipped through Croatia for either a fee, or for part of the shipment, or both'.[26]

And there was also a much earlier report by the UN secretary-general himself – UN Document S/1994/300, dated 16 March 1994 – which confirmed that Operation Deny Flight, which began on 12 April 1993, had not been the great success everyone thought it was, and that by mid-March 1994 1,005 violations of the 'no-fly zone' by what were termed 'non-combat aircraft' had taken place.

A double game was indeed being played on this issue and there were no other possible explanations for the manner in which the Muslims were able to recommence their war with the Bosnian Serbs at the end of March 1995, given that militarily they were a spent force less than 12 months before that. Renewed hostilities with the Serbs under more favourable circumstances had for the Muslims been a cornerstone of the Washington Agreement, but to stand a realistic chance of success they had to be comprehensively supported. With their forces reorganised, and the Croats now technically their allies, the lot of the Bosnian Muslims was steadily improving. However, the problem was that the stronger they grew the less likely it became that they would abide by the terms of the COHA in the longer term.

Much later on some of the main players in these covert activities were prevailed upon to tell the truth before a US Senate Intelligence Select Committee. On 21 May 1996 Richard Holbrooke admitted that he had explored the possibility of a full-scale arming of the Bosnian Muslims in 1994, in spite of the UN arms embargo, because he feared they could not survive another winter on their own. While he denied that the US was actually involved in what subsequently transpired he went on to defend the Clinton Administration's decision to acquiesce to Iranian arms shipments through Croatia to Bosnia. 'Without it the Bosnian government would never have survived from the winter of 1994 to Dayton', he said. 'It's as simple as that.' However, when pressed further by Committee chairman Arlen Specter, Holbrooke also admitted that US technical personnel had become involved in the inspection of some Iranian missiles in trans-shipment to Bosnia because of a report received that the weapons in question had chemical warheads. While the source of this report was not divulged Holbrooke remained adamant that US intelligence agencies were not involved. He claimed that they had never been told of the decision in the first place on the grounds that the whole thing was not in fact a covert operation at all. Rather, it was a diplomatic response to Croatia's enquiry asking if this type of behaviour was OK![27] However, not all of this tied in with other evidence which emerged.

Two days later Deputy Secretary of State Strobe Talbott told the Committee that as far as he was aware the Clinton Administration had decided to keep its collaboration in this matter a secret, although he had in fact informed the CIA on the instructions of Secretary of State Warren Christopher. 'Had it become public it would have stirred up further relations with our principal NATO allies which were already quite tense at the time', he said.

Talbott went on to confirm that on 27 April 1994 the Clinton Administration decided to help Iran ship arms to Bosnia through Croatia by instructing US diplomats in the region to tell Croatia that they had 'no instructions' on what to say about such shipments.[28]

On 30 May Charles Redman and Peter Galbraith, the two US diplomats on the ground in the Former Yugoslavia, confirmed the existence of the US 'no instructions' policy and of having relayed that message to the relevant personnel. Interestingly enough Galbraith was prepared to go a good deal further and stated that 'the [Clinton] Administration was convinced that the arms embargo was fundamentally an error'.[29]

In fact, the Clinton Administration chose to condone a gross violation of a UN arms embargo, which they had supported themselves in the first instance, and they then commenced a devious diplomatic double-game with the remainder of their NATO allies. By deciding to turn a 'blind eye' to what was going on the Clinton Administration may well have eased their own collective conscience on this matter, but it created no end of difficulty for the plethora of agencies attempting to deal with the situation on the ground.

It now transpires also that General Hazim Sadic, formerly the commander of 2nd Corps in Tuzla, had been appointed as military attaché to Turkey in late 1994. He was the one who planned all the drops, as well as security at the drop zones themselves. The supplies came from Iran via Turkish bases in northern Cyprus, and he admits that Armija troops were ordered to fire on UN personnel in order to keep them away.

Brigadier Refik Brdianovic recalls that his troops also fired on UNPROFOR in the Tuzla region and that US personnel were on the ground assisting the Armija to off-load the aircraft. This implies that aircraft actually landed in Tuzla as well, and the equipment in question was in all probability Stinger ground-to-air missiles and some short-range, hand-held anti-tank rockets.[30] None of this happened by accident. It was all planned in detail at the highest levels. The two most senior Americans involved were both major generals. Their names were Jim Campbell and Jack Collins, and they were implementing policy not making it.[31]

Reality in Bihac

Meanwhile back in Bihac a row broke out within the Bosnian Serb leadership with General Milovanovic threatening to resign because his soldiers were cold and hungry, had received little or no pay for months and could no longer continue to operate in this environment. It also emerged that he was about to dismiss several of his field commanders in order to make one last attempt to cut the Pocket in two, but apparently Karadzic had ordered him to stop in order to comply with the terms of the COHA.[32] It then emerged that Karadzic actually tried to sack him because of his reluctance to abide by the terms of the COHA, but Mladic would not hear of it. Some of the civilian population also began returning to the villages from which they had fled before the Serb onslaught in November, and Bill Foxton, a British EC monitor operating in the Pocket, recorded the grim reality of what they found when they got back that cold February morning.[33]

Such was the situation in the villages immediately south of Bihac town in the spring of 1995, and one could easily have been forgiven for thinking that nothing at all had changed since that fateful day in April 1992 when ECMM's Hugh O'Donovan and his team were forced to beat a hasty retreat from Bosanska Krupa as Serb artillery and small arms fire poured in on top of them. But while the fighting continued, and 'normal life', such as it was, continued also, some very strange arrangements were being entered into by all sides.

During February 1995, for example, ECMM confirmed that on average 10–14 trucks belonging to the 5th Corps made daily excursions into Krajina Serb territory and loaded up with a variety of goods, some of which could loosely be described as 'surplus humanitarian supplies'. Accordingly a tin of canned beef which could not be sold in Krajina for 2 DM, because the people had no money to buy it, would make its way into

Bihac Pocket and end up retailing for 8 DM. Of course, none of this was happening accidentally.

The whole operation was strictly controlled by the 5th Corps and a Mr Pivic, known locally as the 'head of the smugglers', who allegedly controlled the entire black market. Pivic also had a 50 per cent stake in Bihac town's infamous discotheque, The Galaxia, which amazingly defied the Serb gunners and continued to operate right throughout the war. His partner in that venture was a battalion commander in the 502 Brigade of the 5th Corps, and with each of them taking 25 per cent of the profits the remaining 50 per cent went straight into 5th Corps' coffers.[34]

For many others, however, survival was still their only focus, and the story of the old lady who traded her curtains, two bath towels, a table cloth and some bed linen for 17 kg of flour was not an exception. The predicament of these ordinary people was not about to improve either if the spring planting of corn seed and potatoes did not take place. UNHCR was ready to buy the necessary 900 tonnes of seed, but not surprisingly there appeared to be no prospect whatever of the Krajina Serbs allowing a convoy of over 90 trucks to pass unhindered into the Pocket.[35] Clearly it would be of no advantage to the black market or its operators to have the people growing food for themselves.[36]

This particularly convoluted picture became further confused with the return of some 5th Corps soldiers who had been taken prisoners of war by the Serbs and were now released as part of an 'exchange programme' supervised and organised by UNMOs and Red Cross officials. The brutality allegedly associated with the incarceration of this group was recounted to Bill Foxton shortly after their release, and while accepting the subjective nature of the interview, their stories remain nonetheless a terrible indictment of the manner in which the Bosnian Serbs conducted their detention. Zlatko Juricic and Sevad Veladzic, two private soldiers in the 5th Corps' 502 Brigade, may never have heard the expression 'post-traumatic stress disorder' before their captivity, but they certainly know all about it now. Their story provides a graphic explanation of why the international community found it necessary to establish an International War Crimes Tribunal in the first instance.[37]

However, it must be pointed out again that no one side in any phase of the Yugoslav conflict ever had a monopoly when it came to brutalising the enemy, and this was as true in Bihac Pocket as it was anywhere else. In a confidential report to ECMM's regional centre in Zagreb, monitors on the ground confirmed that they were equally concerned that war crimes were being committed by elements of the 5th Corps as well as by the Serbs.[38]

New arrangements

One of the more dramatic developments in the overall scheme of things occurred in Zagreb on 6 March when the chief of staff of the Croatian army, General Janko Bobetko, together with the HVO's General Tihomir Blaskic and the Armija's supreme commander, Rasim Delic, attended a meeting at the presidential palace, together with Tudjman, Ganic and Zubak, and announced to the world's press that all three armies had entered into a formal military alliance and established for the first time a joint headquarters. Of course the ink was barely dry on the paper before the Muslims began refuting Croatian assertions that there was now also a single chain of command, but whatever the reality the mere fact that it happened at all was hugely significant. Bobetko would assume chairmanship of the joint command, whose objectives would include the development of closer links with one another in pursuance of the 'Washington Agreement' and 'The 1992 Agreement on Friendship and Co-operation between Croatia and Bosnia', as well as mutual self-defence against the threat of renewed aggression by the Serbs.

Of equal importance was the fact that this announcement came hot on the heels of a number of 'rabble rousing' statements from both Gojko Susak, Croatia's defence minister, and Borislav Skegro, Croatia's deputy prime minister, to the effect that Croatia was now ready militarily and economically to crush the Krajina Serbs once and for all. While all this was in some measure a response to the announcement two weeks previously in Banja Luka of a formal military and political arrangement between the Krajina and Bosnian Serbs, it was also designed to increase the pressure on Knin to reconsider the relative merits of the Z4 plan. Clearly Tudjman had lost all respect for the international efforts aimed at resolution by peaceful means. Instead he preferred to rely on Croatia's new-found friendship with the United States and his well-founded belief that the Clinton Administration would come to his assistance whenever the going got tough.[39]

Meanwhile at UNPROFOR HQ in Zagreb nobody knew whether the troops were going or staying. This uncertainty was compounded by reports from Knin that an internal power struggle had begun between the moderate Mikelic and the combined forces of Babic and Martic, and save for the relative success of reopening the Zagreb–Belgrade highway through Sector West, the economic agreement of 2 December was all but dead.[40] The omens were anything but good, and it was into this uncertain and volatile environment that another American mediator began operating as he introduced a somewhat novel approach to the business of Balkan mediation – he called it 'knocking heads together'.

Richard Holbrooke, the new US assistant secretary of state, who interestingly enough had spent the previous few years as the US ambassador to Germany, had arrived to save the Balkans, and after several rounds of discussion Tudjman announced on 12 March in Copenhagen that the UN could stay for the time being as long as a new mandate was worked out which physically placed UN troops on Croatia's internationally recognised borders with Bosnia-Hercegovina.

He then flew off to New York to talk all this through with Boutros Boutros-Ghali on 17 March, and while attending the ceremony to mark the anniversary of the Washington Agreement both President Clinton and Madeleine Albright were fulsome in their praise for Dr Tudjman's apparent 'U-turn'. In fact a White House communiqué went further and said that President Clinton had expressed to Dr Tudjman his personal gratitude and admiration for Croatia's decision to accept the further presence of UN forces, thereby avoiding a possible renewal of the war and a widening of the conflict in the region.

Armed with this endorsement and whatever additional understandings he had managed to extract in Washington, Tudjman returned to Zagreb and was immediately confronted with considerable dissatisfaction from elements within the Sabor, and also from the refugee and the displaced population who were still crammed into every spare hotel room, private house, flat, bed-sit, apartment, camp site and guest house across the country.[41]

As details of what had been agreed began to emerge it became clear that the main stumbling block had been ensuring that the word 'Croatia' was included in the mandate, as well as agreement to reduce the size of the UN force and the deployment of a civilian police force to monitor the 25 to 30 crossing points with the Republic Srpska (Croatia) and Bosnia along the international border.[42]

Needless to say, all of this came as something of a shock to the Krajina Serbs – although it was of direct relevance to them they were again the last to be informed. Not surprisingly either they were having none of it, but this worried neither Tudjman, Holbrooke nor Akashi, as the major diplomatic initiative concentrated exclusively on appeasing the Croats. Eventually, after much haggling, some amendments were made to the report which Boutros Boutros-Ghali submitted to the Security Council on 26 March, and on the 31st we got three new resolutions, 981, 982 and 983, which established three separate but interlinked UN missions and extended their mandates to 30 November 1995.[43]

In Croatia we would now have UNCRO (United Nations Confidence Restoration Operation) in Croatia. In Bosnia we would still have UNPROFOR, while in the Former Yugoslav Republic of Macedonia (FYROM) we were to have something called UNPREDEP (United Nations Preventative Deployment). In actual fact nothing much was about to change at all and the contentious issues, like the size of the forces and who exactly was going to sit on the international borders, would all be worked out later on.

After a few days' silence Babic released a statement in Knin, in which he specifically pointed to the absence of any 'confidence' between the citizens of Krajina and Croatia, and it was this lack of confidence which had caused them to resist Croatian rule in the first place. From this perspective nothing had happened in the meantime which indicated that they would ever be treated as anything other than second- or third-class citizens in a state dominated politically by Tudjman's HDZ and socially by the Catholic Church.[44] He had a point.

However, these reservations carried no water with the likes of Holbrooke, Galbraith or Stoltenberg, but somewhat amazingly Babic found support from a totally unexpected quarter. On 3 April the Croatian Human Rights Committee issued a statement in which it claimed that ordinary Croats could only have 'confidence' in their *own* judicial system if all current members of the State Judicial Council, and the president of the Supreme Court, resigned from their positions because the method of their appointment had in the first instance been illegal.[45]

End of the COHA

Back in Bosnia the general situation was deteriorating dramatically. UNHCR convoys continued to be denied access to the eastern enclaves of Zepa, Srebrenica and Gorazde, which in turn led to increased suffering by the population and generated even more correspondence between the Pale authorities and Akashi. On the military front the situation was also quite bleak, and when Akashi went to Sarajevo on 12 March in an attempt to keep the COHA on the rails the plane in which he was travelling was fired upon as it landed, leaving a rather large hole in the rear section of the fuselage.

The Serbs were immediately blamed for the attack, but it later emerged, and was confirmed separately by Greek EC monitors on the ground in the city, that the shots were fired from Butimir, which was a Bosnian Muslim government controlled area.

Akashi first met Izetbegovic and then went on to Pale the following day to see Karadzic. Little was achieved, with both sides continuing to hurl abuse at one another. With Zubak and Ganic celebrating the anniversary of the Washington Agreement with Tudjman and Clinton in the United States, Izetbegovic travelled next to Bonn where he made the most amazing statements. He began by effectively advocating renewed conflict as the only means to solve the problems in Bosnia.

'If the Serbs do not accept the Contact Group Peace Plan', he announced, 'then we must fight, we have no other choice.' The very next day he apparently decided to perform a U-turn and declared that the Muslims would not launch an offensive against the Serbs, even if the Serbs failed to accept the CGPP by the time the COHA expired at the end of April. 'We will not start an offensive on the 1st of May, but we will not agree formally to extend the ceasefire', he confidently told reporters.

He concluded by saying that his motto still remained 'when it is a question of war or peace we will negotiate when we can, and fight when we must'. The problem now was which version to believe. It did not take long to find out. As UNMOs and monitors on the ground across Bosnia plotted and reported the redeployment of thousands of Armija troops it was clear to even the most ill-informed observers that something was about to happen – and it did. At 5 a.m. on the morning of 20 March Bosnian government troops launched a huge offensive in north-central Bosnia in an area known as the Majevica hills.

Beginning with an infantry attack in the direction of Lukavica, Stolice and Priboj, and supported by artillery and mortar fire, the government forces set about trying to change the configuration of the Confrontation Line in order primarily to take Tuzla out of Serb artillery range. It did not work, and two hours later, not surprisingly, Serb shells began raining in on Tuzla town. As the morning wore on the attack began to peter out, helped no doubt by some very heavy snowfalls. During the next two days both sides settled into a pattern of minor skirmishing and reciprocal shelling.

At precisely the same time that morning a second attack was also launched by Izetbegovic's troops in the area of Vlasic mountain. Again the objective was to shift the Confrontation Line sufficiently to take Zenica, and if possible Travnik also, outside the range of Bosnian Serb artillery, but this proved too ambitious and before long Serb shells were crashing down on Travnik too.

By Wednesday this assault had evaporated as well, and generally the Muslims were left licking their wounds with precious little to show for their efforts. Attacking uphill against well-prepared defensive positions is difficult enough at the best of times, but attempting it in daylight, and in heavy snow, surely borders on the suicidal. If the Muslims were seeking to record a psychological victory of some description there were several easier targets which they could have opted for without suffering as many casualties as they did.

This of course begs the question as to what was really going on, and who was pulling what strings. It was certainly arguable that the Bosnian government had now adopted a dual approach to the ongoing situation, but on the other hand there appeared to be no correlation at all between the international face of Bosnian politics and the military activity of Izetbegovic's generals on the ground. Either the military commanders were acting independently, which was highly unlikely, or the recent political statements were designed for international consumption only and a hidden agenda was in operation all the time with which all of the key personnel were familiar and concurred. These attacks were a clear, unambiguous, deliberate breach of the COHA, and the international community should have immediately condemned the Sarajevo government for them. This did not happen, and the absence of any formal rebuke effectively gave a clear signal to the Muslims to carry on.

Worse still it then emerged that generals Bobetko, Delic and Blaskic were all actually in Travnik at that time and co-ordinating what had now become combined HV, HVO and Armija operations against the Serbs. Bobetko then appeared on TV explaining what a great job they were all doing, and while this provided clear unequivocal evidence that both Tudjman and Izetbegovic, through their generals, were willing conspirators to breach the COHA not a single reprimand was forthcoming from the international community.[46] In fact the Muslims had never wanted to be part of the process in the first place, and their attitude is best illustrated by the findings of an ECMM team who visited the town of Bugojno in central Bosnia in February 1995.

At this point the entire place had the appearance of an armed encampment as hundreds of Armija troops thronged the dirty battle-scarred town. There was no evidence whatever that anyone was preparing for peace or even attempting to harmonise relations with the local Croat minority.[47] Instead there was overwhelming evidence of military preparation for the next phase of the war where in order to psyche themselves up they had demolished the old partisan graveyard in the centre of the town.[48]

As the days began to stretch into weeks the Armija continued their attacks, with unconfirmed reports suggesting that the Stolice communications relay tower north-east of Tuzla had been captured from the Serbs. However, apart from other small gains around Lukavica, there was nothing to indicate that any major changes to the Confrontation Line had actually taken place. In the Travnik/Vlasic mountain area shelling continued unrelentingly as the Armija continued to press home their attack, but this time the Line was moving significantly with the Serbs vacating anything up to 60 square kilometres. In retaliation, on 24 and 25 March the Serbs shelled Konjic, the supposedly 'safe area' of the Gorazde, and locations to the north and east of Mostar, causing civilian casualties in all three areas.

And then to confuse matters even further it emerged that a meeting had taken place between President Milosevic and Muhamed Filipovic, Izetbegovic's special envoy,[49] where apparently it was agreed that in return for Belgrade's recognition of Bosnia's territorial integrity and sovereignty, and promotion of the principles in the CGPP, the Sarajevo government would be prepared to agree to the abolition of sanctions, and would agree to permit close economic links between the Republic Srpska and Serbia/Montenegro in similar manner to the proposed monetary and customs union between the Federation and Croatia.

The Croatian media immediately began speculating that yet another 'secret agreement' had been concluded, this time between Milosevic and Izetbegovic, which would result in mutual recognition and the acceptance of a 'special status' for the Bosnian Serbs. While there is little doubt that the meeting took place it is highly unlikely that any deal of the nature reported was actually agreed.

A more realistic interpretation would suggest that this was yet another double-cross by Milosevic which was solely intended to put further pressure on Karadzic to accept the CGPP, which in turn would facilitate the lifting of sanctions against both Serbia and Montenegro. The only positive aspect of the meeting was not that anything had been agreed, because in reality nothing had, but rather the fact that for the first time in years Serbs and Muslims had actually managed to sit down together in the same room and talk to one another. It wasn't much progress but at least it was a start.

Meanwhile, Yasushi Akashi spoke of his grave concern that the parties to the conflict appeared determined to plunge Bosnia into a new war. The offensive actions of Armija were, he said, a clear breach of the COHA, and he singled out the Bosnian government for their lack of co-operation in implementing the provisions of the COHA, and appealed for restraint as renewed diplomatic efforts got underway.

Needless to say, all of this fell on deaf ears and at the 7th session of the SDA's Main Board (Convention) in Sarajevo on 27 March it became abundantly clear just where Izetbegovic and his followers were coming from – and even more importantly where they thought they were going. Following some convoluted logic it transpired that they were under the impression they were conducting a diplomatic offensive abroad and simultaneously a military counter-offensive at home.[50]

Haris Silajdzic in his address to the same meeting alleged that more than 70,000 Muslims had fled the area of Sandzak, which straddles the border between Serbia and Montenegro, within the past year as a result Serbian persecution. This was totally without foundation, but such rhetoric virtually ensured that the proposed 'Declaration on the Violation of Human Rights and Freedoms of Bosniac Muslims in Sandzak and other parts of Serbia and Montenegro' would be approved by the Convention with a large majority.[51]

The deliberate introduction of the Sandzak issue, and the attempt to label those who lived there as 'Bosniacs', quite frankly defied logic unless the Muslims now believed that they were sufficiently well armed to take the fight to the Serbs, or knew the United States and Germany were about to enter the equation on their side – or both. Certainly most independent observers were baffled at the arrogance of their new positions.

In a confidential report to all EU foreign ministers, ECMM HQ in Zagreb identified that the Sarajevo government had now begun using the Armija as a political tool. The prospects for the immediate future were considered to be anything but good.[52]

Unification of the Serbs

Meanwhile, in Croatia trouble was now brewing on a number of fronts with the Krajina Serb leadership split down the middle on how far they should trust the Croatian government. On 2 March 20 delegates to Krajina's Assembly tabled a motion of 'no confidence' in Prime Minister Mikelic. This was followed abruptly by a public denunciation of Mikelic by Milan Martic, who also called for his dismissal on grounds of incompetence and corruption. Mikelic, one-time friend of Fikret Abdic and the current advocate of closer links with Croatia proper, then launched a stinging attack on Martic. However, Mikelic survived by 37 votes to 25.

Secure for a while longer Mikelic set about removing those whom he considered to be a direct threat to him within the administration, but ironically the net result of his purge turned out to be a strengthening of Foreign Minister Babic's position. Long term he knew he would find it hard to survive. The issue which could finish him was looming on the horizon. On 21 April Boutros Boutros-Ghali was due to publish his report, which would attempt to reconcile both sides in relation to UNSC Resolution 981 and confirm the continuing presence of the UN in Krajina, but before it was even published reports in Western newspapers stated that Croatia would only accept 'white battalions' in whatever force the UN decided to replace UNPROFOR with. This was immediately refuted by the Croatian government, and on 13 April the Foreign Ministry vehemently denied accusations that Croatia had ever expressed racist or chauvinist attitudes towards members of UN forces from Asia and Africa.[53]

While the denial may have been emphatic not everyone was convinced, and an ECMM report on 20 April threw a totally different light on the matter.[54] Nevertheless, and seemingly undeterred by all this 'bad press', Croatia's foreign minister, Mate Granic, continued to insist that UN troops be deployed along the international border with Bosnia and thereby physically confirm to the world the sovereignty and territorial integrity of Croatia.

While the Croats continued their public campaign to influence the secretary-general's report, the Krajina Serbs, in anticipation of being 'sold out' by the international community, sent a delegation to the 50th session of the Bosnian Serb's Assembly which, conveniently enough, was taking place just across the border in Sanski Most between 15 and 17 April. However, it quickly became clear that this was no 'ordinary' meeting when Milan Martic turned up accompanied by the leaders of Krajina's army and church. On the Bosnian Serb side Karadzic presided over the entire proceedings, with General Mladic also in attendance – as indeed were the leaders of the Serbian Orthodox Church.

From the outset Karadzic launched into a blistering attack on Mladic for his failure to hold the line against both the Muslims and Croats in recent weeks,[55] and some reports suggested that Karadzic had actually tried to relieve him of his command.[56] In reply Mladic attempted to shift the blame to the political authorities for failing to supply him with much-needed fuel and equipment and proclaimed that the continuing rift between Belgrade and Pale was the greatest tragedy for all Serbs. He then delivered a very pessimistic prediction for the future, admitting that in his opinion the BSA did not have the capability to achieve an overall military victory, nor could they count on retaining indefinite control over 70 per cent of Bosnia. He then demanded that the politicians establish optimal war goals in order that his soldiers would at least know what objectives they were dying for.

This was not well received by the politicians, and for many it looked as if the ghost of the 49/51 division of Bosnia was now being advocated by their own military supremo. If that were the case, and it is not beyond the bounds of possibility that Mladic may well have been delivering this specific message on behalf of Milosevic himself, the members of parliament were not prepared to entertain him. Their problem now was that they could no longer trust their top general, or the advice he was offering. All of this seemed to vindicate the attempts made by Karadzic at Prijedor on 14 March to curtail his power and influence. To compound matters further it then emerged that Mladic had recently been having regular meetings in Zvornik with General Perisic, Milosevic's obedient JNA Chief of Staff, and had also been making regular visits to Belgrade,[57] as indeed had several of his top commanders.

Clearly Mladic was not operating on the same wavelength as Karadzic, but there did not appear to be any obvious or immediate solution to the problem. Equally and irrespective of what agenda Mladic was really following, the Bosnian Serbs still needed him and his army to protect them from massive retribution on several fronts, and so for all the wrong reasons he was allowed to remain in power. As the meeting continued Karadzic's contempt for his general became even more evident and eventually the Assembly voted that Mladic should begin to push for a final military victory if an overall political solution was not reached within a short time. With that out of the way the delegates next turned to the even more volatile matter of uniting the military and political resources of both the Bosnian and Krajina Serbs, and after the required debate they agreed to begin a unification process almost at once. If this arrangement became a *fait accompli* it would in all probability be far easier for both groups of Serbs to consolidate their current positions. This was bad news for a large number of people.

It was certainly bad news for the Croatian government who immediately recognised that any attack by them into Krajina might now bring the Bosnian Serbs down on top of them as well. It was even worse news for the Bosnian Croats and Muslims who were now set on a course to try and take back whatever land they could grab in central Bosnia, and it was particularly bad news for the international mediators who condemned the new alliance as a further obstacle to an overall settlement. What none of these people made any attempt to understand was why the Serbs had found it necessary to band themselves together in this manner in the first instance. No one had made any attempt to see the situation from the Serb perspective because had they done so they would immediately have recognised that the Serbs genuinely believed that their 'backs were to the wall' and that the whole world was set against them. And there were compelling reasons for harbouring these beliefs.

In Croatia, Tudjman and his government had become completely indifferent to, and intolerant of, the genuine fears, wishes, aspirations and reservations of the Krajina Serbs. They got away with this because neither the United States nor Germany were prepared to put a stop to it, and were now in any case aligned with the Croats in pursuit of their own long-term objectives in the region as a whole. Equally, the UN organisation on the ground had now become totally impotent and served only as a target for mockery and ridicule, and for the occasional bored sniper in and around Sarajevo. Karadzic's attempts to stabilise the situation in Bosnia continued to be rubbished by all and sundry as the relative success of the Carter initiative received no recognition from anyone.

The BSA were not the ones who broke the COHA, and they were not the ones in daily violation of what remained of it, but nonetheless the Bosnian Serbs, both military and political, continued to be painted as the villains. In this scenario it mattered little what Martic, Karadzic or any other Serb politician tried to say or do, and they were all acutely aware of it. Accordingly they decided to band together in what really amounted to nothing more than a measure of mutual self-defence, but the world condemned them for it.

Karadzic was again accused of promoting the notion of 'Greater Serbia' when nothing of the sort was the case, but it suited other bigger agendas to tout this particular line. In this context, then, the UN bears some responsibility because Akashi knew the real story and in writing to Kofi Annan on 26 April he identified clearly what had really been going on in Sanski Most: 'Reports from the session indicate a serious rift having developed between the military and political leaderships in Pale, aggravated by the ongoing economic blockade and the struggle for limited financial and material resources', he wrote. 'It would appear', he said, 'that Karadzic and the Bosnian Serb political establishment face the prospect of a further erosion of authority; a process tacitly encouraged by Milosevic. The meeting between Milosevic and Mladic in Belgrade on April 21st, which was allegedly convened without Karadzic's knowledge, would support that contention.'[58]

Later in the same document Akashi identified that those aligned in opposition to Karadzic had been meeting secretly in Belgrade and now included Milosevic, Mikelic, Fikret Abdic and Mladic,[59] so it can hardly have come as a great surprise to anyone that Karadzic, Martic and Babic decided to join forces in order to ward off the potential threat which a military alliance of that quartet would pose. But this was never explained properly in the media and before long it became quite clear that the West had abandoned its neutrality in this conflict and was about to commence the business of extracting several 'pounds of flesh' from the Bosnian Serbs, and anyone else remotely connected to them.[60]

And then to compound matters the International War Crimes Tribunal in The Hague released a statement in which it announced that among others Mladic and Karadzic were now under investigation for the alleged commission of war crimes. It made no sense whatever to release a statement of that nature at the very time Akashi, General Smith and the UN civil affairs co-ordinator, Enrique Aguilar, were frantically commuting between Sarajevo and Pale trying to shore up the COHA which was now dying on its feet. Whatever chance they had of convincing Karadzic to cooperate in extending the COHA, or maybe even replacing it with something better, was completely destroyed with this announcement, which could not have been more ill-timed had all the international representatives sat down together and planned it.

Tensions rise between Knin and Zagreb

Meanwhile, back in Croatia, toleration of any Serb, be they of the Krajina or Bosnian variety, had once again hit an all-time low after Dubrovnik airport was shelled again on 19 April. What made this attack different from previous ones was that it took place at the very moment Croatian prime minister, Valentic, two of his cabinet colleagues, the British, American and French military attachés, the local ECMM team and a throng of media personnel were actually lined up on the tarmac to officially reopen the airport.

As they were about to begin the ceremony a 122-mm mortar shell came whistling through the air and impacted near some parked aircraft about 200 metres from the terminal building. Undeterred, the ceremony continued amid the singing of patriotic Croatian songs, and Valentic eventually declared the airport reopened.[61] However, the significance of the interruption was lost on no one and merely confirmed to the ministers present that something would have to be done as a matter of urgency to dissuade the Serbs from continuing with this policy.

One way of frustrating the Serbs was to make it almost impossible for them to travel along the highway between Sectors East and West, although the economic agreement expressly permitted them to do just that. Almost immediately the Croatian police began taking several hours to clear each individual Serb vehicle through their checkpoints. Technically, of course, the Croats were still permitting the Serbs freedom of movement along the road. The problem was actually getting access to it, and before long huge tail-backs developed on the Serb sides which made a mockery of the whole process. This was a calculated provocation by the Croats designed to achieve nothing except a further deterioration in relations between the two sides in the expectation that some incident might occur which would provide President Tudjman with an excuse to send the army across the Confrontation Line in an attempt to evict the Krajina Serbs who had been living in the area for hundreds of years.

By the 24th Milan Martic had almost given them that excuse. Speaking on Radio Knin on the 23rd he said that he was tired of writing warning letters to Boutros Boutros-Ghali and other officials in charge of the negotiating process:

> Since we cannot bring our fuel to the Krajina nor any other material I have informed the UN that I have ordered the highway to be closed for 24 hours commencing on 24 April 06:00 hrs. If this measure does not improve the situation then the RSK leadership will decide on the suspension of the economic relations with Croatia, because we do not want the RSK to be underestimated.

On Sunday there were about 70 Serb trucks on the highway at Lipovac crossing point in Sector East waiting for clearance to continue towards the RSK, first into Sector West and thereafter onwards into Sector North via the Republic Srpska. On Saturday about 400 Serb cars were lined up queuing for petrol at the Croat service station in Nova Gradiska – but were unable to buy any fuel.[62]

The Croatian response was totally predictable, and a government statement was issued immediately to the effect that the Serbs had permanently closed the road. No mention at all was made of the fact that the closure was only to have effect for 24 hours, nor was any explanation given of the Serbs' reasons for taking this action in the first place.

Both sides had now raised the stakes considerably and it was surely no coincidence that on the morning of the 24th Martic found himself chairing a session of his Supreme Defence Council which had to address among other things the matter of whether or not the Krajina Serbs could live with the terms of the latest offering from the UN Security Council – namely, Resolution 988.

After prolonged discussion they concluded that UN peace forces, whatever they were called, should continue to be stationed in Krajina in pursuance of the Vance plan (1992), the Ceasefire Agreement of 29 April 1994 and the Economic Agreement of 2 December 1994. While the name 'UNCRO' was totally unacceptable the Knin government nonetheless remained ready to co-operate with the UN to find a peaceful solution, but only for as long as the UN was prepared to continue treating the Republic Srpska Krajina as a state of the Serbian Nation.

With that out of the way, Martic, Babic and Mikelic then met with the

ICFY co-chairman, Thorvald Stoltenberg, who had just arrived in Knin to discuss the matter of reopening the highway,[63] and no doubt the four of them were very impressed by the 'diplomatic' and conciliatory statement issued that afternoon by Hrvoje Sarinic, on behalf of President Tudjman, which said: 'If the Serbs do not open the highway at 0600 hrs on Tuesday, the Croatian police will do it for them.' Clearly the Croats were making big efforts to avoid an escalation of the problem!

In any event logic and reason prevailed in Knin and at 5 a.m. the following morning the barriers on both sides of the dual carriageway were withdrawn. At the subsequent press conference Martic denied that he had capitulated in the face of the Croatian ultimatum, preferring instead to make another attempt at explaining why he had closed the road in the first place, and in a rare conciliatory gesture concluded the matter by saying 'we will stop the Economic Agreement completely if Croatia blocks the highway, [but] on the other hand, if the situation improves, we will develop our relations with Croatia'.[64]

What he did not know, and Stoltenberg did not tell him either, was that on this issue the Croats had already decided how the matter of the highway was going to be resolved and that their preparations were already well underway. For weeks the Croats had been ignoring the provisions of both the Vance plan and the Ceasefire Agreement of 29 March 1994 by moving personnel, tanks, artillery, mortars, communications equipment and a plethora of other hardware into positions all around Sector West, which would allow them to mount an offensive on the UNPA if and when they got the green light from Zagreb. They had also taken a series of measures to defend themselves from any Bosnian Serb incursion from across the Sava river which might materialise in support of the 18th Corps in Okucani. And this was not done secretly. In fact everyone operating in the area was completely aware of what was going on. To his credit, Henrik Markus, who was now operating as ECMM's liaison officer at the UN's Sector West HQ in Daruvar, sent a detailed report to ECMM HQ on the 24th in which he catalogued exactly what was going on down to the number of troops involved, where they were deployed, what they were actually doing and the number of tanks and guns which were deployed in support of them.[65]

If the Croatian activity was as blatant as this, and there is no doubt whatever that it was, then the question arises as to why no international pressure of any kind was applied to encourage them to stop. The answer to that is very simple – nobody wanted them to stop – and the prevailing strategy, which was primarily of American origin, demanded that the Serbs receive a 'bloody nose', and the sooner the better. The problem now was that Martic had taken the wind out of all their sails by backing down, so another pretext would have to be found before the serious action could begin. And as luck would have it the highway provided that opportunity once again.

Trouble on the roads

On the evening of 28 April an incident took place at the INA petrol station on the Nova Gradiska side of Sector West which caused an already tense situation to escalate out of all proportion. Essentially a fracas broke out when a Croat named Sugic claimed to have identified a Serb named Blagijevic whom he immediately accused of killing his brother at some point during 1991. Sugic then produced a knife and stabbed the Serb several times, killing him in the process. The Croatian police arrested Sugic and took both him and the victim away, but when they then refused to release Blagijevic's remains to his family for burial his brother hijacked two Croatian vehicles, which were driving along the road at 9.40p.m., in an attempt to force the Croatian police to comply with his family's wishes. They ignored him completely, apparently oblivious to the growing tension.

Later, at 10.30p.m., someone opened fire on a white VW Golf as it passed through Sector West and one of the occupants received two bullets in the head. A minibus travelling immediately behind crashed in the confusion and one passenger died instantly having been crushed beneath the vehicle; a second died on the way to hospital. The five who were unhurt were taken away for questioning, this time by the Serbs. At 10.30p.m. UNCIVPOL then decided that it had now become too dangerous to carry out patrols so at midnight the highway was officially closed again, although several people decided to ignore this development and drove up and down it regardless.

By 7a.m. the following day ECMM, UNCIVPOL and UN Civil Affairs were all actively involved in trying to bring both sides together. Eventually they were rewarded for their efforts when at 12.15p.m. the Croatian police and Serb authorities sat down together to iron out their differences. An agreement was reached that all personnel and vehicles involved in the incidents would be handed back at 4p.m. By 6p.m. this exchange was complete, but the highway, which should have reopened one hour later, remained closed.[66] HINA News reported that the road would be open on Monday, 1 May 1995 and Tuesday, 2 May 1995 between 6a.m. and 8p.m., and from Wednesday, 3 May 1995 on a round-the-clock basis.[67] But the Serbs were far from happy, something which was clearly reflected in the advice Colonel Babic, the commander of the Serbs' 18th Corps in Okucani, was now giving to his people: 'Those Serbs who want to go to the petrol station again can do that,' he said, 'but they expose their throats to Croatian blades.'[68]

The Serbs were also well aware of what the Croats were up to just across the Bosnian border in the Livanjsko Polje, and in his daily report from Knin on the night of 30 April Irish EU monitor Jim Fitzgibbon reported on HV build-up activities at several points along the entire Confrontation Line. Fuelling what now amounted to collective paranoia,

Radio Knin began broadcasting a statement by Prime Minister Mikelic that was not designed to promote compromise: 'Attempts from the Croatian side to attribute responsibility to the Serbian side, when the incident has been provoked by the assassination of a Krajina Serb citizen have to be rejected without reservation', he said. 'The highway will remain closed for safety reasons, and a further escalation [of the situation] cannot be excluded.'

In tandem with this the Radio station then reported that the Croatian army was continuing with small-scale combat operations in the Livanjsko Polje and that between 60–70 122-mm mortar rounds had landed in the village of Unitsa, while 30 enemy (HV) vehicles had been spotted in Dabar. This amounted to very bad news, but what very few Krajina Serbs really understood was that the Croats had been operating to a completely different agenda for a considerable time now and were only in need of an excuse to begin a huge new offensive. Equipped with an arsenal of 'new toys' which had been pouring into the country since 1991,[69] Susak, Bobetko and the HV generals had been eagerly looking for an opportunity to play with them, and the closure of the highway, while understandable from the Serb perspective – and perhaps even justified by objective analysis – provided them with the opportunity they were looking for.

Sometime after 2 a.m. on 1 May, which ironically just happened to be a United Nations holiday, a Croatian car was travelling between Pozega and Pakrac along the infamous 'Dragovic road'. Why anyone would risk this particular journey at night, and especially when the overall situation was so volatile, is beyond comprehension, but the facts remain that two Croats took it upon themselves to make this journey along what surely must rate as the loneliest, most eerie stretch of road in the entire world.

This 'Dragovic road' was where hundreds of Serbs used to live before the war, but when the fighting started in 1991 they were routed by the Croats who systematically destroyed their homes and burned their property to ensure they would never ever come back. If one ever wished to see the effects of ethnic cleansing without risking a trip to Bosnia then this was the place to visit. In any event, on this the first morning of a brand new summer, the Serbs high in the hills overlooking the road opened fire on the car and the two occupants were injured.[70]

Croatia launches a special police action

At 2.30 a.m. the commander of the Croatian army's operational zone in Bjelovar contacted the United Nations Sector HQ in Daruvar and announced that a 'special police action' to reopen the highway was about to commence. By 4.30 a.m. all UN troops in Sector West were on full alert, and at 5 a.m. Hrvoje Sarinic made contact with the UN's deputy force commander in Zagreb and admitted that a major Croatian attack on western Slavonia (Sector West) was about to commence in order to reopen the highway; he insisted that this would be a 'limited police action', whatever that was supposed to be.

By the time Roddy de Normann, ECMM's deputy head of Regional Centre Zagreb, which had responsibility for monitoring life in Sector West, was activating his operations staff at 5.15 a.m. the first Croatian troops were already on their way into battle with 500 of them, supported by 12 tanks, pushing eastwards from Nova Gradiska. On the western side of the sector an unspecified number of troops were on the move across the Separation Zone, while 600 special police, a full infantry battalion and an artillery regiment were deployed around Lipik and Pakrac. Before long Bosnian Serb artillery south of the Sava river began engaging the Croatian guns supporting the attack, and by 10.30 a.m. over 360 shells had landed in the general vicinity of Nova Gradiska.[71]

Whatever else this attack might have been it certainly was *not* a 'limited police action'; neither was it an impromptu response to the most recent incident on the Dragovic road.[72] This was a pre-planned, premeditated, deliberate escalation of the conflict, which displayed no regard whatever for the plethora of international treaties and agreements which the Croatian government had supposedly entered into in good faith.

They had now reverted to nothing more than 'jack-boot diplomacy' and 'negotiation at the point of a gun' on the very day that the COHA expired in Bosnia, and with the very real possibility of dragging the Bosnian Serbs into the fighting in Croatia as well. Once again the Croats had chosen to express their gratitude to the contributing countries of the United Nations by treating them with contempt, and by 9 a.m. the Jordanian battalion had begun taking casualties as Croatian artillery and small arms fire rained down on top of them. What exactly this was supposed to achieve is anyone's guess, but clearly the UN were no longer to be treated as the 'dear guests' Franjo Tudjman had been so keen to label them back in January.

By 11 a.m., when Mate Granic arrived to brief the Diplomatic Corps in Zagreb, Croatian forces had advanced up to 3 kilometres into the sector on its eastern side, with another 2,000 of them on their way from Slavonski Brod in order to cut the road between Okucani and Stara Gradiska and thereby prevent any possible link up between the shell-shocked 18th Corps and their spiritual brothers in the Bosnian Serb army south of the Sava river. In his statement Granic persisted with the line that what was taking place was a 'limited police action in pursuit of terrorists' who had provoked the situation in the first place by attacking vehicles passing along the highway and the Dragovic road. He continued to insult his audience by telling them that the aim of the operation was to reopen the highway and provide security for those using it, not to overrun the entire sector, and that Croatia remained committed to a peaceful reintegration of the occupied areas and continuation with the Economic Agreement.

He got away with this preposterous explanation because none of those present knew enough to contradict him, but by lunchtime the truth was beginning to emerge – thanks largely to the presence of ECMM on the ground and some UNMOs operating in the area. Now for the first time a government statement admitted that the Croatian army were indeed involved and closing on the Serbs from all sides. By mid-afternoon it became clear that the operation had three objectives: first to secure the perimeter of the sector; second, to secure the pontoon bridge at Jasenovac; and third, to push along the highway. At this point the Croats began claiming that Jasenovac had fallen that morning and that HV artillery was within shelling range of Bosanska Gradiska and the Stara Gradiska. If this was true then the 18th Corps were in dire trouble, but UN reports suggested that much of this was propaganda and that in fact the Croatian advance was proving far more difficult than first reported.

Contributing in large measure to this was the revelation by UNCRO that 15 members of UNCIVPOL, their two interpreters and 89 members of the Argentinian and Nepalese battalions had been taken hostage by the Serbs in order to provide a human shield against the advancing Croats. In response to this the Croats commandeered several UN vehicles and as a convoy of tanks pushed west along the highway towards Okucani a white UN APC and a white UN Landrover appeared at the head of the HV column.[73] This was 'perfidy' and in clear breach of the Geneva Conventions. Did any one international grouping object? No they did not.

In tandem with this Radio Knin broadcast a general mobilisation of all Krajina Serb reservists and – following the removal of their heavy weapons from the various UN-monitored weapons storage sites, and a meeting of the Supreme Defence Council in Knin – matters took a turn for the worst just after 4p.m. when five artillery shells fell on the city of Karlovac and another four impacted in Sisak. In retaliation for these attacks two Croatian air force MIG 21s took off from Pleso and just after 5.15p.m. attempted to destroy the bridge over the Sava at Stara Gradiska. They failed, succeeding in dropping only two bombs on top of the 18th Corps personnel who were minding the bridge. The introduction of combat aircraft into a 'police action', however, left no one in any doubt as to what Zagreb's intentions really amounted to at this time.

When ECMM's Roddy de Normann eventually got to see Brigadier General Plestina, the Croatian army's senior liaison officer, at 7p.m. he did admit that Croatia was worried about international reaction to this unprovoked attack, but continued nonetheless to promote the 'official line' that this was an operation of 'liberation'. In a convoluted logic he managed to persist with this line while simultaneously admitting that the Croatian strategy was to squeeze the sector from all sides, leaving a narrow corridor in the south through which all the Serbs could escape to Bosnia.[74]

Obviously one man's 'ethnic cleansing' is another's 'operation of liberation' – it just depends on how you interpret it and who happens to be backing you at the time!

In any event, while Plestina was trotting out the HDZ party line, another meeting was underway out in the UN's Pleso Camp near Zagreb airport where Akashi was frantically trying to cobble a deal together which would at least freeze the situation on the ground and thereby enable some dialogue to take place. Having rushed back from Sarajevo where the COHA now lay in tatters, he began what would amount to over six hours of mediation between the Knin and Zagreb governments.

However, and notwithstanding a UN Security Council condemnation of what the Croats were doing, no progress of any description was made. Eventually, at 9.30 p.m., Akashi put forward a UN proposal which contained three essential elements: (a) an immediate ceasefire; (b) the release of all UN personnel held by the Serbs; and (c) a return by all parties to the positions they occupied on the ground as of 30 April.

The Serbs, represented by Mikelic, Prijic and General Loncar, immediately accepted but Sarinic, on behalf of the Croatian government, was having none of it. Instead, and knowing the Serbs would reject it, he demanded that the highway, together with a 2-kilometre strip either side of it, be put under exclusive Croatian control. This was totally unacceptable to the Serbs because the loss of the land link to the Republic Srpska this proposal would create would form a Serb enclave right in the middle of Croatia which would in essence become little more than a large open prison. In that context, and bearing in mind the geographical proximity of Sector West to Jasenovac, the Serb delegation could never agree to what, from their perspective, was little better than herding their people once again into another 'Ustasha concentration camp'.

Sarinic was well aware of this, which of course leads one to suspect that was why he made the suggestion in the first place. At that point, not surprisingly, the talks broke down. As towns and villages throughout Croatia and Krajina observed a black-out that night both sides regrouped and reorganised to face what the morrow would bring. For the Serbs, however, it would just be more bad news, and Foreign Minister Babic knew this only too well. In a statement issued on his behalf that evening he accused the UN of becoming little more than 'an instrument of Croatian foreign policy', given that they were unable and unwilling to take any action to protect the Serbs living in the so-called UN Protected Area of Sector West. By any objective standard he had a case.

When dawn broke the next morning it became obvious that the Croats were intent on resuming where they had left off the previous night as MIG 21 fighters swept up and down the length of the highway. By 6.45 a.m. Croatian artillery was back in action at the rate of five rounds per minute in order to 'soften up' the Serb defences before the next push by the infantry who were now arriving from a variety of bases across Croatia.[75]

By 8.00 a.m. the squeeze on Sector West had recommenced with the position of both the 18th Corps and the civilian population becoming more untenable by the minute. At 10.10 a.m. the Croats unleashed an intense shelling of the Sava bridge at Stara Gradiska, across which over 5,000 civilians had already moved into Bosnia, and launched two air-strikes against the nearby 18th Corps headquarters. The writing was now on the wall, and in fact the Serb commander in Gavrinici had already looked for a ceasefire which would be supervised by the UN. All he got in response was a demand to surrender. Then, at 10.25 a.m., a number of explosions rocked the centre of Zagreb where Dr Jan Gallus, an EC monitor from Slovakia and working with RC Zagreb, was one of the first on the scene.[76]

Meanwhile, back in Okucani the situation had deteriorated further as the Croatian advance continued, and in Pakrac a surrender was now being negotiated for the 800 Serb troops who found themselves totally surrounded by the Croats and only able to survive because they still held the high ground in the area. By 2 p.m., however, Okucani had fallen as thousands of civilians grabbed what few possessions they could carry and fled southwards into Bosnia rather than take their chances with their new conquerors.

And then just before 4 p.m. President Tudjman appeared on television to announce that the action to retake the highway was complete and that western Slavonia had been 'liberated'. In using the term 'liberated' the president clearly chose to indulge in another bout of historical revisionism because had he bothered to consult either the 1981 or 1991 census he would have discovered that this very area had always been overwhelmingly Serb since the days of the Vojna Krajina.

This very point was actually made to Sarinic the following day by ECMM's head of mission, Ambassador Albert Turot (France), when he asked whether some of the concepts in the Z4 plan which pertained to areas which had a Serb majority population might now be implemented in Sector West. The answer he got made it absolutely clear that *no* local political autonomy whatsoever would be granted to the Serbs, and that the priority now was to identify 'war criminals' and try them either before a tribunal in Croatia or else defer proceedings to The Hague.[77]

What Tudjman, Susak, Granic, Sarinic and their HV storm troopers had actually been involved in for the past two days had been nothing short of 'precision ethnic cleansing', and the imposition of their collective will by military force on a Serb minority who genuinely feared for their very lives if compelled to live in the same jurisdiction as people whom they believed to be post-communist neo-fascists. And the international community, the UN, the United States and Germany stood back and let it all happen, effectively without reproach.

At 9 p.m. Haram Basik agreed to surrender his 600 troops in Pakrac to the UN, as well as handing over all heavy weapons within 48 hours and all other lighter equipment within four days, while over 5,000 Serb civilians fled across the Sava bridge into Bosnia. Another salvo of rockets descended on Zagreb the following morning as pictures of Peter Galbraith visiting the wounded in hospital were flashed around the world, and with Sarinic in close support the US ambassador launched into a condemnation of the Serbs for perpetrating these attacks. Needless to say, their was no condemnation whatever of the Croats for starting this latest round of bloodletting in the first instance, but as always that would have been expecting far too much. Galbraith was correct, of course, in so far as he was prepared to go.

The indiscriminate shelling of civilian targets is always wrong, it is a breach of international humanitarian law, and can never be excused no matter what the circumstances, but Galbraith should also have asked why this happened in the first place. There was a Serb perspective, but no one seemed remotely interested in examining it. Instead, and unfortunately, we were treated to yet another round of Orwellian diplomacy.

There appeared to be little or no balance in the diplomatic response to these events and the opinion of those international agents who reported on them seemed to count for nothing. The absence of objectivity in the immediate aftermath of the invasion effectively approved this latest spate of ethnic cleansing and all that went with it. And while bad enough in itself, unfortunately there was much worse to follow.

While all of this was dominating every international news bulletin, Akashi was frantically trying to stop the fighting in Sector West and later announced that he had obtained agreement between the Croatian government and the Knin authorities which would facilitate a ceasefire. Throughout the night Akashi's officials hammered out the details of a plan which would allow UN troops to escort those remaining Serbs who wished to leave as far as the Sava river. Their efforts were rewarded on the morning of 5 May with renewed Croatian air-strikes, which in turn sparked off a fresh battle in and around Pakrac town.[78] The UN Security Council responded to this, at last, by condemning all violations of the old ceasefire agreement of 29 March 1994 and demanded an immediate cessation of hostilities in the Sector. Akashi and General Janvier then set out for Daruvar to implement this demand, but their helicopter was denied permission to land in Sector West by the Croats.

In the midst of this confusion UN troops who thought they were going to be involved in a peaceful separation of the forces now found themselves caught in the middle of renewed fighting and in order to save their own skins they battened down the hatches of their armoured vehicles and left the area as fast as they could. This was absolutely the correct decision, but unfortunately their withdrawal was captured on video by several TV crews who had also wandered into the area. Thus the UN's battered image took yet another punishing body blow.[79] Later that evening the first pictures emerged of lines of Serb fighters being marched away as Croatian troops, with flags waving, were seen 'liberating' several towns and villages in the area. Perhaps the most interesting aspect of this triumphalism was the complete absence of those who had been supposedly liberated – there were none.

As the Croatian army rolled into each town and village with their clean-up teams right behind them, literally washing the blood off the streets, painting white lines on the roads, erecting road signs in Latin script and clearing away all war debris before the international media were allowed into the area, the streets were empty save for a few elderly people who were either too old or sick to embark on a journey into exile. By any stretch of the imagination this was not 'liberation'. This was conquest and a 'land grab'. This was precision ethnic cleansing supported and condoned by the United States. The matter of whether the Croats had been given a 'green light' or an 'orange light', or 'no light at all' was irrelevant. They had approval – and they exploited it to the full.

And the maltreatment of the new Serb POWs seemed to pass almost unnoticed too. ECMM's Gunter Barron appeared on several international TV reports to tell the world that these Serbs were being treated well and that no human rights had been violated, and while from what he saw he probably genuinely believed this to be true the reality was altogether different.

Later that evening more video footage was released which provided evidence of prisoners being publicly humiliated as they were forced to strip to their dirty soiled underwear, and then remain standing *ad nauseam* while being questioned in detail by Croatian policewomen who nonchalantly blew cigarette smoke into their faces while admiring their discomfort.[80] Corralled now into football stadiums and sports halls at Varazdin, Bjelovar and Pozega, over 1,100 members of the 18th Corps began a period of contemplation in which they would ask themselves how all of this could possibly have happened so quickly, and why neither Martic nor Karadzic had come to their rescue. Sector West had fallen to the Croats without any real resistance and had left the Croatian army buoyant and euphoric. Tudjman's gamble had paid off handsomely, and with the international community having given its tacit approval to the whole operation the Croatian president was fortified in his belief that having got away with this once he might well be able to do so again.

At face value it was crystal clear that the balance of forces had now shifted significantly in favour of the Croats, and this would dramatically influence events from now on. But there was also the matter of 'hidden agendas', and the rumour factory began to churn out endless stories which suggested that Sector West had in fact been sacrificed by Milosevic in order to have the economic sanctions lifted in Serbia and Montenegro.

This was certainly close to the truth, and the full story would emerge later on, but the singularly significant aspect of the whole saga was that the fall of Sector West would ultimately prove to mark the beginning of the end for the Republic of Srpska Krajina. Within a very short time the whole deck of cards would come crashing to the ground and the flames of 'pan-Serbian nationalism', as rekindled by Milosevic and Babic in 1989, would soon be extinguished forever.

Leaderless in Knin

As the Krajina Serbs struggled to come to terms with the loss of Sector West and the fact that none of their brother Serbs in Belgrade or Knin had raised a finger to help them, it quickly emerged that this might well be but the first phase of a larger Croatian offensive. However, thanks to the continued intervention of Akashi, and several complaints by UN officials that the Croats had been involved in a number of human rights violations,[81] Tudjman was persuaded to call his troops to heel for the moment.

The last thing Tudjman or Susak needed now was bad international press and so in order to keep their sponsors 'on side' Sarinic paraded before the media to insist again that (a) 'Operation Flash' had been nothing more than a police action to reopen the highway, (b) that really Croatia's relations with Knin had not been damaged at all, and (c) that he hoped both sides could now get on with the business of implementing the Economic Agreement. As outrageous and ridiculous as all of this was, the more Sarinic touted it the more convincing he became, and within a relatively short period this lie became accepted internationally as an adequate explanation for the unprovoked aggression which the Croats had just unleashed.

In Knin the leadership was now split into several different political camps, with the government, police and military in complete disarray. The inevitable in-fighting between Martic, Mikelic and Babic now erupted on a grand scale. Not surprisingly, the first target turned out to be Mikelic himself, who was berated by his colleagues for having gone too far with the Croats in the first place when he signed the Economic Agreement. Next to suffer was General Celeketic who was blamed for the collapse of the 18th Corps and the failure of other units to come to their support. He in turn decided to offer his resignation rather than wait to be fired. In the course of his statement he attributed the fall of Sector West to 'the lack of political and military support from outside the Krajina, which [he] had expected to materialise because it had been previously agreed, and also because of the dirty political games being played [now] by certain individuals'.[82]

Martic then turned to Karadzic for support and a joint session of both the Krajina and Bosnian Serb parliaments was called for 31 May as in excess of 10,000 refugees from Sector West now squabbled between themselves over what pathetic accommodation and shelter they could find. Then, in apparent revenge for the Croatian attack and the subsequent 'ethnic cleansing', several Catholic churches in Banja Luka were destroyed and many Croats still living there were harassed and killed.[83]

In a letter to the Bosnian Serb authorities the Catholic bishop, Franja Komarica, reported the discovery of the charred remains of both a priest and a nun in the ruins of one church and declared that this was the fifth priest from his diocese who had been murdered in the past three years.[84] Equally, in the towns of Tovarnik and Ilok in Sector East Croats were expelled from their homes, and around Knin ECMM's Jochen Kramb, identified that the wealthier Krajina Serbs were in fact systematically leaving the area.[85]

Clearly those Krajina Serbs who understood the real politics of the situation were heading for the relative safety of Belgrade and beyond. Unfortunately for the remainder, who comprised the vast majority of the Krajina Serb population, nobody was telling them anything. And then to compound and confuse matters further, it was announced in The Hague on 9 May that Judge Richard Goldstone had evidence in his possession which established that certain Bosnian Croats, namely Dario Kordic the HDZ leader in Bosnia, and General Tihomir Blaskic his military counterpart,[86] had indeed committed war crimes in central Bosnia in the course of the war.

Two days later the International Tribunal applied to the Sarajevo government to defer jurisdiction to The Hague in connection with these serious violations of international humanitarian law in the Lasva valley in 1992 and 1993. When Goldstone then arrived in Zagreb on 15 May to examine events surrounding the 'liberation' of Sector West, a sense of panic gripped Zagreb. Immediately all posturing and obstructionism ceased, which allowed the long overdue 'Status of Forces Agreement' to be signed between the Croatian government and the UN.

In the short term, then, UN troops would remain in Krajina – but even the most optimistic observers realised that it was but a matter of time before the Croatian army was unleashed by Tudjman once again. Having flexed their muscles once, and got away with it, they continued to receive all the wrong signals from their main sponsors, and almost immediately preparations began for the next offensive.

A huge military parade took place in Zagreb on 30 May[87] and Tudjman was in his element, resplendent in a white uniform with gold braid. He now knew he would not be prevented from launching a second attack on Krajina because Peter Galbraith still had 'no instructions'. All Galbraith communicated to him was 'concern' over the ongoing HV build-up, and ever grateful for American 'concern' Tudjman took this as another green light. Galbraith neither said nor did anything else to dissuade him.[88] In relation to anything the UN might hope to achieve at this time General Peeters, deputy force commander of UNPF, was quite clear when he wrote: 'the presence and action of the UN Force in Croatia has become irrelevant to both sides. We should recognise and admit the situation and we should assess if our present way of thinking is still valid.'[89]

Meanwhile, in Bosnia on 6 May Sarajevo's five months of comparative stability was suddenly shattered when several artillery shells landed in the Muslim suburb of Butmir near the entrance to the famous tunnel under the airport runway[90] which had provided a lifeline to the city in its darkest days.[91] In the context of a return to violence it was hardly surprising that this economic and military lifeline should once again become a target, and on this May morning eight people died and another 40 were wounded as the Serbs began to strangle the city one more time. With the airport closed to humanitarian flights the Serbs' objective was clearly to close the tunnel as well, but as so often in the past this attack only ensured that the besieged citizens of Sarajevo continued their lives with even more determination than before.[92] General Smith apparently requested NATO airstrikes in the aftermath of this latest atrocity, but Akashi turned him down on the basis that the overall situation was now too delicate and tense, and any escalation by the intervention of NATO might only serve to put UN soldiers at greater risk than they already were.[93]

With the whole fabric of the Balkans now crumbling around him Akashi set out for Belgrade and a meeting with Milosevic, Martic, Mikelic and Babic during which they discussed amongst other things the 657 Serbs from Sector West who were still detained in Varazdin and Bjelovar at the pleasure of President Tudjman's investigators![94] They also addressed the matter of the UN's perceived culpability in failing to prevent the Croatian attack and Milosevic said all he had expected was that the UN would 'implement their peace mission, no more, no less'. He went on to say that he wanted a demilitarisation of western Slavonia, with the UN in place to enforce it, and this in turn would allow Serbs to continue living in the area. Knin's position, he said, could not be properly defined until its leaders stopped fighting with one another. Then, in a public reprimand for Krajina's president, Milosevic told Akashi that he had vehemently opposed the shelling of Zagreb, and blamed Milan Martic exclusively for it.

With Milosevic and Mikelic apparently speaking as one voice, Martic now found himself marginalised and isolated as Babic kept his mouth shut and said nothing. Clearly Milosevic had decided to ignore Martic and thereby ensure that Mikelic was the main player from now as discussion focused on ways to decrease tension in Sector West, most notably by guaranteeing the evacuation of the civilian population. When all Akashi could suggest was that Knin be patient and co-operate with the UN, Martic attacked him over the extent to which the Croatian army had been allowed to violate human rights in Sector West. He also accused UNPROFOR and the Security Council of actually abusing the Republic of Srpska Krajina. As the meeting broke up it was crystal clear that as far as Milosevic was concerned two factors had contributed to the fall of Sector West – the ineptitude of the UN troops garrisoned there and the incompetence of Milan Martic.[95]

Martic had become a political liability, and Babic was little better, so it became imperative for Milosevic to now identify with Mikelic, who as the only moderate available in Knin stood the best chance of being accepted internationally. The problem here was that Mikelic had little or no support at home and could only survive if Milosevic waded in behind him. This was now the game plan. With Martic and Babic sidelined in Krajina, and Karadzic unable to blow his nose effectively without General Mladic's agreement, Milosevic convinced himself that he was once again pulling all the strings in the 'pan-Serbian nationalist orchestra'.

As Martic and Babic made their way back to Knin they were in no doubt as to where the key to their survival actually lay, but the problem was how to reconcile that with the certain knowledge that if they adopted a more moderate approach Tudjman would see this as a sign of weakness and roll his HV troops right in on top of them.

In Bosnia the situation was deteriorating as well, and although rumour abounded that Karadzic was on the verge of making a new proposal to the Contact Group there was no evidence on the ground to support this. Instead, on 7 May 11 people died and 14 were injured in Sarajevo.[96] Over 2,200 firing incidents were recorded in the city on 10 May as fighting also intensified in the Posavina Corridor where the Serbs in Brcko, and Bosnian Croats in the Orasje Pocket, hurled tonnes of ordnance at one another and succeeded only in shifting the Confrontation Line marginally.[97]

With the picture now going from bad to worse, Akashi, General Janvier and General Smith flew to Paris for a meeting with the ICFY co-chairman Thorvald Stoltenberg, but nothing new emerged. While they were away, however, the Serbs decided to once again begin curtailing the flow of gas into Sarajevo, and the level of sniper activity was stepped up also. One of the first casualties here was a French UN soldier who was shot while on duty in the city as a member of an anti-sniping patrol. The refusal of the Serb military to allow his immediate evacuation probably cost him his life. He was eventually flown to Paris but died four days later from his injuries.[98]

The very next day a full-scale artillery battle erupted in the suburbs of Sarajevo when, following a Muslim mortar attack on the Serb barracks at Lukavica, over 1,500 assorted shells rained down on the city in reprisal. In addition to this the situation in the Posavina was steadily getting worse and fighting now spread to areas like Gradacac and the Majevica hills north of Tuzla, while a new Muslim offensive got under way around Sarajevo itself and actually succeeded in bringing Pale within Armija artillery range for the first time. From the sanitised environs of UN HQ in New York Akashi condemned this escalation of violence,[99] and expressed all kinds of pessimism for the future, but clearly no one had any interest in what he had to say.

In Bihac Dudakovic launched the 5th Corps on another offensive to the south-east of Bihac town, which immediately sent hundreds of Serbs scurrying off to the relative safety of Banja Luka and Sanski Most. With a total of 4,643 violations of the 'no-fly zone' recorded by UNPROFOR at the beginning of May,[100] and a sharp increase in military activity by all sides clearly evident, every monitoring agency in the region was waiting for events to enter a downward spiral – and on the night of 25 May they were not disappointed.

As hundreds of people gathered outside cafés in the centre of Tuzla, a salvo of artillery rained down on top of them, eventually leaving 71 dead and over 130 wounded.[101] Three days later, in retaliation for several NATO air-strikes, the Bosnian Serbs seized 377 UN soldiers and held them hostage at a variety of locations in order to ward off further punitive attacks. This was immediately effective. Pictures of UN soldiers handcuffed to ammunition bunkers were flashed around the world, and it would take three full weeks of negotiation, and the establishment of a Rapid Reaction Force, to eventually secure their release. Obviously the Carter initiative and the COHA had achieved little more than providing a period of calm during which all of the sides could regroup and rearm.

This was particularly true in the case of both the Muslims and the Bosnian Croats, and although the Federation was in serious political difficulty, both armies appeared to be benefiting dramatically from continued foreign intervention, which we now know to have been primarily of American and Iranian origin.[102] ECMM's Daily Monitoring Activity Report on 17 May confirmed this.[103]

By July 1995 Serb positions on nearly every front had almost become untenable. Day by day tonnes of military hardware made its way to the HV, HVO and Armija troops on the ground.[104] Politically the die had been cast and the necessary military action would follow on in due course. General Delic even set about visiting all his frontline troops in order to make sure they understood that the war had been transformed from a defensive action into what he now also called 'a war of liberation'. He was no doubt influenced in his thinking by the decision of UNPROFOR commander Rupert Smith to begin withdrawing his troops from the eastern enclaves as soon as possible, on the basis that neither the UN nor NATO could actually defend them there anyway. And then in a last throw of the Serb dice Ratko Mladic unleashed the BSA on the eastern Muslim enclaves of Srebrenica and Zepa.

The fall of Srebrenica

Over the next two weeks some of the worst atrocities of the modern Yugoslav conflict would be perpetrated by the Bosnian Serbs, as first Srebrenica and then Zepa crumbled before a relentless BSA onslaught. Why General Mladic permitted what happened to take place will perhaps never be explained until he is forced to answer that question in order to save his own skin if he ever appears before the International Criminal Tribunal in The Hague.

No doubt he will try to suggest that he was only responding to a known UNPROFOR decision to get its own troops out of the enclaves that summer anyway, and he will probably attempt to tell us that the actions of his troops were merely a measured response to Muslim terrorist provocation over the years. The reality, of course, is that whatever explanation he comes up with can never justify the summary execution of nearly 3,000 Muslim men and the hunting down of another 4,000 as they fled in terror across the hills and valleys of eastern Bosnia in a futile attempt to make their way to safety at the Armija's front line near Tuzla in north-central Bosnia. The ICRC figure for those still missing following the BSA's attack on the UN safe area of Srebrenica still stands at 7,079 – 38 per cent of the total number of people missing in the entire Yugoslav wars.[105]

The UN would also bear the brunt of severe criticism for their perceived failure to protect the enclave from Mladic and his thugs; but the truth of that matter is very simple. The Dutch UN battalion was neither mandated, empowered nor equipped to go to war with the Serbs. Mladic was well aware of this, as indeed he was of Akashi's and Janvier's reluctance to call in close air support lest it make an untenable situation (from the UN perspective) appreciably worse. He knew their misgivings and he understood their reservations, and he exploited them all to the full.

The story of Srebrenica is a sickening litany of barbarity, atrocity and murder. The responsibility for it lies exclusively in the hands of Ratko Mladic and his political and military masters in Belgrade who paid his salary at the time and who continue to do so to the present day. In an oft-cited TV interview, given long before the horror of Srebrenica unfolded, Mladic boasted that his preferred military tactics were to shell people out of their minds and to shoot all his prisoners of war. Certainly no one in the international community took this kind of bravado seriously at the time. That was a very serious mistake.[106]

However, before concluding on this matter, and in no way attempting to justify mass murder, in the interest of fairness and balance a number of points must be made:

1. Srebrenica had never been demilitarised in 1993.
2. Neither Izetbegovic nor Naser Oric had any confidence in the UN's safe area policy.

3 Srebrenica was *not* a safe area by any applicable definition.
4 The UN did not have the capability or the manpower to defend it.
5 Prior to July 1995 the Armija forces in Srebrenica had consisted of between 3,000 and 4,000 lightly armed troops.
6 They were organised into four brigades.
7 They were reinforced by a local militia.
8 They carried out systematic attacks on Serb villages from within the enclave and subsequently withdrew into what they considered as *de jure* if not *de facto* UN-protected territory. They were using the UN as cover.
9 As far as the Dutch were concerned, Oric and his two main brigade commanders, Zulfo Tursunovic and Hakija Meholjic, were little more than gangsters who terrorised their own refugee population and profited greatly from the war. They believed that these men jealously protected their own fiefdoms and often would get their men to take up positions close to the Dutch and then open fire on the Serbs, hoping to drag the Dutch into a fire-fight. On other occasions, when they found the Dutch insufficiently accommodating, they would turn off the water supply to their compounds.[107]
10 In May the commander of the Dutch battalion informed UNPROFOR HQ that his unit could no longer be considered operational because no supplies had been getting through.
11 From 3 June onwards there was no co-operation whatever between the Dutch and the local authorities.
12 On 27 June General Janvier issued an order that in the eastern enclaves UN troops could only fire their weapons in self-defence.
13 Most of the Dutch ammunition had in any case become unserviceable, and none of their anti-tank missile systems had been tested since 1994 because the Serbs had refused delivery of the required spare parts.
14 As the Serbs advanced on Srebrenica several Dutch observation posts were systematically overrun and the soldiers taken hostage.
15 On 8 July when OP-F was overrun, the Dutch occupants were permitted to return to Srebrenica town but were then stopped at an Armija road block. When they attempted to move on Private Van Renseen was shot in the head as he tried to get into the back of his armoured vehicle. He died later of his injuries.
16 In the context of murder at Srebrenica Private Van Renseen was also murdered – but by the Muslims, the very people the Dutch and the UN had come to protect in the first place.[108]

Finally, it should not be forgotten that Naser Oric was not in Srebrenica for the final battle. He had been recalled to Sarajevo six weeks previously and Izetbegovic had denied him permission to return. Why was this? This author believes that the upper echelons in the Sarajevo government knew the game was up and decided to spare one of their best and most loyal commanders. They knew that the UN could not defend the enclaves against a serious push by Mladic.

They also knew that Janvier had issued the 'self-defence only' order and that Smith wanted all his troops out of the enclaves as soon as possible. And without any doubt they knew the end-game strategy which Anthony Lake and Bill Clinton were putting together in Washington. Therefore in all probability they knew the enclave situation was a *fait accompli* – if ECMM and UNPROFOR knew it then the Sarajevo government knew it as well. What they could never have envisaged was the manner in which Mladic would deal with the people.

Philip Corwin from UN Civil Affairs in Sarajevo summed up the position rather well when he said that, in his opinion, 'the Muslims of Srebrenica were political capital to the Bosnian government. As long as they remained in Srebrenica they were a strategic asset. In fact in spite of our inability to use the force that was necessary we [the UN] cared more about the Muslim population of Srebrenica than the Sarajevo government did.'[109]

A storm blows through Krajina

In Bihac Pocket the military situation remained calm with only minor alterations to the front lines being effected. However, in some instances there was still a price to be paid for these limited gains – as was the case of the two 5th Corps military police personnel who were captured on Srbljani plateau on 18 May. They were systematically tortured, with their ears, noses and fingers cut off; they were then impaled on two stakes; and both were found naked and dead on the 22nd. They had also had their genitals removed. Such was the barbarity of the conflict and a video made where the bodies were found, and of their condition later in the mortuary, served only to inspire others to greater levels of savagery.[110] And so it went on.

But the most interesting piece of scandal by far in Bihac in May 1995 was the disclosure by a reliable source close to ECMM that a case was being prepared against Hamdo Abdic by General Dudakovic as a result of allegations that Colonel Pivic (he of smuggling fame) and Hamdu Abdic had been with the HVO general Vlado Santic when he 'disappeared' from the Sedra Hotel in Bihac town at 1.20 a.m. on 9 March. The suggestion was that Hamdu had fired the first shot while Pivic finished him off.[111] According to the ECMM source, when Hamdo Abdic was told about his forthcoming prosecution he immediately went to find Dudakovic and the pair of them ended up in a fist fight.[112]

Throughout June and July Abdic forces supported by the Krajina Serbs began one more time to make some headway against the 5th Corps as they pushed southwards from Velika Kladusa. Dudakovic, having managed to consolidate his position by successfully evicting all remaining Bosnian

Serbs from the west bank of the Una river, was also marshalling his forces.[113] He also ordered all telephones disconnected, with the exception of those belonging to the 5th Corps and senior politicians, and when people went to purchase food on the black market there was none available because everything had been commandeered by the 5th Corps.

UNCRO HQ in Zagreb now estimated that over 100,000 professional Croatian troops were fully 'combat-ready'; if one also took account of their 'home guard' and 'reservists' the total number probably exceeded 140,000.

In the Livanjsko Polje the combined HV/HVO offensive continued to gather pace and when the town of Bosanska Gravaho eventually fell on 28 July the Knin authorities declared a state of war. Within hours over 50,000 Krajina Serb troops had been mustered – but almost 7,000 of them were still totally bogged down around Bihac.[114]

On the political front the temperature was now at boiling point as Tudjman began issuing warnings that Croatia would solve the 'Krajina problem' once and for all unless serious peace talks got underway immediately. Yasushi Akashi, who by now had effectively given up on trying to exert any further influence on the Croatian government, warned again about the danger of a full-scale war in the region, but he too understood that 'the writing was on the wall' for the Krajina Serbs. In Geneva a meeting chaired by Thorvald Stoltenberg went into session, but as the delegations present did not represent the highest political level in either Krajina or Croatia the best that could ever be achieved was agreement to begin 'talks about talks'.

On 1 August the Joint Defence Council of the Bosnian and Krajina Serbs met in Drvar and called for immediate military intervention by Belgrade to balance up the situation. Martic declared that he had been given 'assurances' by Milosevic that Serbia would not remain neutral if the Croats attacked Knin, but this was not the message that independent observers understood was coming from Belgrade. In fact the head of the Serbian bureau office in Zagreb, a Mr Knezevic, was openly suggesting for the very first time that the duty of the Krajina Serbs was to be 'citizens loyal to Croatia' and for them to seek their democratic position as a national minority in line with the relevant provisions of the Croatian Constitution.

This philosophy, such as it was, was not well received in Knin where Milan Babic had once again become prime minister on 28 July.[115] Recognising that Krajina could not survive without JNA support, he left immediately for Belgrade to seek out his old sponsor Milosevic, the man who initiated the entire conflict in the heady days of 1990 and 1991 with his vision of pan-Serbian nationalism.[116]

Within the borders of Bihac Pocket the situation remained relatively stable with all manner of light aircraft from Croatia constantly unloading supplies for the 5th Corps at Coralici airfield. However, Sarajevo decided to keep the 'plight' of the enclave right at the top of the political agenda in a determined effort to justify Croatian and/or international intervention in the overall conflict. Foreign ministers Sacirbey and Granic both announced that if the international community failed to do anything to 'save Bihac' then the Armija, with the help of the HV, would do something about it themselves – and since the 'Split Agreement' of 22 July the Croatian army now had an open invitation from Sarajevo to commence operations in Bihac anytime they wished. All any of them were really looking for was an appropriate excuse, notwithstanding that the Pocket was not actually about to fall.[117]

But it didn't matter because virtually all reporting agencies and commentators now realised that the Croats were going to go ahead anyway and launch their offensive to 'liberate Bihac' – one way or the other – and this was subsequently confirmed by US ambassador Peter Galbraith in an interview with the author Tim Ripley.[118]

And then, to no one's great surprise, the whole situation simply erupted in violence when the Geneva 'peace' talks, which were now chaired by Carl Bildt, ground to a halt because the Croats present were not remotely interested in anything other than a military solution.

In response, Milan Babic appeared on television in Belgrade on the evening of 3 August and announced to the world that the Knin authorities would now accept the Z4 plan. Clearly his talks with Milosevic had failed completely and this was his last attempt to convince the Croats to stand down their German-equipped and US-trained army. The political leadership in the Krajina had capitulated. Secession was at an end. Greater Serbia was dead. There was no reason or need to launch a military action against Croatia's Serb community – unless of course the Croats wanted to engage in their own bout of ethnic cleansing and evict over 350,000 ethnic Serbs from their legally held homes and property.

In fact this was precisely the agenda in Zagreb, and Babic's capitulation was ignored. Instead they saw his statement simply as confirmation that Milosevic was not about to commit the JNA to save Krajina. Deputy Interior Minister Sarinic contacted UN HQ in Zagreb and informed General Janvier at 3.20 a.m. on 4 August that Tudjman had decided to unleash the entire HV in an operation to retake Krajina by force. It was of no consequence that the Croats no longer had any excuse to embark on their military adventure. They had been waiting too long. They were armed with tonnes of very expensive military hardware and now it was time to play. HV offensive action would commence one hour and 40 minutes later.

Notwithstanding that this was in breach of the internationally recognised 'Ceasefire Agreement of 29th March 1994', and in complete disregard of the fact that UN peacekeepers were occupying positions through which the main attacks were designed to go, reports from both the UN and

ECMM identified that the first Croatian artillery shells impacted in Krajina at 5.05 a.m.

Attacking on two fronts simultaneously, the 1st and 2nd Guards brigades began a drive through the northern part of Krajina in a planned attempt to link up with the 5th Corps in Bihac Pocket, while in the south the 4th, 7th and 9th brigades, supported by a plethora of other specialist groupings, drove into the RSK in a three-pronged attack on Knin. In Bihac, Dudakovic launched his own attacks westward – in the first instance in an attempt to link up with the 119th and 123rd HV brigades attacking through Plitvice. In order to punch a hole in the Serb defences some of the 5th Corps' initial targets became UN observation posts which were occupied by Polish troops. Four such positions were easily overrun, with the occupants then held captive for a time.

In response to all of these attacks the initial Serb reaction, while somewhat disorganised in the south, proved very determined in the north with both the Kordun and Banja Corps putting up fierce resistance. However, as day number two dawned, with ever-increasing Croatian shelling, it quickly emerged that the RSK Lika Corps were frantically withdrawing into Bosnia. Further south the Serb defences were now crumbling at an unprecedented rate, and without much prompting the Knin authorities packed their bags and abandoned the town to whatever fate lay before it. By 5 p.m. that evening 90 per cent of Krajina was back in Croatian hands, with only small pockets of resistance still holding out around the northern towns of Topusko and Glina.

As the Croats advanced on Knin, burning and looting all before them, UN troops again found themselves subjected to assorted ill-treatment with one of the worst examples occurring when Danish peacekeepers were forced to march in front of advancing HV infantry and tanks in order to provide what essentially amounted to a human shield. That this was an unequivocal breach of international humanitarian law bothered none of the HV commanders on the ground and this unfortunately set the tone for the even worse atrocities which were to follow.

By now several thousand civilians were on the move as they fled before the incessant HV artillery bombardment, and by 2 a.m. on the 6th over 20,000 people had gathered near Topusko. A few hours later the town of Petrinja was captured virtually unopposed after the entire population had fled, and although both military commanders recognised an impending humanitarian disaster they were unable to agree surrender terms which would allow the Serbs to lay down their arms with honour. Accordingly the fighting went on and in retaliation for a Serb artillery salvo on the chemical works at Kutina the Croats targeted an area west of Topusko that night which, coincidentally, just happened to be the location of what had now become one of several huge refugee convoys awaiting a chance to leave for Bosnia and beyond.

The following day another convoy of Serb refugees, trapped near Glina, was targeted directly by the HV artillery. Another convoy was strafed by the Croatian airforce, and when the BSA launched five aircraft against HV positions two of them were shot down. Then the Croats took it upon themselves to vent their anger at this development by again firing in reprisal on the unfortunate refugees, who were simply trying to escape the madness of a situation they barely understood in the first place. Croatian defence minister Susak later accepted that what he called several 'incidents' had occurred, but incredibly described them as 'minor' in nature. Taken in this context his subsequent 'apology' on behalf of Croatia to the Kingdom of Denmark and the Czech Republic for the deaths of their UN peacekeepers as the HV troops ploughed through their UN positions must surely constitute nothing more than a gross insult.[119]

Meanwhile, the 5th Corps were euphoric following their speedy link-up with the HV near Rakovica. Buoyed by this success Dudakovic decided to launch his troops one more time against Velika Kladusa and Fikret Abdic, while simultaneously pushing north-eastwards in an attempt to cut off the Serb withdrawal along the Glina–Dvor road. By now UN and ECMM estimates put the refugee figures at well over 40,000 in Topusko alone, with countless others scattered all over the place. The absolute confusion which reigned was best exemplified by a frantic radio transmission which was received by the UN just after 6 p.m. in which an RSK officer begged for help from the village of Donji Zirovac where a refugee column of women and children were dying all around him. His pleas went unanswered and the shelling continued regardless.[120]

Shortly afterwards the 5th Corps converged on Dvor and became embroiled in vicious hand-to-hand fighting on the outskirts as the Serb rearguard struggled to keep them at bay. Intense mediation then followed and at 7 a.m. on the 8th a ceasefire was agreed which allowed the Serbs to hand over their weapons and then depart for Bosnia unhindered. In order to facilitate this development the 5th Corps were ordered to withdraw from the Dvor–Glina road and thereby allow the pitiful convoys to proceed into exile without further acrimony or loss of life.

Within the space of five days the Krajina region of Croatia had been subjected to an unprecedented systematic ethnic cleansing with over 350,000 people, whose ancestors had first pacified the Vojna Krajina in the late sixteenth century, now condemned to face life as refugees in either Bosnia or Serbia – two places which at that point in time were marginally less hospitable than where they were now leaving. Milan Babic remained in Belgrade and would be instrumental in obtaining agreement from Milosevic to resettle large numbers of his people in both Vojvodina and Kosovo. Those who decided to stay in Bosnia, however, were set to face a much more volatile future, the origins of which were now plain for all to see in the public power struggle which erupted between Mladic and Radovan Karadzic.

But the Krajina Serbs were not the only losers as a result of Operation Storm. Certainly Croatia had solved some of her strategic problems, but victory also involved the unwanted arrival of tens of thousands of people loyal to Fikret Abdic who once again had chosen to abandon their homes in Velika Kladusa rather than take their chances with Izetbegovic, Dudakovic and the 5th Corps.

On previous occasions they had taken refuge in what until recently had been the RSK. Now this was Croatia, the situation had changed dramatically, and 35,000 people were encamped by the side of the road or crammed into filthy conditions near a place called Kuplensko, determined not to return to their homes no matter what agreement was reached or what guarantees were given.[121]

One more time the leadership qualities of Sead Kajtazovic were called into action as several international agencies rushed to the aid of a group who had now become known simply as the 'Abdic Refugees'.[122] Needless to say, Fikret Abdic was not sharing their discomfort preferring instead the luxury of his offices in Rijeka where almost immediately he began plotting his next political moves. For his misguided followers, however, the cyclical nature of Balkan life would continue unrelentingly. The Republic of Srpska Krajina had disappeared and the political experiment known as the 'Autonomous Province of Western Bosnia' (APWB) was at an end.[123]

6

THE END STATE

By April 1995 the International Community had proved incapable of developing any creative or coherent policy when it came to dealing with the Bosnian Serbs. No credit whatever had been given to Radovan Karadzic for his initiative with former president Carter the previous December, the Sarajevo government had all but received US approval to launch its troops on the Vlasic mountain offensive which shattered the Cessation of Hostilities Agreement (COHA), tonnes of military equipment were pouring into Bosnia, the arms embargo had died, US Special Forces personnel were barely disguising their activities throughout the region and UNPROFOR had all but become irrelevant.

In the months following the Croatian army and their US trainers and advisers charged into the heart of Krajina. MPRI had planned it all, and Peter Galbraith had *de facto* given the operation US blessing. The biggest ethnic cleansing of them all was under way live on international television, nobody raised a finger to stop it, and Franjo Tudjman's reunification policy was implemented at the end of a 155-mm artillery gun barrel.

Then, on 28 August, five more mortar rounds were fired into the centre of Sarajevo with one again landing in a crowded marketplace. In the aftermath UN officers were divided on whether the shell, which killed 37 and wounded nearly 80 others, had actually been fired by the Bosnian Serbs. Colonel Andrei Demurenko, a Russian artillery officer, who was also General Rupert Smith's chief of staff, was of the opinion that the shell could not have come from Serb positions. A Canadian officer expressed doubts about whether the bomb had in fact been fired from a mortar tube at all and not dropped from the top floor of a building nearby.

Equally, British and French officers were not initially able to find any evidence that the Serbs had been responsible, and once again the finger of suspicion began to point at the Bosnian Muslims themselves whose leaders, coincidentally, just happened to be attending another international peace conference in Paris. And subsequent leaked reports from Russian military intelligence indicated that they had known on 20 August (eight days previously) that a plan existed to detonate a 'bomb' in

Sarajevo and that this information had already been passed to the US, German and Croatian governments.[1]

In any event, US officers working in UNPROFOR HQ in Sarajevo, assisted it must be said by senior British officers close to General Smith, quickly overruled all of their international colleagues and claimed that they had found a 'fuse furrow' at the site of the impact and Cyrillic markings on what remained of the bomb casing. They were also satisfied that the 'bomb' in question had bounced off the roof of a building nearby en route to the market below, and when adjustments were made to their calculations to allow for this the point of origin could be placed on the Serb side of the demarcation line – just. And on the ground in the city the story was quickly peddled, and believed, that the bombing was in fact revenge for a Muslim attack on a Serb funeral the previous day. Blaming the Serbs tied in nicely with that scenario, and needless to say nobody bothered to enquire why it was that ordinary people attending a funeral had been set upon by a gang of thugs in the first place.

Of equal significance, perhaps, was the fact that UNPROFOR no longer had any troops deployed in either Zepa, Srebrenica or Gorazde – and the Bihac area was now secure. Therefore the way was clear, finally, for the West to go to war with the Serbs without any risk of hostages being taken, and on 29 August NATO announced that it had established 'beyond reasonable doubt' that the Serbs were to blame for the mortar attack. This was wrong. There was plenty of doubt – but clearly it no longer mattered.

To make matters worse the UN report which allegedly confirmed that the Serbs were to blame was immediately marked 'confidential' and has neither been seen nor heard of since. Four years later, in the UN's comprehensive 'Srebrenica Report',[2] the matter of how this highly significant assessment was made is virtually dismissed and considered worthy of no more than seven dismissive lines in parentheses at the end of para. 438. However, several UN officers did not agree with the findings of that investigation, and it must be recorded that at the end of the day it was US officers attached to UNPROFOR who wrote the document, marked it confidential, presented it to Rupert Smith and then passed it on to NATO. Taking all of this in the context of known Russian intelligence warnings and Peter Galbraith's subsequent admission to Tim Ripley that both he and Holbrooke actually knew the bombing was going to happen,[3] one is drawn inescapably to the conclusion that something is seriously wrong with this version of events.

Unfortunately for the Serbs the commander of all UN Forces in Former Yugoslavia, General Bernard Janvier (France), was absent on leave from his HQ in Zagreb while all of this was taking place, resulting in a situation which ensured that any decision to undertake punitive military action against them would now be taken by the UN commander in Sarajevo –

Rupert Smith. The 'Srebrenica Report' confirms at para. 439 that Smith actually wanted to strike immediately but was prevented from doing so because a convoy of UNPROFOR troops were moving through Serb-held territory en route out of Gorazde. However, at 8p.m. that night, when the convoy was safely in Serbia, Rupert Smith decided to undertake punitive military action against the Bosnian Serbs and informed NATO HQ in Naples accordingly.[4] What he apparently failed to do was consult with his superiors in the UN hierarchy, and UN HQ in New York did not become fully aware of his decision until six hours later, at which point they had still not received the famous confidential report on the bombing.[5] Again one is drawn to the conclusion that at best there was something odd about this entire sequence of events.

The truth of what happened in Sarajevo on 28 August 1995 may never be fully explained, but the incident itself served a clear unambiguous purpose. The following morning NATO's planning for air bombardment of the Bosnian Serbs was fine-tuned, and once it was confirmed to Admiral Leighton-Smith that a supporting combined HV/HVO/Armija ground offensive could commence immediately the admiral turned his key as well and NATO *de facto* adopted co-belligerent status with the combined Muslim/Croat forces and their ever-increasing band of foreign advisers.[6]

At 8 a.m. on 30 August, and in conjunction with a 600-round artillery barrage from the guns of the Rapid Reaction Force on Mount Igman, a programme of strategic bombing got under way which included the launching of Tomahawk cruise missiles. Several key BSA installations were quickly demolished, and command, control and communications facilities were blasted to rubble right across the Republic Srpska as Bosnian Muslim and Croat commanders set about launching their ground offensives to redress Bosnia's perceived military imbalance. The 'endgame strategy' had become the 'endgame'. When advised on what was happening President Clinton once again displayed his comprehensive understanding of the problem when he said 'Whooopppeee'.[7]

However, unknown to Clinton, Leighton-Smith or Rupert Smith in Sarajevo, a new European peace initiative was actually underway in the Republic Srpska at the very moment the first NATO bombs began to fall. Seemingly oblivious to the danger involved, ECMM's Spanish head of mission, Ambassador Sanchez Rau, had arrived in Pale on the evening of 29 August in order to meet with Radovan Karadzic. Ostensibly to copper-fasten an agreement whereby water from the south-eastern part of Republic Srpska would be permitted to flow to Dubrovnik, Sanchez Rau and an ECMM team had set off from Podgorica in Montenegro that morning and embarked on a tortuous journey across the mountains to Pale. Before he left, however, Sanchez Rau had made a call to the Spanish Foreign Ministry in Madrid. What was discussed is not known but it appears that Spain was intent on securing a diplomatic coup and finally striking a deal with the Bosnian Serbs when all other measures had failed.

Once again, and in similar fashion to Rupert Smith's failure to fully communicate with New York, nobody at Rau's headquarters in Zagreb had any notion of what was happening. Nobody knew where he was, and nobody knew what he was doing, until a newsflash was broadcast on Bosnian Serb television which stated that five EC monitors had been killed when a NATO air-strike had destroyed their white Landrovers. Javier Solana immediately went before a press conference in Madrid and washed his hands of Sanchez Rau's initiative, disavowed all knowledge of what the Spanish ambassador and head of ECMM had actually been up to, and effectively confirmed that they were all dead.

Fortunately this was not the complete story; Solana had got some of his facts wrong. It later transpired that the monitors, after being accommodated in a hotel in Pale, were in fact roused from their slumber at 3 a.m. on the morning of 29 August and advised to go down into the basement shelter for their own safety. Having maximised the propaganda value of alleging that NATO had killed some of its own people, the Serbs then admitted that in fact the monitors were alive and well, although Karadzic trenchantly refused to meet with them until the bombing was stopped.

Two days later, when it became clear that NATO had no intention of stopping the air war, all five monitors were dispatched to Visegrad on the border with Serbia and eventually released into the custody of Milosevic's chief henchman Jovica Stanisic. Once in Belgrade they were then swept back to Madrid for debriefing where, no doubt, Sanchez Rau had to undertake some interesting explanations. Clearly the entire episode could have ended in disaster, but the fact that to this day the Irish and Dutch monitors who accompanied Sanchez Rau on his abortive peace mission have never been given any inkling of what he was up to, or what agenda he was pursuing, actually speaks volumes in itself and the truth of this diplomatic fiasco will most probably never be fully revealed to the public.[8]

In any event, with the bombing campaign in full flight and NATO planners quickly running out of new targets to attack, Dudakovic again entered the fray on 13 September and launched four brigades of the 5th Corps simultaneously against BSA positions to the east of Bihac Pocket on a 20-kilometre-wide front. Codenamed 'Operation Mistral 2', he retook Bosanska Krupa just after midnight on 14 September and marched into Bosanska Petrovac on the 15th. Mistakenly thinking he had routed the Serbs, when in fact most of them had simply conducted a tactical withdrawal, Dudakovic then decided to abandon his arrangements with the HV and raced for Kulen Vakuf to make amends for his failed attempt to capture the town ten months previously. But it all went horribly wrong and culminated in what is commonly known as a 'blue on blue' near the village of Ostrelj just north of Drvar on the morning of 15 September when the HV and the 5th Corps ended up shooting at, and killing one another.[9] Dudakovic then tried to drive into Sanski Most only to be systematically beaten back by a BSA counter-attack on the morning of 17 September.[10] At this point his offensive ground to a halt, but with the bombing campaign continuing into October it soon became clear that the 'endgame strategy' also involved bombing the Bosnian Serbs all the way to the 51/49 division of their country, which had been the cornerstone of the Contact Group plan for so long.

By now the BSA were in dire trouble right across the country – particularly in the north-west where the biggest threat was no longer coming from the 5th Corps but from over 3,500 HV troops who were now advancing menacingly on Banja Luka in a move consistent with President Tudjman's long-term plans for the ultimate division of Bosnia between Croatia and Serbia. This was clearly on his mind and consistent with everything he had explained in detail to UK Liberal Democrat leader Paddy Ashdown at London's Guildhall on 6 May 1995 on the 50th anniversary of VE Day.

An opportunity to commence this annexation was now at hand and Richard Holbrooke has admitted that he urged Tudjman to take Sanski Most, Prijedor and Bosanski Novi as quickly as possible. Banja Luka apparently was a different matter and Holbrooke claims now that he instructed both Tudjman and his defence minister, Gojko Susak, not to attack it.[11] If Banja Luka fell a huge population transfer would have to take place. In the final analysis this was not something Holbrooke could sanction because it would certainly create far more long-term problems than it would solve. Instead, limited offensives were permitted to continue as the US controlled the ground offensive in order to arrive at a territorial and ethnic balance which saw the eviction of over 100,000 Serbs from their homes across the country in areas which were now controlled by either the Muslims or the Croats. 'You have five days left, that's all', Holbrooke told Tudjman on 5 October. 'What you don't win on the battlefield will be hard to gain at the peace talks. Don't waste these last days.'[12] Further south the Sarajevo government were openly reluctant to exercise any restraint because they perceived correctly that the Serbs were on their knees. But their progress had also slowed down dramatically and so with all sides spent a ceasefire was proposed and agreed to late on 10 October.[13]

It took some time for this message to filter into the most remote regions of the front line, but by 15 October the shooting finally stopped and all sides set about digging themselves into deep defensive positions on either side of the Confrontation Line as the division of Bosnia on strictly ethnic lines became a stark reality. The Dayton Agreement of 21 November, and its signing in Paris on 14 December, formalised these positions, and NATO's 60,000 strong implementation force (IFOR) deployed in theatre to make it work. Bosnia-Hercegovina had been battered into the 51/49 split that most mediators had deemed so appropriate, and yet there were still no guarantees it would work. Time, the continuing presence of NATO and a massive injection of Western finance would all be crucial to any hopes of a long-term resolution, and the United States were now committed for the long haul – whether they liked it or not.

As matters stood at the end of 1995 the United States was finally committed to the one thing it had trenchantly resisted for so long. Thousands of US ground troops were on their way to Bosnia, proof positive that Clinton's policy on Bosnia, if one could even call it that, had been a complete failure. Izetbegovic had finally got his way, and from this point onwards US soldiers, diplomats and politicians could all look forward to being manipulated and abused by the Sarajevo regime as it set about pursuing the next phase of its unification policy; this began four months later on 21 April 1996 when Izetbegovic reviewed a huge military parade in Bihac.

In the presence of Ejup Ganic, Prime Minister Muratovic, generals Delic and Dudakovic, and a huge gathering of foreign diplomatic and military attachés, the president of Bosnia announced to the world that the parade itself was 'a message to both friend and foe to make friends and rejoice, and to warn the enemy never again to raise its finger against our people. I am here to tell you that the struggle for Bosnia-Herzegovina has not finished yet, that it goes on, and to wish you success on this long, difficult and honourable road towards a free and democratic Bosnia. The struggle will continue until Bosnia is unified and democratic.'[14]

Consistent as ever, the reality of military and diplomatic victory was not enough for Izetbegovic, because he perceived it to be a long way short of a final resolution. Prior to leaving Bosnia in 1995 General Rose formed the view that all Izetbegovic's talk about 'creating a multi-religious, multi-cultural State in Bosnia was a disguise for the extension of his own political career and the furtherance of Islam'.[15] The address in Bihac, supposedly to mark the termination of war and the beginning of the healing process, certainly seemed to corroborate that assessment.

In late December 1995 UNPROFOR handed over operations in Bosnia to a NATO implementation force led by Admiral Leighton-Smith. Arriving in full body armour, complete with tanks and helicopters, the message could not have been clearer to the Bosnian Serbs. This force could and would defend itself. Negotiating to secure compliance with agreements was a thing of the past. There were new rules of engagement. Compliance was not optional – it was mandatory – and from now on it would be peace enforcement whether the Serbs liked it or not.

Once again the 'peacemakers' had failed to grasp reality in Bosnia. The Serbs were a spent force. They had nothing left – no aircraft, no tanks, no communications equipment, no money, no economy and certainly no will to continue the fight. They were no longer a threat to anyone – least of all 60,000 heavily armed NATO troops. The problem was always going to be on the other sides, as the Armija, and to a lesser extent the HVO, drank themselves stupid on the euphoria of victory and then went off to collect tonnes of brand new military hardware from US ships unloading at Ploce harbour on the coast. The matter of who would control the victors was never addressed as the next phase of US Balkan policy began to evolve. MPRI were awarded another lucrative State Department contract to train the new Federation army, but nobody seemed to know or care how the monster they were about to create would be controlled in the longer term. Some other US president would inherit Clinton's legacy in Bosnia and be left to grapple with the consequences.

However, before the UN finally terminated its Bosnia operations in December 1995 the last force commander, General Bernard Janvier, took stock of the situation and wrote a significant 'End of Mission' report in which he made a number of telling remarks which speak for themselves:

> From the outset of the mission the force structure, equipment, and tasks were founded upon a false premise. A force based on a Chapter 6 mandate was deployed into a Chapter 7 environment. A peacekeeping force must not be deployed in an area where there is no peace to keep.
>
> Treatment of all warring factions must be patently fair and even-handed if one or all of the factions is not to doubt the impartiality of the UN. The position of Croatia is an excellent example. The Croatians became a de facto host nation to the UN rather than remaining a fundamental part of the problem, their true position. This encouraged them to ignore or, in some famous incidents, abuse UN troops during their offensives in 1995.
>
> The safe area policy was a military and humanitarian disaster in waiting. Insufficient troops were allocated to the task; air power limitations were not recognised; UNSC Res. 836 was lacking in true deterrent effect; the Bosnian Muslims were allowed to use the safe areas for their own military purposes; and the UN troops inside became de facto hostages.

In a remarkably honest document Janvier's assessments were absolutely correct His force will be judged, and judged critically. Those who condemn it will focus on the calamity that was the 'safe area' policy, but in all probability these critics will never have set one foot on a Balkan battlefield nor witnessed at first hand the difficulties a UN force experiences while attempting to operate under Chapter 6 of the UN Charter.

On the other hand, those who praise his force will claim that had UNPROFOR not deployed the lot of the average former Yugoslav citizen would have been infinitely worse throughout the wars of dissolution. Those disposed to this interpretation will also probably identify that it was the duplicitous behaviour of all parties to the conflict which ensured UNPROFOR never achieved the results it might have, and that ultimately in this context the various political and military leaders have only themselves to blame for the wanton destruction and massive loss of life which they chose to inflict each upon the other.

As stated at the outset, and later examined in detail, I firmly believe that Germany's headlong rush to recognise Croatia was fundamentally flawed and that agreeing to go along with it was probably the most critical mistake made by the international community in its attempts to manage, if not control, the dissolution of Former Yugoslavia. I share completely in Lord Carrington's frustrations as he argued in vain against recognition – a position supported by the UN secretary-general, ECMM, and the British, German and American ambassadors in Belgrade. The gift of recognition was a substantial bargaining tool yet it was thrown away for no concession. Europe, it appeared, was preoccupied with doing deals to secure a swift passage for the Maastricht Treaty – Germany conceded to Britain an 'opt out' clause while Britain in turn agreed to support the German push to recognise Croatia.[16]

Thereafter Britain and France sought to deal with Balkan matters at the United Nations only to find the US and Soviet Union vetoing military intervention. The best these two were prepared to countenance was a proposal by the Yugoslav Federation to impose an arms embargo on itself in order to restrict escalation and prevent the illicit flow of arms – a measure which in fact became UNSC Resolution 713 of 25 September 1991 – but there was to be no going back from recognition, or 'preventative recognition' as the Germans were now calling it.[17]

I am also convinced that the failure of the United States to support the Vance–Owen plan was incorrect, especially since in 1995 the Dayton map ended up looking almost identical to Vance and Owen's original document. However, by far the worst offence committed by the US was the commencement of covert military resupply operations to the Bosnian Muslims and the deployment of several special forces and intelligence personnel on the ground throughout the region. These operations were undertaken in clear violation of the United Nations arms embargo on the supply of weapons and military services to the warring parties and provided the Sarajevo government with continuing hope that after one more atrocity the West would finally come to their aid. This double game continued throughout the war and was still being played in Kosovo and Macedonia as late as 2001.

I have no doubt whatever that had the United States desisted from its clandestine and covert activities, and openly supported what the UN was trying to achieve, the international response to the problem would have proved far more effective. At the end of the day the only tangible result of this policy was the prolongation of the war by giving increased expectation to the Muslim side that the US would eventually come overtly to their aid.

Equally, the evolution, administration and failure of the safe area policy is now the subject of its own official UN report[18] – and rightly so. While never condoning murder and loss of life, in this work I have endeavoured to also explain how the Muslim leaders were for the most part the originators of their own difficulties. General Rose wrote of Dudakovic:

> His underlying strategy was familiar to me as it was followed elsewhere by the Bosnian Army – attack on all fronts, retreat into the enclave amid scenes of appalling suffering, call on the UN and NATO to bomb the Serbs. I found him an unpleasant man who demonstrated his total disregard for the safety of his own people by placing his HQ in the middle of the town to protect himself from Serb mortar and artillery fire.[19]

I agree with this assessment because I know it to be true, and all ECMM reports from Bihac over the years have catalogued Dudakovic's flamboyant tactics and blatant disregard for human life, including those of his own soldiers and that of one General Vlado Santic who just 'disappeared' in Bihac Pocket during the early days of March 1995.[20]

Naser Oric was no different. The regime he ran in Srebrenica was almost exactly the same as Dudakovic's operation in Bihac, and the raids he carried out on Serb villages in the Drina valley were fundamentally instrumental in causing the Serbs to mount their own campaign against the enclave, ultimately resulting in its fall and the disappearance of over 7,000 men. In fact the UN's 'Srebrenica Report' traces Muslim attacks on Serb property back further to 1992 and details the ethnic cleansing of Serbs from the town.[21]

The common factor here was that Oric and Dudakovic took their orders directly from Sarajevo and Izetbegovic. He was the one who approved their attacks from within the safe areas; he was the one who tolerated massive smuggling and black market operations; and he was the one who needed his people trapped in enclaves surrounded by the Bosnian Serbs in order to cultivate and promote their status as victims and thereby retain sufficient media interest in their plight. I have no doubt that he believed a constant flow of harrowing imagery from the enclaves would eventually convince the West to intervene on his side – and ultimately this strategy worked, at an unquantifiable price.

Of course, none of this in any way justifies the barbarous attacks on the enclaves by Ratko Mladic and his subordinates in the Bosnian Serb army. And none of it justifies the liquidation of over 7,000 people in the aftermath of the fall of Srebrenica in 1995. However, it certainly does explain why Mladic and others found it necessary to launch the attacks in the first place.

And finally there is the matter of Radovan Karadzic and whether he deserved to be typecast as a psychopath and a butcher. Certainly he has huge questions to answer if and when he appears before the ICTY at The Hague, but Karadzic was never influential within the Bosnian Serb military chain of command which stretched from Mladic on the ground to Milosevic in Belgrade. Equally there is no evidence which suggests that he personally authorised the mistreatment of prisoners or that he advocated a policy of rape, or that he ordered the deaths of Srebrenica's menfolk in July 1995.

In fact, significant evidence exists which shows that, particularly in 1992, Karadzic instructed his security forces to uphold the rules of international humanitarian law; the ICTY is now in possession of these same documents.[22] Of course, the problem is that in his capacity as the president of Republic Srpska Karadzic had clear obligations to speak out against the criminal activities of his army commanders, and he failed to do so. Nevertheless we must be clear that Radovan Karadzic did not have control over the Bosnian Serb army, and Milos Vasic is correct when he states that 'the theory that Radovan Karadzic started it does not hold water. Without Milosevic's full political, logistic, police, and military support, there could have been no war in Bosnia.'[23]

Throughout the course of the modern Yugoslav conflict the concepts of 'perception' and 'reality' have for the most part remained in diametric opposition, with the 'truth' itself often being a relative term – it could mean anything or everything depending on whom you were talking to at any given time. Milos Stankovic got it right when he said:

> We were dealing with pathological behaviour driven by deep-seated perceptions or misconceptions of past injustices. So in a way, truth, whatever that may be, simply wasn't important. All that really mattered were perceptions. People based their analysis and actions on these perceptions. And that was the basis of all our problems in dealing with these people ... They believed they were right, and we thought they were liars for it. We believed in our monopoly of truth, and they saw us as liars. The bottom line is this: if Mladic believed something to be so, regardless of the fact that we knew it not to be that way, the fact that it wasn't so was totally irrelevant. He was always going to base his analysis, and hence his actions, on what he believed to be the case, conditioned as his perceptions were by history and upbringing. Perception based on belief was everything. Truth had nothing to do with it.[24]

Only one group of people could have saved federal Yugoslavia from itself – the Yugoslav National Army (JNA). However, the General Staff allowed themselves to be used and abused by Milosevic and Jovic in pursuit of goals which had nothing whatever to do with 'federalism' and everything to do with one man's quest for power. Milosevic purged the army four times. In 1991 all Slovenes and Croats were forced to leave. Early in 1992 the defence minister, General Kadijevic, and the head of the Security Directorate, General Simeon Tumanov were forced out. Next, 38 senior generals were 'retired', and on 19 May 1992 the JNA was split into the VJ (Yugoslav army) and the BSA (the Bosnian Serb army), with all men born in Bosnia-Hercegovina ordered to transfer to the new entity which was to be commanded by a Milosevic loyalist and pan-Serbian propagandist, General Ratko Mladic. The final purge took place in 1993 when those perceived to be aligning themselves too closely with Karadzic in Bosnia, and Vojislav Seselj in Serbia, were unceremoniously rooted out while thousands of others were ordered to join the ranks of the SARSK (Krajina Serb army) or be retired without pension or gratuity. There was only one way to survive – only absolute and total obedience to Slobodan Milosevic.

Carl von Clausewitz was right when he said that 'war is politics by other means'.[25] Milos Vasic is also correct when he says that it is politics which determines whether an army will be used, abused, or misused.[26] In Yugoslavia the JNA was unable to save the Federation precisely because it was used, abused and misused in order to further the political career of one man, and to advance the lesser careers of a host of unscrupulous underlings who pinned their colours to his coat-tails. That man was Slobodan Milosevic and it is he who bears the lion's share of responsibility for federal Yugoslavia's violent dissolution. There is no distinction or divergence between 'perception' and 'reality' when it comes to the culpability of Slobodan Milosevic. If I have learned nothing else from my time in the Balkans I have learned that.

NOTES

INTRODUCTION

1 Sarah A. Kent, 'Writing the Yugoslav Wars', *American Historical Review*, October 1997.
2 On 24 July 1995, and again on 14 November 1995, Radovan Karadzic and Ratko Mladic were indicted for genocide, crimes against humanity, grave breaches of the 1949 Geneva conventions, and violations of the laws and customs of war, by the International Criminal Tribunal for the Former Yugoslavia.
3 Official Debriefing Report – *Dutchbatt 3 in Srebrenica*, Brigadier-General Van der Wind, 4/10/95.
4 Brendan O'Shea, 'The Life and Times of Ratko Mladic', *Irish Defence Journal*, Vol. 56, No. 1, February 1996.
5 Also applicable in this context are Articles 6 and 39 of the Republic Srpska's Peoples Defence Act, and Article 33 of the Republic Srpska's Internal Affairs Act.
6 Janine di Giovanni, 'Mass Killers Walk Free', *The Mail on Sunday*, 3/3/96.
7 Lindsey Hilsum, 'An Interview with Radovan Karadzic', *Independent*, 16/6/96, p. 12.
8 David Rieff, *Slaughterhouse*, Random House (London), 1995.
9 Roy Gutman, *A Witness to Genocide*, Macmillan (London), 1993.
10 Ed Vulliamy, *Seasons in Hell*, Simon & Schuster (London), 1994.
11 Ibid., p. xi.
12 David Owen, *Balkan Odyssey*, Indigo/Cassell (London), 1996, p. 365.
13 Philip Corwin, *Dubious Mandate*, Duke University Press (London), 1999, p. 216.
14 Michael Rose, *Fighting for Peace*, Harvill (London), 1998, p. 34.
15 Corwin, *Dubious Mandate*, pp. 113, 129.
16 Ibid., pp. 143–144.
17 Lewis MacKenzie, *Peacekeeper – The Road to Sarajevo*, Douglas & McIntyre (Toronto), 1993, pp. 193, 194.
18 Ibid.
19 Milos Stankovic, *Trusted Mole*, HarperCollins (London), 2000, p. 102.
20 Anthony Loyd, *My War Gone By, I Miss It So*, Doubleday (London), 1999, pp. 165.
21 Brendan O'Shea, *Crisis at Bihac: Bosnia's Bloody Battlefield*, Sutton (Stroud), 1998, p. 119.
22 Ibid., pp. 109–111.

NOTES

23 Tim Ripley, *Operation Deliberate Force*, Centre for Defence and International Security Studies, Lancaster University (Lancaster), 1999.
24 Dubravka Ugresic, *The Culture of Lies*, Phoenix House (London), 1998, pp. 39–40.

1 1991

1 Milosevic and Jovic fully accepted the inevitability of dissolution and were concentrating on what the next Yugoslavia was going to look like once the numerous territories in which ethnic Serbs predominated had been annexed.
2 Ed Vulliamy, *Seasons in Hell*, Simon & Schuster (London), 1994, p. 55.
3 Jasper Ridley, *Tito: a Biography*, Constable and Co. (London), 1994, p. 149.
4 At London's Guild Hall, on VE Day 1995, Tudjman proceeded to draw the division of Bosnia on the back of the menu card for Liberal Democrat leader, Paddy Ashdown. The sketch was reproduced in the *Sunday Times* of 7 August 1995.
5 Dusko Doder and Louise Branson, *Milosevic – Portrait of a Tyrant*, The Free Press (New York), 1999, pp. 88–89.
6 Warren Zimmerman, 'The Last Ambassador', *Foreign Affairs*, March/April 1995.
7 In August 1990 Momcilo Djujic, the oldest surviving commander of the Second World War Chetniks, recognised Seselj as his successor to the title of Cetnik Vojvoda (Chetnik Duke) in the magazine *Velika Srbija*.
8 Maja Korac, 'Understanding Ethnic National Identity in Times of War and Social Change', in Robert Pynsent (ed.), *The Literature of Nationalism*, School of Slavonic and East European Studies, University College London (London), 1996, p. 240. See also Robert Thomas, *Serbia under Milosevic*, Hurst & Co. (London), 1999, p. 98.
9 Thomas, *Serbia under Milosevic*, p. 97.
10 Vesna Peric Zimonjic, 'Former Presidents' Aides Singing like Canaries in Corruption Inquiry', *Independent*, 3/4/01, p. 13.
11 This quintet were responsible for the recruitment and subsequent deployment in Croatia, Bosnia and Kosovo of paramilitary units loyal to Milosevic. The most notable formations included The Tigers (Zeljko Raznatovic – alias Arkan), The White Eagles (Dragoslav Bokan), The Yellow Wasps (Dusan and Vojin Vuckovic), The Serbian Falcons (Sinisa Vucinic) The Chetnik Avengers (Milan Lukic) and The Serbian Chetnik Movement (Vojislav Seselj).
12 Order signed by Branko Kostic, federal vice-president, 10/12/91.
13 *Gas Slavonije*, 6/2/96, interview with Gojko Susak, Croatian minister for defence.
14 *Breakdown in the Balkans*, Carnegie Institute Reports 1993.
15 Ibid.
16 Interview with Zimmerman at Glandore, County Cork, Ireland – 24/8/99.
17 Warren Zimmerman, 'The Last Ambassador', *Foreign Affairs*, March/April 1995.
18 *The Death of Yugoslavia*, Part 3, BBC TV, 17/9/95.
19 Lieutenant-Colonel Jonathan Riley, *The Monitor Mission in the Balkans*, ECMM Publication (Zagreb), 1993, p. 6.
20 Doder and Branson, *Milosevic – Portrait of a Tyrant*, p. 93.
21 *The Death of Yugoslavia*, Part 3, BBC TV, 17/9/95.
22 Ibid.

23 Simon Freeman, 'Lies Win Balkan War of Words', *The European*, weekend of 19–21 July 1991.
24 Confirmed to the author in 1999 by Major Frank Kalic, Slovene army.
25 *The Death of Yugoslavia*, Part 3, BBC TV, 17/9/95.
26 On 30 April the EC had already offered Markovic US$4 billion to support the convertibility of the Yugoslav dinar and encourage new markets.
27 *The Death of Yugoslavia*, Part 3, BBC TV, 17/9/95.
28 *Sequence of Events in Former Yugoslavia* (1st edn), ECMM Publication (Zagreb), 19/12/94, pp. 35–36.
29 *Breakdown in the Balkans*, Carnegie Institute Reports 1993.
30 *Sequence of Events in Former Yugoslavia*, p. 44. The Croat village of Kijevo had been under siege since 29 April. On 19 August Colonel Ratko Mladic began shelling the village incessantly. When the military were finished Milan Martic, a police inspector, then burned what remained to the ground. ECMM Team *Bihac Special Report*, 19/10/95. Four and a half years later 19 bodies, all male and aged from 45–60, were found in a mass grave with gunshot wounds both to their heads and abdomens.
31 The first ICRC appeal was made on 2/7/91 and reminded all parties of their obligations to comply with international humanitarian law (IHL). The second was made on 17/7/91 and advised against the misuse of the emblem (the red cross on a white background).
32 Denise Plattner, 'The Penal Repression of Violations of IHL in Non-International Armed Conflicts', *International Review of the Red Cross*, 1990, No. 278, pp. 409–420.
33 Article 3, common to all four Geneva Conventions 1949, para. 1.1, sub-paras. a, b, c, d.
34 Additional Protocol II 1977, Articles 4, 5 and 6.
35 See Yves Sandoz, *A Consideration of the Implementation of IHL and the Role of the ICRC in the Former Yugoslavia*, International Committee of the Red Cross (ICRC), Geneva, Switzerland, 28/9/93, pp. 5–6.
36 Signed in Geneva on 27/11/91.
37 *Breakdown in the Balkans*, Carnegie Reports 1993.
38 Addendum to Memorandum of Understanding 27/11/91, signed on 23/5/92.
39 In a subsequent agreement, signed in Budapest on 7/8/92 by the prime ministers of Croatia and federal Yugoslavia, both entities reaffirmed their commitment to apply the rules of IHL, made specific reference to certain provisions in the four Geneva Conventions and Additional Protocol I, and accepted their obligations to punish war criminals.
40 Diana Johnstone, 'Seeing Yugoslavia Through a Dark Glass – Politics, Media, and the Ideology of Globalization', *Covert Action Quarterly*, Spring/Summer 1999, p. 67.
41 Ibid., p. 67.
42 *Naroda Armija*, Belgrade, April 1992: 'for his exceptional valor in actions undertaken in battle tasks of particular significance to the military forces, and the defense of the country, and for successful, command, leadership, initiative and personal bravery'.
43 Gaja Petkovic, 'Guarantees of the Almighty', *NIN Magazine*, 11/4/94.
44 Helsinki Watch Reports, Croatia, 1992.
45 Doder and Branson, *Milosevic – Portrait of a Tyrant*, pp. 95–96.
46 The Badinter Commission.
47 CSCE meeting, 11 September 1991.
48 8/11/91. ECMM reports from that time indicate the Croatian estimate for JNA

NOTES

troops involved in the fall of Vukovar – 650 tanks, 250 artillery pieces, 100 multiple-launch rocket systems (MLRS) and 45,000 ground troops – to be grossly exaggerated. Only the artillery and MLRS figures can be taken as valid.
49 *Sequence of Events in Former Yugoslavia*, p. 64.
50 Slavenka Drakulic, *The Balkan Express*, Harper Perennial (New York), 1994, pp. 97–98.
51 Michael Ignatieff, *Blood and Belonging*, Penguin (Harmondsworth), 1994, p. 45.
52 Sljivancanin was subsequently promoted to the rank of lieutenant-colonel for his 'successful' management of Vukovar in the aftermath of liberation. In 1994 the International Criminal Tribunal indicted Sljivancanin and two of his colleagues for the murder of 261 people.
53 Aryeh Neier, *War Crimes*, Times Books (Toronto), 1998, pp. 6–11.
54 Mathew Collin, *This is Serbia Calling*, Serpent's Tail Publishers (London), 2001, pp. 48–49.
55 Ibid.
56 The meeting took place in Hotel I on 8/10/91. In attendance were colonels Imra Agotic and Stjepan Adanic for the Croats and General Andrija Raseta and Colonel Arandelo Stamenkovic for the JNA. ECMM was represented by Ambassador Dirk J. van Houten and General Johannes Kosters.
57 A meeting in The Hague on 10/10/91 chaired by Hans van den Broek. The following day leading Serb politicians rejected this plan claiming that the JNA would have to remain in areas where Serbs were in majority.
58 Florence Hamlish Levinsohn, *Belgrade Among the Serbs*, Ivan R. Dee Inc. Publishers (Chicago), 1994, p. 60.
59 Norma von Ragenfeld-Feldman, *The War in Former Yugoslavia and the American New Media*, at http://whatreallyhappened.com/RANCHO/LIE/HK/SATAN.html.
60 Fourth Geneva Convention, 1949, Art. 147.
61 In a BBC *Newsnight* interview with John Simpson, August 1995.
62 See David Fromkin, *Kosovo Crossing*, The Free Press (New York), 1999, p. 127.
63 'In its opinion No. 1 of 29/11/91 the Badinter Commission [correctly] expressed the view that the situation in Yugoslavia was one involving the dissolution of the federal republic and the consequent emergence of its constituent republics as independent states, although the process was not yet complete.'
64 *The Recognition of the Successor States to the Former Yugoslavia*, ECMM Political Section Special Report (Zagreb), 4/12/94, p. 2.
65 Ibid., p. 3.
66 Neither the UN nor the EC suggested that the peoples of Yugoslavia had a right to secede, which flowed from Article 1.2 of the UN Charter.
67 *The Recognition of the Successor States to the Former Yugoslavia*, p. 3.
68 Ibid., p. 4. 'Only if Lord Carrington had been capable of blocking the Serbian aggression against Croatia with the help of the international community could he have pressured non-Serb parties in the conflict into reaching an agreement with Serbia on the key issues before being recognized. The fact that the relevant countries had been increasingly resolute in refraining from the threat of military intervention robbed Lord Carrington of a crucial instrument of pressure.'
69 Riley, *The Monitor Mission in the Balkans*, p. 9.
70 Zimmerman, 'The Last Ambassador'.
71 Misha Glenny, *The Fall of Yugoslavia*, Penguin Books (Harmondsworth),

1993, p. 164. 'Izetbegovic was thus forced by German led EC policy into the same mistake that Tudjman had made voluntarily: he embarked upon secession from Yugoslavia without securing prior agreement from the Serbs.'

2 1992

1. This was the fifteenth ceasefire brokered since the war began in Croatia.
2. Jonathan Riley, *The Monitor Mission in the Balkans*, ECMM Publication (Zagreb), 1993, p. 24.
3. Warren Zimmerman, 'The Last Ambassador', *Foreign Affairs*, March/April 1995, p. 15.
4. *Who are the Bosnian Muslims*, ECMM Special Report (Zagreb), November 1994.
5. Tom Gjelten, *Sarajevo Daily*, Harper Perennial (New York), 1996, p. 33.
6. Warren Zimmerman, *Origins of a Catastrophe*, Times Books (New York), 1996, p. 181.
7. Ibid., p. 182.
8. Ibid., p. 183.
9. Hrvoje Sarinic, Tudjman's chief of staff, later admitted to Zimmerman that Tudjman and Milosevic had discussed their evolving strategy for Bosnia just one week previously in Brussels. He also claimed that Greece and France also supported the break up of Bosnia, something that was patently untrue.
10. Zimmerman, 'The Last Ambassador', p. 15. See also Zimmerman, *Origins of a Catastrophe*, p. 184, for his assessment of Tudjman.
11. Another round of 'partition talks' had taken place in Graz, Austria, on 22 February between Karadzic and Koljevic for the Serbs, and Lerotic and Manolic for the Croats.
12. Ibid., p. 78.
13. A referendum was held concurrently in Montenegro where 75 per cent of the population voted against independence. The Muslims here, 25 per cent of the total, did not participate.
14. Radio Free Europe Reports, 1/3/92.
15. Gjelten, *Sarajevo Daily*, pp. 82–83.
16. Ibid., p. 23.
17. Ed Vulliamy, *Seasons in Hell*, Simm & Schuster (London), 1994, p. 73.
18. 11/5/92: EC ambassadors withdraw from Belgrade. 12/5/92: EC monitors withdraw from Sarajevo and Warren Zimmerman goes home.
19. UNSC Resolution 752, 13/5/92.
20. Helsinki Watch Report, 16/5/92.
21. Carnegie Institute Report on Bosnia, 1993.
22. UNHCR Daily Report, 29/7/92.
23. Lewis MacKenzie, *Peacekeeper – The Road to Sarajevo*, Douglas & McIntyre (Toronto), 1993, p. 193.
24. Ibid., pp. 193–194.
25. Colm Doyle, *The Bosnian Dilemma*, University of Limerick, 1994.
26. David Owen, *Balkan Odyssey*, Indigo/Cassell Publishing (London), 1996, p. 112, and Yossef Bodansky, *Offensive in the Balkans* (International Strategic Studies Association), International Media Corp. Ltd (London), 1995, p. 54.
27. Florence Hamlish Levinsohn, *Belgrade Among the Serbs*, Ivan R. Dee Inc. (Chicago), 1994, p. 312.
28. John Simpson, *Panorama*, BBC TV, 14/1/95.

NOTES

29 *Sequence of Events in Former Yugoslavia* (1st edn), ECMM Publication (Zagreb), 19/12/94, p. 80.
30 ECMM Special Report, 5/10/94.
31 Vulliamy, *Seasons in Hell*, p. 93. 'In the town of Kozarac, there was barely a single house left undamaged, and those that stood intact were occupied by apparently nonchalant Serbs. This town of 25,000 had been 90% Muslim, a 500 year old settlement. Late in May the Serbs had set about its methodical obliteration.'
32 Ibid., pp. 92–93. 'At Celinac near Prijedor the new Serbian civic authorities issued a decree that Muslims were forbidden to ... 1. Move around from 4 p.m. to 6 p.m. 2. Associate or loiter in the streets, in cafes, restaurants, and other public places. 3. Bathe or fish in the river. 4. Drive or travel by car. 5. Gather in groups containing more than three men. 6. Make contact with any relative who was not a resident of Celinac. 7. Sell real estate or exchange their homes without permission and only through official [Serb] channels. 8. Make any telephone call other than from the post office. 9. Leave the town without permission and the necessary documentation. 10. Show contempt for the struggle of the Serbian nation.'
33 UNSC Resolution 757.
34 UNHCR figures for June 1992 reported 1.4 million 'Yugoslavs' as having fled their homes in the face of ethnic cleansing. Twelve months later that figure had risen to over 4 million.
35 BBC interview, 3/6/92.
36 The Croatian Republic of Herceg-Bosna (CRHB) was established by Mate Boban on 21/6/92.
37 Common Defence Pact, 8/7/92. Agreement on Friendship and Co-operation, Protocol on Economic Co-operation, Agreement on BiH Refugee Accommodation, all 21/7/92.
38 Maggie O'Kane, *Guardian*, 29/7/92.
39 Vulliamy, *Seasons in Hell*, p. 125.
40 Aryeh Neier, *War Crimes*, Times Books (Toronto), 1998, p. 134.
41 Vulliamy, *Seasons in Hell*, p. 97.
42 Riley, *The Monitor Mission in the Balkans*, p. 29A. See also Reuters Report/Graphic 1/9/92.
43 Vulliamy, *Seasons in Hell*, pp. 104–105.
44 See ECMM Special Report 3/9/92, and Riley, *The Monitor Mission in the Balkans*, pp. 31–32.
45 Riley, *The Monitor Mission in the Balkans*, p. 33.
46 Marcus Tanner, 'Serb Faces First UN Genocide Trial', *Independent*, 7/8/98, p. 11.
47 Peter Maas, *Love thy Neighbour – A Story of War*, Papermac Books (London), 1996, pp. 38–39. 'At least 2,500 civilians were killed in Kozarac in a seventy-two hour period. It was a slaughterhouse. The survivors were sent to the prison camps.'
48 Ibid., p. 36. '"This is a great moment in the history of the Serbian people", he chanted, priest like. Kovacevic was a madman from birth. There was a certain vulgar justice to the fact that a man who was reared in a concentration camp ended up running his own string of camps as an adult.'
49 Vulliamy, *Seasons in Hell*, p. 9.
50 On 13 March 1997 Milan Kovacevic was indicted for war crimes and charged with complicity in genocide. On 10 October 1997 he was arrested by S-FOR troops in Prijedor and immediately flown to The Hague. On 23 June 1998 additional charges were brought against him. (See International Criminal Tribunal for Former Yugoslavia 'Bulletin' No. 21, 27/7/98, p. 10.) In his last

letter to his brother he wrote: 'Tell all the people never to surrender. It is better to die than to come here. It is hell.' (See 'Hague Court Hit by Blunders' by Marie Colvin, *Sunday Times*, 16/8/98, p. 15.) On 1 August he was found dead in his cell, his abdominal aorta having burst during the night.

51 Lara Marlowe, 'Cleansed Wounds', *Time*, 14/9/92, p. 34.
52 See Annex A, this chapter (p. 59). The matter of this document's existence was put to Florence Hartman spokesperson for the International Criminal Tribunal in The Hague by journalists from the 'Nedeljni Telegraf' (Belgrade) in May 2001. Ms Hartman did not confirm the existence of this order, but more importantly she did not deny its existence either. (Full report 'Nedeljni Telegraf' [Belgrade], 23 May 2001.)
53 Extract from 1995 ICTY Indictment.
54 The ultimate irony here, of course, is the fact that these very same camps, and particularly Omarska, were designated in October 1995 as refugee centres and used to accommodate thousands of distraught Serbs who were forced to flee their homes in western Bosnia before the advancing Croat/Muslim forces – yet another example of the cyclical nature of life in the Balkan quagmire.
55 See Annexes A, B and C, this chapter (pp. 59–62). ICTY spokesperson Ms Hartman did not deny the existence of these documents.
56 Norma von Ragenfeld-Feldman, 'The War in Former Yugoslavia and the American Media', http://whatreallyhappened.com/RANCHO/LIE/HK/SATAN. html.
57 Andrew Bell-Fialkoff, 'A Brief History of Ethnic Cleansing', *Foreign Affairs*, Summer 1993, p. 120.
58 Jaques Merlino, 'The Truth from Yugoslavia is Not being Reported Honestly', *Foreign Affairs*, 1993.
59 Peter Brock, 'The Partisan Press', *Foreign Policy*, Winter 1993/94, pp. 152–172.
60 Pursuant to UNSC Resolution 780 of 6/10/92 an Expert Commission was established to examine in detail the question of detention camps in Bosnia-Hercegovina. When the report was published in May 1994 it stated that the Commission had located 173 mass graves and 715 detention centres, the operation of which broke down as follows: 237 Serb, 89 Muslim, 77 Croat, four mixed Muslim/Croat where they were co-operating with one another, and a further 308 where it was unclear who was in control.
61 Eagleburger was still making negative contributions over two years later when he attempted to ridicule the December 1994 President Carter initiative.
62 Daniel Benjamin, 'Hatred Ten Times Over,' *Time*, 17/8/92, p. 26.
63 Wiliam Mader, 'Frustration with Bad-faith Talks', *Time*, 14/9/92, p. 36. Also referred to by Colm Doyle in his paper 'The Bosnian Dilemma', University of Limerick, July 1994.
64 From an address to the Royal United Services Institute for Defence Studies on 6/7/92, and also referred to by Colm Doyle.
65 UNSC Resolution 781, 9/10/92.
66 Carnegie Endowment for International Peace, *Report on Former Yugoslavia 1989–1993*.
67 Permanent Peace Conference moves to Geneva, Switzerland, 3/9/92.
68 UNSC Resolution 776.
69 *New York Times* of 17/9/92, and ECMM Weekly Reports, September 1992.
70 ECMM Reports 1992, and eyewitness observation and investigation by the author in 1994.
71 UNSC Resolution 780, 6/10/92.
72 Janes Sentinel estimated that in 1993 the Sarajevo government still spent over US$60 million on the procurement of weapons and ammunition which were

transported covertly into central Bosnia from Italy, Slovenia, Croatia and Hungary, and during the period April 1992 to April 1994 they also estimated that the HVO received equipment worth US$660 million, the BSA US$476 million, and the Armija US$162 million. So much for an arms embargo.
73 The Prijedor Agreement, 1/11/92.
74 This was the first mention of something which would be implemented later, on 4 August 1994 in fact, and become known as 'The Drina Blockade'.
75 Carnegie Report on the Former Yugoslavia, 1993.
76 CSCE and US observers reported widespread irregularities in the process.

3 1993

1 Milos Stankovic, *Trusted Mole*, HarperCollins (London), 2000, p. 78.
2 Lieutenant Colonel Bob Stewart, *Broken Lives*, HarperCollins (London), 1993, p. 213.
3 Croatian weekly newspaper, 8/1/93.
4 UNSC Resolution 802.
5 David Owen, *Balkan Odyssey*, Indigo/Cassell Publishing (London), 1996, pp. 102–111.
6 Ibid., pp. 125–126. Lord Owen states that Ruder Finn Global Public Affairs (US) were paid US$10,000 per month by the Croatian government to promote a positive image of Croatia in the US. He confirms that they were also employed by the Sarajevo government.
7 UNSC Resolution 764, 13/7/92.
8 UNSC Resolution 771, 13/8/92.
9 UNSC Document No. S/24657.
10 UNSC Resolution 780, 6/10/92.
11 UNSC Document No. S/25274.
12 Michael G. Roskin, 'The Bosnian-Serb Problem: What We Should, and Should Not Do', *Parameters* (US Army War College Quarterly), Vol. XXII, No. 4, Winter 1992/93, p. 31.
13 Stankovic, *Trusted Mole*, p. 104.
14 Naser Oric had previously served as one of Slobodan Milosevic's personal bodyguards while he was a police officer in Belgrade.
15 Stankovic, *Trusted Mole*, p. 132.
16 UNSC Resolution 816 did not include any provision to bomb ground targets.
17 Stankovic, *Trusted Mole*, p. 145.
18 UNSC Resolution 819, 16/4/93.
19 UNSC Resolution 820, 17/4/93.
20 General Morillon's 'Srebrenica Agreement', 17/4/93.
21 On 6 May the UNSC adopted Resolution 824 which stated that: Acting under Chapter 7 of the Charter, the Council declares that Sarajevo and other threatened areas like Tuzla, Zepa, Gorazde, Bihac, and Srebrenica shall be treated as safe areas and should be free from armed attack.
22 Stankovic, *Trusted Mole*, pp. 150–153. 'We dropped into a scene of almost uncontrolled chaos. It was estimated that some 55,000 refugees were crammed into this small town. People hung from every balcony of the shabby apartment blocks, the walls of which were pocked by scars and shell holes. The first casualties had arrived. I nearly puked when I saw what lay inside. The stench was over-powering, a mixture of stale sweat, faeces, and sweet rotting putrification.'
23 Ibid., p. 152.
24 Stewart, *Broken Lives*, pp. 278–299.

25 *Time*, 20/6/94. Report by James O. Jackson on the work of the International War Crimes Tribunal in The Hague.
26 In an interview on 4/8/95 with Captain Cathal O'Neill, personal staff officer to the force commander, General Wahlgren.
27 Assembly meetings rotate between the major towns in the Republic Srpska.
28 Yugoslavia in this context means Serbia and Montenegro.
29 Momir Bulatovic (president of Montenegro), Vitali Churkin (Russian envoy), Richard Bartholomew (US envoy).
30 *The Death of Yugoslavia*, Part 5, BBC TV, 2/10/95.
31 ECMM Special Report, 15/1/95.
32 *Time*, 3/5/93, p. 44.
33 Decision of the Security Council, 6 May 1993. The vote to establish the 'safe areas' was carried by 15 votes to nil. There was no detail – this was to be worked out later.
34 In an interview with Captain Cathal O'Neill, 4/8/95.
35 *The Death of Yugoslavia*, Part 5, BBC TV, 1/10/95.
36 Ibid. Comment by Jose Maria Mendeluce, UN negotiator at the time.
37 It is also worth noting at this point that when another 'safe area', Bihac Pocket, came under sustained attack in November 1994, 18 months after these dramatic events in Srebrenica, neither the UN nor anyone else could at that point decide what constituted the designated 'safe area', nor had they any notion what their obligations actually were *vis-à-vis* its protection.
38 The geographic boundaries of the six so-called 'safe areas' were never defined. As far as the UN was concerned they believed their obligation was to protect the population, while the Sarajevo government demanded the safeguarding of territory.
39 Report of the secretary-general pursuant to paragraph 2 of Security Council Resolution 808 (1993) – UNSC Document S/25704, 3/5/93, para. 29, p. 8. 'The international tribunal shall prosecute persons responsible for serious violations of international humanitarian law committed in the territory of the Former Yugoslavia since 1991. This body of law exists in the form of both conventional law and customary law. The part of conventional international humanitarian law which has beyond doubt become part of international customary law is the law applicable in armed conflict as embodied in: the Geneva Conventions of 12 August 1949 for Protection of War Victims; The Hague Convention (IV) Respecting the Laws and Customs of War on Land, and the Regulations annexed thereto of 18 October 1907; the Convention on the Prevention and Punishment of the Crime of Genocide of 9 December 1948; and the Charter of the International Military Tribunal of 8 August 1945.'
40 Report of the secretary-general pursuant to paragraph 2 of Security Council Resolution 808 (1993) – UNSC Document S/25704, 3/5/93, paras, 37, 38, 39, p. 10.
41 Preamble to the Fourth Hague Convention Respecting the Laws and Customs of War on Land, 18/10/1907, para. 8.
42 Article 6, Statute of the International Criminal Tribunal for Former Yugoslavia.
43 Report of the secretary-general pursuant to paragraph 2 of Security Council Resolution 808 (1993) – UNSC Document S/25704, 3/5/93, para. 54, p. 14.
44 Ibid., para. 55, p. 14.
45 Article 21.4.d of the Statute of the International Criminal Tribunal for Former Yugoslavia outlines that the accused must be tried in his presence. Trials *in absentia* are not permitted.
46 With the establishment of the second International Criminal Tribunal for Rwanda in 1994 the Security Council attempted once again to remove any

remaining distinctions between the rules applicable in international and non-international armed conflicts.
47 Adam Roberts, 'The Laws of War: Problems of Implementation in Contemporary Conflicts', in *Law in Humanitarian Crisis*, Vol. 1, European Commission Publication, 1995, p. 75.
48 Official presidential statement on Bosnia, 6/5/93.
49 Two mosques destroyed in Banja Luka, 7/5/93.
50 Appeal by force commander to Tudjman to intervene in Mostar, 9/5/93.
51 *The Death of Yugoslavia*, Part 5, BBC TV, 1/10/95.
52 Ibid.
53 ECMM Report 23/6/93, para. 3.
54 Stankovic, *Trusted Mole*, p. 201.
55 Ibid.
56 The Washington Accord, 22/5/93.
57 NATO defence ministers meeting in Brussels, 25–26/5/93.
58 Brendan O'Shea, *Crisis at Bihac*, p. 15.
59 Misha Glenny, *The Fall of Yugoslavia*, Penguin Books (London), 1993, p. 152.
60 Quoted in *Vanjska Politika Srijeda*, 2 Veljace 1994, by Aleksandar Milosevic and translated by Croatian Assistance Team ECMM.
61 Lewis MacKenzie, *Peacekeeper – The Road to Sarajevo*, Douglas & McIntyre (Toronto), 1993, p. 165.
62 Laura Silber and Alan Little, *The Death of Yugoslavia*, Penguin/BBC (London), 1995, p. 262.
63 ECMM Report/Info Cell, 11/5/93.
64 ECMM Report, 11/7/93. Abdic had no difficulty signing. For him it was the only way forward.
65 The Washington Accord, 22/5/93.
66 Brendan O'Shea, *Crisis at Bihac*, p. 20.
67 Letter, Abdic to Izetbegovic, July 1993.
68 Talks began on 27 July 1993 with Karadzic, Boban and Izetbegovic, and also involved the participation of presidents Tudjman, Milosevic and Bulatovic, as appropriate.
69 10 July 1993. Signed at Makarska, Croatia, an agreement on the delivery of humanitarian aid in the whole area of Bosnia-Hercegovina under the control of the Croat and Muslim forces in the presence of representatives from all international humanitarian agencies.
70 ECMM Weekly Mil./Pol. Summary, 29/9/93.
71 ECMM Sequence of Events, 29/8/93, p. 115.
72 Ibid., 31/8/93, Geneva.
73 Taken from the letter of the president of the Initiative Committee, Professor Asim Dizdarevic to the president of the Bihac District Assembly, Ejub Topic, on 11/9/93.
74 Brendan O'Shea, *Crisis at Bihac*, p. 22.
75 ECMM Weekly Consolidated Report, 29/10/93.
76 ECMM Weekly Report, 11/11/93.
77 Stankovic, *Trusted Mole*, pp. 143–144. 'We discovered that Americares had a reputation for busting into war zones aggressively and unilaterally without diplomatic clearance. They had been very active in supplying Mujahideen in Afghanistan. Some of the press who seemed to know even more claimed that Americares was the baby brother of Air America, the CIA front airline that was so active in Vietnam, Cambodia, and Laos'.
78 Brendan O'Shea, *Crisis at Bihac*, p. 26.
79 RC Zagreb Daily Reports, 4–5/12/93.

80 UNPROFOR/G2 Assessment Review, April 1994. The Republic of Srpska Krajina forces were not operating under a unified command structure but were functioning instead as independent units, very much doing their own thing and following their own agendas.
81 ECMM Weekly Mil./Pol. Summary, 30/12/93.

4 1994

1 Fikret Abdic interviewed by Aleksander Milosevic in Vanjska Politika, 2/2/94.
2 RC Zagreb Daily Report, 17/2/94.
3 RC Belgrade Daily Report, 23/2/94.
4 Special Report – HRC Zagreb, 3/3/94.
5 *Time*, 14/2/94.
6 Laura Silber and Alan Little, *The Death of Yugoslavia*, BBC/Penguin (London), 1995, p. 344.
7 Tim Spicer, *An Unorthodox Soldier*, Mainstream Publishing (Edinburgh), 1999, p. 130.
8 Boutros Boutros-Ghali, *Unvanquished*, Random House (New York), 1999, p. 145.
9 Paul Adams, 'Marketplace Massacre', in *From Our Own Correspondent 5*, BBC Books (London), 1994, p. 93.
10 Central to Serb acceptance of the agreement was the deployment of Russian UN troops around Sarajevo.
11 Washington Agreement, 18/3/94.
12 HQ ECMM Special Report, 21/9/94.
13 Boutros Boutros-Ghali had also threatened to impose sanctions against Croatia if they continued their involvement in Bosnia.
14 *Time* 14/3/94: 'In return for his co-operation in this marriage, Croatian President Tudjman was promised western financial aid and unspecified help in recovering the Krajina region from the Serbs.'
15 Defense and Foreign Affairs Strategic Policy, 31/10/95.
16 One of the main casualties of this process was the hardliner Mate Boban. He was replaced by far more pragmatic and moderate politicians in the personages of Ivo Komsic and Kesimir Zubak.
17 The influence of Peter Galbraith should not be underestimated in securing this agreement.
18 The Ceasefire Agreement of 29 March 1994 came into effect at 9.00 a.m. on 4 April.
19 Brendan O'Shea, *Crisis at Bihac*, p. 43.
20 Mladic's daughter actually committed suicide apparently because she could no longer cope with the barrage of criticism the other students threw at her in relation to the manner in which her father was conducting military operations in Bosnia.
21 A human mule train travelled most nights across the mountains, through Serb lines, in order to bring in supplies of everything from food, to medicines, to ammunition.
22 Rose called this dilemma 'The Mogadishu Line' in a reference to events in Somalia on Sunday, 3 October 1993 when the US army lost 18 soldiers dead and 72 injured.
23 Silber and Little, *The Death of Yugoslavia*, p. 362.
24 Brendan O'Shea, *Crisis at Bihac*, p. 45.
25 Michael Rose, 'A Year in Bosnia – What Has Been Achieved?', *The RUSI Journal*, June 1995.

26 512 Fighter Squadron, based in Ramstein, Germany, operating from Aviano, Italy.
27 Prior to this call for close air support (CAS) the UN was represented in Gorazde by just a small number of unarmed observers (UNMOs). The forward air controllers (FACs) were only inserted just before the CAS request was put to Akashi.
28 'The Rules of Engagement for these strikes required the Forward Air Controllers (FACs) to have the target in their line of sight, simultaneous two way radio communication with the attacking aircraft, and a valid expectation of causing limited collateral damage before the final instructions could be given to the pilots from the ground' – Barbara Starr, *Janes Defence Weekly*, 16/4/94.
29 Brendan O'Shea, *Crisis at Bihac*, p. 46.
30 International aid workers put the figure at over 300 dead and over 1,000 wounded since the attack began. Bosnian government figures were considerably higher, but as usual contained a gross distortion of the truth.
31 This number was later increased to 474 when UNPROFOR occupied a further 14 observation posts.
32 Silber and Little, *The Death of Yugoslavia*, pp. 371–372.
33 Gaja Petkovic, 'Guarantees of the Almighty', *NIN Magazine*, 11/3/94.
34 Andre Lejoly, *Federation Building in Bosnia-Hercegovina*, ECMM SR, 30/11/94. Lejoly's assessments were absolutely correct.
35 Silber and Little, *The Death of Yugoslavia*, p. 374.
36 Reuters Sarajevo, 26/7/94.
37 Brendan O'Shea, *Crisis at Bihac*, p. 55.
38 Reuters, 28/7/94. John Steinbruner of the Brookings Institution in Washington DC: 'The international community will have to go in on the ground in sufficient numbers to impose or induce a settlement by taking the military option away from all the militias and this will not occur until the United States joins the enterprise. This is face-the-music time.'
39 ECMM Weekly Information Analysis Summary, 29/7–4/8/94.
40 Silber and Little, *The Death of Yugoslavia*, p. 380.
41 Brendan O'Shea, *Crisis at Bihac*, p. 56.
42 Ibid.
43 Unofficial estimates of Milosevic's support for the Bosnian Serbs in 1994 ranged as high as 20 per cent of Serbia's GNP.
44 Reuters Sarajevo, 5/8/94.
45 Reuters Zagreb, 5/8/94.
46 Brendan O'Shea, *Crisis at Bihac*, pp. 56–57.
47 Reuters Pale, 7/8/94.
48 This was what General Rasim Delic announced in June 1994 as the 'Liberation War' in which the Muslims set out to recover all territories where prior to the conflict there had been a Muslim majority.
49 ECMM Daily Monitoring Activity Report, 7/8/94.
50 Beta News/Reuters Pale, 9/8/94.
51 Tanjug News/Reuters Belgrade, 10/8/94.
52 Mike McCurry announced that there was no agreement on tightening sanctions or a timetable for lifting the arms embargo against the Muslims (Reuters Washington).
53 The French were first to announce that if the arms embargo was lifted they would withdraw their troops from UNPROFOR. Defence Minister François Leotard announced on French TV-TF1 that he had already informed the US Administration of this decision.
54 RC Zagreb, Daily Report of 16/2/94.

55 RC Zagreb, Daily Report of 17/2/94.
56 CC Plitvice Daily Report of 17/2/94; Team Bihac Daily Report of 18/2/94; RC Zagreb Daily Report of 19/2/94.
57 Team Kostajnica Daily Report of 26/2/94.
58 RC Zagreb Daily Report of 11/3/94.
59 Team Bihac/RC Zagreb Daily Reports of 2/3/94.
60 BH Command was the name given to that element of UNPROFOR operating in Bosnia-Hercegovina. Still based in Kiseljak, its new commander, General Sir Michael Rose, would shortly move the whole operation to Sarajevo.
61 WTN Interview/RC Zagreb Daily Report, 25/3/94. His troops, he said, had become 'the machines of peace in the logic of war'.
62 RC Zagreb Daily Report, 1/4/94.
63 Brendan O'Shea, *Crisis at Bihac*, p. 67.
64 ECMM Special Report, 16/12/94. Allegations that 2,000 people were detained there was a gross exaggeration, but a camp did exist and was later discovered by Robert Fisk of the *Independent*.
65 On 21/4/94.
66 This picture would be constructed over time by the brigade intelligence officer and his staff, drawing on all information as it came to hand including the interrogation of prisoners of war.
67 RC Zagreb Daily Reports, 10–12/5/94.
68 Team Bihac Daily Report, 13/5/94.
69 Team Bihac Daily Report, 20/5/94.
70 RC Zagreb Daily Report, 11/6/94.
71 RC Zagreb Daily Report, 13/6/94.
72 ECLO North/RC Zagreb Daily Reports, 15/6/94.
73 In an interview with Commandant Fergus Hannon, 15/3/96.
74 The practice of identifying newly liberated villages on the radio quickly stopped when the Krajina Serbs began to tune in, and having identified the locations on the map promptly shelled them.
75 Team Bihac Daily Report, 15/6/94.
76 Team Bihac Daily Report/Source Frenchbatt, 17/6/94.
77 Team Bihac Daily Report, 17/6/94.
78 RC Zagreb Daily Report, 24/6/94.
79 RC Zagreb Daily Report, 1/7/94.
80 Brendan O'Shea, *Crisis at Bihac*, p. 79.
81 Team Bihac Daily Report, 7/7/94.
82 No relation to Fikret. The name 'Abdic' is as common in Bihac Pocket as 'Murphy' is in Ireland.
83 Brendan O'Shea, *Crisis at Bihac*, pp. 83–85.
84 Roderick de Normann, 'The Miracle of 5 Corps', *Janes Intelligence Review*, 1996.
85 Bill Foxton, 'Bihac Pocket – A Tactical Appreciation', ECMM Papers, 17/2/95.
86 RC Zagreb Daily Report, 10/7/94.
87 ECMM Special Report, D/HoM Ops, 22/7/94, Part 1.
88 Ibid., Part 2.
89 Reuters Zagreb, 3/8/94.
90 Reuters Zagreb, 10/8/94.
91 HINA News Agency, 10/8/94.
92 Reuters Zagreb, 10/8/94.
93 Head of Mission's Special Report/ECMM Papers, 13/8/94.

NOTES

94 Zarko Modric, 12/8/94.
95 In August 1995 another ECMM head of mission would also embark on a solo run and find himself in Pale when NATO bombs began to explode all around him. Getting to the bottom of that story would prove extremely difficult also.
96 RC Zagreb Daily Reports, 15/8/94, 17/8/94.
97 RC Zagreb Daily Report, 20/8/94.
98 RC Zagreb Daily Report, 21/8/94.
99 RC Zagreb Daily Report, 22/8/94.
100 Abdic's control over his people can be attributed to the fact that he was their elected representative. However, he also controlled an Austrian bank account into which former residents of the Pocket now working elsewhere in Europe were encouraged to deposit money.
101 Vjesnik, 23/8/94.
102 Special Report to ECMM HQ, 22/8/94.
103 Richard Meares/Reuters, 4/8/94.
104 Team Bihac Daily Report, 23/8/94.
105 Team Glina Daily Report, 24/8/94.
106 Team Karlovac Daily Report, 25/8/94.
107 RC Zagreb Daily Report, 25/8/94.
108 It later emerged that the Croats had convinced themselves that this was an opportunity for the Serbs to infiltrate into Croatia.
109 'Feed The Children' Report, 26/10/94.
110 CC Topusko Daily Report, 26/8/94.
111 An ECMM team in Batnoga on the 27th estimated that up to 90 per cent of those present would go back to Velika Kladusa if they had a free choice – Team Plaski Daily Report, 27/8/94.
112 Brendan O'Shea, *Crisis at Bihac*, pp. 91–100.
113 Galbraith also tried to convince Abdic that under the Washington Agreement the Bihac region would enjoy far greater autonomy than it had before and for that reason he should accept the amnesty and return.
114 Both ECMM and UNPROFOR also provided further confirmation that most of the houses in Velika Kladusa had indeed been looted, and in some cases Muslim refugees from other parts of Bosnia had also begun moving into the recently abandoned properties – Team Plaski Daily Report, 28/8/94.
115 Team Plaski Daily Report, 29/8/94.
116 RC Zagreb Daily Report, 2/9/94.
117 Team Velika Kladusa Daily Report, 7/9/94.
118 Team Bihac Daily Report, 9/9/94.
119 Team Velika Kladusa/UNHCR Reports, 12/9/94.
120 RC Zagreb Daily Report, 13/9/94.
121 RC Zagreb Daily Report, 13/9/94.
122 Team Bihac Daily Report, 15/9/94.
123 On 16/9/94 Slovenia agreed to allow 85 of the refugees at Turanj, who apparently had correct documentation, to pass through the country en route to locations elsewhere in Europe. The Serbs, however, had other ideas and refused. These people would eventually escape their ordeal, but not before bureaucracy and officialdom on all sides had registered their authority and in some cases been paid off.
124 To this end a new radio station came on the air, 'Radio Krajina Cazin', and broadcasting from Korenica provided the inhabitants of Batnoga with a daily diet of anti-5th Corps propaganda.
125 ECTF was the European Community Task Force whose function was to

co-ordinate the allocation and distribution of humanitarian aid in the region, given that the EU was paying for over 80 per cent of it.
126 Michael Cleary, Report to head of ECTF, Visit to Batnoga, 19/10/94.
127 Captain Mike Stanley's real name was Milos Stankovic. He was an officer in the Parachute Regiment of the British army and because of his Serb origins, and the fact that he spoke Serbo-Croat, he was assigned as an interpreter with senior British commanders in UNPROFOR between 1993 and 1995.
128 Milos Stankovic, *Trusted Mole*, HarperCollins (London), 2000, pp. 343–346.
129 Vecernji List, 17/11/94.
130 The napalm did not detonate.
131 Brendan O'Shea, *Crisis at Bihac*, p. 105.
132 Reuters/Evelyn Leopold, 19/11/94.
133 At 9.39 a.m. on 21/11/94 two Sagger missiles also impacted on the presidency building in Sarajevo. This of itself would have warranted a response had the Udbina raid been cancelled for any other reason.
134 It also emerged at this time that Croatia had for some time been resupplying Dudakovic at night, by air, employing civilian aircraft normally used for 'crop dusting'. These planes took off from Osijek, Varazdin, Zagreb (Lucko) and other places, and landed at Coralici airfield near Cazin. The legality or otherwise of this activity was addressed by no one.
135 Brendan O'Shea, 'The Rise and Fall of the 5th Corps', ECMM Papers, 9/12/94.
136 UNPROFOR Report Z-1714, 15/11/94.
137 UNPROFOR Fact Sheet, 31/11/94.
138 UNPROFOR Report Z-1714, 15/11/94.
139 EU monitors in Korenica were informed by the president of the municipality that three people had been killed in the raid, with a further three taken to hospital in Knin (UNPROFOR Chronology, 21/11/94).
140 Letter, Mladic to De Lapresle, 09/20–1051, 22/11/94.
141 Letter, Karadzic to Akashi, 22/11/94.
142 Letter, Akashi to Karadzic, 23/11/94.
143 Daily Sitrep HQ BH Forward Command Sarajevo, 23/11/94.
144 ECMM Daily Briefing, 25/11/94.
145 Ibid., para. 11.
146 Ibid., para. 5.G.
147 Reuters Sarajevo, 24/11/94.
148 Team Bihac Capsat Message to HQ ECMM, 11.30 p.m., 24/11/94.
149 Chaired by General Rose; General Ratko Mladic and General Rasim Delic also attended.
150 Reuters Sarajevo, 25/11/94.
151 News Report ECLO Sarajevo, 25/11/94.
152 Reuters Dhaka, 25/11/94.
153 ECLO Sarajevo Daily Report, 26/11/94.
154 In his letter to Karadzic on the 28th the secretary-general appeared to be genuinely pursuing a resolution of the problem.
155 Boutros Boutros-Ghali, *Unvanquished*, Random House (New York), 1999, p. 214.
156 Leonid Kerestedzhjiyants (Russia), Peter Galbraith (US), Geert Ahrens and Alfredo Cordella (ICFY) and Jean-Jacques Gaillarde (EU).
157 Gotovina was later indicted for war crimes by the ICTY.
158 ECMM Weekly Information Analysis Summary No. 107.
159 At the CSCE meeting in Budapest French foreign minister, Alain Juppe, was

apparently clear that '[i]f there is no diplomatic progress over the next few weeks, we need to be ready and prepared to start a possible withdrawal operation'.
160 Result: Yes 142, No 0, Abstentions 18. The only European countries to abstain were Russia and Belarus.
161 Vjesnik (10/12/94) and WIAS 108.
162 Reuters, 11/12/94.
163 Reuters Sarajevo, 21/12 94. 'An anti-tank rocket fired from a rebel Croatian Serb position blew up a U.N. armoured vehicle in a Bosnian government enclave [Bihac] on Monday and four Bangladeshi peacekeepers were wounded, U.N. officials said.'
164 *Time* No. 52, 1994; UNMO Reports/Team Bihac Daily Report, 12/12/94.
165 Di-Mari Ricker, 'Closing a War', *ABA Journal*, January 1996, p. 69.
166 Reuters, 15/12/94.
167 Confirmed to the author by ECMM sources working on the ground near Sarajevo that morning. *Time*, Vol. 144, No. 26, p. 84, who clearly had no faith in either Karadzic or his ability to deliver on his self-imposed preconditions, were only too happy to also report that this attack had been launched by the Serbs. They were wrong.
168 Reuters Sarajevo, 18/12/94.
169 Hanley and his two colleagues eventually crossed the Drina river very late that night having been delayed and questioned at several points along the way. They were even interrogated by so-called 'Interpol' agents (read Milosevic's secret police) in Belgrade where, incredibly, the trio were accused of being international smugglers!
170 Reuters Pale, 19/12/94.
171 The veracity of this letter was confirmed to the author by Joyce Neu in 1999.
172 Reuters Pale, 20/12/94.
173 All Reuters, 21/12/94.
174 ECLO Sarajevo, 22/12/94.
175 RC BiH Weekly Report, 24/12/94.
176 Krezimir Zubak admitted as much to ECMM in the course of the meeting with Ambassador von Stulpnagle on 16/12/94.
177 Brendan O'Shea, *Crisis at Bihac*, pp. 129–131.
178 Reuters Zagreb, 18/12/94.
179 Team Karlovac Daily Report, 22/12/94.
180 RC Zagreb Daily Report, 22/12/94.
181 On the morning of 26 December the refugees in Turanj had been made ready for the return journey to Velika Kladusa but none of these vehicles had enough fuel. On this occasion once the permission was granted for the convoy to proceed to Cazin the fuel was produced in Turanj by UNHCR.
182 Reuters Sarajevo, 27/12/94.
183 Team Glina Daily Report, 29/12/94.
184 Philip Watkins, 'Meeting in Pale', ECMM Special Report, 30/12/94.

5 1995

1 Philip Watkins and Christopher Geidt, 'Meeting with General Delic', ECMM Special Report, 6/1/95.
2 Belgrade Telegraph/Wias No. 113, 3/2/95.
3 HINA News, 12/1/95 (9.33 p.m.).
4 HINA News, 12/1/95 (9.33 p.m.).
5 WIAS 111, 20/1/95.

6 RC Zagreb Daily Report, 13/1/95.
7 Signed in Washington on 29 November 1994. See ECMM Sequence of Events, 1st edition, 19/12/94.
8 ECMM Economics Section Special Report No. 22, 6/10/95.
9 'The Balkans – Turning a Blind Eye', *Newsweek*, 15/4/96.
10 ECMM Economics Section Special Report No. 22, 6/10/95.
11 RC Zagreb Daily Report, para. 2a, 13/1/95.
12 The Z4 plan proposed to allow the Serbs to retain their own president, government, flag, language, radio, TV, social welfare system, police force and to raise their own tax revenue. However, in the Sabor, Croatia's national parliament, the Krajina Serbs were to have only ten out of 148 seats in the House of Representatives (6.7 per cent), and nine out of 77 seats in the House of Counties (11.7 per cent). Access to the top jobs in central government would be on an 'ethnic pro-rata basis' with only one member of the Krajina government guaranteed a cabinet post in the national equivalent.
13 Robert Owen would later become the administrator of Brcko, pursuant to the Dayton Agreements.
14 In an interview with Tim Clifton, political secretary, ECMM HQ, 23/1/95.
15 ECMM Weekly Information Analysis Summary No. 114, 10/2/95.
16 Personally witnessed by the author.
17 Correspondent series, *Allies and Lies*, BBC TV, 2000.
18 To drop equipment in the area of Tuzla West the lake was the final navigation marker. From there the crew could pick out the drop-zone lights and, coming in at 400 feet and 250 knots with the pallets ready on rollers, all that was necessary was to lift the nose of the plane and the cargo went straight out of the back complete with parachute.
19 'Night and Day', *The Mail on Sunday*, 24/9/95.
20 UN Sector North-East Report No. 1020, 19 2123 B, February 1995.
21 'Night and Day', *The Mail on Sunday*, 24/9/95.
22 While there is no disputing the fact that the United States was using Brac as a base from which to launch RPVs, or 'drones', on high-tech reconnaissance flights over Bosnian Serb positions, the reporting of so many C-130 flights is not consistent with this operation.
23 'Defence and Foreign Affairs Strategic Policy' of 31/10/95 also reported the deployment of US Special Forces personnel, *on active duty*, in support of both the Bosnian Croats and the Bosnian Muslims.
24 ECMM Special Report, 23/295.
25 Interview with General Cosic, *Janes Defence Weekly*, 19/11/97, p. 32.
26 Cable: Akashi to Annan, 'BiH Violations of the Arms Embargo', 18/7/94.
27 Reuters Washington, 21/5/96.
28 Reuters Washington, 23/5/96.
29 AFP Washington, 30/5/96.
30 Correspondent series, *Allies and Lies*, BBC TV, 2000.
31 The *Sunday Times* (5/3/95) also reported the involvement of Turkish aircraft in the resupply operation at Tuzla. See also *Defence and Foreign Affairs Strategic Policy*, 30/4/96, p. 3.
32 Marcel Cintelan, RC Belgrade Special Report, 31/1/95.
33 Bill Foxton, Team Bihac Special Report, 14/2/95.
34 Bill Foxton and Oscar Meyboom, 'The Economy in Bihac Pocket', ECMM Investigation Report, 1/3/95.
35 Bill Foxton, Team Bihac Special Report, 1/3/95.
36 Brendan O'Shea, *Crisis at Bihac*, p. 167.

NOTES

37 Bill Foxton and Luc Vermeulen, Team Bihac Special Report, 23/3/95.
38 ECMM/Team Bihac Special Report, 5/3/95. 'At body and prisoner of war exchange meetings each side tries to discover how many of each [dead or alive] the other side has. Neither side wishes to admit to more dead bodies than the other side. However it has been reported recently to us that one body was delivered which was so fresh that rigor mortis had not yet set in. In another case a body had been decapitated so cleanly at the neck that it was in itself suspicious.'
39 ECMM WIAS No. 118, 10/3/96, para. 10/Assessment.
40 The Krajina Serbs were not exclusively to blame for this state of affairs. It had been agreed that the Croats would provide the necessary new parts to enable resumption of some electricity production at the Obrovac power station. However, they failed to deliver the parts, retaining them instead as a bargaining chip for further negotiations.
41 Total number of registered displaced persons/refugees in Croatia on 12/1/95 was 383,039. Another 56,887 Croats had relocated themselves to other countries, with over half of this figure now resident in Germany. (Source: Croatian government official figures.)
42 ECMM WIAS 119, 17/3/95.
43 UNPF Chronology of Events, p. 34.
44 WIAS 122, 6/4/95, para. 5.
45 All the judges had been appointed by prime ministerial decree, something which was not permissible by law.
46 UN SRSG Weekly Situation Report, 5/4/95.
47 ECMM Special Report, 'No Surrender – No Compromise', 24/2/95.
48 UN G2 Sector SW Special Report, 19/2/95.
49 UN SRSG Weekly Situation Report, 5/4/95.
50 Izetbegovic's address to the 7th Session of the SDA's Main Board in Sarajevo, 23/3/95.
51 ECMM WIAS No. 122, 6/4/95.
52 ECMM Coyug 1/1 April 1995, 'Use of Armija for Political Ends'. 'The offensive actions launched by the Armija before the period of the COHA had expired demonstrates, and represents, a more robust posture from the Muslim politicians.'
53 Croatian Foreign Ministry statement of 13 April 1995.
54 ECMM/WIAS, 20/4/95. 'Non-European units of the UN contingent in Croatia have repeatedly been targeted in the Croatian government controlled media as being "lazy, incompetent and stupid".'
55 Throughout the war Mladic at all times remained a general in the JNA and was paid in that capacity from Belgrade – as indeed were several of his subordinate commanders.
56 RC Belgrade Special Report, 24/4/95.
57 Ibid. Mladic made two visits to Belgrade in April 1995, neither of which were authorised by Karadzic.
58 UN SRSG Weekly Report, 26/4/95.
59 Also reported in Nasa Borba and VIP News in Belgrade, 24/4/95.
60 The level of distrust between Karadzic and Mladic had become so bad that the police, who had always been completely loyal to Karadzic, were now reorganised along military lines in a praetorian guard.
61 ECMM Team Dubrovnik Special Report, 19/4/95.
62 ECMM Daily Briefing No. 9872 for 22/23 April 1995, 24/4/95.
63 ECMM Daily Briefing No. 9873 for 24 April 1995, 25/4/95.
64 ECMM Daily Briefing No. 9374 for 25 April 1995, 26/4/95.

NOTES

65 ECLO West Special Report, 24/4/95. 'The HV [Croatian army] seems to be ready to take the northern part of the UNPA at any time.'
66 ECMM Reports: (a) RC Zagreb Special Report, 30/4/95; (b) ECLO Highway Daily Report, 29/4/95; (c) ECLO West Daily Report, 29/4/95; (d) Team Slavonski Brod Daily Report, 29/4/95.
67 RC Zagreb Daily Report, 30/4/95.
68 RC Zagreb Weekly Assessment 23–29 April 1995, dated 30/4/95.
69 Defence and Foreign Affairs Strategic Policy, October/November 1992, pp. 10–11.
70 Brendan O'Shea, *Crisis at Bihac*, pp. 200–201.
71 ECMM Coyug No. 1, 1/5/95.
72 ECMM Daily Briefing No. 9879, 2/5/95.
73 RC Zagreb Log, 1/5/95.
74 RC Zagreb Log, 1/5/95 (7 p.m.).
75 For example, at 7.15 a.m. that morning the 104 Brigade had just arrived from Varazdin and were busy forming up in Novska, while the 81st Independent Guards Battalion had moved into Pakrac (RC Zagreb Log, 2/5/95).
76 Jan Gallus (Slovakia), Humanitarian Cell RC Zagreb/Special Report, 2/5/95.
77 Meeting between Sarinic and Ambassador Turot, 3/5/95.
78 UNPROFOR Sequence of Events, 1995.
79 ITV News Report by Paul Davies.
80 ECMMs were present at the POW processing centre in Bjelovar and the manner in which some monitors were unwittingly or otherwise manipulated by the Croatian media handlers brought about a stiff rebuke from Senior Monitor Roger Bryant, who in two special reports on 7 and 8 May drew the attention of monitors to the provisions of international humanitarian law.
81 ECMM WIAS No. 127, 11/5/95.
82 ECMM WIAS No. 128, 18/5/95.
83 UN Sequence of Events, 7/5/95.
84 ECMM Daily Monitoring Activity Report No. 9892, 13–14/5/95.
85 ECMM WIAS No. 129, 25/5/95.
86 ECMM Daily Monitoring Activity Report No. 9882, 6–7/5/95.
87 Brigadier General P. Peeters, 'The Aftermath of Sector West', UNPROFOR Document, 13/6/95.
88 Marcus Tanner, *Croatia – A Nation Forged in War*, Yale University Press (London), 1997, p. 296.
89 Peeters, 'The Aftermath of Sector West', para. 4, p. 5.
90 Asim Metiljevic, 'Digging a Lifeline for Sarajevo', *Transition Magazine/OMRI*, 31/5/96.
91 In January 1993 work began to connect Butmir with Dobrinja, with 40 people working four shifts per day. Both sides finally met at 1.07 a.m. on 13 July 1993.
92 ECMM Daily Monitoring Activity Report No. 9886, 6–7/5/95.
93 Ibid., No. 9888, 9/5/95.
94 Ibid., No. 9889, 10/5/95.
95 ECMM Daily Monitoring Activity Report No. 9889, para. 9, 10/5/95.
96 RUSI International Security Review, 1996, p. 119.
97 The Bosnian Croats admitted that they had lost about 200 square metres of ground at a cost of three dead and 35 wounded: ECMM DMA Report No. 9889, 10/5/95.
98 UN Sequence of Events, 15/5/95.
99 UN Sequence of Events, 16/5/95.
100 UN Document S/1995/5, 9/5/95.
101 Richard Caplan, *Post-mortem on UNPROFOR*, London Defence Studies No.

NOTES

33. The Centre for Defence Studies, Kings College and Brasseys (London), 1996, p. 17.
102 ECMM WIAS, 25/7/95. 'US engagement in this area has become more and more obvious and US diplomats seem to have become the favourite supporters of ABiH [Muslims] and HVO [Bosnian Croats].'
103 ECMM Daily Monitoring Activity Report, para. 7, 17/5/95.
104 Yossef Bodansky, *Some Call it Peace*, International Media Corp. Ltd/ISSA (London), 1996.
105 David Rohde, *A Safe Area*, Pocket Books (London), 1997, p. 350.
106 See also Jan Willem Honig and Norbert Both, *Srebrenica, Record of a War Crime*, Penguin (London), 1996.
107 Philip Corwin, *Dubious Mandate*, Duke University Press (London), 1999, pp. 204–205.
108 See 'Report Based on the Debriefing on Srebrenica', 4.10.95, by Brigadier General O. van der Wind.
109 Corwin, *Dubious Mandate*, pp. 211–212.
110 ECMM Team Bihac Daily Report, 23/5/95.
111 ECMM Team Bihac Daily Report, 22/5/95.
112 ECMM Team Bihac Daily Report, 30/5/95.
113 Groups known as the 'Visivubus' were mobilised and comprised the elderly. Those less than 60 were called up for ten-day training periods and employed near the front line in observation roles.
114 ECMM WIAS, 31 July/3 August, 1995.
115 The last meeting of the Parliament of the Republic of Srpska Krajina took place in Topusko on 28 July 1995, where Milan Babic became prime minister.
116 Milosevic addressed two letters to Izetbegovic and Mladic on 1 August urging them to conclude an immediate ceasefire.
117 ECMM Team Bihac Daily Reports, 21–28/7/95.
118 In an interview with Tim Ripley, Zagreb, 21/12/97. See also Tim Ripley, *Operation Deliberate Force*, Centre for Defence and International Security Studies, Lancaster University (Lancaster), 1999.
119 ECMM WIAS, 4–10/8/95.
120 Roderick de Normann, 'Operation Storm', *Janes Intelligence Review*, November, 1997.
121 ECMM WIAS, 11–17/8/95, and ECMM Humanitarian Activity Report No. 33/95, 18–24/8/95.
122 ECMM Team Karlovac Special Report, 13/9/95.
123 Brendan O'Shea, *Crisis at Bihac*, pp. 217–220.

6 THE END STATE

1 Yossef Bodansky, *Offensive in the Balkans*, International Media Corp. Ltd/ISSA (London), 1995, p. 15.
2 Report of the secretary-general pursuant to General Assembly Resolution 53/35 – The Fall of Srebrenica – 15/11/99, A/54/549, para. 438: '(The secrecy surrounding the UNPROFOR investigation into this incident gave rise to speculation, fuelled by the Serbs, that there was doubt as to which side had fired the mortar rounds. A review of United Nations documentation however confirms that UNPROFOR considered the evidence clear: all five rounds had been fired by the Bosnian Serbs.)'
3 See Tim Ripley, *Operation Deliberate Force*, Centre for Defence and International Security Studies, Lancaster University (Lancaster), 1999. Galbraith

admitted to Tim Ripley that both he and Holbrooke knew the bombing was going to happen.
4 This was the so-called 'dual key' system whereby no action could be taken until both the UN and NATO keys were turned to 'on'.
5 Report of the secretary-general pursuant to General Assembly Resolution 53/35 – The Fall of Srebrenica – 15/11/99, A/54/549, para. 441.
6 Tim Ripley believes that Leighton-Smith turned his 'key' the minute news broke of the bombing in Sarajevo on 28 August and that the air war would have gone ahead even if the HV/HVO/Armija ground offensive had failed to materialise.
7 Bob Woodward, *The Choice*, Simon and Schuster (New York), 1996, p. 270.
8 In subsequent interviews with Irish ECMM monitor Jim Fitzgibbon who accompanied Sanchez Rau.
9 In fact, co-operation became so bad that on 19 September Galbraith had to arrange a meeting in Zagreb between Tudjman and Izetbegovic in order to sort it all out and only managed to finally resolve the matter after a screaming fight with Defence Minister Susak when 'extreme' US pressure was brought to bear. Thereafter HV commanders gave Dudakovic a very wide berth and on 25 September General Momir Talic launched a BSA counter-attack which seemed to catch Dudakovic completely by surprise.
10 'An Exercise in Force Protection', Major J. W. Ogden LD, 'C' Sqn., The Light Dragoons (UK), Implementation Force, Bosnia, February 1996.
11 Richard Holbrooke, *To End A War*, Random House (New York), 1998, pp. 160–161.
12 Ibid., p. 199.
13 This left unfinished business in several areas where no clear physical delineation had been achieved on the ground, and not surprisingly several reasons were concocted to justify a postponement of the general ceasefire to afford the Muslim and Croat forces an extra few days to consolidate their positions and secure a number of key road junctions which would be vital in terms of resupply once the Confrontation Line was finally frozen.
14 Yossef Bodansky, *Some Call It Peace*, International Media Corp. Ltd/ISSA (London), 1996, p. 130.
15 Michael Rose, *Fighting for Peace*, Harvill Press (London), 1998, p. 38.
16 Martin Bell, *In Harm's Way*, Hamish Hamilton (London), 1995, p. 38.
17 Susan L. Woodward, 'The West and the International Organisations', in *Yugoslavia and After*, edited by David A. Dyker and Ivan Vedjvoda, Longman (London), 1996, p. 131.
18 Report of the secretary-general pursuant to General Assembly Resolution 53/35 – The Fall of Srebrenica.
19 Rose, *Fighting for Peace*, p. 99.
20 Brendan O'Shea, *Crisis at Bihac – Bosnia's Bloody Battlefield*, Sutton Publishing (Stroud), 1998, p. 173.
21 Report of the secretary-general pursuant to General Assembly Resolution 53/35 – The Fall of Srebrenica, paras. 33–40.
22 In fact an entire collection of such papers is now freely available at www.karadzic.net.
23 Milos Vasic, 'The Yugoslav Army and the Post Yugoslav Armies', in *Yugoslavia and After*, edited by David A. Dyker and Ivan Vedjvoda, Longman (London), 1996, p. 131.
24 Milos Stankovic, *Trusted Mole*, HarperCollins (London), 2000, pp. 278–279.
25 Carl von Clausewitz, *On War*, Princeton University Press (Princeton, NJ), 1976.
26 Vasic, 'The Yugoslav Army and the Post Yugoslav Armies', p. 116.

SELECT BIBLIOGRAPHY

Almond, Mark, *Europe's Backyard War*, Mandarin Books (London), 1995.
Baerlein, Henry, *The Birth of Yugoslavia*, Leonard Parsons (London), 1922.
Bell, Martin, *In Harm's Way*, Hamish Hamilton (London), 1996.
Bodansky, Yossef, *Offensive in the Balkans*, International Media Corp. Ltd/ISSA (London), 1995.
Bodansky, Yossef, *Some Call it Peace*, International Media Corp. Ltd/ISSA (London), 1996.
Boutros-Ghali, Boutros, *Unvanquished*, Random House (New York), 1999.
Campbell, Greg, *The Road to Kosovo*, Westview Press (Boulder, CO), 2000.
Caplan, Richard, *Post-Mortem on UNPROFOR*, Centre for Defence Studies/Brassey's (London), 1996.
Civic, Christopher, *Remaking the Balkans*, Pinter Publishers (London), 1991.
Collin, Mathew, *This is Serbia Calling*, Serpent's Tail (London), 2001.
Corwin, Philip, *Dubious Mandate*, Duke University Press (London), 1999.
Djilas, Milovan, *Wartime*, Secker and Warburg (London), 1977.
Djilas, Milovan, *Rise and Fall*, Macmillan (London), 1985.
Doder, Dusko and Louise Branson, *Milosevic – Portrait of a Tyrant*, The Free Press (New York), 1999.
Drakulic, Slavenka, *The Balkan Express*, Harper Perennial (New York), 1993.
Dyker, David A. and Ivan Vejvoda, *Yugoslavia and After*, Longman (London), 1996.
Eyal, Jonathan, *Europe and Yugoslavia: Lessons from a Failure*, Royal United Services Institute for Defence Studies (London), 1993.
Fromkin, David, *Kosovo Crossing*, The Free Press (New York), 1999.
Gjelten, Tom, *Sarajevo Daily*, Harper Perennial (New York), 1996.
Glenny, Misha, *The Fall of Yugoslavia*, Penguin Books (London), 1993.
Glenny, Misha, *The Balkans*, Granta Books (London), 1999.
Gow, James, *Legitimacy and the Military*, Pinter Publishers (London), 1992.
Gow, James, Richard Paterson and Alison Preston (eds), *Bosnia by Television*, British Film Institute (London), 1996.
Gow, James, *Triumph of the Lack of Will*, C. Hurst & Co. (London), 1997.
Gutman, Roy, *A Witness to Genocide*, Macmillan Publishing (London), 1993.
Halberstan, David, *War in a Time of Peace*, Bloomsbury (London), 2003.
Honig, Jan Willem and Norbert Both, *Srebrenica, Record of a War Crime*, Penguin (London), 1996.

SELECT BIBLIOGRAPHY

Hukanovic, Rezak, *The Tenth Circle of Hell*, Little Brown & Co. (London), 1996.
Hurd, Douglas, *The Search for Peace*, Little Brown & Co. (London), 1997.
Jasarevic, Senudin, *Aggression on the Bihac Region*, Una-Sana Canton (Bosnia), 1995.
Judah, Tim, *The Serbs*, Yale University Press (London), 1997.
Loyd, Anthony, *My War Gone By, I Miss It So*, Doubleday (London), 1999.
Maas, Peter, *Love Thy Neighbour – A Story of War*, Papermac Books (London), 1996.
MacKenzie, Lewis, *Peacekeeper – The Road to Sarajevo*, Douglas & McIntyre (Toronto), 1993.
Malcolm, Noel, *Bosnia – A Short History*, Macmillan Publishing (London), 1994.
Neier, Aryeh, *War Crimes*, Times Books (Toronto), 1998.
O'Shea, Brendan, *Crisis at Bihac – Bosnia's Bloody Battlefield*, Sutton Publishing (Stroud), 1998.
Owen, David, *Balkan Odyssey*, Indigo/Cassell Publishing (London), 1996.
Pavlowitch, Stevan, *Tito: Yugoslavia's Great Dictator*, C. Hurst & Co. (London), 1992.
Rieff, David, *Slaughterhouse: Bosnia and the Failure of the West*, Random House (London), 1995.
Ripley, Tim, *Operation Deliberate Force*, Centre for Defence and International Security Studies, Lancaster University (Lancaster), 1999.
Rodhe, David, *A Safe Area*, Pocket Books (London), 1997.
Rose, Michael, *Fighting for Peace*, Harvill Press (London), 1998.
Russell, Alec, *Prejudice and Plum Brandy*, Michael Joseph (London), 1993.
Shawcross, William, *Deliver Us From Evil*, Bloomsbury (London), 2000.
Silber, Laura and Alan Little, *The Death of Yugoslavia*, BBC/Penguin (London), 1995.
Spicer, Tim, *An Unorthodox Soldier*, Mainstream Publishing (Edinburgh), 1999.
Stankovic, Milos, *Trusted Mole*, HarperCollins (London), 2000.
Stewart, Bob, *Broken Lives*, HarperCollins (London), 1993.
Tanner, Marcus, *Croatia – A Nation Forged in War*, Yale University Press (London), 1997.
Thomas, Robert, *Serbia under Milosevic*, Hurst & Co. (London), 1999.
Thompson, Mark, *A Paper House*, Vintage Books (London), 1992.
Tudjman, Franjo, *Horrors of War*, Evans & Co. (New York), 1996.
Ugresic, Dubravka, *The Culture of Lies*, Phoenix House (London), 1998.
Vickers, Miranda, *Between Serb and Albanian*, Hurst & Co. (London), 1998.
Vulliamy, Ed, *Seasons in Hell*, Simon & Schuster (London), 1994.
Woodward, Bob, *The Choice*, Simon & Schuster (New York), 1996.
Woodward, Susan, *Balkan Tragedy*, Brookings Institution (Washington), 1995.
Zimmerman, Warren, *Origins of a Catastrophe*, Times Books (New York), 1996.

INDEX

Abdic, Fazilla 134
Abdic, Fikret 94–5, 100–1, 126, 225n91; APWB 107, 136, 138; Bihac 97, 104, 124; Boban 101; Dudakovic 101–2, 105, 128–31, 199; ECMM 107, 135; Ganic 96, 98; Izetbegovic 95, 96, 98–9, 125, 131; Karadzic 101; Krajina Serbs 101, 127, 195–6; Mikelic 126; Rose 131; Tudjman 99–100, 126, 134; UNPROFOR 132; Velika Kladusa 100, 125, 128, 132, 136–7, 200; von Stulpnagel 136
Abdic, Hamdo 129, 195
Agreement on Friendship and Co-operation between Croatia and Bosnia 168
Agrokomerc 94–5, 100–1
Aguilar, Enrique 177
Ahmetovic, Dzemal 154
Ahmic, Elma 81
Ahmici killings 81
air-strikes 120, 140, 192
Akashi, Yasushi 4; arms supplies 164; Belgrade meeting 190; Boutros-Ghali 6; Carter 150; ceasefire 186; COHA 173, 177, 184; Croatia 196; Gorazde 114; human rights violations 188; Izetbegovic 170–1; Karadzic 7, 142, 145; Milosevic 190; Paris meeting 191; refugees 134; Rose 113; Sanski Most 176; Sarajevo 5, 108, 190; UNPROFOR 141
Albanians, ethnic 21, 22
Albright, Madeleine 66–7, 112, 140, 169
Alic, Fikret 45–6, 50
American Historical Review 1
Americares 102–6, 221n74
ammunition 102–3, 160; *see also* arms supplies
Annan, Kofi 141, 162, 164
anti-Serb sentiment 37–9, 57–8, 140, 151–2, 202

Argentinian UN troops 183
Armija 55; ammunition 160; Confrontation Line 172; Gorazde 114–15; HVO 56, 104; Izetbegovic 53; Sarajevo 173; UNMO 171; Vares 102, 122
arms embargo 55, 58, 71, 102–3, 119, 160
arms supplies 161–6, 196–7, 207, 219n72, 226n123
Arria, Diego 85
Ashdown, Paddy 205
Athens conference 83–4
atrocities 6–7, 13–14, 19, 44, 107–8, 195
Autonomous Province of Western Bosnia 126–8, 130, 200; Abdic 107, 138; 5th Corps 124–5; US 136; Velika Kladusa 100–1, 131, 132–3, 154

Babic, Milan 174; Croatian Human Rights 170; Karadzic 176–7; Knin 169–70; Martic 168, 176–7, 190, 191; Milosevic 196; Republic of Srpska Krajina 28, 31; resettlements 199; Tudjman 146, 158; UN 184; Vance Plan 30; Z4 plan 146, 197
Badinter Commission 2, 26, 27, 28, 215n63
Baker, James 12, 21, 37
Bangladeshi UN troops 144, 147–8
Banja Luka 114, 168, 189, 205
Batnoga 134, 135–6, 137, 138
Belgrade 10, 27–8, 82–3, 190
Bell, Martin 81
Biden, Joseph 78, 89, 103
Bihac District Assembly 100–1
Bihac Pocket 124–8, 129; Abdic 97, 104, 124; arms supplies 196–7; atrocities 195; black market 166–7; British UN troops 142; casualties 56; Dudakovic 101, 124, 127–30, 139–41, 192, 195–6, 198, 204–5; ECMM 7, 105, 128, 129–30, 138,

235

INDEX

Bihac Pocket *continued*
228n37; 5th Corps 127–8; Karadzic 143; Krajina Serbs 154–6, 157; Mladic 107; NATO 142, 144; Rose 143, 144, 154; Sarajevo 101–2; Silajdzic 143; Tudjman 7–8, 100; UNHCR 167
black market 82–3, 166–7
Blaskic, Tihomir 155, 168, 171–2, 189
Boban, Mate 36, 56, 92, 99, 101, 104, 222n16
Bobetko, Janko 57, 168, 171–2, 181
Bodansky, Yossef 38–9
Bonal, Francis 143
Bosanska Bojna 97–8, 101
Bosanska Gravaho 196
Bosanska Krupa 36, 140, 166, 204
Bosanska Petrova 204
Bosanski Brod 36
Bosnia 1, 29, 32, 33, 41, 117; Clinton 92–3; election results 21; HVO 54; refugees 37; Tudjman 31–2; UN peacekeepers 42; UNO 37; UNPROFOR 169
Bosnia-Hercegovina 20, 32, 34, 95, 205–6, 221n67
Bosnian Muslims: arms embargo 119; arms supplies 161–6; bombing of mosque 33; civilian attacks 33, 37, 70–1; Croatia 9; displaced 55–6, 122; human shields 161; HVO 102; Karadzic 33; leaders 38; Mladic 41; NATO 6; prison camps 44, 47; rape 47, 65, 67; restrictions 217n32; Sarajevo 58–9, 192; Srebenica 193; UN hostages 207; US 163, 164–6, 208–9; Vance–Owen plan 66
Bosnian Serb Army (BSA) 55; COHA 176; HV 205; HVO 91–2; JNA 211; Karadzic 46, 122–3; Mladic 46, 57, 175, 192, 209–10, 211; Una valley 128
Bosnian Serb Assembly 82, 84
Bosnian Serbs 29, 66; Contact Group 118, 123, 138–9; Cosic 82, 93; Croatia 183–5; EC Summit 147; highway blockades 177–8, 179; hostages 192; Izetbegovic 31, 71; Krajina Serbs 56, 188–9; leadership 42; media 121–4; Milovanovic 166; NATO 93, 94, 206–7; no-fly zone 77; Owen 78; Pale 22–3, 34; prison camps 3, 89; Republic of Srpska 34–5; UN 85–6, 143, 148; UN Charter 155; Vance–Owen plan 78, 82, 84–5, 88, 91; war crimes 76; *see also* anti-Serb sentiment
Bourke, Jim 129
Boutros-Ghali, Boutros 36, 57, 65; Akashi 6; Izetbegovic 114, 145; Karadzic 145; Krajina 174; safe havens 94; Sarajevo 59, 108, 143–5; Tudjman 169; Vance–Owen plan 89
Brdianovic, Refik 166
Brioni Agreement 15–16
British UN troops 55, 142
Brock, Peter 50
Brussels peace-plan 16–17
Bryant, Roger 134, 230n78
BSA *see* Bosnian Serb Army
Bulatovic, Momir 84, 120
Burns, John 48, 49–50
Bush, George 12, 58

Cailloux, Bruno 129–30
Campbell, Jim 166
Canadian UN troops 74, 78, 79, 81–2, 163
cannibalism rumours 68, 71
Carrington, Lord 4, 52–3, 215n68; Belgrade 27–8; ceasefire 21–2; Cutilherio 36; Germany 2, 27, 208; peace talks 25, 34, 43
Carter, Jimmy: COHA 2, 152, 176; Izetbegovic 150, 152; Karadzic 151, 155–6, 201; Sarajevo 148–53; Silajdzic 150
Catholic Church 170, 189
ceasefire: Akashi 186; Bihac Pocket 125; Carrington 21–2; Carter 153; Delic 109; Dudakovic 143; Geneva 25; Karadzic 36, 42; Sarajevo 109; Silajdzic 104, 143; Srebenica 80; violations 186
Ceasefire Agreement (1994) 178, 179, 197–8
Celeketic, Milan 153, 188
Cerska 70–2
Cessation of Hostilities Agreement (COHA) 154–6, 170–3, 182, 201; Akashi 173, 177, 184; BSA 176; Carter 2, 152, 176; Delic 157–8; Izetbegovic 155, 157–8; Karadzic 2, 155–6, 166, 177; Milosevic 152
Cetin, Hikmet 104
Christopher, Warren 6, 67, 77, 83, 108, 119
Churkin, Vitali 88, 113–14, 114, 115, 117, 118
Claes, Willy 150
Clausewitz, Carl von 211
Cleary, Michael 138
Clinton, Bill 92–3; Athens 83; Christopher 67; Contact Group plan 123; ethnic cleansing 187; Holbrooke 165; Karadzic 93; Owen 66–7; Rapid Reaction Force 203; Srebenica 195; Tudjman 169; US State Department 78; Wiesel 85

INDEX

close air support (CAS) 113, 223n25
CNN 25, 85–6, 112, 140; Karadzic 148, 149, 151–2
COHA *see* Cessation of Hostilities Agreement
Collins, Jack 166
Conference on Security and Co-operation in Europe (CSCE) 12, 14–15, 36–7
Confrontation Line 106, 171, 172, 178, 180
Contact Group 116–20, 123, 138–9, 155, 172, 191
Corwin, Philip 4, 5, 195
Cosic, Dobrica 57–8, 66, 82, 84, 93, 94
Cosic, Kresimir 164
Croatia 10–12, 15–17, 20–1; Akashi 196; arms embargo 71; Bosnian Serbs 183–5; Confrontation Line 106; displaced people 16–17, 18, 23; ethnic cleansing 8, 197; European Community 20, 90; Germany 2, 11, 26–8, 208; JNA 40; Krajina Serbs 26, 168; Mostar 53; Republic of Srpska Krajina 200; UN 37, 182; UNCRO 169; US 158–9, 168; *see also* HV
Croatian Army *see* HV
Croatian Human Rights Committee 170
Croatian National Guard 11
Croatian Republic of Herceg-Bosna 42, 63
Croats 6–7, 11, 104, 189; Bosnian Muslims 9, 81, 109–10; ethnic cleansing 197; highway blockades 182; Krajina Serbs 7, 110, 146; Kupres 35–6; Livanjsko Polje 180–1; propaganda 144; Sector West 187; UN Protected Areas 65; Zagreb 144
CSCE 12, 14–15, 36–7
Cutilherio, Jose Pires 34–6
Cvetkovic, Dragisa 9
Czech Republic 199

Damjanovic, Sretko 76
Danish UN troops 198, 199
David, Filip 24
Dayton Agreement 205, 208
De Lapresle, General 111, 142, 162, 164
Delanovic, Sefija 134–5
Delic, Rasim: ceasefire 109; COHA 155, 157–8; military alliance 168, 171; parade 206; war of liberation 192; Watkins 157
Delimustafic, Alija 96–7
Delors, Jacques 55
demilitarisation 80, 97–8, 101
demonisation of Serbs 18, 43, 50
Dempsey, Judy 46
Demurenko, Andrei 201

Department of Peacekeeping Operations, UN 141
Dequen, Colonel 137
detention centres *see* prison camps
displaced people: Croatia 16–17, 18, 23; Krajina Serbs 65; Muslims 55–6; Sarajevo 42; Serbs 8, 43, 186; statistics 37, 57, 143–5
Dizdarevic, Asim 100
Dole, Bob 14
Doyle, Colm 38, 39–40, 81
Dragovic Road 54, 181, 182
Drekovic, General 101, 102, 160
Drina valley 70, 120
Dubrovnik 24–5, 177
Dudakovic, Atif: Abdic 101–2, 105, 128–31, 199; arms supplies 226n123; Bihac Pocket 101, 124, 127–30, 139–41, 192, 195–6, 198, 204–5; Boric 125; ceasefire 143; parade 206; refugees 134; Rose 209; Sky News 160–1; Talic 232n9; Velika Kladusa 133, 199
Dutch UN troops 193, 194
Dvor–Glina road 199

Eagleburger, Lawrence 14–15, 51, 53, 57–8, 149–50, 218n61
EC monitors 2, 20, 126, 136–7, 153, 226n128
ECMM 1–2, 4; Abdic 107, 135; arms supplies 163–4; Bihac Pocket 7, 105, 128, 129–30, 138; Brioni Agreement 16; Bugojno 172; Germany 27; helicopter casualty 31; highway blockades 179; international humanitarian aid 166–7; Karadzic 155; Milosevic 83; Mladic 155; prison camps 46; prisoners of war 230n78; Separation Zone 133; war crimes 167; weapons factories 161; Zagreb 8
Edwards, Wayne 63
Epocha 46
Etherington, Mark 7
ethnic Albanians 21, 22
ethnic cleansing 40–3, 76, 187; Croatia 8, 197; Krajina 199; liberation 184; Pakrac 54; precision 185, 187; rape 65; Zaklopace 37
European Community 20, 22, 43, 90, 147, 155
European Community Task Force 225n115

Feed the Children 135
Feldman, Norma von Ragenfeld 49–50

Ferhadija mosque 33
5th Corps: APWB 124–5; Bihac Pocket 127–8; Milovanovic 143; prisoners of war 167; Velika Kladusa 101, 133
Filipovic, Muhamed 172
Fischer, Joschka 18
Fitzgibbon, Jim 180
forward air controllers (FACs) 113, 223n25, n26
Foxton, Bill 7, 166, 167
Frankfurter Allgemeine Zeitung 18
French UN troops 74, 124, 191

Galbraith, Peter: arms supplies 165; Carter 150; ethnic cleansing 187; hospital visits 186; Krajina 201; and Redman 110; refugees 135–6; Ripley 7, 197, 202; Susak 232n9; Tudjman 189–90; Z4 159
Ganic, Ejup 28; Abdic 96, 98; Carter 152; media 68; parade 206; US 70; Washington Accord 170; Zagreb meeting 168
Geidt, Christopher 153, 155
Geneva 25, 57, 65–6
Geneva Conventions 17, 68, 183
Geneva International Conference on the Former Yugoslavia 54, 99–102
Genscher, Hans Dietrich 14, 15, 20
Germany: Badinter 27; Bosnia 29; Carrington 2, 27, 208; Croatia 2, 11, 26–8, 208; Kadijevic 23; WEU 19
Gharekhan, Chinmaya 161–2
Gligorov, Kiro 9
Globus 65, 144
Goldstone, Richard 189
Gorazde 111–16; casualties 114; media 112; Mladic 94, 111–12, 114, 121; siege 53; Silajdzic 112, 115; UNHCR 170; UNPROFOR 203
Gorbachev, Mikhail 22
Gore, Al 66–7
Gornji Vakuf 63–4, 65, 104
Granic, Mate 104, 134, 147, 158–9, 174, 182–3, 197
Guardian 74, 152
Gutman, Roy 3–4, 48, 49–50

Hadzic, Goran 31
Hadzihasanovic, Enver 63
Halilovic, Sefer 86, 95
Hanley, Tom 149, 151, 227n158
Hannay, Sir David 86
Hassain, Ismail 148
helicopter evacuation 74–5, 78

Herak, Borislav 50, 76
highway blockades 120, 122, 180; Bosnian Serbs 177–8, 179; Croatians 182; ECMM 179; Granic 182–3; reopening 181–8
HINA News 180
Holbrooke, Richard 164–5, 168, 202, 205
Hollingworth, Larry 78
hostage taking 192, 207
Hrvatska Television 24
Hulls, Brian 74
human rights violations 188
human shields 161, 198
Hurd, Douglas 118
HV 157, 159, 197–8, 205
HVO: Armija 56, 104; Bosnia 54; Bosnian Muslims 102; Bosnian Serb army 91–2; escalation 55; Granic 147; HV 157

ICRC (Red Cross) 16–17, 37, 44–5, 91–2, 193, 214n31
Ignatieff, Michael 23
Independent 152, 163
international community: apportioning blame 42; death threats 4; foreign troops 54–5; international humanitarian aid 67; Karadzic 139, 201; media 3–4; no-fly zone 53; precision ethnic cleansing 185; prison camps 49–59; Serbs 82; Tudjman 187
International Conference on Yugoslavia 17
International Criminal Tribunal for the Former Yugoslavia 68–70, 210, 212n2
international humanitarian aid 4, 55, 125, 134; abuses 72; blockades 122; Bosnia-Hercegovina 221n67; boycotts 67; ECMM 166–7; international community 67; Krajina Serbs 137, 166–7; NATO 70; protection 53; Srebenica 74; *see also* refugees
international humanitarian law: civilian attacks 186; Geneva Conventions 17, 68; ICRC 214n31; tribunal 87; violation 189, 198, 220n39
International War Crimes Tribunal 49, 86–8, 93, 110, 167, 177, 189
international war law conventions 59–62
ITN news 50
Izetbegovic, Alija 33, 66; Abdic 95, 96, 98–9, 125, 131; Akashi 170–1; Armija 53; Boban 56, 99; Bosnian Serbs 31, 71; Boutros-Ghali 114, 145; Carter 150, 152; Christopher 67; COHA 155, 157–8; Contact Group plan 118; Cutilherio

INDEX

plan 34; federal state 9; MacKenzie 5, 51–2; Makarska Agreement 99; military parade 206; New York 54; Oric 194–5; referendum 20; Rose 206; Sarajevo 43, 59, 95–6; Srebenica 74; state of war 42; Tudjman 32, 56; UN troops 28–9; UNPROFOR 36; Vance–Owen plan 30, 76, 91

Jajice 63–4
Janvier, Bernard 186, 191, 193–5, 197, 202–3, 207–8
Jarnak, Ivan 134
Jasenovac camp 43, 47, 184
JNA 5, 16, 211; border crossings 13; Croatia 40; ethnic Albanians 21; Ignatieff 23; Markovic 12; Mladic 229n54; ten-day war 12–13; volunteers 10; Zagreb 22
Jones, Pauline Neville 139
Jordanian UN troops 182
Jovic, Borisav 12, 211, 213n1
Juppe, Alain 93, 118, 150, 152, 226n148
Jusic, Zlatko 126, 127, 131

Kadijevic, General 14, 16, 21, 23, 25, 31, 211
Kajtazovic, Sead 135–6, 137, 200
Kalshoven, Frits 69
Karadjordjevo meeting 9
Karadzic, Radovan 3, 5, 48–9, 65; Abdic 101; Akashi 7, 142, 145; anti-Serb sentiment 38; Athens 83; Babic 176–7; Bihac 143; Boban 36, 92; Bosnia 32; Bosnian Muslims 33; Boutros-Ghali 145; BSA 46, 122–3; Carter 151, 155–6, 201; ceasefire plans 36, 42; Clinton 93; CNN 148, 149, 151–2; COHA 2, 155–6, 166, 177; Contact Group plan 117, 118–19, 155, 191; Cutilherio plan 34; ECMM meeting 155; Greater Serbia 20–1; HVO/Armija 104; ICTY 210; indicted 212n2; international community 139, 201; Lisbon Peace conference 39–40, 43; London Peace conference 43; marginalized 82, 83; Martic 176–7, 188–9; media 47–8, 67; Milosevic 21, 89, 119, 173; Mladic 90–1, 115–16, 174–5; New York conference 72; peace proposal 139; Rau 203–4; Republic of Srpska 3, 36, 58, 90, 210; Rose 139; Sarajevo 35–7, 53, 158; US State Department 49; Vance–Owen plan 65, 67, 75–6
Karlovac 135, 183

Kent, Sarah A. 1
Kijevo village 214n30
Kinkel, Klaus 90, 118, 158
Klujic, Stepan 34
Knin 168, 169–70, 178–9, 188, 189
Kohl, Helmut 15
Koljevic, Nikola 31, 35, 143, 155
Komarica, Franja 189
Kordic, Dario 189
Kosovo 21, 22
Kovacevic, Milan 47–8, 217n48, 217–18n50
Kozarac 46, 47–8, 217n31
Kozyrev, Russian Foreign Minister 91
Krajina 134, 135, 174, 199, 201
Krajina Serbs 65; Abdic 101, 127, 195–6; Bihac Pocket 154–6, 157; Bosnian Serbs 56, 188–9; Croatia 26, 168; Croats 7, 110, 146; EC Summit 147; evicted 8, 65; international humanitarian aid 137, 166–7; Knin 189; Lika Corps 105; Mikelic 173–4; Radio Knin 183; Sector West 188; Tudjman 176, 178; UNHCR 134; UNPROFOR 125, 135; Vance Plan 30–1; Velika Kladusa 140; Z4 160; Zagreb–Belgrade highway 153
Krajisnik, Momcilo 114, 115, 117, 119, 120
Kramer, Klaus 7
Kucan, Milan 10, 12, 13
Kukanjac, Milutin 95
Kuljis, Denis 144

Lake, Anthony 195
Le Hardy, C. A. 162
Leighton-Smith, Admiral 112, 114, 203, 206, 231–2n6
Lejoly, Andre 116–17
Letic, Edi 6
Levinsohn, Florence Hamlish 25
Lilic, Zoran 94, 117
Lisbon Peace conference 37, 39–40
Livanjsko Polje 147, 180–1, 196
looting 225n104
Los Angeles Times 163
Loyd, Anthony 6
Lukavica 191–2
Lukic, Vladimir 105

Macedonia 16, 169
Macek, Vladko 9
MacKenzie, Lewis 4, 5–6, 38, 43, 51–2
McLeod, Charles 46
Maher, J. P. 25
Makarska Agreement 99
Markovic, Ante 12, 14, 16–17, 21, 22, 25

INDEX

Markus, Henrik 141, 179
Marlowe, Lara 48
Martic, Milan: Babic 168, 176–7, 190, 191; Karadzic 107, 176–7, 188–9; Kijevo 214n30; Mikelic 174; Milosevic 190–1, 196; UNPROFOR 160–1, 191; UNSC Resolution 988 178; Zagreb–Belgrade highway 153
Maslenica bridge 21, 65, 99
Maurice, Frederic 37
Mayhew, Barney 46
media v, 2, 3–4, 13–14, 68; Bosnian Serbs 121–4; Gorazde 112; Karadzic 47–8, 67; Milosevic 16, 24; Mladic 90–1; prison camps 47–8; reality 2; Tudjman 99, 188; Western 90–1, 140
Meholjic, Hakija 194
Merlino, Jaques 50
Mesic, Stipe 15, 25, 89
Michelis, Gianni de 15
Mikelic, Borislav: Abdic 126; Babic/Martic 153, 168, 174; Economic Agreement 188; Krajina Serbs 173–4; Milosevic 146, 190; Radio Knin 181
Milosevic, Slobodan 3, 58, 211, 213n1; Akashi 190; Athens conference 83–4; Bosnian Serb Assembly 82; Brioni Agreement 15–16; Bulatovic 120; COHA 152; Contact Group plan 117–18; Cosic 57–8, 66; ECMM 83; Filipovic 172; Karadzic 21, 89, 119, 173; Kertes 10; Markovic 22; Martic 190–1, 196; media 16, 24; Mikelic 146, 190; Mladic 116, 176; Republic of Srpska 75; Sector West 187–8; Slovenia 13; Tudjman 9, 66; UN 31; UN Security Council 42
Milovanovic, Manojlo 74, 143, 166
Misetic, Bosiljko 160
Mitterrand, François 42
Mlaco, Dvezd 4
Mladic, Ratko 18–19, 212n2; arms supplies 164; Athens 84; Belgrade 4–5; Bihac Pocket 107; Bosnian Muslims 41; BSA 46, 57, 175, 192, 209–10, 211; Contact Group 119; daughter's death 111, 222n19; De Lapresle 142; ECMM meeting 155; Gorazde 94, 111–12, 114, 121; JNA 229n54; Karadzic 90–1, 115–16, 174–5; Kijevo 214n30; media 90–1; Milosevic 116, 176; Milovanovic 74; Republic of Srpska 5; Rose 4–5, 112; Smith 5, 164; Srebenica 3, 86, 193–5; UN 74–5; UNPROFOR 142
Moldestad, Ovind 161

Morillon, Phillipe 73–6, 77, 78, 79–80, 85, 86
Mostar 36, 53, 56, 88–9, 103, 118
MPRI 110, 159, 207
Muratovic, Hasan 4, 154, 206
Muslim-Croat Federation 109–10, 160–1
Muslim Democratic Party 101
Muslims *see* Bosnian Muslims
Mutual Defence Accord 9
Myers, Dee Dee 151, 152

National Council proposal 66
NATO: air-strikes 120, 140, 192; Bihac Pocket 142, 144; Bosnian Muslims 6; Bosnian Serbs 93, 94, 206–7; casualties 204; dual key system 231n4; international humanitarian aid 70; no-fly zone 76, 109, 160, 161–2; Sarajevo 120–1; Tuzla 161–2; UNPROFOR 125–6, 206; Vance–Owen plan 75
Nepalese UN troops 183
New York peace conference 71, 72
New York Times 49
Newsweek 66, 159
no-fly zone: Bosnian Serbs 77; enforcement 78; international community 53; NATO 76, 109, 160, 161–2; UNPROFOR 192; violations 121, 164, 192
Nobilo, Mario 147
Normann, Roddy de 182, 183
Nova Gradiska 180, 182
Nuremberg Tribunal 87

O'Donovan, Hugh 7, 166
Ogata, Sadako 37, 104
O'Kane, Maggie 74
Operation Deny Flight 121
Organisation of Islamic States 57, 93
Oric, Naser 75; demilitarisation 80; Izetbegovic 194–5; Morillon 73; Srebenica 70–1, 77, 78, 209; Stankovic 80
Osobodjenje 33
Owen, David 4, 103; Abdic 98; Americans 117; Athens 83; Bosnian Serbs 78; Clinton 66–7; Gorazde 115; Permanent Peace Conference 53; Sarajevo 38; *see also* Vance–Owen plan
Owen, Robert 160

Pakrac 54, 185, 186–7
Pale government 22–3, 34, 82–3
pan-Serb cause 41, 188, 196
Peace Conference on Yugoslavia 21

INDEX

Pecigrad 127, 131
Peeters, General 190
Perisic, General 175
Permanent Peace Conference 53
Peruca dam 65, 99
Pivic, Colonel 167, 195
Plavsic, Biljana 35
Pleso Camp 184
Pohara, Armin 89
police stations attacked 16
Polish UN troops 105, 135, 136, 198
politics of hate 23
Poos, Jaques 15
Posavina Corridor 191
post traumatic stress disorder 167
Prevention and Punishment of the Crime of Genocide Convention 87
Prilic, Jadranko 105
prison camps 19, 43–6, 50–1; Bosnian Muslims 44, 47; Bosnian Serbs 3, 89; ECMM 46; international community 49–59; media 47–8; Mladic 19; refugee centres 218n54; Tudjman 89–90; UNHCR 89; UNSC Resolution 780 218n60
prisoners of war 167, 187, 230n78
propaganda 14, 24, 144

Radio Knin 181, 183
Radio Television Serbia 24
rape 47, 65, 67
Rapid Reaction Force 192, 203
Raseta, General 30
Rau, Sanchez 203–4
Raznjatovic, Zeljko 41
Rechil-Kir, Josip 11
Red Cross *see* ICRC
Redman, Charles 110, 117, 165
refugees: Batnoga 134, 135–6, 138; Bosnia 37; Dudakovic 134; evacuation 77; Galbraith 135–6; Krajina 134, 135; prison camps 218n54; Sector West 189; Separation Zone 137; Topusko 198; Turanj 133, 134, 135, 154, 227n169; UN 135–6; UNPAs 37; UNPROFOR 136; Velika Kladusa 154, 200; *see also* displaced people; international humanitarian aid
Regional Joint Commission 157
Reismuller, Johann Georg 18
Republic of Srpska: Bosnian Serbs 34–5; crossing points 169; Europe 155, 203; highway blockade 120, 122; Karadzic 3, 36, 58, 90, 210; landlink 184; Lilic 117; Milosevic 75; Mladic 5; Vukovar 23

Republic of Srpska Krajina: Babic 28, 31; Croatia 200; Lika Corps 198; Lilic 117; Sector West 188; UN 178; UNPROFOR 191, 222n76
Rieff, David 3–4
Ripley, Tim 7, 197, 202, 231–2n6
road blocks *see* highway blockades
Roberts, Adam 88
Rose, Michael: Abdic 131; Akashi 113; Bangladeshi UN troops 147; Bihac Pocket 143, 144, 154; Dudakovic 209; Izetbegovic 206; Karadzic's peace proposal 139; Lilic 117; Mladic 4–5, 112; Mogadishu Line 222n21; NATO 120; Sarajevo 115, 124, 162–3, 164; Silajdzic 144–5
Rosso, Ante 104, 109
Ruder Finn Inc. 39, 49, 50, 66
Ruhe, Volker 15
Russian eight-point plan 71
Russian Federation 110

Sacirbey, Muhamed 68, 71, 197
Sadic, Hazim 165–6
Saetersdal, Lieutenant 162
safe areas *see* UN, safe areas
Saint, C. 'Butch' 110
sanctions 22, 42, 119, 121, 155
Sandzak issue 173
Santic, Vlado 195, 209
Sarajevo: Akashi 5, 108, 190; Armija 173; arms supplies 219n72; Bihac Pocket 101–2; Bosnian Muslims 58–9, 192; Bosnian Serbs 53; Boutros-Ghali 59, 108, 143–5; bread queue massacre 5, 37–40; Carter 148–53; casualties 191; ceasefire 109; Contact Group 172; Izetbegovic 43, 59, 95–6; Karadzic 35–7, 53, 158; Lukavica 191–2; market square 6, 108, 153, 201–2; NATO 120–1; Owen 38; politics 4, 5, 42; recognition 28; Rose 115, 124, 162–3, 164; siege 53, 154, 190; Silajdzic 38, 39, 105; Smith 190, 201; Srebenica 78–9; truce 30; UN Civil Affairs 120; UNPROFOR 108, 123–4; violence 33–4, 107–8
Sarinic, Hrvoje: Akashi proposal 184; ceasefire 111, 179; highway reopening 179, 181–2, 188; Janvier 197; population transfers 9; Turot 185; US ambassador 186
SARSK 57, 211
Sava bridge 183, 185, 186
school children killed 78

INDEX

Sector West: ceasefire 186; Croats 187; Jasenovac 184; Krajina Serbs 188; Milosevic 187–8; Nova Gradiska 180; refugees 189; reopening of road 168, 181–2
Separation Zone 111, 133, 137
Serbian Orthodox Church 123
Serbs 10–11; atrocities 13–14, 49; Batnoga 137; blamed 5, 6–7, 202; checkpoints closed 142; Croatia 20; demonisation 18, 43, 50; displaced 8, 186, 205; international community 82; prisoners of war 187; refugees 198–9; school children killed 78; UNPAs 184; weapons collection points 114; wedding party 33; *see also* Bosnian Serbs; Krajina Serbs
Seselj, Vojislav 10, 11
Sicel, Bozidar 131
Silajdzic, Haris 68; arms embargo 55; Bihac 143; Carter 150; ceasefire 104, 143; Contact Group 117; EC proposals 43; Gorazde 112, 115; Granic 134; Rose 144–5; Sandzak issue 173; Sarajevo 38, 39, 105; Vienna Agreement 116
Simpson, John 39
Skegro, Borislav 168
Skela village 17
Sky News 112, 140, 160–1
Slavonia 11, 185
Slovenia 10, 12–15, 21, 37
Smith, Rupert: COHA 177; Mladic 5, 164; Moldestad 161; Paris meeting 191; Sarajevo 190, 201; Srebenica 195, 202–3; withdrawal 192
Solana, Janvier 204
Soskocanin, Vukasin 10
Spegelj, Martin 11
Srebenica 73–5; Bosnian Muslims 193; Canadian peacekeepers 81–2; ceasefire 80; fall of 193–5, 210, 231n2; hunger 71; Mladic 3, 86, 193–5; Oric 70–1, 77, 78, 209; safe area 78–80; Smith 195, 202–3; UNHCR 170
Srebenica Agreement 79
Srebenica Report 202, 203, 209
Stanisic, Jovica 10, 204
Stankovic, Milos 4, 219n22, 225n117; Americares 221n74; Armija/BSA 92; COHA 155; Croat–Muslim war 6; Oric 80; truth 210–11; Tuzla 103; Zametica 139
Stanley, Mike *see* Stankovic, Milos
Stara Gradiska 183, 185
Starcevic, Ante 31–2

Stari Most bridge 103
Status of Forces Agreement 189
Steinbruner, John 119
Stewart, Bob 4, 55, 63–4, 81
Stoltenberg, Thorvald 4, 77, 91, 162, 179, 191, 196
Stulanovic, Sefik 135
Susak, Gojko: Banja Luka 168, 205; Galbraith 232n9; HV 181, 199; media 188; Mostar 118; Osijek 11; truce 30

Talbott, Strobe 165
Talic, Momir 232n9
ten-day war 12–13
Thatcher, Margaret 78
Thoms, Jan Uwe 137
Time 66, 85, 227n156
Topusko 198, 199
Totic, Colonel 80–1
Travnik 171, 172
truth 1, 4, 14, 24, 68, 210–11
Tudjman, Franjo: Abdic 99–100, 126, 134; Babic 146, 158; Baker 12; Bihac Pocket 7–8, 100; Boban 56; Bosnia 31–2; Boutros-Ghali 169; Brac Island airport 84; Carter 150; Catholic Church 170; Clinton 169; Croatian National Guard 11–12; expansionism 32, 93; Galbraith 189–90; Germany 26; Greater Croatia 109; Holbrooke 168, 205; HV 197–8; international community 187; Izetbegovic 32, 56; Kadijevic 25; Krajina Serbs 176, 178; Macedonia Federal Presidium session 16; media 99, 188; military parade 189; Milosevic 9, 66; Mostar 118; prison camps 89–90; propaganda 144; reunification 201; Slavonia 185; UN 182; UNPROFOR 153, 158; US 85, 159; Vance–Owen plan 91; Vance Plan 31; Wahlgren 89; Western intervention 57; Zadar 65; Zagreb meeting 168
Tuffelli, Monique 143–5
Tumanov, Simeon 211
Turajlic, Hajika 64, 65
Turanj 133, 134, 135, 154, 227n169
Turks 32, 161
Turot, Albert 185
Tursunovic, Zulfo 194
Tuzla 74, 103, 106, 157, 161–2

Ugresic, Dubravka v, 8
Una valley 128
UNCIVPOL 98, 180, 183
UNCRO 169, 178, 183, 196

INDEX

UNHCR 37, 57, 122, 143–5; Bivac Pocket 167; denied access 170; end of humanitarian aid 70; free passage 104; HVO/BSA 91–2; Krajina Serbs 134; prison camps 89; Velika Kladusa 126–7

UNICEF mobile health clinic 136

United Nations (UN) 142; arms embargo 160; Babic 184; Croatia 182; Department of Peacekeeping Operations 141; dual key system 231n4; hostages 73–5, 183, 192, 207; international humanitarian aid 67, 125; Krajina 174; Milosevic 31; Mladic 74–5; observers 82; Pakrac 186–7; Pleso Camp 184; refugees 135–6; Republic of Srpska Krajina 178; safe areas 85, 86, 93–4, 111–12, 220n37, n38; sanctions 121; Sarajevo 5; Srebrenica Report 202; Tudjman 182

United Nations Charter 155, 207

United Nations Civil Affairs 120, 180

United Nations General Assembly 37

United Nations Mixed Military Working Group 78

United Nations peacekeepers 3, 42, 65; Argentinian 183; Bangladeshi 147–8; Bosnian Serbs 85–6, 143, 148; Canadian 74, 78, 79, 81–2, 163; Czech 199; Danish 124–5, 198, 199; Dutch 193, 194; French 74, 124, 191; Jordanian 182; MacKenzie 43; Nepalese 183; Polish 105, 135, 136, 198; statistics 25; Turkish 161

United Nations Protected Areas 30, 37, 65, 146, 179, 184

United Nations Security Council 42, 58, 68–70; Resolution 713 22, 208; Resolution 721 25; Resolution 757 42; Resolution 764 68; Resolution 771 69; Resolution 780 51, 218n60; Resolution 808 69, 86–7, 220n39; Resolution 819 78, 85; Resolution 820 79; Resolution 827 88; Resolution 836 207; Resolution 947 158; Resolution 958 140, 141; Resolution 981 174; Resolution 988 178

UNMOs 128, 130, 142, 171, 223n25

UNPREDEP 169

UNPROFOR 4; Abdic 132; Akashi 141; Americares 103; arms supplies 163; Bosnia 169; demilitarisation 97–8; Gorazde 203; Izetbegovic 36; Knin reports 168; Krajina Serbs 125, 135; MacKenzie 38; Martic 160–1, 191; Mladic 142; NATO 125–6, 206; no-fly zone 192; Polish battalion 105; refugees 136; Republic of Srpska Krajina 191, 222n76; Sarajevo 108, 123–4; Separation Zone 111, 133; status 141–5, 159–60, 201, 208; Tudjman 153, 158; Vance Plan 37; Velika Kladusa 148; weapons collection points 43, 110; Z4 plan 146–7

USA (United States of America): airbase 84; airdrops 70, 71–2; anti-Serb sentiment 151–2; APWB 136; arms supplies 207; Bosnian Muslims 163, 164–6, 208–9; Croatia 158–9, 168; Defense Training and Advisory Programme 164; State Department 49; troops 89; Tudjman 159; Vance–Owen plan 208; Yugoslav consulates 37

Valentic, Nikica 177
Van den Broek, Hans 15, 20, 28
Van Renseen, Private 194
Vance, Cyrus 4, 34, 36, 53, 55, 59, 76–7
Vance–Owen plan 58, 63–8, 208; Bosnian Muslims 66; Bosnian Serbs 78, 82, 84–5, 88, 91; Boutros-Ghali 89; Izetbegovic 30, 76, 91; Karadzic 65, 67, 75–6; Mostar 88–9; NATO 75; Tudjman 91
Vance Plan 30–1, 37, 54, 178, 179
Vares 102, 122
Vasic, Milos 210, 211
Velika Kladusa 132–5, 138, 141; Abdic 100, 125, 128, 132, 136–7, 200; APWB 100–1, 131, 132–3, 154; Dudakovic 133, 199; EC monitors 136–7; 5th Corps 101, 133; Krajina Serbs 140; looting 225n104; refugees 154, 200; UNHCR 126–7; UNPROFOR 148
Vienna Agreement 116
Viera de Mello, Serge 120
Virovitica Four 11
Vlasic mountain attack 171
Vojvodina 10, 199
von Stulpnagel, Paul Joachim 131, 136, 155
Vukovar 23–4, 41
Vulliamy, Ed 3–4, 45, 48
Vuono, Carl 110

Wahlgren, General 89
war crimes 23–4, 76, 167, 189; *see also* International War Crimes Tribunal
Washington Accord 93, 98, 116, 168, 169, 170
Washington Post 66
Watkins, Philip 153, 155, 157
weapons collection points 43, 110, 114, 120, 130

INDEX

weapons factories 161
Webb, Justin 74
Western European Union 19, 53
Western media 90–1, 140
Wiesel, Elie 85
Williams, Michael 123
Woerner, Manfred 94, 114
World Health Organisation 73
World-wide Television News 125
wounded 74–5, 79

Yeltsin, Boris 22, 83, 88, 119
Yugoslav consulates 37
Yugoslav State Council 14
Yugoslavia 12, 17, 36, 54

Z4 plan 228n12; Babic 146, 197; Galbraith 159; Knin 168; Krajina Serbs 160; Turot 185; UNPROFOR 146–7

Zadar 21, 65
Zagreb: Croats 144; demonstrations 10–11; ECMM 8; JNA 22; military parade 189; Mladic 57; Russian Federation 110; three army meeting 168
Zagreb–Belgrade highway 153, 168
Zagreb/Knin Economic Agreement 146
Zaklopace 37
Zamaklaar, Dragan 48
Zametica, Jovan 139
Zemunik airport 99
Zenica 80–1, 161, 171
Zepa 3, 170
Zetra concept 32, 160
Zimmerman, Warren 9, 12, 31, 32, 36
Zubak, Kesimir 116, 117, 155, 168, 170, 222n16

For Product Safety Concerns and Information please contact our EU
representative GPSR@taylorandfrancis.com
Taylor & Francis Verlag GmbH, Kaufingerstraße 24, 80331 München, Germany

www.ingramcontent.com/pod-product-compliance
Lightning Source LLC
Chambersburg PA
CBHW062135300426
44115CB00012BA/1935